HITLER'S PROFESSORS

HITLER'S PROFESSORS

The Part of Scholarship
in Germany's Crimes Against
the Jewish People

Max Weinreich

Yale University Press
New Haven and London

Originally published in 1946 by the Yiddish Scientific Institute—YIVO—as part of the YIVO English Translation Series. Published in 1999 with a new Foreword by Yale University Press.

Printed in the United States of America.

Library of Congress Cataloging-in-Publication Data

Weinreich, Max, 1894–1969.
    [Hitlers profesorn. English]
    Hitler's professors : the part of scholarship in Germany's crimes against the Jewish people / Max Weinreich.
        p.   cm.
    Originally published: New York : Yiddish Scientific Institute—YIVO, 1946. With new introd.
    Includes bibliographical references and indexes.
    ISBN 0-300-05387-8 (alk. paper)
    1. Antisemitism—Germany. 2. Learning and scholarship—Germany—History—20th century. 3. Germany—History—20th century. 4. Germany—Intellectual life. 5. Holocaust, Jewish (1939–1945)—Causes. I. Title.
    DS146.G4W3913   1999
    943.086—dc21   98–48936
                     CIP

A catalogue record for this book is available from the British Library.

The paper in this book meets the guidelines for permanence and durability of the Committee on Production Guidelines for Book Longevity of the Council on Library Resources.

10   9   8   7   6   5   4   3   2   1

Foreword to the Second Edition

More than half a century has passed since Max Weinreich published *Hitler's Professors*. In the long list of scholarly publications on what is now known as the Holocaust, this was both a pioneering work and a preeminent one. Completed in March 1946, it was originally written in Yiddish and appeared in two consecutive issues of *YIVO-bleter,* the Journal of the Yiddish Scientific Institute (today, the YIVO Institute for Jewish Research) in New York. Weinreich was closely associated with YIVO, under whose auspices this book is now reprinted.

Weinreich published his findings, which constituted a formidable indictment against the German intellectual elite, while the Nuremberg Trials were in their final weeks. Many of his conclusions anticipated the work—and the verdict—of historians writing decades later. He has much material, for example, on the anti-Jewish propaganda that permeated every aspect of German life, including the evolution of the pernicious film *Der ewige Jude* (The eternal Jew), and he points out in one of his many fascinating footnotes that the man who prepared an earlier exhibition under the same name— which included photographs, filmstrips, and other material portraying Jews from a viciously racist perspective—was a famous historian of journalism, Karl d'Ester of the University of Munich, the city in which the exhibition was first shown in December 1937.

Hitler's Professors is written with great passion. Drawing on published (and often widely publicized) writings, Weinreich conveys through the quotations that he has selected the anger he felt on reading these materials for the first time. As early as 1924, he points out, two Nobel Prize winners, Philipp Lenard and Johannes Stark, were among the signatories of a newspaper appeal in support of Hitler, who, they said, "with his comrades in struggle appear to us like God's gifts out of a time that has long passed, in which races still were purer, men were still greater, minds less deceived."

Building on a formidable bibliography of books, pamphlets, and articles in the immediate aftermath of the war, Weinreich provides erudite evidence of the scale and ramifications of Nazi support in German intellectual life. He examines in great detail the intellectual support and encouragement inside Germany for Nazi policy toward the Jews. In the first months of Hitler's rule, this intellectual imprimatur sanctioned the burning of banned books. From there, events moved slowly but steadily toward mass murder. Even before Hitler came to power, Lenard was heard to say (as recalled by Stark): "And that's just why the Jews must be sunk to the center of the earth." The reason: Stark had spoken to him "with sorrowful air about the mighty Jewish influence in trades, in economy, in politics, in the press, and in scholarship."

Such pseudoscientific scholarship gave the political actions of the Third Reich intellectual validity. It was spewed out without pause throughout the Nazi era, including the very period when mass murder was at its most intense.

One of of the pioneering sections of Weinreich's book deals with the anti-Jewish research institutions set up on German models in Italy, France, Lithuania, Croatia, Hungary, and Denmark. Another shows how the mass murder of Jews in the East, which began with the German invasion of the Soviet Union in June 1941, was accompanied by the apparatus of pseudoscholarship. This was exemplified in General Keitel's order of 12 September 1941, which stated that "the fight against bolshevism demands in the first place also reckless and energetic action against the Jews, the main carriers of bolshevism."

The anthropologists of the Third Reich widely promoted this image of a political disease carried by race. Two days before Keitel's order, the intellectual magazine of anti-Semitism, edited by the political historian Wilhelm Ziegler, published an article stating that the world would have to thank "German mind and German courage for causing to perish forever the most extreme product of Jewish anti-mind [Ungeist] and hatred at the gates of Europe."

The misuse of science and of language in the service of false science is starkly illustrated in these pages. Students and scholars will find that Max Weinreich, writing so closely to the tragedy that engulfed and destroyed the world he had known and loved, was able to convey the steps whereby the mass murder of six million people was justified, sustained, and encouraged by those whose training and culture ought to have encouraged their humaneness and marked them for intellectual and scientific leadership but instead made them the willing, even enthusiastic servants of evil.

By the time he wrote this book, Max Weinreich was an eminent scholar of European Jewry. His area of greatest expertise was the Yiddish language. His achievements in its study, in both Poland and the United States, were remarkable. The historian Lucy Dawidowicz has written that he, "more than any other man or institution, succeeded in gaining for Yiddish prestige and status it had never before enjoyed."[1]

Weinreich, the son of a merchant, was born under the rule of the Russian tsar in the small town of Goldingen (Kuldiga), Latvia, on 22 April 1893.[2] His native language was German, but he also became fluent in Russian. He began his education in his hometown in a predominantly non-Jewish gymnasium where the language of instruction was Russian, but because of the school's anti-Semitism he moved to a Jewish gymnasium in the city of Dvinsk in 1908 to complete his schooling. It was at this new school that he befriended a member of the youth wing of the Bund, the Jewish Workers Union, and was quickly drawn to the Yiddish language. By the time he was thirteen he had mastered the language and become a correspondent for a Yiddish daily newspaper, *Die Hofnung* (Hope), published by the Bund in Vilna. His first translations of European literature into Yiddish were published when he was fifteen. By the age of sixteen, he was publishing original articles in Yiddish.

Having moved to the Russian capital of St. Petersburg, Weinreich graduated from the Classical Gymnasium in 1912 with the

1. This, and all subsequent quotations from Professor Dawidowicz, are taken from Lucy S. Dawidowicz, *The Jewish Presence: Essays on Identity and History,* Holt, Rinehart and Winston, New York, 1977, chapter 11, "Max Weinreich: Scholarship of Yiddish."

2. Max Weinreich's year of birth is usually given as 1894. But in his handwritten "Lebensrauf" for the University of Marburg he writes it distinctly as 1893. (Hessisches Staatsarchiv Marburg)

much-prized Gold Medal, the highest honor. He then studied German linguistics, history, and politics at St. Petersburg University, where he joined a Bundist student circle and wrote for Bundist publications.

After the Bolshevik revolution of 1917, the twenty-four-year-old Weinreich left Russia for Vilna—then (briefly) a part of independent Lithuania—where he edited a Bundist daily newspaper. In 1919 he made his way to Germany, studying German philology at Berlin University and later at the University of Marburg, where in 1920 he embarked on a doctorate in the history of Yiddish linguistic studies. Having received his Ph.D. in 1923 he returned to Vilna (by then part of Poland), married Regina Szabad, a member of one of the city's leading Jewish families, and taught at the Yiddish Teachers' Seminary. He became an editor of the Vilna Yiddish daily newspaper *Der Tog* and a prolific writer, serving as a correspondent for the New York newspaper *Der Forverts* (The Jewish daily forward), to which, wrote Robert King, "he continued to contribute until his last years, shuddering, no doubt, to see his articles appear in the visibly un-Yivo archaic orthography of the *Forverts*."[3]

In Vilna, Weinreich's work on behalf of the Yiddish language was that of a determined and brilliant pioneer. In 1924, aged thirty, he responded enthusiastically to the call for the establishment of a Jewish research institute and became a representative of the Vilna organizing committee from which YIVO emerged. At the first YIVO conference in 1925, he was elected president of the Institute, with responsibility for research and publications. For fourteen productive and fulfilling years he served and guided the Institute, around which a wealth of Yiddish studies and records focused. "It became his life's goal," wrote Lucy Dawidowicz, "to fashion from this folk language a refined and supple instrument, a tongue fit for learned discourse, and to win prestige for it among Jews and non-Jews. This he achieved." Weinreich believed that research and study were not only to be of the highest scholarly quality in themselves, but were also, in Dawidowicz's words, "to serve the intellectual needs of Jews, to increase their

3. Robert D. King, *The Weinreich Legacy* (Fifth Annual Avrom-Nokhem Stencl Lecture in Yiddish Studies), Oxford Centre for Postgraduate Hebrew Studies, Oxford, 1988.

self-understanding, to fortify them intellectually against anti-Semitism and self-depreciation, and to help them develop a healthy sense of self-esteem." Before he was forty, Weinreich had already published several books on Yiddish grammar and orthography, had edited three volumes of linguistic studies, and was editor of *YIVO-bleter,* the bimonthly scholarly journal started by YIVO in 1931.

Weinreich left Vilna in 1932 to study at Yale University for two years as a Rockefeller Foundation Fellow at the International Seminar on the Impact of Culture on Personality. From the United States he returned to Europe, to Vienna, to continue his study of the impact of culture on personality. In Vienna he also studied the therapeutic function of research, working under Siegfried Bernfeld, a disciple of Freud. Two years later, back again in Vilna, he organized the collecting of more than three hundred autobiographies written by young Jews. These autobiographies became the basis for his 1935 book, *Der veg tsu undzer yugnt,* on the problems of Jewish youth growing up in a society that legitimized anti-Semitism. Weinreich believed that, through research and study, Jews could learn self-esteem and help heal the wounds inflicted on their personalities by the often-hostile surrounding society.

In August 1939 Weinreich represented YIVO at the International Linguistics Congress in Brussels. The German invasion of Poland on the first day of September prevented his return to Vilna, as it also prevented the return of many leading Zionists, who were then at their annual congress in Switzerland, to their homes throughout Poland. With difficulty due to wartime conditions he made his way to the United States. At the age of forty-six he had a new home in a new land, fortunately in a city where Yiddish was still a living language, a vibrant mode of thought and expression.

As soon as Vilna fell under Soviet control following the Nazi-Soviet partition of Poland in October 1939, the future of YIVO and all its works was clearly in danger. Weinreich, as its research director, set about reorganizing the Institute in New York. Among his achievements in his new—and final—home was the establishment of the YIVO Center for Advanced Jewish Studies and the publication of the *YIVO Annual of Jewish Social Science.* Vilna, meanwhile, had been occupied by the Germans in summer 1941 and its Jewish

population, estimated at 80,000 at the time of the German invasion,
was marked out for murder, many in the nearby death pits of Ponar.
Fewer than 6,000 Vilna Jews survived the war, mostly those who
joined the partisans in the forests. Many of the survivors left soon
after the war for the United States, Israel, and other distant havens.
The vibrant Yiddish life and Jewish culture and scholarship of the
"Jerusalem of Lithuania" did not survive the destruction of Vilna
Jewry.

In New York, Weinreich continued to work with incredible energy and devotion to maintain and enhance the study of Yiddish and
its scholarly applications. In 1947 he was appointed a professor at
City College of the City University of New York, supervising Yid-
dish studies. He was later a visiting professor at the University of
California, Los Angeles (1948), and Columbia University (1959–60).
Over the course of an incredibly productive decade, he organized several major conferences and colloquiums on Yiddish Studies (1958),
Yiddish Dialectology (1965), Jewish Participation in Movements
Devoted to the Cause of Social Progress (1964), Multilingualism and
Social Change (1967), the Economy of Polish Jewry in the Interwar
Period (1967), and Yiddish in American Jewish Life (1968). These
were formidable achievements that contributed to the spread of linguistic, social, and historical knowledge. The culmination of Weinreich's work was his comprehensive four-volume history of the Yiddish language. Together with his son Uriel (who tragically prede-
ceased him), he ensured that the Yiddish language would always be
established on a plinth of gold.

It was inevitable that Weinreich would write about the terrible
impact of the Nazi destruction of the communities that had constituted the Yiddish heartland. He studied thousands of documents
that were brought to YIVO immediately after the Holocaust, many
of which had been top secret during the war itself. He also read
some five thousand German wartime publications. He based his thesis that "German scholarship provided the ideas and techniques
which led to and justified unparalleled slaughter" on this research.

In her 1969 American Jewish Year Book article eulogizing
Weinreich, who died in January of that year, Lucy Dawidowicz
points out that, for Weinreich, "scholarship had been an instrument

for Jewish survival, but the Germans had turned it into a tool for Jewish death." Weinreich's research showed that many German writers and thinkers, professors and scholars, who before 1939 had been part of the mainstream of German intellectual life had been willing, even enthusiastic, participants in that process. It was these scholars—in whose milieu Weinreich himself had worked in Berlin and Marburg—who, he wrote, "supplied Nazism with the ideological weapons which any movement, particularly a German movement, needs for its success." At each stage of the evolution of the destruction of European Jewry "the German rulers had theorists at hand who praised their achievements in reducing the Jews and supplied the academic formulae and the scholarly backing for each further step in German policies, until the 'extinguishment' of the 'eternally hostile forces' was accomplished to the best of the murderer's abilities." Special research institutions and publications were created as "instrumentalities in Germany's war against the Jews."

Weinreich stressed that every scientific and intellectual discipline was enlisted to serve the cause of the Jewish issue, an issue, he wrote, that "from the very outset was recognized as a decisive weapon in Germany's strife for conquest." He had studied the writings of physical and cultural anthropologists, philosophers, historians, jurists, economists, geographers, demographers, theologians, linguists, and physicians. In a forceful aside, he commented: "Only the names of the engineers who so ingenuously constructed the gas chambers and death furnaces for the time being remain in obscurity; but their deeds speak for their efficiency." Even those names are now known; indeed, one such firm of engineers is, at the time of this writing, seeking compensation from the German government for lost revenues due to its postwar tribulations.

Martin Gilbert

CONTENTS

HITLER'S PROFESSORS

... It is necessary that the whole scholarship of a people so deeply moved serve the leaders of such a movement in making understandable their national, political, and supranational aims ... with its full political, scholarly knowledge of things, with its full information on foreign countries and the world.

> PROFESSOR KARL HAUSHOFER, *Der nationalsozialistische Gedanke in der Welt*, Munich, 1933, p. 48.

... The international Jew! ... We have been following his footsteps for so many years and probably for the first time we have in this Reich elucidated in a methodical, scholarly way this human problem and phenomenon....

> HITLER, in an address to his Old Guard, November 11, 1941.

... Today we can proudly state that scholarship contributed its share to the success of the Führer's great plans....

> PROFESSOR MAX CLARA, *Deutsches Hochschulverzeichnis, 1941/1942*, Leipzig, 1942, p. IV.

Planning and Preparation

I

THE PROBLEM STATED

This study is a report on the part of German scholarship in Germany's crimes against the Jewish people.

In 1939 there were in Europe, including the European part of the Soviet Union, about nine and a half million Jews. About eight and a quarter million fell under Nazi domination. Of these, according to German Secret Police estimates placed before the International Military Tribunal at Nuremberg, four million were killed in the extermination camps while two million more met death in other ways. Attorney General Tom C. Clark, in his letter to the Yiddish Scientific Institute of December 10, 1945, too, considered that according to the best information "six million Jews were slaughtered by the Germans and their satellites." But this is not the whole account. Among those left on former Hitler-dominated territory there are extremely few children, and many are alive merely in a technical sense, ill and destitute, beyond any hope of recovery. To appreciate the ratio of casualties, we may recall that the number of battle dead in the European war is estimated at fourteen million out of a population of well over five hundred million. And these six

5

million Jews that cannot be accounted for were not soldiers.
Jewish citizens in Poland, in England and France, in Russia, in the
United States, and in all other Allied countries served in the armed
forces, and the Jewish share in those who will never return is equit-
able. The battle deaths, however, are not included in the figure of
six million. They were a civilian population which was murdered, murdered in premeditation, as evidenced by Hitler's solemn
statement in his Reichstag address of January 30, 1939, that if a
new war were to break out, its result would be "the annihilation of
the Jewish race in Europe." No other prophecy of Hitler materialized;
this one nearly did.

"History," to quote from Justice Robert H. Jackson's opening
address before the Nuremberg Tribunal,[1] "does not record a crime
ever perpetrated against so many victims or one ever carried out
with such calculated cruelty.... Determination to destroy the Jews
was a binding force which at all times cemented the elements of this
conspiracy." Whose conspiracy? It will not do to speak in this connection of the "Nazi gangsters." This murder of a whole people was
not perpetrated solely by a comparative small gang of the Elite Guard
or by the Gestapo, whom we have come to consider as criminals.
As is shown by Hitler's threat, afterwards frequently repeated by
himself and his henchmen, as the literature of the Nazi Party, the
Reich government, and the Wehrmacht shows, the whole ruling class
of Germany was committed to the execution of this crime. But the
actual murderers and those who sent them out and applauded them
had accomplices. German scholarship provided the ideas and techniques which led to and justified this unparalleled slaughter.

Everyone's feeling naturally revolts against such a stupendous
accusation. Frankly, the present writer, too, would have considered
it an exaggeration on the basis of the casual evidence available until
recently. But when, after the defeat of Germany, German publications
(which now number about five thousand) began pouring into
the library of the Yivo, the previous scattered impressions gathered
into a coherent picture. To subject the conclusions arrived at to even
closer scrutiny, other extensive collections of German literature were
examined.[2] Thus the present report, based upon a good many thou-

---

[1] Justice Jackson's address, *New York Times,* November 22, 1945. The above mentioned
German Secret Police estimates, *New York Times,* December 15, 1945.

[2] Beside the library and archives of the Yiddish Scientific Institute—Yivo, the author
examined the collections of the New York Public Library, the Columbia University Library,
the Jewish Library of Information of the American Jewish Committee, the Institute of Jewish
Affairs of the World Jewish Congress, the Jewish Labor Committee. The Yivo owes its own

sands of books, pamphlets, periodicals, and documents, provides ample evidence that there was participation of German scholarship in every single phase of the crime. The ideas underlying the ultimate "action" were developed in advance with the necessary philosophical and literary trimmings, with historical reasoning, with maps and charts providing for the details with well-known German thoroughness. Many fields of learning, different ones at different times according to the shrewdly appraised needs of Nazi policies, were drawn into the work for more than a decade: physical anthropology and biology, all branches of the social sciences and the humanities—until the engineers moved in to build the gas chambers and crematories.

But could it not be, we are tempted to ask in a last effort to save at least a bit of our belief in the fundamental integrity of scholarship, that Hitler's accomplices were merely sham scholars, nobodies elevated in rank by their Nazi friends and protectors, who produced what is described as "scurrilous literature"? Even this consolation is baseless. The scholars whom we shall quote in such impressive numbers, like those others who were instrumental in any other part of the German pre-war and war efforts, were to a large extent people of long and high standing, university professors and academy members, some of them world famous, authors with familiar names and guest lecturers abroad, the kind of people Allied scholars used to meet and fraternize with at international congresses. The younger academic people might have stayed a little longer on the waiting list as "Privatdozenten" except for the fact that several thousand positions were vacated through the dismissal of Jewish or liberal professors; but, technically, the young Nazi instructors more often than not were qualified for the positions they were offered just as the scientific periodicals and publishing houses with which they became affiliated have been known to every specialist abroad in his respective field. If the products of their research work, even apart from their rude tone, strike us as unconvincing and hollow, this weakness is due not to inferior training but to the mendacity inherent in any scholarship that overlooks or openly repudiates all moral and spiritual values and, by standing order, knows exactly its ultimate conclusions well in advance. But as far as ascertainable facts, methods, and techniques go, we shall do well not to underestimate German "Jew-knowledge" of the last dozen years and to remember what Wilhelm

collection of books and documents mainly to the efforts of its staff member Z. Szajkowski (Sz. Frydman).

Grau had to say at the opening of the Frankfort "Institute for the Study of the Jewish Question" on March 26, 1941:

> . . . The Institute acknowledges its indebtedness to the method-
> ical critical school which has been developed in German scholarship
> in the last hundred years and has enhanced Germany's reputation
> in the world as well as [its indebtedness] to the great compre-
> hensive force in exposition which the best and most gracious Ger-
> man scholars possessed. . . .[3]

The reader is requested to bear in mind that this study deals with only one specific angle of Jewish experiences in Europe. No attempt is being made to chronicle what the Jews have suffered at the hand of Germany since 1933; apart from the chapters in which hitherto unknown facts and documents are communicated, a general knowledge of the facts is taken for granted. Nor is it intended to depict here the techniques by which the six million Jews were put to death. Necessary as such reports are, one should not be expected here. The present survey, as its title suggests, is concerned solely with the participation of German scholarship in Germany's crimes against the Jewish people since 1933. This particular frame of reference will explain why such notorious criminals as Goering or Streicher are mentioned only accidentally, mostly in connection with the research institutions they appeared in and Frick or Bormann are mentioned hardly at all, whereas others decidedly lower in the hierarchy will be spoken of extensively. Likewise, we are not interested in epitomizing anti-Jewish literature as such, and many products of it may be entirely absent from our survey. On the other hand, a definition of the peculiar function of scholarship in preparing and justifying anti-Jewish policies cannot avoid discussion of some "un-Jewish" subjects, e.g., the policies of "space" and "refolking"; for neither the place of the "Jewish ques-tion" in the whole system nor the implications of its "solution" can be properly understood if not read against this more general back-ground.

Since the sources are not easily accessible and only very few of them have been translated into English, we quote rather freely. The most important excerpts concerning the Jews are given in facsimile in the appendix; some original documents in the possession of the Yivo are reproduced in the text. There are considerable difficulties in translating such specific terms as *Volk* (people, nation, folk), *Wissen-schaft* (scholarship, science), *Weltanschauung* (philosophy, ideology,

---

[3] *Weltkampf* I (1941), 19.

Weltanschauung), or the different compounds of *Art* (species). The heaviness of some sentences in the quotations is due to our desire to render the German original as closely as possible; frequently, the original term is added in parentheses.

Despite the tremendous amount of quotable material, much of which had to be left out, many particulars have, of course, remained unknown. We have had access to a number of documents classified "Only for the use of officials (Nur für den Dienstgebrauch)," "Secret (Geheim)" or even "Secret Reich Matter (Geheime Reichssache)," but still the records of many conferences and decisions can be unearthed only by delving into the Central Archives of the National Socialist Party (Hauptarchiv der NSDAP) formerly located at Barerstrasse 15, Munich 33, or the SS archives reportedly discovered last August in Berlin.[4] Many secret Nazi documents of the highest significance have been presented at the Nuremberg trial, and in many cases reference to them has been introduced into this survey, which was essentially ready at the time the Nuremberg Tribunal started its proceedings. But the prosecution at Nuremberg has limited itself to pressing the case, for the time being at least, against a score or so of top politicians, administrators, and military. Concerning the rôle of German scholarship under Hitler, archival sources have not yet been made accessible by the Allied authorities. Thus, in several instances, we had explicitly to point to gaps in our survey. Fundamentally, however, the picture is complete and the evidence here submitted seems to be sufficient to form a judgment. What we are going to prove is that German scholars from the beginning to the end of the Hitler era worked hand in glove with the murderers of the Jewish people and that the official indoctrination literature of 1944-1945 which openly proclaimed: "The Jew must be annihilated wherever we meet him!" repeated to the letter the "facts" and "reasons" contained in the scholarly literature. To a degree, this may be said even of the actual orders to kill.

---

[4] Cf. *The New York Times,* August 21, 1945: "Berlin, Aug. 20 (U. P.)—Conclusive proof that the extermination of Europe's Jewry was plotted by the Nazi inner circle was discovered in the files of Philip Hoffmann, chief of the infamous SS Race and Resettlement Office, American Army authorities reported today. The files revealed that Reinhard Heydrich, 'hangman' of the Nazi party, who was late assassinated in Czechoslovakia, extended invitations to a luncheon on Jan. 20, 1942, to thirteen high Nazi and Reich government officials to discuss the complete liquidation of the Jewish question. Attached to the invitations were photostatic copies of a letter from Hermann Goering charging Heydrich with solution of the question.' "

II

GERMAN SCHOLARSHIP 1918-1933. THE EARLY YEARS
OF THE HITLER REGIME

Why did German scholars associate themselves with nazism? The charitable reply "what else could the poor little fellows do?" certainly is out of place. One should merely recall the behavior of many scholars in the countries overrun by Germany under circumstances that were incomparably more trying. We shall see that German scholars of conviction or courage could remain silent or even venture, if only in a whisper, an opinion of their own. But the number of such scholars was exceedingly small.

This is not the place for a discussion of whether the "German spirit" always indulged in dreams of world domination. For our purpose, it is sufficient to note that from 1919 to 1933 only a small number of German scholars were intellectually opposed to what in the course of time turned out to be the philosophy of national socialism.

For the field of history, a highly conclusive survey was made by Oscar J. Hamman in a paper, "German Historians and the Advent of the National Socialist State." Dr. Hamman thus sums up the results of his painstaking study:

> As a whole it may be said that the German historians, save for a republican minority, needed little "co-ordination." The Germany of the future which most historians had visioned and wished for approximated in many fundamental respects the Nazi state of today [1941] . . . Since 1933 [we observe] but the intensification of tendencies which already were pronounced before the advent of the Nazi regime.[5]

Mr. Hamman attributes the pro-Hitler philosophy of the historians to their reluctance to accept the establishment of Germany's war guilt in the Treaty of Versailles. To a degree, this is true, as witness the following statement, disarming in its naiveté, by the well-known historian Manfred Laubert of the Universities of Breslau and Berlin in the 1942 preface to the new edition of his book *Die preussische Polenpolitik* (Cracow, 1944); be it remembered that Laubert was in the Nineteen-Twenties a contributor to the leading Jewish *Monatsschrift für Geschichte und Wissenschaft des Judentums* and used to send out reprints of his articles with friendly greetings to Jewish scholars abroad:

---

[5] *Journal of Modern History*, XIII (1941), 161-188.

Over two decades have passed since the first edition of this book. Intended, to begin with, as a scientific militant tract against the *diktat* of Versailles and as an exhortation to the German people, it at that time conveyed the belief: "Our resurrection will to a great extent depend upon the shape things will assume in the East" (p. 4). This expectation has been fulfilled surprisingly soon and beyond all hopes by the Campaign of the Eighteen Days and by the formative will of the Führer.... I believe the general outline had been drawn rightly and thus no revision was needed.

As an explanation of the root causes, Mr. Hamman's argument seems to miss the point that history in Germany repeated itself. German scholarship in the post-Versailles period played exactly the same rôle in supporting Germany's drive for world domination as in the days of the Kaiser, when Werner Sombart construed the fundamental contrast between the English and the Germans, whom he conceived as "merchants" and "heroes," respectively.[6]

Pronouncements of that kind would be too numerous to quote, so we may refer merely to the ill-famed manifesto of the ninety-three German professors which scholars in the Allied countries were too quick to forget after 1918.

But one man of that period surely deserves particular attention because he was one of the first scientists to appear proudly among Hitler's followers. Philipp Lenard, the famous physicist, had won the Nobel Prize before the first World War. In August, 1914, he summed up his deliberations on England and Germany in the following sentence: "It is . . . not new that England nearly always was a political monster."[7] Still, among the names of German scientists whom Lenard praised at that time we find Goldstein of Berlin and Heinrich Herz, who had been his teacher and sponsor. Some years later Lenard became so enraged against the Jews that he even construed a German physics (Deutsche Physik) as opposed to Jewish physics represented by Einstein. As early as May 8, 1924, after Hitler had been sentenced to imprisonment because of the Munich putsch, Lenard published in the *Grossdeutsche Zeitung*[8] an ecstatic statement in favor of Hitler and the Nazi party. This statement, co-signed by

---

[6] During World War II, the concept *Händler* vs. *Helden* reappeared and in addition, as could be expected, British *Händler* spirit was identified with Judaism. Cf. Dr. Werner Dittrich in *Der Weltkampf* (Munich), December, 1939, p. 495: "Once more shopkeeper spirit and state spirit, Semitedom and Nordic men clash. We have no doubt about who is going to be this time Rome and Carthage, respectively...."

[7] Philipp Lenard, *England und Deutschland zur Zeit des grossen Krieges* (Heidelberg, Winter, 1914, 16 pp.).

[8] An organ of the pre-Hitler "Greater-Germany" movement.

Johannes Stark, another famous German physicist, who had won the
Nobel Prize in 1919, contained the following passage:

> As recognized natural scientists we should like herewith to
> announce in conformity with out innermost feeling that in Hitler
> and his comrades we discern the same spirit which we always looked
> for, strove toward, developed out of ourselves in our work that it
> might be deep going and successful; the spirit of clarity without
> residue, of honesty toward the outer world, and simultaneously of
> inner unity, the spirit which hates any compromise work because
> of its insincerity. This, however, is exactly the spirit which we early
> recognized and advanced in the great scholars of the past, in Galileo,
> Kepler, Newton, Faraday. We admire and adore it likewise in
> Hitler, Ludendorf, Pöhner and their comrades; we recognize in them
> our nearest relatives in spirit.... It is clear, complete personalities...
> that we wish to have, just as Hitler has. He and his comrades in
> struggle appear to us like God's gifts out of a time that has long
> passed, in which races still were purer, men were still greater, minds
> less deceived.[9]

The allegiance so boldly professed under the Weimar republic
brought ample reward when "God's gift" attained power. At the
inauguration of a "Lenard Institute" at the University of Heidelberg
on December 13, 1935, Johannes Stark took occasion to declare:

> Jewish physics which... came into being during the last three
> decades and has been made and publicized both by Jews and by
> their non-Jewish pupils and imitators appropriately found its high
> priest in a Jew, in Einstein. Jewish advertising wanted to make him
> the greatest natural scientist of all times. Einstein's theories of
> relativity, however, in essence were nothing but a heaping of arti-
> ficial formulae on the basis of arbitrary definitions and transforma-
> tions of the space and time coordinates.... Jewish formalism in
> natural science is to be rejected by all means....
>
> When after the Jewish-Marxist rebellion [of November 1918]
> Jewry dominated the governments and the street, Lenard recognized
> in the overwhelming influence of Jewry the decisive cause of the
> distress of the German people, and he did not keep this recognition
> to himself but expressed it. When on the day of the funeral of the
> shot Jew Rathenau all state enterprises were supposed to close, he
> instinctively [sic] did not pay attention to this directive.... With
> pleasure I even today recall a conversation which I had with Lenard
> in 1928 or 1929. I explained with a sorrowful air how mighty
> Jewish influence was in trades, in economy, in politics, in the press,
> and in scholarship. Lenard's eyes flamed up, and waving his arm

---

[9] J. Stark, "Philipp Lenard als deutscher Naturforscher," *Nationalsozialistische Monatshefte*, no. 71, Feb. 1936, pp. 106-112.

he said: "And that's just why the Jews must be sunk to the center of the earth." [10]

A year later, Lenard was awarded the state science prize and Alfred Rosenberg, in presenting it at the party convention in Nuremberg, while the Führer himself looked on, said in part:

> ... As a thinker Professor Lenard taught that science is not equal to science, that racial souls alien to each other also create quite different scientific psychological worlds. On the one hand [there are] perceptibly strong ideas and symbols as expressions of Europeanism, on the other hand, imageless dogmatizing and pseudo-logical verbal skirmish as testimony of Jewish nature. [11]

Stark, younger and more agile, was requited in a more practical way than was Lenard. After the National Socialists seized power, he was appointed president of the time-honored and highly efficient research institute known as Physikalisch-Technische Reichsanstalt and is known to have actively participated in the German researches on atomic power. In a pamphlet, issued in the second year of the Nazi regime, he republished Lenard's 1924 panegyric on Hitler and then— a rather early confession—spoke of the "great importance" of his Reichsanstalt "for national defense." Appropriately connecting the military tasks with the racial policy of the Nazis which had just started, Stark made the following statement, the whole significance of which became known very much later:

> It is on this biological cognition that an important part of National Socialist ideology is founded. And out of it National Socialist state leadership deduces the guiding principles for its folk-political measures [leading to] the racial species-improvement (rassische Aufartung) of the German people. Its measures tending to eliminate the Jewish influence, which is detrimental to the folk, upon the German people are founded on biological science.... [12]

As early as 1933, i.e., even before Stark had published his pamphlet, the Saxonian branch of the National Socialist German Teachers Union published a "vow of allegiance" by nine professors, some of them rectors of their universities. Their statements, collected in a

---

[10] *Ibid.*

[11] *Der Parteitag der Ehre vom 8. bis 14. September 1936. Offizieller Bericht ...* (München, Eher, 309 pp.), p. 52. — On June 7, 1942, on the occasion of his 80th birthday, Lenard in the presence of high dignitaries was promoted to be Ehrensenator of the University of Heidelberg. Cf. *Postarchiv* 70 (1942), 275-281.

[12] Johannes Stark, *Nationalsozialismus und Wissenschaft* (München, Zentralverlag der NSDAP, Franz Eher Nachfolger, 1934, 20 pp.), pp. 16, 18.—In order not to extend unduly the bibliographical references in the forthcoming footnotes, I should like to call attention to the fact that the Verlag Franz Eher Nachfolger in Munich (later: Munich and Berlin) was the official publishing house of the National Socialist German Workers Party (NSDAP). From this point, it will be referred to merely as Eher.

book, were of course written in German, but as "German science" appealed

> to the intelligentsia of the whole world to cede their understanding to the striving German nation—united by Adolf Hitler— for freedom, honour, justice and peace, to the same extent as they would for their own nation,

the book also contained translations of the statements into English and several other languages.[13] The following quotations, for convenience's sake, are taken from the English text of the publication. Professor Dr. Eugen Fischer, Rector of the University of Berlin, ended his address with the exclamation: "The Leader, Hail and Victory." Professor Dr. Martin Heidegger, the Freiburg philosopher of renown, couched his thoughts in the philosophical language to which he was accustomed but the meaning of his words could escape nobody:

> . . .To know means to us: to have power over things in reason and to be ready to act.... The National Socialist revolution is not merely the taking over of an already existing power in the state by another party sufficiently large enough to do so, but this revolution means a *complete* revolution of our German existence.... Hail Hitler.

Professor Dr. Friedrich Neumann, Rector of the Göttingen University, said in part:

> We demand that each separate people of a real independent will of culture may be allowed to develop its own idea of race and its own style of life up to the highest mark of perfection.

The other authors, who all expressed their views in similar vein, were: Professor Dr. [Arthur] Golf, zoologist, University of Leipzig; Professor Dr. E[manuel] Hirsch, theologian, University of Göttingen; Geheimrat Professor Dr. W[ilhelm] Pinder, historian of art, University of Munich; Professor Dr. [Ferdinand] Sauerbruch, surgeon, University of Berlin;[14] Professor Dr. D. [Friedrich Karl] Schumann, theologian, University of Halle.

It would be very desirable indeed to have studies like Dr. Hamman's of other fields of German scholarship.[15] But even a most sketchy

---

[13] *Bekenntnis der Professoren an den deutschen Universitäten und Hochschulen zu Adolf Hitler und dem nationalsozialistischen Staat. Vow of Allegiance of the Professors of the German Universities and High-Schools* [sic] *to Adolf Hitler and the National Socialistic State.* [Title and text also in Italian, French, and Spanish.] Überreicht vom Nationalsozialistischen Lehrerbund Deutschland/Sachsen ([Dresden, 1933], 136 pp., 4°).

[14] If any proof is needed, this is the proof that Sauerbruch had been openly Nazi since the early days of the Third Reich; that he was loyal to the last is shown below, p. 231. As a matter of fact, his Nazi affiliation was a secret to nobody. Why, then, did the Russians in 1945 appoint him to a high position in the Berlin municipal administration and need months to discover his political physiognomy?

[15] For the field of philosophy, cf. Wladimir Eliasberg, "German Philosophy and German Psychological Warfare," *The Journal of Psychology* 14 (1942), 197-215; for the field of psychology, David P. Boder, "Nazi Science," *Chicago Jewish Forum* I (1942), pp. 23-29.

survey will convince us that historical science was by no means an exception and that literally every discipline was pervaded with intense nationalism that waited for the organizing hand of the Führer. The scholars whom we have so far met are but the beginning of an imposing list.[16] Without the slightest attempt to be exhaustive, one should by no means overlook the far- (but not far-enough) sighted geopolitician, Professor Dr. Karl Haushofer (University of Munich), and Professor Dr. Ewald Banse, the early apostle of defense science (Wehrwissenschaft), who under the veil of defense actually expounded military science. In jurisprudence, we are reminded of the brilliant Carl Schmitt, who back in the peaceful years of the republic gained fame by developing the concept of "friend-foe relation": the foe, both in home and foreign politics, is the stranger, the one who is different; with him, no compromise is possible and the contest can terminate only in the annihilation of one of the conflicting sides.[17] No less decided in his sympathies was the prominent international jurist, Professor Dr. Victor Bruns, Director of the world-famous Institut für ausländisches Recht und Völkerrecht (Institute of Foreign and International Law). Minor, but by no means negligible, persons in this field were Georg Dahm, Professor of Penal Law at Kiel, and Otto Koellreutter, Professor of Public Law at Munich. All of these had intellectually, if not in organization, been in line with the "Movement" even before the Nazi party seized power. The same applies to philosophers like Max Wundt (University of Tübingen) or Erich Rothacker (University of Bonn), linguists like Leo Weisgerber (University of Rostock), Georg Gerullis (University of Königsberg), and Max Deutschbein (University of Marburg), sociologists like Max Hildebert Boehm (University of Jena) and Hans Freyer (University of Leipzig),[18] a psychologist like Erich Rudolf Jaensch (University of Marburg), and many others who did not hesitate to profess their ideas under the Weimar Republic. Dr. Theodor von Vahlen, professor of mathematics at the University of Greifswald, was "dismissed from his post in Republican times because he has removed a Republican flag from the University building." But he was

---

[16] We refrain from quoting the names of over hundred scholars who joined the above-named eight speakers in their "vow of allegiance" and who were listed on the last pages of the Bekenntnis. . . .

[17] Carl Schmitt, "Der Begriff des Politischen," Archiv für Sozialwissenschaft und Sozialpolitik 58 (1927), 1-53. Later republished in pamphlet form. It was no accident that his leading papers were translated into Italian, Spanish, and Japanese.

[18] It was Freyer who in a much spoken-of booklet Revolution von rechts (Jena, Diederichs, 1931, 73 pp.), had proclaimed: "A new front forms on the battlefield of the bourgeois society: the revolution from the right. . . . It is going to overcome the old parties, their stale programs, and their dusty ideologies. . . ." (p. 5).

given a chair in Austria, where the graduate schools had become Nazi nests even before 1933, and in 1938 he was made president of the Prussian Academy of Sciences.[19]

It is not surprising, then, that the attractive power of national socialism became infinitely greater after 1933, when the "revolution from the right" had not only come but, by all indications, had come to stay. It is hard to recall even single acts of defiance against the regime such as did occur in Italy, where a number of professors refused to take the oath of allegiance to fascism. Contrary cases, on the other hand, are too many to be counted, and only specimens can be offered. Erich Rothacker in the last chapters of a scholarly work discussed in dead earnest the contributions of Hitler, Rosenberg, Darré to the philosophy of history.[20] Others, who had not grasped in time the course of events, then were eager to climb on the bandwagon. Otto Hoetzsch, for instance, the well-known historian of Eastern Europe, though thoroughly conservative, in contrast to the Nazis, in the Weimar years had advocated an understanding with the Soviet Union. But in a preface, dated March, 1934, to a volume of collected papers, he inserted the following paragraph:

> . . . The fact that we again really seriously can think of it [the Eastern problem], we, and consequently also the author, owe to the national uprising of 1933, to its Führer and his followers in this special field.[21]

Hans Naumann, the famous historian of literature and culture, "gave the address and his sanction for burning books banned by the Nazis in the market place in Bonn on 10th May, 1933." [22] He tried to reproject the Führer principle into the Middle Ages and in taking over the rectorship of the Bonn University in 1934, closed his speech with a eulogy of the man "with the beloved name," "the most intrepid, the most irreproachable of all and therefore our Führer." [23]

---

[19] Paul E. Kahle, *Bonn University in Pre-Nazi and Nazi Times* (1929-1939). *Experiences of a German Professor* ([London, 1945], 38 pp.), p. 33.

[20] Erich Rothacker, *Geschichtsphilosophie.* Handbuch der Philosophie (München, Oldenbourg, 1934, 150 pp.).

[21] Otto Hoetzsch, *Osteuropa und der deutsche Osten* (Königsberg, Ost-Europa-Verlag, 1934, 431 pp.).

[22] Kahle, *op. cit.,* p. 9.

[23] Hans Naumann, *Der Hohe Mut und das Freie Gemüte* (Bonn, Gebr. Scheur, 1934, 16 pp.).—For the anniversary of the founding of Bismarck's Reich, January 18, 1935, the University of Bonn invited as a guest speaker a lieutenant general whose speech, at a rather early date, contained the following confession: "Out of soldierdom, out of fighterdom the Third Reich has grown.. Soldierdom, fighterdom are its foundations and its hopes. Because solely under the protection of military force Germany's economy, culture and civilization can prosper." Cf. Oskar Vogl, Generalleutn. a. D. *Grosse Soldaten als Wegbereiter deutscher Einheit.* Festrede zur Reichsgründung [at the University of Bonn] am 30. Januar 1935 (Bonn, Scheur, 1935, 18 pp.).

The historian Professor Dr. Willy Andreas of the University of Heidelberg terminated an address on the Reformation by praising "the unity of folk, leadership, and Reich." [24] In the field of vital statistics men like Friedrich Burgdörfer, whom we shall meet more than once in our further discussion, joined the camp early and willingly.

It would be the easiest thing in the world to extend this long list of highly respectable "guild" scholars who fell in line with nazism. But the names that have appeared in the preceding pages certainly prove one thing: that national socialism was in no way alien to German universities at the time of Hitler's advent.

Highly instrumental in bringing the universities into the Nazi network was the Nationalsozialistischer Deutscher Studentenbund (National Socialist German Students Union) and, even more so, the Nationalsozialistischer Deutscher Dozentenbund (National Socialist German University Instructors Union). From the very outset, the latter achieved, through actions of its individual members or cells, far more than its numerical strength warranted, and eventually dominated the field entirely.

Two groups deserve the place of honor among those who made their scholarship subservient to Nazi ends: the physical anthropologists and biologists, and the jurists. We shall soon see that the whole structure of anti-Jewish thought and action was erected upon the so-called "racial science." This science was exploited by Streicher, who in his speeches confused albumin with sperm and, therefore, became easy prey of haughty critics abroad, but it was concocted by some world-famous scholars like Erwin Baur, Ernst Rüdin and, perhaps most of all, Eugen Fischer. Then, the jurists distinguished themselves. They spared no effort in molding the abstruse ideas of the new rulers into clear-cut articles of laws and directives and in defending the legality of the measures taken.

III

HOW THE SCHOLARS CAME INTO THE NAZI CAMP

Against the evidence just submitted there stands out the undeniable fact that during their first years the Nazis did not feel quite at ease with the universities and preferred either to establish new

[24] Willy Andreas, in *Der deutsche Mensch* (Stuttgart, Deutsche Verlagsanstalt [1935], 180 pp.), p. 64.

institutions of their own, such as the Akademie für deutsches Recht
(Academy of German Law) and the Reichsinstitut für Geschichte
des neuen Deutschlands (Reich Institute for the History of the New
Germany), or to take possession of institutions that were not directly
affiliated with universities. In this category, the Deutsche Hochschule
für Politik (German Graduate School of Politics) in Berlin and the
Deutsche Akademie in Munich, also known as the Akademie zur
wissenschaftlichen Erforschung und Pflege des Deutschtums (Academy
for the Scientific Investigation and Cultivation of Germandom) deserve to be mentioned prominently. We shall have to deal with these
institutions repeatedly in our subsequent discussion.

To be sure, the commanding posts at the universities were not
lost sight of and the first year of the regime already saw many rector-
ships firmly in "safe" hands. Ernst Krieck, for instance, appointed by
the Nazis Rector of the Frankfort University immediately after the
seizure of power, had been an ardent Nazi for many years; as early
as 1925 he had declared:

> The future... depends... on the question of whether there still
> are nucleus people (Kernmenschen) who possess instinct and cour-
> age really to dominate, tautly to form, and inconsiderately to purify
> public life.[25]

In Berlin, Eugen Fischer assumed the rectorship. Naumann's rôle
in Bonn has been mentioned already. Nonetheless, the Nazis distrusted
the universities. In such a spirit of suspicion Krieck at an assembly of
Heidelberg students exclaimed angrily: "They [the old-time pro-
fessors] ought not to get away with the statement: we always were
nationalistic (national); we [National Socialists] ought to continue
the struggle in a radical manner." [26]

Many an old-fashioned professor must have shaken his head over
this lack of gratitude on the part of one who, despite his close affinity
with nazism, had received an honorary doctor's degree from the
Heidelberg Faculty of Philosophy while the professors' salaries were
still paid by the republic. But then, there was no end of shocking
pronouncements. Krieck's colleague, Professor Dr. Wolf Meyer-Erlach,

---

[25] Ernst Krieck, *Menschenformung* (2. Auflage, Leipzig, Quelle und Meyer, 1933, 371
pp., 1st ed., 1925). — In the preface to the 14th edition of his book *Nationalpolitische
Erziehung* (Leipzig, Armanen-Verlag, 1933, 186 pp.), dated Frankfort on-the-Main, August,
1933 (1st ed., 1932). Krieck in his overbearing manner pointed out: "This book . . . contributed a good deal to the [National Socialist] revolution in that it won over for the Movement
entire strata of the educated to whom the elementary popular movement was accessible only
by way of understanding and conceiving, not by becoming involved immediately. . . . It was
the first attempt to penetrate national socialism philosophically."

[26] Cf. *Der Heidelberger Student*, no. 3, May 29, 1935.

Rector of the University of Jena, about the same time expressed himself this way:

> The struggle is not yet over. Enough cobwebs are still hanging in the corners and nooks of the universities. There are still instructors and students whose eyes are turned backward, toward eternal yesterday's life. But we know that ... the future is more potent than the past....[27]

Other professors and student leaders, who had been engaged for years in the struggle for complete nazification, in 1935 and 1936 were prepared to acknowledge no more than limited gains.[28] Only around 1936, after about 1,500 professors had been dismissed for racial (and, to a much smaller degree, also for political) reasons,[29] the regime felt more secure, though complaints about the aloofness of the "guild" scholars were not lacking for some years more.[30] A keen American observer in a study covering the year 1936 was able to establish the fact that "the institutions of higher learning have been brought thoroughly into line with the sentiments and ambitions of the national government." [31]

By this time we have come to understand the phenomenon which previously appeared as a contradiction. The Nazi distrust of the old professional stock was inspired mainly by their totalitarian aspirations. In the old academic atmosphere, people had been accustomed to detached discussions, they had acquiesced in the existence of the Weimar "Judenrepublik (Jews' republic)," they even themselves had sometimes associated with Jews. In Nazi action and propaganda, on the other hand, everything had to be brand new so as to achieve the maximum of dynamism. The Nazis were not content to see people agree with them more or less; they wanted people to accept them without any mental reservations and to renounce all former ties, if any.

---

[27] From Meyer-Erlach's introduction to the dissertation by Hans Joachim Düning, *Der S. A.-Student im Kampf um die Hochschule (1925-1935)* (Jena, 1936). The mere fact of a rector's writing a preface to a doctoral dissertation was quite startling.

[28] E.g., Dr. Richard Oechsle, Gaustudentenbundsführer in Baden, in *Der Heidelberger Student*, No. 5, January 23, 1936; [Professor] Georg Dahm in *Zeitschrift für deutsche Kulturphilosophie* II, 3 (1936), 211.

[29] The figure as computed by Edward Y. Hartshorne, Jr., *The German Universities and National Socialism* (London, Allen & Unwin [1937], 184 pp.). The *Zeitschrift für freie deutsche Forschung,* Paris, 1938, pp. 157-158, listed two scores of professors who, for similar reasons, were dismissed in 1937.—The degree to which German professors conformed to the ideological requirements of the Nazi state can conveniently be gauged by deducting from the number of dismissed professors those who were eliminated for *racial* reasons, i.e., Jews or descendants of Jews. The rest would represent those who, though racially impeccable, ostensibly opposed the Nazis. We may say in advance that their number was extremely small.

[30] Cf. e.g., Walter Frank, *Deutsche Wissenschaft und Judenfrage* (Hamburg, Hanseatische Verlagsanstalt, 1st ed. [1937], 2nd ed., 1940, 51 pp.).

[31] Hartshorne. *op. cit.*

This demand, by the way, is characteristic of Nazi policy in general and probably a result of deep psychological insight; we shall recall that Hitler carefully avoided being identified with former nationalistic groups and cliques. For this reason the old-timers among the professors, too, were looked at askance. But their aloofness against which the great Nazi champions (Krieck, Walter Frank. Jaensch) inveighed did not apply to Hitler's ideals as such. It stemmed rather from the repugnance of intellectuals toward the profanity of language and the vulgarity of reasoning, often deliberate, which used to be a feature of nazism in the period of its struggle for power. At that time, educated people still were able to see, even if they were pleased by the contents, that *Mein Kampf* was written in the verbose, strained style of a self-taught person which often sounded like a parody of itself; that Rosenberg's *Der Mythus des 20. Jahrhunderts* (The Myth of the Twentieth Century) could not qualify for a review in a respectable periodical; that Feder's treatises on economics were low-class journalism. As to the anti-Jewish publications, like Artur Dinter's *Die Sünde wider das Blut* or Hans F. K. Günther's first tracts on racialism or the incessantly reprinted *Protokolle der Weisen von Zion* (Protocols of the Elders of Zion), they did not show up very well either as compared with the average academic production and frequently were subjects of laughter. As time went on, however, the Nazis not only became the source of power and wealth and the seekers after Germany's greatness, but also learned how to handle footnotes and quotations. Thus, the situation had changed remarkably, and one German scholar after another, if only he was not tainted by Jewish family connections, proceeded to discover his National Socialist heart. The well-known democratic Professor Dr. Willy Hellpach of the University of Heidelberg, who in 1925 had run for president of the Weimar republic as a candidate of the liberal Democratic Party, in 1928 had gone so far as to advocate intermarriage with Jews and to state clearly:

> The Germans are no race folk (Rassenvolk). He who wants to make such a one out of them, who wants to found their folkdom on race, their national consciousness on race instinct, inevitably becomes a destroyer of Germandom.[32]

But after some years of penitence, even Professor Hellpach joined the faithful.

---

[32] Willy Hellpach, *Politische Prognose für Deutschland* (Berlin, Fischer, 1928, 519 pp), p. 9.

To get insight into the procedure of nazification, it is instructive to read the above mentioned pamphlet by Kahle, whether or not one agrees with its suggestions for the future.[33] And once nazification was achieved, German scholarship proceeded from a single fundamental idea, expressed by Krieck in the following way:

> Each folk in each period must form its life according to its own law and fate and to this law of its own, scholarship, with all other spheres of life, is also subject.
>
> . . . The idea of humanism, with the teaching of pure human reason and absolute spirit founded upon it, is a philosophical principle of the eighteenth century caused by the conditions of that time. It is in no sense binding upon us as we live under different conditions and under different fate.[34]

In endless verbal variations we encounter this master idea:

> Such a folk-bias carries its certainty in itself and not in logical criteria of truth, because the latter do not attain to the metalogical, such as symbol, myth, fate, heroism, or providence.[35]

Or, as a German philosopher expressed it in a cautious attempt to defend philosophy against the "spirit of the time":

> The "German man," the "Nordic man" is being made the *canon* against which the validity of views on the world is being measured.[36]

"Views on the world," as we have known since September 1, 1939, from the very outset meant exactly that; the Nazis did not stop at Germany's borders. As a matter of fact, they never seriously concealed their intentions; they simply adroitly maneuvered. In a pamphlet published by the Deutsche Akademie in the early days of the regime, Karl Haushofer pleaded for understanding abroad by submitting that

> the National Socialist idea in the world has . . . the same double face as the mystic Janus: one that overlooks world distances in

---

[33] Cf. footnote 19. To grasp Professor Kahle's views—and he certainly is representative of a good many pre-war German liberal professors — it is sufficient to read the following sentences concerning the German students' organizations which between 1919 and 1933 had been real hotbeds of reaction but later were dissolved by the Nazi regime because of their Monarchist leanings: "In pre-Nazi times German students were not particularly interested in politics. . . . The students were organized in the 'Verbindungen'. . . . The Verbindungen called 'Corps' were rather exclusive. . . . In the Corps Borussia [at Bonn] . . . the members were all princes, counts and barons. . . . Nothing was so unpopular in German universities as the suppression of the old 'Studentenverbindungen.' The reintroduction of these institutions . . . migh prove helpful in bringing back the students to normal pre-Nazi University life. There is no doubt that these institutions were by no means perfect, and several alterations would be necessary in any case, but with such modifications these institutions might be able to compensate the students for such attractions in the Nazi organization as appealed to the young people" (pp. 23, 37-38).

[34] Ernst Krieck, *Das nationalsozialistische Deutschland und die Wissenschaft* (Hamburg, Hanseatische Verlagsanstalt [1936], 35 pp.), pp. 24, 31. — The address was read at the celebration of the 550th anniversary of the Heidelberg University, in the presence of many guests from abroad.

In many subsequent quotations, too, "Volk" is rendered by *folk*, in order to preserve somewhat of the mystical flavor it possesses in the German language.

[35] Professor Dr. Walter Schulze-Sölde, *Politik und Wissenschaft* (Berlin, Junker und Dünnhaupt, 1934, 62 pp.).

[36] Theodor Litt, *Philosophie und Zeitgeist* (Leipzig, 1934, 61 pp.), p. 15.

spanning the globe and another that can be comprehended only in the very own folk soil of each race.[37]

But the world obstinately wanted to see only one face of Janus, the one turned inward. Victor Bruns bluntly applied the master idea to foreign politics:

> . . . The unjust treaty as an embodiment of power is a negation of the conception of law and consequently of the legal order. Its removal is a requirement of the law itself.[38]

He made it abundantly clear that it was the Reich, and solely the Reich, which was to define what was just or unjust. But though he was enthusiastically seconded by Carl Schmitt and his thesis was unanimously adopted by German political science, the outer world refused to identify the undertone of "today Germany—tomorrow the world" and, instead, preferred to believe that national socialism was an internal, purely German affair.

IV

ALFRED ROSENBERG, THE APOSTLE OF RACIALISM

In Nazi definition, a *folk* consists of several *race* components. The German folk, for example, is said to be predominantly Nordic but also to contain strains of Faelic, Dinaric, Mediterranean, Baltic, and other race blood. The Norwegian folk possesses more Nordic components and therefore ranks even higher than the German in hierarchy. The English folk is said to consist of practically the same components as the Germans, only in different proportions. Consequently, both Norwegians and the English are cognate (artverwandt) to the German folk. If they deviate from their right way in history it is because miscegenation has led to deterioration of the stock. As to the Eastern European peoples, the noble elements are represented among them to a much lesser degree; for that reason they are less valuable folks or, in common parlance, lower races. Finally, the Jews are essentially a counter-race (Gegenrasse); they are alien in species (artfremd), since they are a mixture of the Near-Eastern (vorderasiatisch) and Oriental races, with some other minor admixtures.

Anthropologists outside Germany unanimously refuse even to discuss seriously the German race classification, let alone to draw from

---

[37] Karl Haushofer, *Der nationalsozialistische Gedanke in der Welt* (München, Callwey, 1933, 48 pp.), p. 46.

[38] Victor Bruns, *Völkerrecht und Politik* (Berlin, Junker und Dünnhaupt, 1934, 27 pp.), p. 23.

it any conclusions of a practical nature. But since the Germans religiously adhered to this dogma, we might at least expect that the passages on "folk" and "folk bias" quoted in the previous chapter be recognized as contradicting the doctrine of race. Nothing of the kind. This would presuppose more deference to "pure reason" and more discrimination in the use of terms than the Nazis were interested in. While they accused their opponents of being vague, they themselves cared little for exactness, since greater things were at stake. Professor Dr. Alfred Baeumler, a foremost German university teacher in philosophy, wrote:

> For centuries, the racial-soul and folk (rassenseelisch-völkische) peculiarities *in spite* of all universalistic counteraction were able to produce a unity of culture. Finally, the power abated. The international Jew, by making use of money thinking, elevated himself to world domination and threatened to destroy all waxing creative power; bolshevism was about to annihilate the nations physically as well. Just then the distress of the time in the most threatened folk gave rise to the will and the cognition which led to regeneration. Instead of the vague mixture of general concepts and values which used to be called the spirit of humaneness or the idea of Western culture, national socialism set up an organically founded *Weltanschauung*. It did not content itself with piecemeal curing of the symptoms but attacked the evil at its roots.[39]

Thus spoke a man who had won his spurs in editing Bachofen and Nietzsche and finally became Alfred Rosenberg's bard. It is indeed fitting that our discussion on Nazi Weltanschauung should start with a quotation from a eulogy of Rosenberg since, after the seizure of power, he was the key person in streamlining anti-Semitism and in bringing it in line with the general new philosophy. To rely on Baeumler again:

> The struggle of the Führer against Versailles was the struggle against the Jewish democratic myth. It was Rosenberg's task to carry this struggle on a plane of principles up to the end.[40]

Or, in again reverting to the subject:

> In days to come one will adore in Rosenberg one of the greatest German educators against halfness.... He early recognized that the deeper and more significant the contrasts that wrestle with each other, the more valueless a compromise.[41]

[39] Alfred Baeumler, *Alfred Rosenberg und der Mythus des 20. Jahrhunderts* (München, Hoheneichen-Verlag, 1943, 111 pp.), p. 97.
[40] *Ibid.*, p. 69.
[41] *Ibid.*, p. 107.

Rosenberg's career is well known and does not need to be dwelt upon here. It was he, it seems, who in 1923 first proclaimed Hitler to be Germany's *Führer*. He was a prolific speaker and writer, the editor-in-chief of the *Völkischer Beobachter* from its inception and, what interests us particularly here, the founder in 1924 of *Der Weltkampf, Monatsschrift für die Judenfrage aller Länder*, a periodical with which we shall have to deal many times. Later on, he started the *Nationalsozialistische Monatshefte*, as the theoretical organ of the Movement. His *Mythus des 20. Jahrhunderts* was second only to *Mein Kampf* as a bestseller.[42] Rosenberg's speeches often came out in pamphlet form and also were widely distributed through private channels and through the machinery he had established. Hardly an issue of any publication of his failed to fulminate against the Jews. In speaking about the "Protocols of the Elders of Zion," which he quoted without end and published many times, he unscrupulously admitted that their provenience was obscure, but, he added, his own intuition was the best proof of their authenticity. He was a reckless writer:

> Rosenberg the journalist does not attack Mr. Schmidt or Mr. Cohen; he attacks the demon who has become visible and who is the mortal enemy of Germandom. He creates the feeling in his readers: this is a matter of life and death; it can only be you or we.[43]

But not his literary production alone made Rosenberg the single person most responsible for what happened to the Jews in Europe under Nazi domination. What made him particularly dangerous was the combination of a mind prone to indulge in speculations and an unquestionable organizational talent. Some "pure theorists" were more meticulous in using sources and more precise in chiseling out their formulations, such as Professor Dr. Walter Frank, whom we shall meet soon; and certainly other Nazis have more actual killings on their consciences than this lover of Goethe, Schiller, Kant, and Schopenhauer, with his impeccable, if a little overstressed, manners. But Rosenberg was the man who brought theory and practice together, who not only supplied the ideology but also built the organization to promote it. There was no exaggeration in the word-

---

[42] The German official bibliography *Deutsche Nationalbibliographie*, no. 28 of 1941, lists the sum total of all editions of *Mein Kampf* as 7,100,000 copies; the latest copy in the Yivo library, published in 1943, bears the imprint: sum total of all editions 9,840,000 copies. Rosenberg's *Mythus*, according to *Deutsche Nationalbibliographie*, no. 36 of 1941, up to September of that year had been printed in 950,000 copies; a 1943 edition in the Yivo library belongs to "1026.-1075. Tausend," which means an additional 125,000 copies within two years. The *Mythus* first appeared in October, 1930.

[43] Baeumler, *op. cit.*, p. 19.

ing of the address that was handed to Rosenberg together with the award of the German national prize for art and science at the Reichsparteitag der Arbeit (Party Convention [in Honor] of Labor) in Nuremberg in 1937 in the Führer's presence:

> ... Only later days will be able to measure fully how strong is the impact of this man on the intellectual and philosophical formation of the National Socialist Reich.

As the head of the "Foreign Affairs Office" of the Nazi party, even before 1933, Rosenberg was the foremost advocate of the *Ostpolitik* which eventually was to carry Germany's military forces to the very Volga and Caucasus. In the provinces under his rule, the so-called Eastern Occupied Territories (besetzte Ostgebiete) the first mass murders of the Jewish population started in the summer of 1941. This period we shall discuss later,[44] but it is a safe guess that just as the sensational consummation of the "Campaign of the Eighteen Days" had been achieved by careful preparations, just as the attack on the Soviet Union was no improvisation, so the "radical solution of the Jewish question" was not contrived on the spur of the moment. As Baeumler testified: "He who really *wishes* to save the German people from the Jewish grip, will refrain from nothing in pursuing his objective." [45]

On Jan. 24, 1934, Rosenberg was made Beauftragter des Führers für die Überwachung der gesamten geistigen und weltanschaulichen Schulung und Erziehung der Nationalsozialistischen Deutschen Arbeiterpartei (Commissioner of the Führer for the Supervision of the Total Intellectual and Philosophical Schooling and Training of the National Socialist German Workers Party). The following offices were organized, each liberally staffed: Office of Schooling (Amt Schulung), Office of Philosophical Information (Amt weltanschauliche Information), Office of Literature (Amt Schrifttum), Office of Research (Amt Wissenschaft), Office of Pre-History (Amt Vorgeschichte), Office of Art Cultivation (Amt Kunstpflege), Press Office (Amt Presse).[46]

---

[44] Just for the record, it is useful to note the following passage on the Eastern scheme in Baeumler's book: "[In the Foreign Affairs Office of the Nazi party] the problems of the East were given particular attention.... For reasons easily understandable, today [1943] no more particulars about the initiative of the Foreign Affairs Office in different fields can be given" (p. 105).

[45] *Ibid.*, p. 88.

[46] Carl Johanny, Oscar Redelsberger. *Volk, Partei, Reich.* 2. Auflage (Berlin, Deutscher Rechtsverlag, 1943, 300 pp.), p. 98.
   More "offices" or "main offices" were added later, such as for Party Training Apparatus (Parteiamtliche Lehrmittel) and, most important, the Main Office on supra-State Powers (Hauptamt Überstaatliche Mächte), in which the struggle against the Jews was concentrated. A review of ten years' activities of the Rosenberg Office was given in the *Nationalsozialistische Monatshefte*, no. 161 (1944), 1-6.

Even while the Party was still in the ascendancy, Rosenberg was able to attract one by one ambitious younger academic people eager for recognition and remuneration by assigning them special tasks in the rapidly growing Nazi machinery. As the Weimar Republic gradually decayed, more and more scholars had come to derive their inspiration from Hitler and his prophet. Now, with the founding of the Office of Research within the Commissionership, Rosenberg's opportunities for displaying his organizational talents multiplied a thousandfold. And he certainly made full use of them. In 1938, an even closer relationship between Rosenberg and the academic world was established. That year, the University of Halle-Wittenberg requested him

> to give his particular support to this university which is at once time-honored, close to present-day problems and promising for the future, and personally to convey through it to the academic youth of the German people the ideological possessions of the National Socialist Weltanschauung.[47]

An Alfred Rosenberg Foundation was called into being to make available 100,000 marks annually to young scholars.

In his first address after his appointment as Commissioner, Rosenberg at a most solemn function in the presence of the highest officials, the diplomatic corps, and the international press on February 22, 1934, spoke thus:

> This heroic attitude [of national socialism], to begin with, departs from the *single* but *completely* decisive avowal, *namely from the avowal that blood and character, race and soul are merely different designations for the same entity*. In the development of the victorious National Socialist movement, a deep mystery of blood revealed itself which seemingly had died in the World War and yet was regenerated in this new movement. Under *this* sign, the cell-building of the German soul, of the German people proceeded again. And around this recuperating, newly born blood circulate all thoughts of those who wanted to struggle for this new Germany and for the great time coming. A concomitant of this experience was the rise of a new science, of a new scientific *discovery* which we call racial science.[48]

The foreign guests who were invited to Rosenberg's performance probably could not make much out of this involved statement, which was a comparatively easy passage in the entire address. Some of them, who had yawned at *Der Mythus des 20. Jahrhunderts* or laughed at

---

[47] [Karlheinz Rüdiger]. *Das Werk Alfred Rosenbergs. Eine Bibliographie* (München, Eher [1941], 31 pp.), p. 28.
[48] Alfred Rosenberg. *Der Kampf um die Weltanschauung* (München, Eher, 1938, 24 pp.).

some of its more intelligible statements, such as that Socrates was to be considered an international Social Democrat,[49] did not expect any better. But the German audience got the hint perfectly, and reviewers vied with each other in the use of superlatives.

V

RACIAL SCIENCE: EUGEN FISCHER, ERNST RÜDIN, AND OTHERS

Nobody needs reminding that the emphasis upon race emanated from Hitler himself. In *Mein Kampf* he had announced:

> The total educational and training work of the folk-state must find its crowning-point in that it burns instinctively and rationally the sense of race and the feeling of race into the hearts and minds of the youth entrusted to it.[50]

In his speech at the Nuremberg Parteitag (Party Convention) of 1933, the first after his coming into power, he again took occasion to declare:

> National socialism professes . . . the heroic teaching of evaluating blood, race, and personality as well as the eternal laws of selection and thus consciously puts itself in unbridgeable contradiction to the philosophy of pacifist-international democracy and its effects.

In preaching this new gospel, the scientists were not found wanting. One of the first universities to open an Institut für Erbbiologie und Rassenforschung (Institute of Hereditary Biology and Race Research) was the University of Frankfort on-the-Main; a staff member of this institute, as we shall see, later obtained prominence in the death factory of Oświęcim. The director of the institute, Professor Dr. Otmar Freiherr von Verschuer, in his inauguration speech pointed out that four roads had led to modern racial science: anthropology, eugenics, medical constitution-research, and experimental genetics (Erblehre). Gobineau, Mendel, and others had successfully worked in the field but only a generation after these champions it became possible to tie up genetics very closely with the history of the state. Adolf Hitler, he stressed, was the first statesman to recognize genetics as a necessity for the state and the folk.[51]

In the beginning, also, the term "political biology" was in vogue. The Munich publishing house of J. F. Lehmann, which had pioneered in racialism in days when the world knew nothing of Hitler,

---

[49] Rosenberg, *Der Mythus* . . . , p. 286.
[50] Pp. 475-476.
[51] *Das Archiv*, 1935, p. 450.

initiated a series, "Politische Biologie," and its editor, Dr. Heinz Müller, in his preface to a book by the well known statistician Burgdörfer suggested:

> A National Socialist biology . . . must find the bridge to culture and politics just as . . . National Socialist politics ought to be only biological, i.e., that which takes into account the laws of life. To this principle everything else in German life must be subordinated. The science of our people, too, on the basis of this Aryan biological value-gauge has to serve their struggle for existence and the preservation of their healthy life and of the race defining it in that it prepares and hands over as a weapon and equipment to the materializer, the man of politics, the fighter what is important and interesting for the struggle of the people for existence.[52]

Insistence upon race meant, of course, pressing the Jewish issue both in theory and practice. There is substantial agreement that nazism would never have made such headway except for its harnessing the power of hate against a conspicuous minority, strongly marked throughout the centuries, "who were few enough to be helpless and numerous enough to be held up as a menace," as Justice Jackson put it at the Nuremberg trial. The Jew could be represented as the embodiment of everything to be resented, feared, and despised. He was a carrier of bolshevism but, curiously enough, he simultaneously stood for the liberal spirit of rotten Western democracy. Economically, he was both capitalist and socialist. He was blamed as the indolent pacifist but, by strange coincidence, he was also the eternal instigator to wars.

As far as the Jews were also the conspicuous competitors, above all in trade and in the professions, they were taken care of in the anti-Jewish legislation of the first months of Nazi domination. For highly practical reasons, shopkeepers, lawyers, and physicians in numbers had joyfully adopted the Nazi program long before the Party had ascended to power, and now their reward had come. But the Nazis wanted not merely to disfranchise the Jews and to take their wealth away. Likewise, the "Aryanization" of the universities and scientific periodicals which came in the wake of the seizure of power was more than the forcible installation of competitors in positions for

---

[52] Friedrich Burgdörfer, *Völker am Abgrund* (München, Lehmann, 1936, 76 pp.).—On the Lehmann firm and its rôle in the rise of nazism, see *Fünfzig Jahre J. F. Lehmanns Verlag, München* (München, Lehmann, 1940, 216 pp.). This book on p. 67 contains a very pertinent paragraph describing the peculiarity of German racial science as compared with eugenics: "In the period after the [first world] war, Jewish-democratic and clerical circles, particularly in Berlin, attempted to neutralize racial hygiene under the name of eugenics. . . . With the strengthening of the National Socialist movement soon new studies came into existence which were to serve the idea of racial hygiene. . . ."

which they previously had striven in vain. Anti-Semitism to the new rulers was a means to greater ends. Downing the Jews would bring the Reich a good deal nearer to downing Christianity, too, which would leave national socialism the complete conqueror of German souls. Moreover, as the international situation would be heading toward a showdown, fanning up anti-Semitism would disrupt the countries to be attacked and, from the very outset, gain for Germany the favor of large elements who would profit from expropriating the possessions of the Jews. In one of the last chapters we shall hear an astute Nazi testify that anti-Semitism has been nazism's secret weapon.

Thus, anti-Jewish feelings and convictions had to be inculcated in every German and, beyond that, in every person anywhere in the world. This end, the Nazis knew in their German deference to scholarship, could be effected only through science. Volkmar Eichstädt, a learned librarian of the Prussian State Library in Berlin, author of a comprehensive anti-Jewish bibliography, suggested:

> Research into the contest, full of struggle and finally victorious, of our German folk with the racially alien element of Jewry leads us nearer to recognizing our German nature itself and it thereby not only multiplies our knowledge but also strengthens our will to a folk life.[53]

The scheme was simple and yet fascinating. The law of nature concerning "the survival of the fittest" should be presented so as to admit no exceptions. The unfit is doomed to *Ausmerze* (extinction) and if he does not go voluntarily, he must be helped out of existence. This law of nature would be, then, made to apply also to groups or, in a more mystical term, to races; and in the order of fitness the Jews would appear as the lowest group predestined for *Ausmerze,* while the top folk of the Germans would emerge as the crown of creation. The term *Ausmerze* should be remembered. As a metaphor, it appears in Nazi literature as early as in the Twenties, e.g., in Rosenberg's *Mythus*:

> ... The most glowing nationalism ... is the message which one day will melt down all slags to extract the noble and to extinguish the ignoble.[54]

In the Thirties, selection (Auslese) and extinction (Ausmerze) are the pivots of the racial doctrines that dominate German political

[53] Volkmar Eichstädt, "Das Schrifttum zur Judenfrage in den deutschen Bibliotheken," *Forschungen zur Judenfrage* VI (1941), 253-264.
[54] P. 85.

and intellectual life. In the Forties, *Ausmerze* is used, as we shall see, to designate and, with the air of scientific authority about it, to sanction the annihilation of the Jewish people all over Europe. The concept had not been developed in vain.

To begin with, only internal measures were discussed and thus interference from abroad was avoided. After all, Germany, in doing away with the Jews, discriminated only against her own citizens, and this discrimination was nobody else's business, as the world was only too ready to concede. By the same token, if Germany's eugenists indulged in suggesting forcible sterilization for certain groups of the population, it was their right to do so. As a matter of fact, the Congress of the International Union of Eugenic Organizations in Zurich in 1934 detachedly and on a purely theoretical level discussed the question of German racial policies on the basis of the Nazi Professor Karl Astel's paper. Astel was an SS staff member, too.

Rosenberg's Training Commissionership, in spite of all the importance attached to it, was not considered sufficient to pump this new revelation into the German people. A special Rassenpolitisches Amt der NSDAP (Racial-Policy Office of the National Socialist German Workers Party) was created for this particular purpose, and Walter Gross, M.D., whom we shall meet many times as our discussion proceeds, was made its head. Furthermore, the Nazi regime very early took up "political biology" as a technical administrative task and Dr. Achim Gercke, expert for race study in the Reich Ministry of Interior, thus elucidated the principles he expected to follow in his work:

> First of all, we have the negative side in our work which translated into race technique means: extinction (*Ausmerze*). In its last consequence, it amounts to *sterilization of those hereditarily inferior.* Let them not bother us with the old and false humanitarian ideas. There is in truth only one humane idea, that is: *"furthering the good, eliminating the bad."* The will of nature is the will of God. Let us look around.... How does nature work for millennia with her creatures? She sides with the strong, good, and victorious one and separates "the chaff from the wheat." We simply fulfill the commandment, no more, no less.[55]

Erwin Baur, director of the Kaiser Wilhelm Institut for Breeding Research, wrote in the same book:

> Every farmer knows that should he slaughter the best specimens of his domestic animals without letting them procreate and should

---

[55] Cf. Charlotte Köhn-Behrens, *Was ist Rasse?* 2. Auflage (München, Eher, 1934, 125 pp.), p. 64.

instead continue breeding inferior individuals, his breeds would degenerate hopelessly. This mistake, which no farmer would commit with his animals and cultivated plants, we permit to go on in our midst to a large extent. As a recompense for our humaneness of today, we must see to it that these inferior people do not procreate. A simple operation to be executed in a few minutes makes this possible without further delay.... No one approves of the new sterilization laws more than I do, but I must repeat over and over that they *constitute only a beginning.*[56]

It is worthwhile stopping for a moment to take cognizance of the fact that the above paragraph was written by a biologist of worldwide reputation: apart from his many studies in heredity he was with Professor Dr. Eugen Fischer, whom we have encountered already as the first Nazi rector of the Berlin University, and Professor Dr. Fritz Lenz, co-author of the famous two-volume work on genetics and eugenics that has been used as a university textbook far beyond Germany's borders. A younger representative of the discipline and an ardent Nazi, Professor Dr. Otmar Freiherr von Verschuer of the Frankfort University, in a textbook issued during the war,[57] gratefully acknowledged the lasting contribution of "the leading textbook of Baur-Fischer-Lenz..., to whom belongs the chief merit of the inner upbuilding of our science" and considered it "a particular favor of fate" that he had been privileged to work as student and assistant under "these three great pioneers of racial hygiene."

In the fourth edition of this three-author work, published in 1936, Lenz proved by the following statement that at that time a scholar with courage could still be somewhat of a non-conformist:

> If here, in the first place, the *differences* in the endowment of the Jews and Teutons (Germanen) were stressed, it should not be overlooked, however, that in external mental dispositions (Anlagen) they resemble each other, and this is particularly true if "Teutons" are to designate people of the tall blonde race....[58]

But even he concluded his discussion with a spirited paragraph on the historical rôle of national socialism "in paving the way for a sound selection in the sense of purification, improvement and elevation of the race" (p. 773); and the Near-Eastern-Oriental character

[56] *Ibid.,* p. 35.

[57] Otmar Verschuer, *Leitfaden der Rassenhygiene* (Leipzig, Georg Thieme, 1941, 260 pp.).

[58] Prof. Dr. Baur, Prof. Dr. Eugen Fischer, Prof. Dr. Lenz, *Menschliche Erblehre und Rassenhygiene,* Band I: *Menschliche Erblehre* (München, Lehmann, 1936, 796 pp.), p. 756.— The reviewer of the *Zeitschrift für die gesamte Staatswissenschaft* said of it: "A standard work of which there is no equivalent in other countries."

of the Jews, a formulation which seems to have been coined by Eugen Fischer,[59] is taken for granted together with its implications.

As to Fischer, it is instructive that he was forced to acknowledge:

> The racial extraction [of a person] is really not always easy to establish . . . and in some parts of the population [one finds] a very strong crossing of Northern, Eastern-Baltic, Alpine, Dinaric [elements] . . . and one sees a tremendously variegated picture of single individuals.[60]

On the other hand, he too was heart and soul for human breeding (". . . races with hereditary dispositions increasable through breeding. . . The Nordic race, bred in the sharpest selection. . . ," *ibid.,* pp. 316-317), and, most significantly, he saw fit to bow in reverence before the champion of the German racial idea, Hans F. K. Günther. "In the excellent presentation of Hans F. K. Günther," Fischer took pains to acknowledge, "we possess . . . a first class *Rassenkunde des deutschen Volkes*" (p. 279). To feel the full weight of this statement we must recall that even in Germany Günther's just cited book on the racial composition of the Germans used to be the target of ridicule before the Nazis made him a university professor to reward him for his contribution to their cause. To them he was valuable indeed. "It is Günther's undeniable merit," the pugnacious *Kampfruf* wrote in the period of struggle for power, "to be transforming racial knowledge from a secret science of a few initiated into a concern of the whole German people. He supplied the National Socialist movement with the mental equipment for that political utilization of this problem, which use is of so decisive an importance for the future of the German people." [61]

From Günther and Fischer, whom we shall encounter again repeatedly, we may now turn to Dr. Ernst Rüdin, for many years Professor of Psychiatry at the University of Munich. He not only served nazism with his pen by contributing to and editing a two-volume work on "Genetics and Eugenics in the Folk State" and several smaller books but also actively participated in preparing German racial legislation. Witness the fact that on the occasion of his 65th birthday Rüdin was awarded the Goethe medal for art and science by the Führer and honored by the following telegram from the Minister of the Interior Dr. Wilhelm Frick:

---

[59] Cf. Gerhard Kittel in *Forschungen zur Judenfrage* III, 131: "Kein geringerer als Eugen Fischer." The "Jewish nose," Kittel informed, was of Near-Eastern provenience.

[60] *Ibid.,* p. 296.

[61] Cf. p. [281] of the book listed in footnote 63.

To the indefatigable champion of racial hygiene and meritorious pioneer of the racial-hygienic measures of the Third Reich I send... my heartiest congratulations.[62]

Rüdin's name appears together with two others on a rather early commentary on German eugenic legislation intended primarily for physicians. A full professor and Director of the Kaiser Wilhelm Institute for Genealogy and Demography, Rüdin would not have shared authorship with small fry, but the two co-authors were worthy of the honor. Arthur Gütt, M.D., was a high official (Ministerialdirektor) in Frick's Ministry of the Interior. Falk Ruttke, doctor of jurisprudence, on the basis of the secret Nazi documents which we produce in chapter XXXIX, is now revealed as the author of the "infamous Nuremberg Laws," as General Eisenhower termed them in his first order issued on German soil. The leading ideas of the authors were expressed in the introduction to the volume:

> Our whole cultural life for decades has been more or less under the influence of biological thinking, as it was begun particularly around the middle of the last century, by the teachings of Darwin, Mendel, and Galton and afterwards has been advanced by the studies of Ploetz, Schallmeyer, Correns, de Vries, Tschermak, Baur, Rüdin, Fischer, Lenz, and others. Though it took decades before the courage was found, on the basis of the initial findings of the natural sciences, to carry on a systematic study of heredity, the progress of the teaching and its application to man could not be delayed any more. It was recognized that the natural laws discovered for plants and animals ought also to be valid for man, and this could fully and completely be confirmed during the last three decades both through family research (Familienforschung) and through the study of bastards and twins.[63]

In another volume devoted to the subject and also written by three esteemed scholarly co-authors, Professor Dr. Martin Staemmler stated:

---

[62] *Allgemeine Zeitschrift für Psychiatrie und ihre Grenzgebiete,* III (1939), 408.— The New York newspaper *PM* of August 21, 1945, quoted a letter addressed to Rüdin by Frick as early as 1933 reading: "I hereby tender you assignment as my honorary representative at the Society for Race Hygiene and the German League for Heredity Science and Racial Improvement. The theory of inheritance and race hygiene are of the utmost importance for the structure of the Reich and for improvement of the race of the German people; therefore, I would like you to carry through the reconstruction work in closest collaboration with my ministry." In 1944, when he was seventy, Rüdin, again according to *PM*, received from the Führer a bronze medal bearing the Nazi eagle and praising him as the "pathfinder in the field of hereditary hygiene."

[63] Dr. med. Arthur Gütt, Dr. med. Ernst Rüdin, Dr. jur. Falk Ruttke, *Gesetz zur Verhütung erbkranken Nachwuchses vom 14. Juli 1933* ... (München, Lehmann, 1934, 272 pp.), p. 13.—The leading German legal weekly *Juristische Wochenschrift* in its issue of May 11, 1935, published a large paper by Dr. Ruttke "Erb- und Rassenpflege in Gesetzgebung und Rechtsprechung des 3. Reiches" on the penetration of legislation and jurisdiction of Germany with racial concepts.

I believe and hope just after the events of the last years that German idealism, heroism and spirit of sacrifice are still alive.... Let us, therefore, free the Nordic soul from the fetters of materialism; then it will again attain its former bloom. Then we will again recognize it as what we would like to set before our people as the breeding aim.[64]

He continued:

Extinction and selection are the two poles around which the whole race cultivation (Rassenpflege) rotates, the two methods with which it has to work.... Extinction is the biological destruction of the hereditary inferior through sterilization, the quantitative repression of the unhealthy and the undesirable.... The ... task consists of safeguarding the people from an overgrowth of the weeds....[65]

Later in the same study, we find a paragraph which anticipates the ideas underlying German policies during the war:

Race cultivation has the task of changing the quantitative ratio of the good hereditary traits to the bad in favor of the former, in disfavor of the latter. In other words, it should see to it that more persons should be born with good hereditary traits than those with bad. It should try by all means to find out people with full value, normal and super-value traits (selection!), to promote them and to receive from them large progeny; secondly, it must try by all means to find out people with subvalue traits and to repress them in their progeny (extinction); it must in the third place defend the people from internal racial disruption by not admitting alien racial elements to it.[66]

One of the Nazi leaders, Hans Schemm, who until his death in 1937 was a Bavarian cabinet member, aptly epitomized the situation by stating: "national socialism is applied biology."

The section of the Nazi party that made the most of applying biology in a manner now thoroughly known to the world was Himmler-Kaltenbrunner's Elite Guard (SS, Schutzstaffel), proclaimed by Himmler to be "a National Socialist soldierly order of Nordically defined men." It is not surprising, therefore, that an instruction book[67] classified as restricted and issued by the chief of the SS and SD (Sicherheits-Dienst, Security Service) after October, 1941, i.e., at a time when the wholesale extermination of the Jews in the occupied Eastern territories was already in full swing, abundantly quoted from Erwin

---

[64] Dr. Alfred Kühn, Dr. Martin Staemmler, Dr. Friedrich Burgdörfer, *Erbkunde, Rassenpflege, Bevölkerungspolitik. Schicksalsfragen des deutschen Volkes*. Her. von Dr. Heinz Woltereck (Leipzig, Quelle und Meyer, 1935, 298 pp.), p. 134.

[65] *Ibid.*, pp. 134-135.

[66] *Ibid.*, p. 157.

[67] Nur für den Gebrauch innerhalb der Sicherheitspolizei und des SD. Der Chef der Sicherheitspolizei und des SD. *Der Rassegedanke und seine gesetzliche Gestaltung*. Heft 1 (n.p., n.d. [after October, 1941], 65, III pp. 4°).

Baur, Friedrich Burgdörfer, Arthur Gütt, Ernst Rüdin and the book by Kühn-Staemmler-Burgdörfer just referred to.

In a feeling of justice one may remind oneself that, after all, the question of race vs. environment is controversial and that similar, though not identical, formulations on race improvement could perhaps be found in some writings on eugenics outside Germany as well. But when two people seem to say the same thing they may say something different. I submit that it is not only the words that count but, even more so, the emotional, intellectual and moral climate in which they are uttered. As a matter of fact, we heard the Nazis themselves quite openly admit the disparity between their "racial hygiene" and "neutral" eugenics. It makes all the difference in the world whether a discussion is carried on in the cool atmosphere of specialized literature under a democracy that gives each side equal opportunity of expression, or a controversial issue is made the basis of legislation and administrative practice in a country ruled by an implacable dictatorship. Books that in Hitler's Germany opened with a quotation from Hitler's *Mein Kampf,* like the Staemmler volume, and began: "It is an imperishable merit of the National Movement not only to have politically united our people and filled it with new vigor..." should not be granted the honor to be considered part of a scientific discussion; they were instruments in a ruthless struggle for power that soon was to engulf the whole world. The German "racial scientists" were not merely exponents of an idea; simultaneously, they were the only legislators and the enforcers of the law, with every opponent virtually gagged.

As a matter of fact, the Hitlerite scholars were afraid of the impression they might produce abroad; but they relied — and for a long time they were right in doing so—on the capital of prestige that German scholarship had accumulated. The following quotation, remarkable also in its wording apart from the content, is a case in point:

> Since January 1, 1934, the law of July 1, 1933, on preventing hereditarily-ill progeny has been enforced. Thereby a years-long controversy about the admissibility of sterilization, about the way of executing it and the extent of its application has been concluded. In a sense, this concerns not only Germany but also Europe and the rest of the world. Though the world war, in which almost the whole world fought against Germany, pushed back German influence abroad with regard to power politics, still neither our former adversaries nor the traitors to their country who fled abroad

succeeded in destroying the authority of German scholarship. German scholarship is still a model to foreign countries because for decades it has done pioneering work. Thus, if we do not ourselves jeopardize German scientific research and the reputation of German training particularly in the field of medicine, this is going to remain so in the future, too, and German influence in general is going to grow increasingly along with the political regeneration of the German people.[68]

It would be amusing, were it not tragic, to compile the passages of Nazi literature throughout the years with all their efforts to reconcile the extravagances of their Nordic theory with the necessity of recognizing the individual merits of prominent Germans who deviated from the racial norm. Similarly, different interpretations had to be advanced as to what was to be considered desirable and worthy of perpetuation as both Hitler and Goebbels, not to speak of many minor gods, in their appearance very definitely diverged from the proclaimed Nordic ideal.

But as to the Jews, everything was clear from the moment the definition of a Jew was introduced into the law. True, the term "Aryan" later was dropped in favor of "persons of German or cognate (artverwandt) blood," ultimately to be supplanted by the simple term "German" as opposed to "Jew." [69] At a still later stage, it occurred to the Nazi scholars that "anti-Semitic," too, was a misleading term since it would include also opposition to the Arabs on whom Nazi Germany relied heavily in preparing her blueprints for world conquest.[70] But these were vacillations only as to terminology. As to the essence of racialism, simultaneously admired as a science and revered as religion, there was no trembling, no step back or aside. The objective was fixed early and then the *Ausmerze* procedure was gradually mapped out and followed up to the inexorable end when it was no longer a metaphor nor a term referring to breeding.

VI

LEGAL AND POLITICAL SCIENCE: HANS FRANK, CARL SCHMITT, AND OTHERS

The situation in which an idea is set forth is important in any other scientific field just as in "racial science." It may be all right for a legal theorist to express his doubts as to the classical principle

---

[68] Gütt, Rüdin, Ruttke, *op. cit.*, p. 13.

[69] Otto Paul, "Kommen wir ohne das Wort 'arisch' aus?" *Weltkampf* I (1941), 100-101.

[70] Cf., p. 111.

of *nulla poena sine lege* (no penalty without a law). But it was quite
a different matter when this principle was defied in 1934 Germany[71]
in a series "The German State of Today (Der deutsche Staat der Gegenwart)," initiated by Carl Schmitt, in which over a dozen most
prominent German jurists joined in justifying the foundations of the
Third Reich. As one author in this series explained,[72] the idea of
"neutral research" was dead in his country, which had made research
"the institutional reality of the spiritual realm." Translating this do-
minant philosophy for the needs of practical jurists, Landesgerichts-
präsident Dr. Dietrich of Hechingen in a technical legal periodical
was able to conclude that a crime committed for the greater glory
of the Reich, as the Nazis understood it, was no crime at all:

> . . . We can therefore conclude that if the law is to be inter-
> preted rightly, the national goal is to be considered without further
> ceremony a motive for excluding guilt.... Thus the judge who
> already has the courage freely to interpret the law may now find
> the right way in the appropriate situation. In this, he also treads
> old Teutonic paths. As is well known, among our forefathers the
> inner enemy used to be outlawed and became a man without honor,
> without right and peace, an *outcast*. Each folk member could openly
> slay him so long as he was not at a sanctuary. "Infamous is the
> nation that does not stake everything on its honor." Exterminating
> without remainder the inner enemy is doubtlessly part of restituting
> German honor.[73]

A realistic picture of what happened in Germany, therefore, can
be gained only if the words of her scientists are confronted with the
deeds of her political, industrial, and military leaders. In doing so,
by the way, we merely comply with the wish of the German scholars
themselves, who ardently desired to be considered part and parcel of
the German system. Be it stressed again that in this book we deal
exclusively with those aspects of nazified German scholarship which,
directly or indirectly, refer to the Jews. Otherwise, we should have
to consider additional hundreds of persons and additional thousands
of publications.

Among the jurists, there was even the closest organizational co-
operation with the new state, as well as real sympathy. As early as
June 26, 1933, the Akademie für deutsches Recht (Academy for
German Law) was founded, which a year later was made a cor-

---

[71] Dr. Heinrich Henkel, *Strafrichter und Gesetz im neuen Staat* (Hamburg, Hanseatische Verlagsanstalt, 1934, 71 pp.).
[72] Professor Dr. Paul Ritterbusch, *Idee und Aufgabe der Reichsuniversität* (Hamburg, Hanseatische Verlagsanstalt [1935], 29 pp.).
[73] *Deutsche Juristenzeitung*, June 1, 1933.

poration of public law. From the very outset it was headed by Dr. Hans Frank, Reich minister, who during the war as Governor General in Poland won the reputation of one of the worst Nazi satraps and was put on the list of the top war criminals for the Nuremberg trials.[74] This Akademie was responsible for the whole Nazi legislation, including the preparation of the Nuremberg Laws. Hans Frank himself had seen in the "Aryan paragraph" "a beacon for the German people, nay, for the whole world." [75] No other witness for the commanding rôle of the Akademie für deutsches Recht is needed, since we have the testimony of Hans Frank himself. In 1938, he published a little book in which he praised the National Socialist seizure of power as "the greatest revolution in world history" and reiterated the basic right (Urrecht) of each folk "to shape its state institutions in a way that suits it for its existence" (p. 12). About his Akademie whose membership was most distinguished (see index), he had this to say:

> During the last years no larger law of the German Reich was published in which the Akademie für deutsches Recht did not have its full share (massgeblichen Anteil)…. At present this work is being done in over forty committees (Ausschüsse). In the committees of the Akademie für deutsches Recht, Department of Law Shaping (Rechtsgestaltung), the representatives of German legal science, of the Reich ministries, of the Party authorities, of the professional (ständische) organizations, etc., are united in harmonious work to develop the legal life of the Reich that it serve the Führer and the German folk.[76]

Undeniably the members of the various committees had a busy time. The questions raised by the new legislation were many and intricate. For instance, the difference between "Reich citizen (Reichsbürger)" and "state citizen (Staatsbürger)" had to be established in legal terms. The substitution of "German and cognate blood" for "Aryan," no doubt, was preceded by meticulous studies. Then, what about "hybrids (Mischlinge)"? They required classification. Article two of the Nuremberg Laws: "Extramarital relations between Jews and state citizens of German or cognate blood are prohibited" led to a most painstaking investigation in the Zeitschrift der Akademie für

---

[74] He is not to be confused with Walter Frank, the historian with whom we shall have to deal soon or with Karl Hermann Frank, who "distinguished" himself in occupied Bohemia-Moravia.

[75] Hans Frank [with 25 contributors, many of them university professors]. Deutsches Verwaltungsrecht (München, Eher, 1937, 536 pp.), p. 158.—All members of the Akademie für Deutsches Recht as of 1934 are listed on pp. 78-83 (II) in Das deutsche Führerlexikon 1934/1935 (Berlin, Stollberg, 1934, I, 552 pp. + II, 148 pp.).

[76] Dr. Hans Frank, Rechtsgrundlegung des nationalsozialistischen Führerstaates (München, Eher, 1938, 56 pp.), pp. 6, 7, 12.

deutsches Recht into the minutiae of what actually was to be considered extramarital relations. Likewise, the courts wanted to be advised as to what constituted a household in the sense of the law which
forbade male Jews to engage in their households female domestic
help of German or cognate blood under forty-five years of age. Should
a Jew who rents a room in an apartment and takes only one meal
a day there be considered a member of the household? And would
a seamstress who comes into a Jewish household for a week or so
fall under the definition of domestic help? All these problems had
to be given serious thought in legal literature.[77]

In addition to the jurists who rallied around the Akademie für
deutsches Recht, another group was eager to combine theory with
practice, the Reichsgruppe Hochschullehrer des Nationalsozialistischen Rechtswahrerbundes (University Instructors Group of the National Socialist Lawyers Union). Presided over by Carl Schmitt,
it held a conference on "Jewry in Jurisprudence" on October 3rd and
4th, 1936. Representatives of several ministries and institutions, including the Institut zum Studium der Judenfrage to which we are
devoting a special chapter, took part. One of the guests of honor,
Julius Streicher (a top defendant at Nuremberg), was prevented
from coming but wired his greetings, which were read to the
audience. The proceedings of the conference were published in a
series of pamphlets under the general heading: "Das Judentum in der
Rechtswissenschaft (Jewry in Jurisprudence)" by Deutscher Rechtsverlag, Berlin.

Papers were presented on the following subjects: Jewry and Eco-
nomics (Dozent Dr. Klaus Wilhelm Rath, U. of Göttingen); Jewish
Influence in Constitutional Law and Political Science (Professor Dr.
E[dgar] Tatarin-Tarnheyden, U. of Rostock); Jewry in Adminis-
trative Law Study (Professor Dr. [Theodor] Maunz, U. of Freiburg);
Jewry in Civil Procedure (Dozent Dr. [Horst] Bartholomeyczyk,
U. of Breslau); Jewry in Commercial Law (Professor Dr. [Hans]
Würdinger, U. of Breslau); Positivism, School of Free Law, Science
of Legal Sources (Professor Dr. Erich Jung, U. of Marburg); Jewry
in Criminal Law (Professor Dr. [Karl] Klee, U. of Berlin); Jewry
in Criminal Procedure (Professor Dr. [Karl] Siegert, University of
Göttingen); The Influence of Jewish Theorists on German International Law (Dozent Dr. Norbert Gürke, U. of Munich); Jewry in

---

[77] Cf. Dr. Bernhard Lösener, Ministerialrat, Dr. Friedrich Knost, Oberregierungsrat,
Die Nürnberger Gesetze, 5. Auflage (Berlin, Vahlen, 1942, 296 pp.).

International Private Law (Professor Dr. [Horst] Müller, U. of Freiburg); Jewish Criminality (Professor Dr. [Johann] von Leers, U. of Jena); Jewry in Criminal Psychology (Dr. M[ax] Mikorey, member, Akademie für deutsches Recht); Jewry and Competition (Dr. Jur. Otto Rilk).

The tone for the whole conference was set by Carl Schmitt, himself a member of the Akademie für deutsches Recht, who in his introductory address declared:

> The great speeches of the Führer and his fellow-combatants at the Parteitag der Ehre (Party Convention [under the Sign] of Honor) in Nuremberg have shown us with stirring clarity the present battle situation in the ideological contest with Jewry.

And further:

> . . . We must free the German spirit from all Jewish falsifications, falsifications of the concept "spirit (Geist)" which made possible for Jewish emigrants to call "unspiritual (ungeistig)" the marvelous struggle of Gauleiter Streicher.[78]

VII

THE BEGINNING OF THE NEW ANTI-JEWISH SCIENCE: GERHARD KITTEL

Even in the Middle Twenties Hitler was aware of the necessity of presenting anti-Jewish ideology in a scholarly coating. The crude writings of the Rohlings and the Ahlwardts, he felt, could not be relied upon:

> . . . The timbre [of these older anti-Semites] . . . mostly was such as again to arouse in me doubts because of the partly shallow and extraordinarily unscientific argumentation in defense of the statement.[79]

By 1936 he had succeeded. Within a few years, the fight against the Jews was no more confined to shabby tracts by unknown authors; it had made its entrance into the respectable academic world of Germany.

To show the great distance that anti-Jewish research covered within a few years, it is helpful to quote from a review of an old-fashioned anti-Semitic publication republished under Hitler. Dr. Karl Georg Kuhn of the University of Tübingen, writing in the leading *Historische Zeitschrift,* complained:

---

[78] *Das Judentum in der Rechtswissenschaft . . . 1. Die deutsche Rechtswissenschaft im Kampf gegen den jüdischen Geist* (Berlin, Deutscher Rechtsverlag, 1935, 35 pp.), pp. 14-15.

[79] *Mein Kampf,* p. 60.—Even people who before Hitler had devoted their whole literary careers to "unmasking" the Jews, such as the historian of literature Dr. Adolf Bartels, were kept at a respectful distance, and Fritsch's *Handbuch der Judenfrage* was adopted, after the author's death, only after a substantial overhauling.

That is not the right way: to take a translation [of Shulhan Aruh IV] made one hundred years ago by a converted Jew [Loewe], to provide it with a fervent anti-Semitic title and no less fervent anti-Semitic introduction and to think to have served national socialism by publishing this. On the contrary, our science in new Germany, in this fought-for position, is being discredited by such a procedure. We cannot work, nor ought we today to work on the Jewish question by simply taking over and solely providing with a new façade the old [material] that had been created from quite different philosophical points of view; we must start from the sources and approach the problems quite in a new way.[80]

In the early months of their regime, when the Nazis had yet very little to offer by way of scientific presentation of the Jewish problem, they must have doubly appreciated the services rendered them by one of the first university scholars who openly joined in their fight on the Jews. This was Dr. Gerhard Kittel, at that time full Professor of Theology at the University of Tübingen, a not so great son of a great scholar but still a recognized authority in the Old Testament, a man who had mingled with Jews and could quote their "hidden" books in the original Hebrew. Kittel observed:

> Leading National Socialists again and again stressed, and rightly so, that "only those who fully master the [material on the] Jewish question are entitled to make it a subject of public pronouncements." [81]

He obviously referred to himself. No wonder then that this little book intending to show the incompatibility of Jews with non-Jews created a sensation. True, he emphasized the Christian point of view more than a die-hard Nazi would have done; but, on the other hand, it was rather pleasant for the Nazis to have a theologian of high standing testify that "the National Socialist Labor Party clings to a positive Christianity." Kittel took pains in proving that the century and a half of Jewish emancipation should be considered a historical mistake. The Jew, he contended, always had been outside the larger community; thus he should not share in its activities and should be kept in the position of an alien. But in taking this decision "racial or emotional viewpoints" alone should not prevail; "the real and full reply," he stressed,

> is given only when one succeeds in building the Jewish question on a religious foundation and in giving the struggle against Jewry a Christian interpretation.

[80] *Historische Zeitschrift*, 156 (April-Oktober 1937), p. 315.
[81] Gerhard Kittel, *Die Judenfrage* (Stuttgart, Kohlhammer, 1933, 78 pp.), p. 9.

It is erroneous to ask, Kittel advised the readers as his discussion
developed, "whether individual Jews are honest or dishonest Jews,
whether individual Jews perish unjustly or whether it serves those
individuals right." [82] He freely admitted the hardships brought upon

> quite a few nice, noble, educated people [who] *break down men-
> tally and perish* because their avocation is destroyed, the con-
> tents of their lives are annihilated, and they do not know where and
> how they shall rebuild something new. We, on the German side,
> shall never neglect the deep and bitter tragedies which the present
> developments constitute for such people. It never was the way of
> the German to laugh at another man's distress! [83]

This certainly sounded somewhat unusual to orthodox Nazi ears,
but little did it matter if only the outcome of the interpretation was
fundamentally in unison with the Nazi program. It was. The sentence
immediately following the exclamation mark began with the words:
"It will be the task of all right-minded people to mitigate hardships"
but then the qualification was added: "inasmuch as this is possible
without weakness and without impairing the fundamental necessities."
And the next paragraph stressed again:

> But indeed, *we ought not to become soft!* We ought not out of
> weakness to permit conditions to continue which have proved a
> failure both for the German and the Jewish people.

To do justice to Kittel, we must report that one of his chapters
contained the following statement:

> *Extirpation* (Ausrottung) *of Jewry by violence* is not worthy
> of a serious discussion: if the systems of the Spanish inquisition and
> the Russian pogroms did not manage it, it will certainly be im-
> possible to achieve in the twentieth century. There is no inner sense
> in this idea either. A historical state of affairs, as exemplified by
> this people, can be resolved by the extirpation of the people only in
> demagogical slogans but never in history itself. The sense of a
> historical situation always consists in that it sets us a task we have
> to master. To kill all Jews does not mean, however, to master the
> situation. [84]

But this calm discussion of the extirpation of a whole people by
violence (the entire discussion is quoted; there is not a word more
on the subject) proceeded solely from the angle of expediency. No
moral issues, no religious inhibitions seemed to be involved. This way
of thinking, no doubt, was entirely to the Nazi taste. Some ten years
later they had changed their minds and come to the conclusion that
"killing all Jews" in their hands would be the best thing to do, and

---

[82] *Ibid.*, p. 12.   [83] *Ibid.*, p. 61.   [84] *Ibid.*, p. 14.—Italics in original.

then the professor of theology, in the meantime promoted from small Tübingen to the University of Vienna, followed suit. But at the time Kittel wrote the just quoted statement, matters had not advanced thus far.[85] It was still 1933, and we may recall that during their first years the Nazis were eagerly looking over the frontiers for the impression they were making, although the punishment inflicted upon the half million German Jews at that time, as compared with what happened later to the Jews of Germany and of entire Europe, seems hardly worth mentioning. In 1933, the Nazi government even employed a certain Jakow Trachtenberg to extort declarations from Jewish organizations in Germany to the effect that actually no wrong was done to the Jews, which statements later were made into a book, published expensively in three languages and widely circulated abroad.[86]

At this initial stage the idea presented to the world can thus be summed up: the Jews are incompatible with the German folk, since they consist of incompatible racial components. "No less a figure than Fischer" had established beyond any doubt, as Kittel testified,[87] that the Jews consisted chiefly of representatives of the Near-Eastern and the Oriental races, with minor admixtures of other races. As to which other races were involved, there were differences of opinion, but scholarly controversies did not delay the course of political action. Germany, so the argument ran, is obviously entitled to shape her fate without "foreign" interference. The alleged persecutions of the Jews are nothing but atrocity propaganda of "escaped traitors." At a press conference in the Ministry of the Interior, Dr. Frick vigorously denied any intention of persecuting the Jews. The Jews had simply been assigned to their own area and might act as they pleased among themselves without, of course, annoying their hosts, he asserted.

Even after the promulgation of the Nuremberg Laws "for the protection of German honor and German blood" on September 15, 1935, the line was maintained. A semi-official publication proudly protested:

> . . . The liberalistic—contrary to nature and suicidal—thesis claiming "equality of everything bearing a human face" is sup-

[85] Throughout the Nazi era Kittel was actively engaged in anti-Jewish research in conjunction with Walter Frank's institute and, afterwards, with Goebbels' "Antijüdische Aktion." We shall see how he gradually succeeded in throwing overboard more and more reservations.

[86] Die Greuelpropaganda ist eine Lügenpropaganda sagen die deutschen Juden selbst. Atrocity Propaganda Is Based on Lies Say the Jews of Germany Themselves. . . . (Berlin, Jakow Trachtenberg Verlag, 1933, 142 pp.)—The text is in German, English and French. The preface, dated Berlin, May 15, 1933, and signed J. Trachtenberg, stated: "May this book rehabilitate not only Germany's honour but that of the world as well!"

[87] Cf. footnote 59.

planted by the evaluation of the person on the basis of folkdom and attainment....

Certainly, the National Socialist state defended itself against Jewish double-crossing . . . but the National Socialist state *by no means* destroyed the economic existence of the Jews, nor did it destroy their *cultural* existence within the *Jewish* framework . . . clean separation.... As the old champion party-member Julius Streicher proclaimed on August 15 [1935] at a mass meeting in the Berlin Sportpalast, "the greatest disgrace of Germany was the time in which the Jew could dare to rule Germany according to Talmudic laws." [88]

A scholar who undertook to justify "the extinction (*Ausmerzung*) of all Jewish influences" on scientific grounds, Dr. Wilhelm Köhler, maintained in November, 1936:

The racial legislation of the Third Reich, stemming as it does from the requirement of the blood and anchored in the irrefutable obligation toward the folk feeling, has put an end to the incomplete and mostly wrong policy toward the Jews in the past. In Germany the Jewish question since September 1935 has been cleared. By a clear delimitation Jewry in our fatherland has been once and for all pushed back into its bounds and rendered innocuous. [89]

"Once and for all...." But it soon turned out that the regime was insatiable, as in any other domain of Nazi policy. As Hitlerism embarked upon an expansionist policy and ultimately upon war, the Jewish issues, too, were changed accordingly and the pressure was intensified. That this change had been foreseen was indicated even by the writers who professed to be content with the "solution" of the Jewish question achieved by the Nuremberg Laws. The same Köhler, directly after the passage quoted above, ended the paragraph with the following unmistakable threat:

. . . This truly statesmanlike act was, however, not merely a result of an emotional reaction, but to a prominent degree the outcome of the most profound *knowledge* of the danger that threatens us from Jewry. Thus, we Germans, now as before, are duty bound again and again to strengthen and to keep alert our knowledge of the methods and aims of Jewry all the more since *world* Jewry, whom Adolf Hitler unmasked, prepares itself for the last decision... And from the mistakes made by the former generations out of inertia, self-interest, confusion of concepts and feelings, we can and must learn not for the sake of dead knowledge which paralyzes

---

[88] Gerd Rühle, *Das Dritte Reich . . . Das dritte Jahr 1935* (Berlin, Hummelverlag, 1936, 518 pp.), pp. 280, 282-283.—Italics in original.

[89] Dr. Wilhelm Koehler, *Studien zur Geschichte der Judenfrage* (Berlin, Schlieffen-Verlag, 1937, 156 pp.), p. 7.—The author belonged to the old General Staff group; witness the publishing house and the fact that the chapters of the book first had appeared in *Deutsches Adelsblatt.*—Italics in original.

strength but in order to be able militantly and courageously to carry the weapons which shall conquer in the present and coming struggles.

More poignantly, but exactly in the same spirit, Himmler himself announced also in 1936:

> We shall see to it that never more in Germany, the heart of Europe, will there be an opportunity to kindle the Jewish Bolshevist revolution of the subhuman from within or through emissaries from outside. We know of the existence and the doings of all these forces and the day even the smallest attempt takes place, be it today, be it in decades or in centuries, we shall ruthlessly be to them a merciless executioner's sword.[90]

VIII

WALTER FRANK. THE REICHSINSTITUT FÜR GESCHICHTE DES NEUEN DEUTSCHLANDS (REICH INSTITUTE FOR THE HISTORY OF THE NEW GERMANY)

We now turn to the historian Walter Frank, who, down to the spring of 1941, was most prominent in organizing and integrating anti-Jewish scholarship in Germany. While still a youth, he "had become acquainted with the practical mass struggle against Jewry in Nuremberg at Julius Streicher's rallies," he proudly confessed.[91] In his studies at the University of Munich he was guided by Karl Alexander von Müller, President of the Bavarian Academy of Sciences and a leading pro-Hitlerite historian long before Hitler attained power. In 1927, Frank was graduated with a doctoral dissertation on Dr. Adolf Stöcker, the militant anti-Semite of the eighties.[92] Some other monographs followed, each of them either directly or indirectly unmasking the "international Jew," among them a study on the French

[90] Heinrich Himmler, Reichsführer SS, *Die Schutzstaffel als antibolschewistische Kampfsorganisation* (Münich, Eher, 1936, 31 pp.), p. 31. In the same pamphlet, *ibid.*, Himmler vividly described the rôle of his SD (Sicherheits-Dienst) which later was to play such a prominent part in the annihilation of the Jews: ". . . Those who somehow and somewhere must have a bad conscience with regard to the Führer and the nation shall fear us. For those people we have built up an organization which is called *Sicherheitsdienst* [Security Service], and likewise we, the SS, supply the men for service in the *Geheime Staatspolizei* [Gestapo, Secret State Police]."

[91] Walter Frank, *Die deutschen Geisteswissenschaften im Kriege. Rede, gehalten am 18. Mai 1940 an der Universität Berlin* (Hamburg, Hanseatische Verlagsanstalt, 1940, 29 pp.).— The Wehrmacht considered the paper of such importance that a special edition was ordered as "Sonderschrift des Oberkommandos der Wehrmacht, Abteilung Inland." Cf. *Deutsche Nationalbibliographie*, Reihe B, 1944, p. 1361.

[92] Walter Frank, *Hofprediger Adolf Stoecker und die christlich-soziale Bewegung* [1. Auflage, Berlin, 1928]; 2. Auflage (Hamburg, Hanseatische Verlagsanstalt, 1935, 450 pp.).— The "Hanseatische Verlagsanstalt" in Hamburg not only was the permanent publisher for the Reichsinstitut but in general ranked high among the publishing houses favored by the Nazis and is likely to have had close party connections.

Third Republic.[93] Simultaneously, Frank was active in the Nazi movement.

Obviously, Hitler's entry into the Reich Chancellery was the great hour for Walter Frank. A dynamic personality and a powerful speaker, he was the right man for the regime to use in creating one of the energy centers which in time would conquer the more rigid universities. Thus, the Reichsinstitut für Geschichte des neuen Deutschlands (Reich Institute for the History of the New Germany) was founded and its direction by order of the Führer entrusted to Frank. In contrast to the former Historische Reichskommission, which offered only first-hand documentation, this Reichsinstitut had been conceived from the very outset as a source from which interpretations of German and world history in the spirit of national socialism would emanate.

The opening of the Reichsinstitut on October 19, 1935, was staged as a first-class event and high dignitaries of the Party and the Government, among them Rudolf Hess and Alfred Rosenberg, were present. In the following years, Rosenberg kept conspicuously aloof from the institute; Hess' continual interest, on the other hand, eventually proved its undoing.

While emphasizing the militant National Socialist character of the new institution, in his fiery introductory address, and blaming the senile detachment of the "guild" scholars, Frank nevertheless took pride in mentioning those scholars of established reputation who had been invited to join the new institute. Of historians he named Erich Marcks and Karl Alexander von Müller as well as Heinrich von Srbik, who, from his Vienna chair, had always supported the Nazi movement. Alfred Baeumler, Ernst Krieck, and Hans F. K. Günther were also among the honorary members appointed. A year later Frank was able to report that the budget of his institute had been increased sixfold,[94] though he did not mention actual figures. In any case the publications became frequent; many of the papers which appeared in the volumes of the Reichsinstitut's *Forschungen zur Judenfrage* were also issued separately.

Of primary interest to us is the Forschungsabteilung Judenfrage (Research Department for the Jewish Question) created within the Reichsinstitut in the spring of 1936 as the result of a meeting held in October, 1935, at the Reich Ministry for Science with the partici-

93 Walter Frank, *Nationalismus und Demokratie im Frankreich der dritten Republik (1871-1918)* (Hamburg, Hanseatische Verlagsanstalt, 1933, 652 pp.).
94 *Historische Zeitschrift* 155 (1936-1937), 448-450.

pation of representatives of other Reich authorities. Walter Frank, director of the whole institution, thus defined its anti-Jewish purposes:

> In German politics, Israel's kingdom terminated in the spring of 1933. In German scholarship, however, Israel through its governors reigned longer.... In the camp of national socialism [there was] at the beginning . . . only a minority of solitary adherents scattered over the whole country....
>
> We don't want dictatorship but we want the leadership in the scientific life of our nation.... In this process of an army-formation the Reichsinstitut . . . is the first army corps....
>
> We know that cleverness alone, without instinct and without power and without a little bit of madness in addition, never has stormed any rampart of history. But we know, too, that a great people is not governed without intelligence and without ability and without knowledge.... The time of the sciences and the universities, therefore, is *not over*. But the time has arrived for a *renewed* scholarship and a *renewed* university.[95]

The first Conference (Tagung) of this Department was opened in Munich on November 13, 1936. The large auditorium of the University was secured and a galaxy of honorary guests was present. Among them was the Deputy of the Führer, Reich Minister Rudolf Hess, and several years later Frank still took occasion to remark that Hess' presence "underscored the revolutionary importance" of the manifestation. All ministries, including the Ministry of War, had sent their representatives, as had nine universities. The Rectors of the Universities of Erlangen, Frankfort on-the-Main, Heidelberg, Jena, and Tübingen had come personally; besides, there were represented the Universities of Berlin, Giessen, and Munich and the Schools of Technology of Dresden and Munich. Walter Gross, of the Racial-Policy Office of the Party, too, was among the guests. Karl Alexander von Müller was one of the principal speakers. Historical research does not conduct the immediate struggles for power, he declared,

> but it can forge the weapons for these struggles.... Owing to the support of the Movement and the State [we are going] to call into being here in the immediate vicinity of the State Library and its treasures which are irreplaceable also for our work and through a large complementary professional library of our own a unique scientific laboratory for this [Jewish] question....[96]

Frank too underscored that the Department was creating "large-scale technical opportunities . . . through the foundation of the largest

---

[95] Walter Frank, *Deutsche Wissenschaft und Judenfrage* (Hamburg, Hanseatische Verlagsanstalt, 1937, 51 pp.), p. 47.—Italics in original.

[96] *Historische Zeitschrift* 155 (1936-1937), 448-450.—According to the same source, three representatives of the Wehrmacht—Assmann, Foerster, and Haehnelt—were made permanent members of the Reichsinstitut.

European library on the Jewish question," but he also stressed the primary importance of the political struggle. The Jews, he declared, "have been trying to forge around Germany the iron ring of their international might," but in the long run they will be unable to prevent "that the links in this ring will be loosened and that Adolf Hitler's Germany will rise up over Europe ever more powerful and visible." [97] Among the listeners to this grandiloquent address was Commanding General von Reichenau "as the representative of Reich War Minister Field Marshal General von Blomberg," — the same von Reichenau who, by 1941 himself a field marshal, in that year, as we shall see later, exhorted his soldiers on the Eastern Front to "understand the necessity of hard but just expiation on the part of Jewish subhumanity" and "to free the German people once and for all from the Asiatic Jewish danger." He had learned the lesson thoroughly.

The following fifteen scholars were appointed members of the Department: Professor Dr. Johannes Alt, U. of Würzburg, for the history of literature; Professor Dr. Hans Bogner, U. of Freiburg i. Br., for ancient history; Director General Dr. Rudolf Buttmann, Munich, for library science; Professor Dr. Hans Alfred Grunsky, U. of Munich, for the history of philosophy; Professor Dr. Gerhard Kittel, U. of Tübingen, for research into religion; Professor Dr. Franz Koch, U. of Berlin, for the history of literature; Dr. Karl Georg Kuhn, U. of Tübingen, for talmudic research; Professor Dr. Philipp Lenard, U. of Heidelberg, for the natural sciences; Dr. Ottokar Lorenz, for economic history; Professor Dr. Herbert Meyer, U. of Göttingen, for legal history; Dr. Wilhelm Stapel, Hamburg, for the history of literature; Professor Dr. Rudolf Tomaschek, Dresden School of Technology, for the natural sciences; Professor Dr. Max Wundt, Tübingen, for the history of philosophy; Oberregierungsrat in the Propaganda Ministry, Dr. Wilhelm Ziegler, Berlin, for political history. In addition, division heads were appointed on problems of Eastern Europe and Russia, of Palestine, of the Romance-speaking countries, and of the Anglo-Saxon countries, as well as scholars in racial science and archival science.

While the Reichsinstitut itself was to continue to be located in Berlin, it was announced that the location of the Department was in Munich, Ludwigstrasse 22-b, and that Dr. Wilhelm Grau was

[97] Ibid.

appointed Acting Director (Geschäftsführender Leiter) to work with research associates and a staff of specialists in different fields. Dr. Grau was no novice in anti-Jewish research. Like Frank himself, he was a student of Karl Alexander von Müller's in Munich. In 1931, he tells us in the preface to his first study on "Anti-Semitism in the Later Middle Ages," [98] he became interested in the Jewish problem and in 1933 received his Ph.D.; the study just referred to had been accepted in lieu of the required dissertation. It turned out later that he had used the materials collected by a Jewish historian (interpreting them in his own way, of course), [99] but this was not considered by the Hitlerites a blot on his shield. The Faculty of Philosophy of the University of Munich offered a large grant for the publication of the study and Grau was put in charge of the department of literature on Jews of the leading scholarly periodical *Historische Zeitschrift*. On October 1, 1935, he was made division head (Referent) for Jewish problems at the Reichsinstitut and a year later was promoted to the position of Acting Director of the Department.

Grau was not merely an armchair student; much more than a scholar, he was an administrator with vision and energy. In a paper read in 1936 in Karlsruhe at the annual conference of the Association of German Historical Societies he demanded that two fundamental requirements be fulfilled:

(1) The Jewish stocks of the Frankfort Municipal Library (Stadtbibliothek) should be "designated for an explicitly German end,"

(2) Jewish archives should be confiscated or, as he put it,

German archival officials . . . shall be no conservative natures that faithfully preserve intact what has been placed into their hands but they must be conquerors who daringly take hold of what their archives do not possess but should possess. [100]

---

[98] Wilhelm Grau, *Antisemitismus im späten Mittelalter. Das Ende der Regensburger Judengemeinde, 1450-1519* (München, Duncker und Humblot, 1934, 201 pp.).—A second edition was published in 1939.

[99] Cf. *Zeitschrift für Geschichte der Juden in Deutschland*, 6 (1935), pp. 17-24. Grau's rejoinder, *ibid.*, pp. 186-198. This discussion shows that some objections to Nazi teachings still could be raised in Germany at that time.

[100] Some years later quoted by Grau himself in *Weltkampf* I (1941), 16-17, from his paper: "Die Geschichte der Judenfrage und ihre Erforschung," *Blätter für deutsche Landesgeschichte*, her. vom Gesamtverein der deutschen Geschichts- und Altertumsvereine, 83 (1937), 163-173.—The rather cautious wording probably was due to the presence of historians from abroad at that time. In recalling the Karlsruhe conference five years later, Grau complained that he had to deal with "opposition from abroad . . . even in the presence of German listeners"—indeed, quite an awkward situation in Nazi Germany. For the first time, Grau had developed his ideas on "The Jewish Question as a Task of Historical Research" in *Deutsches Volkstum*, September, 1935; the paper appeared in pamphlet form in the Hanseatische Verlagsanstalt, Hamburg, at the inauguration of the Reichsinstitut. In his postscript to the second edition, which appeared a year later, Grau was able to inform his readers that the University of Tübingen, as the first among German universities, had been authorized by the Reich Minister for Science to give regular courses in the history of the Jewish question.

As early as the beginning of 1937 he expressed the conviction that the Jewish problem had international implications and thus anticipated the "solution" of the Forties:

> The German Jewish question today appears particularly as a problem of economic and international policy. Whether Germany will solve her Jewish question forever and whether the world is on its way to the solution will depend on whether there will be successful steering in these domains in the years to come.[101]

It was, therefore, a well-deserved compliment when the *Literarisches Zentralblatt* of January 31, 1936, declared: "It is to be assumed that owing to Grau's studies the racial idea, until now rather externally connected with historical science, is going to become an integral part of this science."[102]

IX

THE REICHSINSTITUT FÜR GESCHICHTE DES NEUEN DEUTSCHLANDS, 1935-1938. WILHELM GRAU

The second Conference of the Department was held, again at the Munich University, from May 12 to 14, 1937. In addition to members of the Forschungsabteilung of the institute proper, we are informed [103], the following persons participated: General Ritter von Epp, Reichsstatthalter in Bavaria; Gauleiter Mutschmann, Reichsstatthalter in Saxony; Dr. Boepple, State Secretary in the Bavarian Ministry of Education, and other representatives of the State and Party. "As Dr. Grau, Acting Director of the Forschungsabteilung, indicated, there was no question of any official representation; it was active participation in this closed working conference and thus actual common work of science, [National Socialist] Movement, and State."

The scope of the research to be conducted by the Department already had been expanded to comprise also the natural sciences. The history of the Jews, it was maintained, can be explained only in terms of their peculiar racial amalgamation, and "these are problems which the worker in the field of *Geisteswissenschaften* cannot answer any more for himself but only with the biologist specializing in heredity"[104] and the natural scientist in general. Thus the appointment

---

[101] Wilhelm Grau, *Die Judenfrage in der deutschen Geschichte* (Leipzig, Teubner, 1937, 32, VIII pp.), p. 37. Originally published in *Vergangenheit und Gegenwart* 26, Heft 4 and 5. Second edition, 1937; third edition, 1940.

[102] P. 80.

[103] *Historische Zeitschrift* 156 (1937), 667.

[104] Karl Georg Kuhn, *Die Judenfrage als weltgeschichtliches Problem* (Hamburg, Hanseatische Verlagsanstalt [1939], 51 pp.), p. 34.—This paper, read at the 1938 Tagung of the Reichsinstitut, terminated in a quotation from Adolf Hitler: "We understand the challenge [of the Jews], we are prepared to meet it."

of the following new members was announced: Dr. Johannes Stark, of the Physikalisch- Technische Reichsanstalt, and Professor [Rudolf] Mentzel, president of the Deutsche Forschungsgemeinschaft, for the natural sciences; Dr. Arthur Gütt, Ministerialdirektor in Frick's Ministry of the Interior; Dr. Friedrich Burgdörfer, Director in the Reich Office for Statistics, to be in charge of population research; Professor Dr. Otmar Freiherr von Verschuer and Professor Ludwig Schemann, in charge of the fields of heredity and race. Then Dr. Grau gave a report on the structure, the activities, and the tasks of the Department (library, archives, consultation services, research projects, and publications), and finally called the conference to order with a few remarks on its specific character. This specificness the report depicted as follows:

> Particularly noteworthy are the methodical innovations introduced by the Forschungsabteilung Judenfrage. Already at its first annual conference scholars of all important branches of natural and cultural sciences joined to work together on one subject. The course of this second conference in its papers, discussions, and private conversations showed that the many personal and scholarly relations established anew here have quietly brought to maturing many a valuable contribution to the Jewish question which together with others permits hope for a well-rounded picture of the Jewish question in all spheres of life.[105]

The reporter—Dr. Clemens August Hoberg of Frank's research staff—then stressed the fact that Julius Streicher had actively participated in the Conference; we may recall that Streicher about half a year earlier had been invited to another scholarly conference in Berlin:

> A further methodical innovation consisted in the active participation in the conference on historical science of men who have been making history. In the course of this development addresses were presented by Gauleiter Streicher, "My Political Struggle against Jewry," and by the retired Col. Nicolai, "How the Chief of Information Service of the Supreme Command in the [First] World War Saw the Influence of the Jews during the World War." These addresses showed how important it is that the present-day historian, in contact with history-making personalities, cultivate also the tradition of contemporary history which due to the telephone and "traveling diplomacy" frequently threatens to become lost without written residue. Moreover, this sympathetic contact (Fühlungnahme) between science and politics serves the unity of the spiritual life

[105] *Historische Zeitschrift* 156 (1937), 669.

of the nation in that the historian forges the weapons for the man of politics and deepens for him the view of the historical wrestling of the present out of past history and at the same time on his part receives from the man of politics new formulations of questions and new insights.

In such frank wording, this seems to be the first avowal of complicity between Nazi practice and Nazi theory. It is helpful, therefore, to hear also Dr. Grau's testimony:

> For the first time a methodical innovation was introduced at this working conference of the Department...; for the first time leading men in active life spoke within the framework of a scientific body.... Colonel Walther Nicolai and Gauleiter Julius Streicher [spoke] about topics from the history of the last few decades not on the basis of literary source material, but as persons who in leading positions have experienced and participated in forming the events.[106]

Grau not only promised to maintain this procedure at the annual conferences to come, but insisted that he was fully aware of the particular honor which had been bestowed upon his institution:

> We know that the particular trustworthiness of our working circle is an unavoidable prerequisite of such a procedure. The confidential character peculiar to such communications also requires that we refrain from any kind of publication.

One will certainly not go amiss in presuming that many facts concerning the eventual policy of Germany against the Jews could be disclosed by opening the archives of this peculiar research institution.

A year later, from July 5 to July 7, 1938, prominent representatives of Party and State and the members of the Reichsinstitut gathered at the University of Munich for a third Conference. "For the first time reporters of the daily press were admitted in order to stress that the institute was not only the headquarters for research but also a teaching pulpit." [107] At that time, it appears, Dozent Dr. Karl Georg Kuhn of the University of Tübingen, orientalist and Semitist, and Dr. Clemens August Hoberg, of Munich, historian and philosopher, were, among others, staff members of the Forschungsabteilung Judenfrage. "With them is associated a large circle of experts who belong to the general Sachverständigenbeirat (Advisory Council of Experts) of the Reichsinstitut." [108]

[106] "Vorbemerkung," *Forschungen zur Judenfrage*, II (1937), 7.
[107] *Historische Zeitschrift*, 159 (1938-1939), 218-221.
[108] Cf. Historische Zeitschrift, 162 (issued September 18, 1941, but, obviously, very much belated), 560, and Kuhn, *op. cit.*, p. 34.

Before introducing the first speaker, Frank made the disclosure "that the Reich now has appropriated the necessary particular amounts for building up within the framework of the Reichsinstitut a large European library in the Jewish question." Rudolf Hess in an official statement issued on October 12, 1937—and we must not forget the weight each pronouncement by Hess carried—had told of his particular interest in the building-up of this library.[109]

At the time of this Conference, Grau was no longer connected with the Reichsinstitut. From volume 158 (March-October, 1938) his contributions also disappeared from the *Historische Zeitschrift;* his place was taken by the more reliable Dr. Volkmar Eichstädt. As Grau had been one of the pillars of anti-Jewish research and was to play an even more important part again, we are naturally interested in the reasons for his absence. Frank did not mention them in his report. His only indirect reference to Grau was the announcement that in the summer of 1938, the Forschungsabteilung Judenfrage had been transformed into the Hauptreferat Judenfrage, "led by myself." Only two years later, in a discourse at the Berlin University, Frank rather reluctantly disclosed that he had to part with Grau because of the latter's Catholic-clerical leanings. As early as 1934, Frank took occasion to remind the audience, he had criticized, in a book-review published by Rosenberg,[110] Grau's contention that modern anti-Semitism constituted a decline from religious anti-Semitism in the Middle Ages. Grau, in following up this suggestion, had eliminated one of the incriminating sentences in the second edition of his book, Frank went on, but other passages pointing in the same direction remained unchanged and the general impression was that Grau still clung to his theories, as evidenced by an article he wrote in 1938 in the periodical *Wille und Macht.*

Frank did not mention in this charge why he had engaged Grau in spite of his heresies and not only collaborated with him for some years but also praised him unreservedly at the opening session of his

---

[109] The *Völkischer Beobachter,* Berlin edition, of October 13, 1937, carried the following report: "Munich, October 12th. The Deputy Führer, Reichsminister Rudolf Hess, received the Director of the Research Department for the Jewish Question, Reichsinstitut für Geschichte des neuen Deutschlands, the President of the Bavarian Academy of Sciences, Dr. Karl Alexander von Müller, and the Acting Director, Dr. Wilhelm Grau. They reported to him about the research activities and the erection of the Munich library for the history of the Jewish question. On this occasion the Deputy Führer was offered the first volume of the recently published *Forschungen zur Judenfrage.* He again expressed the active interest which he personally and the National Socialist German Workers Party feel for the work of the Research Department"— Cf. also: Walter Frank, *Die deutschen Geisteswissenschaften im Kriege,* p. 15, *Historische Zeitschrift* 157 (1937-1938), 444.

[110] *Die Bücherkunde,* 1934, 11/12.

Department in 1936. We are led to believe that behind this divergence of opinion for which Grau allegedly was dismissed there was some clash along other lines. At any rate, Grau did not submit. Ambitious and flexible, he emerged after some years of eclipse as Rosenberg's man in the grandiose Frankfort Institute for Research into the Jewish Question and while Frank had already become a mere shadow of himself the highly official *NS Briefe* greeted the third edition of a paper by Grau with the words: "An essay like this cannot be sufficiently recommended." At the Frankfort institute, in addition, Grau could reach beyond theorizing: having started with research into medieval persecutions of the Jews he was to finish by being instrumental in events against which the persecutions of the Middle Ages look like child's play.

X

THE REICHSINSTITUT FÜR GESCHICHTE DES NEUEN DEUTSCHLANDS, 1938-1941. HESS, STREICHER, KEITEL AS PATRONS

To the 1938 Munich Conference "history-making personalities" were again invited, and again Julius Streicher scored a triumph:

> In his lively and fascinating speech lasting several hours, he [Streicher] called upon German historians to establish immediate contact with the nation and with the people.... Adolf Hitler said in the beginning of the Movement: "A fighter doesn't lecture, he speaks from his heart." The Gauleiter was happy to find that in the circle of the Reichsinstitut a new spirit dominated. Here were men who felt young and also had the courage needed to write history from their hearts.[111]

Before the session adjourned, Frank repeated the statement he had made in his opening address that the Reichsinstitut looked upon itself as "the center of anti-Semitism in German science." He praised Streicher, "the political front-fighter of the mass meetings," who had taught the audience "his science experienced in practice," and was happy that "the gap between cognition and action, between mind and politics created by a sick epoch was beginning to close." [112]

Hoberg, again reporting for the *Historische Zeitschrift,* was most enthusiastic about the outcome of the Conference. The members of the Reichsinstitut, he declared, had been welded into a community of interest and it was impossible to list the wealth of suggestions and ideas which came up during the discussions:

[111] *Historische Zeitschrift* 159 (1938-1939), 220.
[112] "Vorbemerkung," *Forschungen zur Judenfrage,* III (1938), 7.

Here there is really the spiritual center in which the creative forces stream together to enhance each other. In linking his concluding speech to the remarks of Gauleiter Streicher, Walter Frank said that it is indicative of true wisdom to dissolve apparent entanglements into large simple cognitions. These large simple cognitions emerged out of essential lines of the papers presented and also of the discussions in a concord that was surprisingly harmonious. National Socialist scholarship has to organize itself from all disciplines into a new totality in accord with the policy on the Jewish question. Obviously not only the Jewish question is the foundation of this totality. The new unity stems from the National Socialist Weltanschauung, from the essential ground of its body, the idea of race and folk. This unity is therefore possible only—this presumably is one of the most conspicuous outcomes of the Conference—as the embracing universality of the German spirit in which anti-Semitism instead of pure negation is a constructive, necessary element of the whole.[113]

The fourth annual Conference, the last of which we have knowledge, was held in Munich on July 4-6, 1939. The papers read there were published in the fourth volume of the *Forschungen zur Judenfrage*, but no organizational report seems to have been issued. Walter Frank in his prefatory notice to the volume[114] had this to say:

No further elaboration is needed to show to what degree the present moment underscores the importance of these *Forschungen zur Judenfrage*. The war forced upon the German nation by the Western plutocracies has evidenced more than any other event that the strictly scholarly work on research into the Jewish question constitutes one of the weightiest contributions to the spiritual rearmament of our people and to the enlightenment also of the other nations of the world.

We do not know whether any further conferences on Jewish topics were held by the Reichsinstitut after the outbreak of war. At any rate, the *Forschungen zur Judenfrage* continued to appear until 1944 and the series grew to nine large volumes. The following thirty-five scholars, mostly university professors, contributed to this series (the Roman figure in parenthesis indicates the volume, or volumes, in which their papers were published): Johannes Alt (I), Hans Behrens (IV), Hans Bogner (I, II), Erich Botzenhart (III), Friedrich Burgdörfer (III), Rudolf Craemer (V), Volkmar Eichstädt (VI), Wilfried Euler (VI), Julius [Giulio] Evola (IX), Richard Fester (VI), Eugen Fischer (III, VII), Walter Frank (I, III, IV,

[113] *Historische Zeitschrift*, 159 (1938-1939), 221.
[114] Dated Berlin, September 29, 1939.

V, VIII), Karl Richard Ganzer (III), Oscar Grosse (V), Hans
Alfred Grunsky (II, IV), Johannes Heckel (I), Heinrich Heer-
wagen (IV), Clemens August Hoberg (IV, IX), Otto Höfler (IV),
Gerhard Kittel (I, II, III, IV, V, VII, IX), Franz Koch (I, II),
Karl Georg Kuhn (I, II, III), Ottokar Lorenz (II), Herbert Meyer
(I), Hermann Meyer (IX), Herbert Michaelis (VIII), Kleo Pleyer
(II), Bolko Freiherr von Richthofen (VIII), Joseph Roth (IV),
Günter Schlichting (VI), Wilhelm Stapel (I, II), Bruno Thüring
(IV), Otmar Freiherr von Verschuer (II, III), Max Wundt (I, II),
Wilhelm Ziegler (II, IV).

Apart from the Conferences of the Jewish Department, conferences on general topics of German history were also held by the
Reichsinstitut in Berlin. But it seems that even at those occasions the
Jewish problem was paramount. There was, for instance, the Berlin
meeting of December 1, 1938. No report on it seems to be available,
but it is referred to in the advertisement placed at the end of Kittel's
book of 1939, where the publications of the Reichsinstitut on both
Jewish and general problems are listed:

> German scholarship in a struggle against World Judaism! "Just
> as the outrage of World Judaism was followed by the political and
> economic counterblow of the Reich, so in scholarship there will be
> a reply in that we continue to strengthen the anti-Jewish wing of
> our research work" (Walter Frank, at the Berlin conference of the
> Reichsinstitut, December 1, 1938).[115]

As is well known, the "political and economic counterblow of
the Reich," i.e., the November pogroms throughout the nation,
ushered in the final elimination of the Jews from German life.

On a gathering of the institute in Berlin, held in January and
February, 1939, the *Völkischer Beobachter* of February 2, 1939, remarked in part:

> Hitler youth, young German workingmen and students sat with
> women and men of all strata of society, and in deep moral earnest-
> ness listened to the words of German scholars.

At one of those sessions which were devoted to "Jewry and the
Jewish Question," Dr. Hans Alfred Grunsky, full Professor of Philosophy at the University of Munich, spoke on Spinoza.

---

[115] Gerhard Kittel, *Die historischen Voraussetzungen der jüdischen Rassenmischung* (Hamburg, Hanseatische Verlagsanstalt [1939], 48 pp.), p. [47].
  In Nazi usage, *Freveltat des Weltjudentums* designated the shot directed by Hershl
Grinshpan on November 7, 1938, against the member of the German embassy in Paris, vom
Rath. Official Nazi documents recovered in Berlin prove beyond doubt that the wave of
murder, arson, and pillage which swept the Reich three days later was planned long in advance
and that official orders went out to police and party members to participate. Cf. *The New
York Times*, September 21, 1945.

Spinoza, as Grunsky proved, was a trade-Jew like his co-racialists who, only camouflaged as a Teutonic mystical thinker, thought of creating a new Tora that would bring all nations under the laws of the Talmud.[116]

As evidence shows, Walter Frank's ascent continued well into the war; but after the spring of 1941 he merely continued his activity as writer and editor without ever again attaining any prominence. It is, therefore, safe to assume that it was the flight of his protector Rudolf Hess to England that marked the decline of Walter Frank. Shortly before that time he had reached his zenith: he had been received in audience by General Field Marshal Keitel and the press had stressed in that connection that the Reichsinstitut with its anti-Jewish research "was resolved and in a position to make a recognized contribution to the spiritual conduct of the war." [117]

On May 18, 1940, Frank, with tremendous acclaim, delivered at the University of Berlin his last public address known to us. It was a speech on fundamentals, intended both to sum up past experience and to show the way into the future.[118] He repeatedly expressed appreciation for Hess' support of his Reichsinstitut and in his feeling of security went so far as to label Rosenberg a "publicist" in his anti-Jewish efforts. Little did he know that Rosenberg's team would soon completely outdistance him.

As additional subject-matter for German anti-Jewish research Frank mentioned the problems of Eastern-European Jewry. This, he said, "results from the mere regulatory political task which the German Reich has now [after the defeat of Poland in 1939] undertaken with regard to the Polish space and thereby also with regard to the greater part of Eastern Jewry." But, he urged, the main objective was still the study of the thoroughly Westernized Jew. The Eastern-European Jew ("the Galician," as Frank put it), with a language of his own and his own peculiar way of life, could be made to fit much more easily into the stereotype of the inimical alien, but Frank did not want the easy way:

> It will always remain a task of paramount importance to unveil the so-called "noble," "educated," "German" Jew and to expose him as the most dangerous type of the alien parasite. It is easy to show

---

[116] *Deutsche Justiz, Amtliches Blatt der deutschen Rechtspflege,* Her. Dr. Franz Gürtner, Reichsminister der Justiz, 101, I (1939), 235.

[117] *Die Judenfrage* of June 5, 1941, in a note devoted to volumes V and VI of *Forschungen zur Judenfrage* which were about to appear. Cf. footnote 91, which contains another proof of the high interest of the Wehrmacht in Frank's work.

[118] Cf. footnote 91.

a Galician Jew as a member of the "Asiatic horde" on Europe's soil. This is harder when the "Asiatic" meets us in the civilized form of a Baruch Spinoza or Moses Mendelssohn, of a Friedrich Gundolf or an Albert Einstein, a Maximilian Harden, Walther Rathenau or a Benjamin Disraeli. The Reichsinstitut in this respect already has done extraordinary work.

He wound up his speech by showing the broad vistas that had opened through "the rise of our *folk,* defined as it is by the Aryan *race,* to the new *Reich":*

> . . . the victory of National Socialist Germany over the Western democracies will lead to a *spiritual revolution in the European West,* too. When, under the assault of the German battalions, the rotten systems and ideologies of the West begin to totter, the superior results of political science produced by the new Germany can and must invade the vacuum that will arise.
>
> Along with the critical mission of political science there will be also a *constructive mission.* It will consist in showing the German people itself and the surrounding world the way of the Germans to the Reich and to the regulating mission of this Reich in Europe... Taking its departure from a gigantic creative foreign policy and a new German Greater Reich, [the new political science] again will be able and forced to shape the history of great-power and world politics in a new sense, far beyond purely diplomatic historiography.
>
> All this scholarship will have the objective not only of informing people who *know* but also of educating people who possess the *will.*
>
> And if we succeed in combining the depth and thoroughness of German scholarly method with the glowing force of political will, then the prophecy of Christoph Steding will materialize that *a new political science of the German Reich will assume leadership in the scholarship of Europe.*[119]

XI

GOEBBELS' INSTITUT ZUM STUDIUM DER JUDENFRAGE (INSTITUTE FOR THE STUDY OF THE JEWISH PROBLEM). WILHELM ZIEGLER

Not all Nazi institutions devoted to anti-Jewish research achieved as much as the Reichsinstitut, but all of them, of course, deserve our attention. To evaluate them correctly we must see them within the general framework of Nazi politics. Now that the gleaming façade

---

[119] *Ibid.,* pp. 12, 17, 18.—Italics in original.
   Christoph Steding. *Das Reich und die Krankheit der europäischen Völker* (Hamburg, Hanseatische Verlagsanstalt, 1938, 772 pp.). This book, edited by Frank after the author's death, tended to show that for the Teutonic nations surrounding Germany the only way out of their spiritual crisis would be to unite, under Germany's leadership, into a Greater-Teutonic Reich. The book was so popular that in 1943 a third edition was issued.

of uniform will and action has broken down, we have come to see that a continual sequence of feuds between factions and even individuals went on behind it. They did not differ in ideology in general nor, for that matter, in their goal of radically "solving the Jewish question" or even as to the application of the sternest measures in the course of action; what did go on was a contest for power. Goebbels, who always seems to have been lagging behind in his effort to make his talk as important as the action of others, never personally appeared among the guests of honor at Frank's Reichsinstitut; as a matter of fact, he might have construed Frank's invectives against the incompetent anti-Jewish writers who do the cause more harm than good as directed against himself and his staff. He, therefore, lent his support to another institution, the Institut zum Studium der Judenfrage (Institute for the Study of the Jewish Problem) in Berlin which in the course of time drew ever nearer the Ministry of Public Enlightenment and Propaganda to become finally, though not overtly, one of its agencies. While the organ of this institute at least casually mentioned the Reichsinstitut and Frank, it seems to have ignored Rosenberg to the degree of mentioning the opening of his Frankfort Institute for Research into the Jewish Question—a front-page event which took place in March, 1941—as late as in the Jan. 1, 1943, issue. Dr. Giselher Wirsing, a Rosenberg man who was given a prominent place at the opening of that Frankfort institute, in a Propaganda Ministry report (now in the Yivo archives) of 1944 was branded as having at one time shown "an explicitly pro-Soviet attitude." On the other hand, except for his appearance at the inauguration, Rosenberg did not participate in Frank's institute nor pay any attention to it, and his *Nationalsozialistische Monatshefte,* as we shall see, did not wholeheartedly approve of Frank's *Forschungen zur Judenfrage.* Ultimately Rosenberg erected an anti-Jewish institute of his own, in which he installed nobody else than Grau, the man who had been dropped from Frank's staff.

The Institut zum Studium der Judenfrage appeared on the scene even a little earlier than Frank's Jewish Department. At the start, its director was Eugen von Engelhardt [120] who, however, soon was superseded by a man of learning, Dr. Wilhelm Ziegler, a high official (Regierungsrat) in Goebbels' ministry. In the years of the republic,

---

[120] He was author of: *Jüdische Weltmachtpläne* [1. Auflage, 1936], 2. Auflage (Leipzig, Hammer-Verlag, 1943, 104 pp.). The book, essentially, is an interpretation of the Protocols of the Elders of Zion, spiced with plenty of abusive language.

Ziegler had been a prolific writer on the severity of the Versailles Treaty and on the "lie of war-guilt." Two of Ziegler's aides at the Institut, Hans Georg Trurnit and Karl Friedrich Wiebe, also were subordinates of Goebbels. We may assume, therefore, that the connection with Goebbels' ministry was established with Ziegler's taking over, about 1935, though the earliest direct evidence available belongs to 1938. In that year and the following ones there is the strongest evidence imaginable that the Institut was but one of the many camouflaged branches of Goebbels' ramified agency. Among the rubble that was the Propaganda Ministry in Berlin, two accounting sheets were recovered that are now in the archives of the Yivo and reveal the secret. In 1938, out of the amount of 3,750,000 Reichsmark appropriated for "home propaganda," 50,000 were set aside for the Institut zum Studium der Judenfrage (actually, 68,500 Reichsmark were spent); in 1939, although the total amount for "active propaganda" was reduced to 3,250,000 Reichsmark, the Institut was to be given 60,000 Reichsmark.[121]

Under Ziegler's direction, the money was not spent in vain. At least seven books, some of them voluminous, were published over the years, several of them in two editions, dealing with such topics as Jews and bolshevism, Jews and labor, the Jews in Germany, and the like. One book of a scholarly nature, Klaus Schickert's on the Jews in Hungary,[122] will be referred to later; the author, like Walter Frank and Grau, was a pupil of Karl Alexander von Müller's. In addition, a periodical *Mitteilungen über die Judenfrage* was launched in 1937, issued intermittently as a semi-monthly and weekly. In 1940, the title was changed to *Die Judenfrage in Politik, Recht, Kultur und Wirtschaft*. For the benefit of newspaper editors who might wish to make use of the material, the *Mitteilungen* originally were printed only on one side of the paper and re-publication was invited. On the contrary, a supplement, *Judentum und Recht,* was marked: "Not for publication. Confidential material."

The initial editor, Hans Georg Trurnit, a co-author of a voluminous anti-Jewish book,[123] was replaced in May, 1939, by Dr. Wolff

[121] The Yivo archives also own a dozen or so stencils pertaining to the Institut's routine activities; they, too, were found in the ruins of Goebbels' ministry.

[122] Klaus Schickert. *Die Judenfrage in Ungarn. Jüdische Assimilation und antisemitische Bewegung im 19. und 20. Jahrhundert* (Essen, Essener Verlagsanstalt, 1937, 201 pp.) = Die Juden im Leben der Völker. Schriften zur Judenfrage der Gegenwart, her. vom Institut zum Studium der Judenfrage, Berlin.

[123] *Weltentscheidung in der Judenfrage. Der Endkampf nach 3000 Jahren Judengegnerschaft.* In Verbindung mit dem Institut zum Studium der Judenfrage hrsg. von Dr. Willi Fr. Könitzer und Hansgeorg Trurnit (Dresden, Zwingerverlag, 1939, 303 pp., ill. 4°).

Heinrichsdorff; in April, 1940, Wolfgang Fehrmann became editor; in December, 1942, when Fehrmann went into military service, Horst Seemann took his place. Other frequent contributors were Friedrich Löffler, Leipzig, and Dr. L. Franz Gengler. Dietrich Wilde, a lawyer, was in charge of the supplement.

The Institut first was located Berlin W9, Bellevuestrasse 11a. Later it moved to Wilmersdorferstrasse 95, Berlin-Charlottenburg, and there opened a library "which collects the entire material necessary for the required struggle with world Jewry," as a most respectable scientific periodical phrased it.[124]

On December 12, 1939, the mimeographed sheet of Goebbels' ministry, the *Nachrichtenblatt des Reichsministeriums für Volksaufklärung und Propaganda* (no. 27) carried the following announcement:

> The Institut zum Studium der Judenfrage is located in Berlin W9, Postdamer Strasse 17 and is now called "Antisemitische Aktion."

From that time on, the new name of the institution appeared on the head of the *Mitteilungen zur Judenfrage* and, later, of *Die Judenfrage* and continued until the issue of February 15, 1942 (vol. VI, no. 4); then, without any explanation for the change, the institution was again renamed "Antijüdische Aktion." The facts discussed subsequently will make it clear that the change was caused by Germany's increased interest in the Arabs whose pro-Axis leaders resented the term "anti-Semite." Under the new designation it continued until the very end of 1943, when *Die Judenfrage*, without warning, ceased publication. During 1943, a new organ of the "Antijüdische Aktion" made its appearance, *Archiv für Judenfragen, Schriften zur geistigen Überwindung des Judentums,* each issue containing 64 pages in book size and edited by Friedrich Löffler. He was a veteran contributor to many anti-Jewish reviews and former editor of the Leipzig *Hammer,* "the oldest anti-Jewish periodical in Germany,"[125] which had ceased publication in 1940. In 1944, we shall meet Löffler as an expert on anti-Jewish research in connection with the international anti-Jewish congress that was planned by the

[124] *Zentralblatt für Bibliothekswesen* 57 (1940), 67.

[125] Cf. Löffler's letter to the Propaganda Ministry of December 2, 1939, at present in the Yivo archives.—Of the *Archiv für Judenfragen,* the Yivo possesses 3 issues, marked Gruppe A1, Heft 1, 2, and 3, respectively.—A catalogue of the library of the Antijüdische Aktion is known to us from a bibliographical entry: *Bibliothek der Antijüdischen Aktion. Bücherverzeichnis. Nach Verfassern geordnet.* Bd. 1-3. 1: A-F. 2: G-N. 3: O-Z ([Berlin] 1943, 4º). Typescript, mimeographed.

Reich authorities for the fall of that year and was referred to in state papers under the code word "K44."

Because *Die Judenfrage* showed little pretense of being a scholarly publication, there is no need for us to go into the details of its contents. Only its general orientation in the years when the Jewish question already was being finally "solved" will interest us later, when we shall reach those years in our presentation. At that time we shall also come back to the *Archiv für Judenfragen,* which undoubtedly had scholarly intentions.

As far as our information goes, the Antijüdische Aktion, like another of Goebbels' agencies, the Anti-Comintern (see page 113), toward the end of the Nazi era was absorbed into a new enterprise of the Propaganda Ministry, the *Zentralforschungsinstitut* (Central Research Institute), although neither the Aktion nor the Anti-Comintern lost their identity completely.

XII

WALTER GRUNDMANN. THE INSTITUT ZUR ERFORSCHUNG DES JÜDISCHEN EINFLUSSES AUF DAS DEUTSCHE KIRCHLICHE LEBEN (INSTITUTE FOR THE STUDY OF JEWISH INFLUENCE ON GERMAN CHURCH LIFE)

It would lead us too far afield to elaborate on all phases of the Nazi fight against the Christian religion as an outgrowth of Judaism, a fight which was countenanced by Rosenberg even before the seizure of power. In its broader aspects, it belongs under the adjustment of religion to the Hitler regime, i.e., to general contemporary history of Germany. But we ought not to overlook one particular institution, the Institut zur Erforschung des jüdischen Einflusses auf das deutsche kirchliche Leben (Institute for the Study of Jewish Influence on German Church Life). Though less glamorous than others, it still played its part among the five anti-Jewish research institutes of the Hitler era. In exertion of energy, for one thing, it was second to none.

In academic and theoretical circles, the "de-Judaization" efforts, too, had started early and Professor Dr. Ernst Bergmann of the University of Leipzig, whose name is best known in this connection, was only one of the pioneers. In the very first year of the Hitler era a Privatdozent of the University of Königsberg, in discussing Luther's attitude toward the Jews, had come to the conclusion:

> The Jewish question . . . has not been bred by agitators, it is not merely an internal German question, it is a question of world his-

tory,. . . which... must be seen not in the scope of mere humaneness but *sub specie aeternitatis* or, rather, by facing the cross.[126]

But not until 1939 were these anti-Jewish efforts given an organizational foundation; until that time, they were single-handed and somewhat erratic. On April 4 of that year, a number of Land Churches (Landeskirchen) founded the just mentioned Institut,[127] with Oberregierungsrat Leffler as director (Leiter) and Professor Dr. Walter Grundmann, of the University of Jena, as research director (Wissenschaftlicher Leiter). Grundmann thus defined the aims of his institution in a letter to the Ministry of Propaganda:

> The activities of the Institut tend to develop the scientific conclusions from the race and folk conceptions of the National Socialist Weltanschauung for the religious sector of German life. The men united in the Institut, as National Socialists, from the very outset took this stand as opposed to the previous theology and science of religion, which do not accept these conceptions and therefore are barren for the religious future of the German people.[128]

The official inauguration of the Institut took place at the Wartburg where German minstrels in the Middle Ages held their famous contest and Luther completed his translation of the New Testament. Grundmann here delivered himself of a speech on "The de-Judaization of Religious Life as the Task of German Theology and Church." [129] On March 1-3, 1940, the first conference was held at Wittenberg. Eight papers were read which later were edited by Grundmann under the title "Christianity and Judaism. Studies in Their Mutual Relationship." [130] During the year 1940, Grundmann published a book which was to show that Jesus was not a Jew:

> From the recognition of the unity of psychic attitude and blood inheritance, which has been granted to our time, it follows from necessity that in all probability Jesus, since he could not be a Jew

[126] Lic. Erich Vogelsang, Privatdozent in Königsberg, *Luthers Kampf gegen die Juden* (Tübingen, Mohr, 1933, 35 pp.), p. 35.—German scholars in the Nazi era frequently reverted to the subject of Luther's attitude toward the Jews. Cf. Prof. Dr. Theodor Pauls, *Luther und die Juden* (Bonn, Gebr. Scheur, 1939-1940, I, 140 pp., II, 104 pp., III, 98 pp.); Theodor Pauls, Werner Petersmann, 'Entjudung selbst der Lutherforschung in der Frage der Stellung Luthers zu den Juden (Bonn, Gebr. Scheur, 1940, 23 pp.).

[127] Originally the name ".. . zur Erforschung und Beseitigung des jüdischen Einflusses. . ." (for the Study and Elimination of Jewish influence . . .)" was contemplated.

[128] This letter, dated May 31, 1941, as well as the other original documents mentioned in this chapter, is now in the possession of the Yivo.

[129] The address appeared in pamphlet form: Walter Grundmann, *Die Entjudung des religiösen Lebens als Aufgabe der deutschen Theologie und Kirche* (Weimar, 1940, 22 pp.). In 1937, Grundmann had published *Deutsche Theologie*. A year later, the following book of his appeared: *Die Gotteskindschaft Jesu und ihre religionsgeschichtlichen Voraussetzungen* (Weimar, Verlag Deutsche Christen, 1938, 168 pp.), which the leading *Deutsche Literaturzeitung* (1940, No. 47/48) praised as being "free from Judeo-Christian distortion."

[130] *Christentum und Judentum. Studien zur Erforschung ihres gegenseitigen Verhältnisses* (Leipzig, Georg Wigand, 1940, 248 pp.).

on the basis of his psychic specificness (seelische Artung), was not a Jew by blood either.[181]

In setting forth this thesis Grundmann could lean upon an older colleague, Professor Dr. Emanuel Hirsch of Göttingen, who, notwithstanding his Jewish-sounding name, was a pure Aryan and who had been among the first university teachers to come out for Hitler (see p. 14). Hirsch in a book on the essence of Christianity had stated:

> [In Galilee] non-Aryan and Aryan peoples . . . time and again left their traces in the population. Science has no reason to define Jesus' blood origin in any more definite way than by "non-Jewish." [132]

On March 3-5, 1941, the second conference of the Institut was held at Eisenach.[133] The speakers included four professors of the University of Jena (Grundmann, Eisenhuth, Meyer-Erlach, Wagenführer); two of the University of Giessen (Bertram, Euler); and one each from the universities of Berlin (Hempel), Greifswald (Koepp), and Leipzig (Leipoldt). Land bishop Schulz (Schwerin) pointed to the Teutonic German element which ought to be the center of present-day church life and bitterly attacked the kind of theology that opposed this view. Pastor Dr. Hunger spoke on "Jewish Psychoanalysis and German Pastordom," and Professor Grundmann announced the formation of a research team of psychologists, jurists, etc., within the Institut. All speakers, the report tells us, "recognized the necessity of removing from Christian teachings everything that is Jewish or influenced by Jewry." At a church service in Eisenach excerpts were read from "God's Message," an adaptation of the New Testament from which everything Jewish was eradicated.[134]

An eight-page report presented by Grundmann to the Ministry of Propaganda in the summer of 1941 and now in the Yivo archives, listed the following research projects of the Institut, each consisting of a number of studies: (1) The person of Jesus Christ; (2) The beginnings of Christianity; (3) Palestine; (4) Problems of Catholicism (including "the influence of Judaism on Catholicism from the blood-racial and spiritual-religious point of view" and "the attitude of

---

[181] Walter Grundmann, *Jesus der Galiläer und das Judentum* (Leipzig, Georg Wigand, 1940, 246 pp.), p. 205.

[132] E[manuel] Hirsch, *Das Wesen des Christentums* (Weimar, Deutsche Christen, 1939 165 pp.). Anhang: "Die Abstammung Jesu," pp. 158-165.

[133] Cf. *Weltkampf*, I (1941), 112-113.—The transactions were published, under a somewhat modified name, as *Germanentum, Christentum und Judentum*, Vol. II.

[134] *Die Botschaft Gottes* (Weimar, Verlag Deutsche Christen, 1940, 96, XII pp.).—Mention is also made of a gathering in Heidelberg, April 15-17, 1941, at which papers were read by Professors Odenwald (Heidelberg), Meyer-Erlach and Wagenführer (Jena) and Leipoldt (Leipzig).

the Catholic Church toward Judaism"); (5) The history of the Teutonic-German faith; (6) Archives of German piety; (7) Guidance of souls and cult; (8) Problems related to the fateful struggle of the German people. In addition, the practical work (Gestaltungsarbeit) of the Institut was presented, such as the adaptation of the New Testament, or the large project called "The History of God with the Germans and the Germans with God" ("Die Geschichte Gottes mit den Deutschen und der Deutschen mit Gott"), which was to be undertaken by a number of renowned poets headed by Wilhelm Kotzde-Kottenrodt.

It was a matter of grief for Grundmann and his group that they did not possess a scientific review of their own. After the previous attempts to obtain the permission of the Ministry of Propaganda had failed, Grundmann again tried his luck on June 24, 1941, a few days after Germany's attack on the Soviet Union, by pleading:

> The new political situation created for the German liberation struggle by the alliance of Jewish bolshevism with Jewish plutocracy, raises a number of religious problems, too.... The Institut considers as its essential task cooperation as a pioneer in this field, witness the works of Prof. Meyer-Erlach initiated by it on "The Influence of Judaism on English Christianity" (Transactions of the Institut, vol. I, distributed as an offprint in 25,000 copies) and "Is God an Englishman?"

The permission was refused and the Institut had to content itself with its newsletter called *Verbandsmitteilungen*. One of its issues carried the report that Professor Dr. h.c. Ernst Krieck had been elected corresponding member of the Institut.

A year later, in 1942, the industrious institute was able to convene for a third conference, held in Nuremberg from June 9 to 11. The transactions were published in an imposing volume of over four hundred pages,[135] to which Professors Bertram, Grundmann, Odeberg, and Werdermann, among others, contributed; the last author devoted over thirty pages to "the danger of Judaizing in religious education and how to overcome it." Grundmann within the same year succeeded, moreover, in editing another volume, for which he himself wrote a paper of almost eighty pages on ancient religion in the light of racial science, and in which considerable space was devoted to "Old Testa-

---

[135] *Sitzungsberichte der dritten Arbeitstagung des Instituts zur Erforschung des jüdischen Einflusses auf das deutsche kirchliche Leben vom 9. bis 11. Juni 1942 in Nürnberg* (Leipzig, Georg Wigand, 1943, 424 pp.) = Germanentum, Christentum und Judentum, Vol. III.

ment and Judaism." [136] Among the authors represented in the volume were Professors Leipoldt and Odeberg. [137]

To the same year belongs a book by Professors Grundmann and Karl Friedrich Euler on "The Religious Face of Judaism," [138] which was prepared explicitly for "the historical vindication and justification of Germany in the struggle against Jewry." This justification, as we shall later see, fell in a time when the annihilation of the Jewish people was already in full swing. Euler set out to prove that the ancient Hebrews (=Chabiru) never were a people and that the Jews always had been a racial mixture which, however, through breeding and selection received the shape (Ausformung) of a special race. An appendix on "The Yiddish Language as the Expression of Jewish Psyche (Geistesart)" was added. Grundmann in his part of the volume expounded the eternal hatred of the Jews toward the whole non-Jewish world and the tendency of the Jews to appropriate every sublime idea, including Christianity.

The Institut also founded a research team on "Teutondom and Christianity" which until August, 1943, had held at Weissenfels near Lützen two "Nordic conferences," "well attended also by foreigners from the North."

A word should be said about the attitude of the Nazi government toward the ideas and actions represented by the Jena institute. It may be gratuitous to state that no institution of any kind, let alone one concerned with problems of Weltanschauung, could have existed in Nazi Germany without official approval. But in this case too the surface unanimity of the regime was misleading. The presence of a representative of the Ministry for Church Affairs at the 1939 Wartburg session gave the gathering the first green light and when Grundmann's book on Jesus was rather boldly attacked by the Marburg Professor of Theology, H. von Soden, in *Deutsches Pfarrerblatt* 46, 13/14 (April 5, 1942), an intervention of the Ministry of Propaganda forced the editor to agree to publishing a rejoinder by the author. But there was no agreement within that ministry itself.

---

[136] The volume, entitled *Die völkische Gestalt des Glaubens*, is known to us only through a casual reference.

[137] The contents of several publications of Grundmann's Institut are given by B. Weinryb in *Jewish Review* III (1945), where also several other Nazi writings against the Jews are discussed.

[138] Karl Friedrich Euler and Walter Grundmann, *Das religiöse Gesicht des Judentums, Entstehung und Art* (Leipzig, Wigand, 1942, 176 pp.). Known to us from a note in *Die Judenfrage*, Dec. 15, 1942, and from an extensive review by [Professor Dr.] Wilhelm Koepp of the University of Greifswald in *Europäischer Wissenschafts-Dienst* III (1943), 30-31. The item on the Nordic conferences in the next paragraph is also taken from that review.

Grundmann's continuous efforts to obtain the permission for a periodical were treated in a dilatory way, and an internal note of the
Propaganda Ministry gave the following reasons for this attitude:

> The endeavors of this organization and its leading men such as
> Prof. Grundmann are well meant. But there is no interest either in
> assimilating (angleichen) Christian teaching in national socialism
> or in proving that a re-shaped (umgestaltetes) Christianity is not
> fundamentally Jewish (keine jüdische Grundhaltung aufweist).[139]

On a specific occasion, even a more negative attitude was revealed.
When several persons of the Ministry of Propaganda were invited
to a meeting of the Institut in Berlin on January 15, 1942, at which
Professors Grundmann and Werdermann were to lecture, a high
official of the Ministry noted in pencil on the invitation: "If such
lectures at present are considered desirable at all, they should be
watched." Another of Goebbels' officials contemplated asking the
Party Chancellery, i.e., the supreme authority of the Party, for a decision on how to treat the Jena Institut, but whether such a request
was ever made is not known. At any rate, the Institut was still
in existence in the summer of 1944, when (see p. 227) Professor
Dr. Georg Bertram, of the University of Giessen, is quoted as being
"at present" its Research Director. What happened to Grundmann
can only be guessed.

XIII

PREPARING FOR WAR: THE CONCEPTS OF FOLK AND SPACE

The development of the three institutes dealt with in the previous
chapters has been brought down the war years in order not to interrupt
the chronological flow of events. Presently, we shall have to resume
our survey at the point we broke off, namely, at the promulgation
of the Nuremberg Laws which, in contrast to what was expected,
brought with them an intensification of anti-Jewish legislation and
practice. In the field of research, the same holds true: after 1935,
the scholars' contribution to the struggle against the Jews grew im-
mensely both in quantity and in ardor. This intensification was in
unison with the spirit of the era. "Co-ordination" (the nearest possible,
but by no means adequate equivalent for German *Gleichschaltung*)
of scholarship with the regime had made further progress. The Hochschule für Politik in Berlin, always compliant since the advent of

---

[139] These items as well as the ones in the following paragraph are taken from documents
now in the Yivo archives.

Hitler, in 1937 was by decree of the Führer reorganized "to disseminate and strengthen the formation of knowledge and will in the spirit of national socialism." But by that time everything had become political. In retrospect, German scholarship of that period looks like a gigantic assembly line working toward one aim.

"Today, national socialism knocks at the door of every scholarly discipline and asks: what have you to offer me?", the dean of German linguists, Professor Dr. Eduard Hermann of the University of Göttingen, observed. He deplored that Indo-European scholars had "failed to show . . . the National Socialist government to what extraordinary degree their science is able and competent to cooperate in the highest objectives of the National Socialist movement...." [140] Another scholar in this field, Glaesser, prepared an "Introduction into Racial Linguistics" which was published by Winter in Heidelberg, one of the most respectable scientific publishing houses of the country.[141] Professor Dr. Lutz Mackensen of the University of Greifswald, a distinguished student of cultural anthropology, in a paper on the state of his field of knowledge in the era of national socialism, argued like this: "Recently K. Saller, *Der Weg der deutschen Rasse* (second edition, Leipzig, 1934), again maintained that *Rasse* is nothing ready, but a permanent process. This will be pleasant reading to the Jewish 'race students.' " [142] "Present day German psychology," Erich Rudolf Jaensch, one of the most representative scholars in the field, declared, "has long since abandoned the rôle of the mere onlooker and put itself with the greatest decisiveness at the service of the community and of action directed to the betterment of mankind." [143]

Although we came to know Jaensch as a rather early convert to nazism—in 1933 he had extolled the Prussian spirit as "related to the spirit of the SA and the SS" [144] — his reference to mankind was

140 Eduard Hermann, "Was hat die indogermanische Sprachwissenschaft dem Nationalsozialismus zu bieten?" *Göttingische Gelehrte Anzeigen*, 199 (1937), 49-59.

141 Edgar Glaesser, *Einführung in die rassenkundliche Sprachforschung* (Heidelberg, Winter, 1939, 174 pp.).

142 Lutz Mackensen, *Volkskunde in der Entscheidung* (Tübingen, Mohr, 1937, 48 pp.), p. 46.

143 E. R. Jaensch, *Jugendanthropologie und Neuformung des Menschentums* (Leipzig, Barth, 1937, 89 pp.).—Late in 1944, a German psychologist reported: ". . . the extinction of Jewish psychoanalysis [in the Third Reich] . . . After the predominance of alien species (artfremd) [was eliminated]—incidentally, it was in existence not only in psychology but in mathematics and medicine as well—the outlook has become free." Cf. Georg Schliebe, in *Internationale Zeitschrift für Erziehung* XIII (1944), 211-243.

144 Professor Dr. Erich Jaensch, *Die Wissenschaft und die deutsche völkische Bewegung* (Marburg a/Lahn, Elwert, 1933, 75 pp.), p. 64.—Under the Nazis, it became customary among "Aryan" scholars to bring the Jewish moment into scientific discussions. For instance, the famous student of Semitics, Professor Dr. C. Brockelmann, in reviewing B. Landsberger,

not intended as a joke. He meant something different. It was the time when "the mystic Janus," to use Haushofer's rhetorical language, was about to turn his face. The first period of the regime was devoted to inner consolidation; it could not be frequently enough repeated that national socialism was no article for export. The learned writings of well-known and aspiring scholars in the rapidly expanding "Science of Foreign Countries (Auslandswissenschaft)"—the University of Berlin even founded a special school in this field—played up "understanding (Verständigung)." No fundamental issues could divide the European nations, it was asserted in accordance with Hitler's speeches of that period; Germany had no aggressive intentions whatsoever. Not only England and France but even Czechoslovakia and Poland were accorded this gentle handling until the time was ripe. For instance, a group of recognized historians headed by the celebrated Professor Dr. Albert Brackmann of the University of Berlin, in a large volume preaching *Verständigung* with Poland, spoke these reasonable words:

> ... We shall here proceed not from the opposition between the two peoples [Germans and Poles], but from the fact that the two peoples for more than a thousand years lived in the closest community of space and, therefore, were in particularly close political and cultural relationship.... [We wish] to put history at the disposal of the understanding of the contacts thus originated.... because the historian is no judge of the past and no legislator for the future, but a servant of truth.[145]

This devotion to truth, to be sure, did not prevent Brackmann, immediately after the Campaign of the Eighteen Days, from judging the past by "proving" that Poland never was capable of independent existence.[146] But while Hitler prepared for war, the Brackmanns helped to veil his intentions.

Die Fauna des alten Mesopotamiens, invoked the spirit of the renowned anti-Semite Lagarde to castigate what he considered a distortion of facts by the author: "The procedure [was] ... to discredit a fellow-researcher by distorting the facts ... Such methods about which Lagarde complained frequently enough previously were unfortunately very popular in certain circles of our science but now in the Third Reich they, I hope, will disappear completely." Professor Dr. Richard Thurnwald and Professor Dr. Walter Krickeberg became involved in a lengthy argument about who had entrusted book reviews to Jewish contributors and favored Jews in general. Cf. *Zeitschrift für Ethnologie* 70 (1938), 119-124 and *Archiv für Anthropologie,* N. F., XXIV (1938), 298-302.

[145] Albert Brackmann, Her., *Deutschland und Polen* (München, Oldenbourg, 1933, VI, 273, XVIII pp.), p. III.

[146] Albert Brackmann, *Krisis und Aufbau in Osteuropa. Ein weltgeschichtliches Bild* (Berlin, Ahnenerbe-Stiftung-Verlag, 1939, 68 pp.).—From the moment Poland had dared to defy Hitler, the German scholars to the last man advanced a new theory (ridiculous, of course, to anyone acquainted with Polish politics): that Piłsudski had wanted *Verständigung* with the Third Reich and readily would have given in to Hitler in 1939, but that his disciples had betrayed his legacy. Cf. Dr. Helmut Schubring, *Deutscher Friedenswille gegen polnischen Nationalhass im Einsatz der deutschen Presse 1933-1939* (Berlin, Junker und Dünnhaupt, 1941, 182 pp.).

A second, parallel track of German policies became visible after the Saar victory, the reintroduction of compulsory military service, the Nuremberg Laws—all pressed into one year 1935. Though peace continued to be a subject for oratorical declamations, he who had his eyes open should have seen the shaping of events. Today, in the light of hindsight, it is truly inconceivable how stubbornly the world refused to believe that the war was being set in motion, though the Nazis openly and consistently professed their will to war even before they acknowledged their rearmament, or rather the complete militarization, of the nation. "We fall in without arms," a very early song by the prominent Nazi poet Hans Baumann began, the Baumann of "tomorrow the world": "We fall in without arms, we march without weapons; a young army in its own land—what is this army for?" And the second stanza provided the candid answer: "We stand ready for the Germany of tomorrow; that's why we must march today." [147]

But not only the marching songs of the Labor Service, the SA, the SS down to the Hitler Youth were one passionate hymn celebrating war and defying the rotten outer world; not only did the orators at mass meetings and the radio announcers harp upon the same theme, but also the serious magazines and the scholarly periodicals and books had been gradually seized by this obsession. "The field is open for audacious minds, as it has not been for five hundred years," Rosenberg declared.[148]

True, the Germans did not inform the world that their lexicographers were preparing as early as 1936-37 new questionnaires on soldier's speech for a new emergency,[149] just as utmost secrecy surrounded the creation in the Nazi party of a war organization with the significant name of *Mob* (mobilization) in 1937.[150] But in sufficient numbers outright acts were committed in broad daylight. One by one research institutions devoted to the problems of total war

147 "Wir treten ohne Gewehre an, / marschieren ohne Waffen / ein junges Heer im eignen Land! / Was hat das Heer zu schaffen? // Wir steh'n für das Deutschland von morgen bereit. / drum müssen wir heute marschieren...." *Liederbuch der Nationalsozialistischen Deutschen Arbeiterpartei* (München, Eher, 1937, 98 pp.), p. 80.

148 Alfred Rosenberg, *Weltanschauung und Wissenschaft* (München, Eher [1937], 13 pp.), p. 9.

149 August Miller, "Die deutsche Soldatensprache und die Arbeit an ihr," *Deutsche Kultur im Leben der Völker... Deutsche Akademie* VII (1941), 395-6. As is now established by the evidence introduced at the Nuremberg trial, Dr. Hjalmar Schacht was appointed Commissioner General for War Mobilization as early as in 1935.

150 Since this fact never seems to have been mentioned in non-Nazi literature, the following outright confession from the nearly official Parry publication, Carl Johanny and Oscar Redelberger, *op. cit.*, p. 123, is worth quoting: "The Party *did not want war....* However, the *Führer* knew, too, that *the decision on peace or war rested not with him alone. In due time he therefore prepared his Party for the emergency.* As early as 1937 . . . within the staff of the Deputy Führer [Rudolf Hess] a separate department was formed which created a *Mob-Organization* comprising all gaus, districts, local organizations, ramifications and affiliated associations (Gliederungen)."

mushroomed into existence: War and Army Academy, the Military Science Department of the General Staff of the Army, the Military Science Department of the Navy, the Aerial War Academy, etc., etc. German publishing houses competed with each other in putting out scholarly studies on "Economic Mobilization," "Population Development from the Point of View of War Economy," "The Military Economy of Total War," and so on; in addition, the war potential of other nations was diligently studied. Thus, the well known German maxim was complied with that politicians, diplomats, fifth columnists, and spies should be firmly backed by social sciences. Even the thin terminological veiling of "Defense Science (Wehrwissenschaft)" instead of "War Science (Kriegswissenschaft)" was dropped more and more frequently; inasmuch as the former still occurred, it was defined as being more inclusive, referring more to the totality of the forthcoming war than the traditional compound beginning with *Kriegs-*.[151] In 1936, the "Annual Reports on War Economy" made their appearance, and no effort was made to conceal the editor's affiliation with the Reich War Ministry.[152] On August 13, 1937, the Reich Minister of Education ordered the registration of all persons knowing foreign languages, whether or not they used this knowledge professionally. Each such person, it was added, must be prepared to offer his or her services in case of need.[153] How could the meaning of these signs be mistaken?

But Hitler was right in stating that there would be no repetition of 1914-18. He was right in claiming that instead of the rigid militaristic concepts of the Kaiser, he was in possession of a dynamic philosophy. Haushofer, his inspirer and interpreter, in looking backward at the outbreak of the war, put it this way:

> It was just a mistake [of the old-school nationalists] . . . to believe that the colonial problem was the key to solving all international questions. The German living space (Lebensraum) in the first place [*sic*] was concerned about not being throttled at home! *Therefore* Danzig and the [Polish] Corridor were of more importance to it than a West African colonial empire patched together by bartering....[154]

In bold, if somewhat crude, strokes the program had been outlined as early as in *Mein Kampf* written in 1924, and in the Middle

<hr>

[151] Cf. *Handbuch der Wehrwissenschaften*, a highly official publication started in 1934, *s.v.*

[152] *Kriegswirtschaftliche Jahresberichte* I (1936)... Kurt Heise, Major V <E> im Reichskriegsministerium (Hamburg, 1936, 234 pp.).

[153] *Das Archiv*, 1937, p. 543.

[154] *Zeitschrift für Geopolitik* XVI (October, 1939), 776.—Italics in original.

Thirties the blueprint was ready. The date is hard to establish, but after the first years of the regime, the concept of *Lebensraum* became uppermost in German minds. Haushofer, the teacher of Rudolf Hess, had made the term popular the world over through his own writings and those of his staff, which was said to consist of a thousand people. Derived from Lebensraum, newly coined but quickly sanctioned compounds like "thinking in terms of space (Raumdenken)," "perceiving space (Raumfühlen)," "arranging space (Raumordnung)" found their way into the open. *Raum* had become an almost mystical term on one level with *Rasse* (race) and *Blut* (blood). A belated report confessed that

> soon after the National Socialist upheaval (Umbruch) students of all departments at different graduate schools offered themselves, outside of curricular work, for projects which we may call Raumforschung (space research) ...[155]

During 1935, by several laws and decrees (February 15, March 29, June 26, December 18) a Reich Agency for Space Arrangement (Reichsstelle für Raumordnung) and a Reich Board for Space Research were created; the participation of many prominent scholars under the leadership of Professor Dr. Konrad Meyer was secured and a splendidly printed journal made its appearance.[156] It was greeted by the Reich and Prussian Minister of Education with the following dedication printed on the front page:

> The entrance of science into the study and arrangement of space will by necessity introduce it into the fundamental questions of national socialism: Blood and Soil, Folk and Space. Through this task, German scholarship will both take and give power.

Superficially, the interest of German Raumforschung was limited to the territory of Germany. But extensive group and individual study trips abroad, particularly to the adjacent countries, and careful reports on pertinent foreign literature tended to widen the scope of the findings from the outset.

At first glance, it is surprising to see this enthusiasm develop over research into such highly specialized subjects as changing landscapes or foresting wasteland. Other topics dealt with by the new Reich Agency for Space Arrangement again seemed utterly academic.

---

[155] Gerhard Isenburg, "Die Arbeitsgemeinschaft für wirtschaftliche Raumordnung," in: Hochschule für Politik, Forschungsabteilung *Jahrbuch 1939* (Berlin, 1939), pp. 435-443. Quotation from p. 437.

[156] *Raumforschung und Raumordnung. Monatsschrift der Reichsarbeitsgemeinschaft für Raumforschung*, Heidelberg-Berlin, Kurt Vowinckel Verlag, 1. Jg., Heft 1, Oktober, 1936, 4°.— It will be noted that the journal was entrusted to the same publishing house from which *Zeitschrift für Geopolitik*, and most of the geopolitical literature in general, was issued.

But the meaning was clear to the initiated. The reviewer of "Space Arrangement in Greek City Construction" emphasized that "the book shows, to begin with, the close interrelation between all mental and artistic creativity of a race and, moreover, the tendency toward clarity in the Greek people that is cognate [to the Germans] (artverwandt)." [157] The study on "The Colonizing Work of Frederic the Great" was termed "an instructive attempt to make the past the touchstone of current tasks." [158] The first wartime issue of *Raumforschung und Raumordnung* (III, 8/9), in a leading article signed by the new editor, Professor Dr. Paul Ritterbusch, quite naturally spoke of "the necessary incorporation of the Reich Board for Space Research and Space Arrangement into the war-effort research."

Indeed, behind the innocent front, which German scholars liked to compare to the National Planning Board of the USA, powerful engines were being erected to ram the very structure of Europe—and we now know how nearly they succeeded. Rearranging a village, it turned out, meant laying out plans for giving German settlers on Polish or Soviet soil habitations that would suit them most. Changing the landscape meant transforming the monotony of the Polish or Russian plain into something that might please the Herrenvolk when they took over the Eastern Space (Ostraum). This very designation, *Ostraum,* which began coming into the open more and more frequently, was to show the average German that he would move into a historical-cultural vacuum which he would have to model for the first time in modern history, and German scholarship was quick to supply the "evidence" that at least one-half of European Russia, not to speak of the territory between the Baltic and the Black Sea, was in essence German "culture soil (Kulturboden)." So the second half of Russia, once conquered, would come in handy as a useful, if amorphous, appendix.

After nobody had objected to the incorporation of Austria, everything indeed must have seemed possible. Karl Alexander von Müller, no enthusiastic youngster, exclaimed:

> . . . By this enlargement [of its territory] the National Socialist state, owing to its own unheard-of concentration of power has reached a peak in the national development of our folk. The most

---

[157] *Deutsche Mathematik* 3 (1938), 346. " 'To be German means to be clear,' the Führer said," was the conclusion of the reviewer, Professor Dr. Hamel of Berlin. Cf. footnote 270.
[158] *Neues Bauerntum*, 1938, Heft II.

beautiful political dream of our youth stands before our eyes as a reality. . . .

And he went on to say:

> Thus this German folk, which so long wavered on its road and more than once seemed to lose itself, does take its place among the great solid nations of Europe with the youngest and most concentrated momentum. And we believe and hope its ultimate consolidation will mark the beginning of the recovery of our continent and the first step in rebuilding it in a better way.[159]

What "recovery of our [European] continent" meant was intimated by other theorists of the regime, for instance, by Ernst Krieck who on January 18, 1939—the anniversary of the founding of Bismarck's Reich—stated at the University of Heidelberg:

> The Teutons are the nobility folk of world history. If we want to prove this in history again, we must remove from our existence Asiatism in any shape that has penetrated our being, the poison and the illness of the European peoples. This is the racial renascence. 1938, the year of Greater Germany, calls to the German people to lift up our eyes that we be adequate to the deeds of the Führer and the greatest of the German missions.[160]

Other nations could not interfere because they simply were not entitled to. That somewhat unexpected contribution was made by Carl Schmitt in a paper read at the University of Kiel on April 1, 1939.[161] With usual brilliancy, he set out to show that now that the German state had become a Reich, it was one of the carriers and creators of a new international order. Within its "greater space (Grossraum)" the German Reich sets the law itself; if need be, the Reich "is able . . . to reject the interference of powers that are alien to the space and do not belong to the folk (raumfremde und unvölkische)." The buoyant septuagenarian Haushofer went into raptures over this theory:

> . . . a planetary outlook, . . . keen formulations, . . . world-spanning demands of spatial-political justice: a high goal of mankind and the highest of German geopolitics.[162]

---

[159] *Historische Zeitschrift* 158 (1938), 2.

[160] Ernst Krieck, *Volk unter dem Schicksal* (Heidelberg, Winter, 1939, 10 pp.), p. 10.

[161] Carl Schmitt, *Völkerrechtliche Grossraumordnung mit Interventionsverbot für raumfremde Mächte* (Berlin-Wien, Deutscher Rechtsverlag, 1939, 88 pp.).

[162] *Zeitschrift für Geopolitik* XVII (März, 1940), 151.—To measure the speed with which German megalomania was moving upward in those fateful years, it is worth noting that the *Nationalsozialistische Monatshefte*, no. 129 (Dezember, 1940), pp. 90-91, attacked Schmitt's proposition. The antithesis Staat vs. Reich, the reviewer argued, could imply that other states, too, could become reichs; actually, only the German folk can create a Reich.

XIV

ON THE EVE OF WAR: JEWRY=BOLSHEVISM.
PETER-HEINZ SERAPHIM

This human law of non-interference, of course, admirably supplemented the divine law of racial inequality that had been established earlier. While still posing as promoters of "understanding,"
German scholars were dexterous enough to interpret even their race
concept as an instrument of peace. France ought to accept Germany's
offer of cooperation, a much acclaimed author urged in 1937:

> Germany's policies are race policies in the highest sense, because
> they refuse to oppress other races and folkdoms and respect them
> as the highest and most valuable possessions entrusted to man by
> creation. Thereby France receives guarantees which she has never
> experienced.[163]

The conclusion drawn from statements of this kind always was
the same: that Europe was in terrible danger if the idea of *Rasse*
was not assigned its proper place. Here the Jews came into the elaborate scheme. The Jews were blocking the path of real "understanding," both the "international Jews" entrenched in strategic positions
in the respective countries and the "traitors" who had barely escaped
Nazi violence. Thus, anti-Jewish propaganda, as a means of under-
mining morale among Germany's prospective adversaries in the on-
coming war, was run through different channels. While cheap tracts
against the Jews were translated into as remote languages as Lithuanian
and Lettish, Jewish preponderance in literature and social life of all
countries was "exposed" on a scholarly level: "the Jew" had managed
to "Judaize" the leadership strata in such countries as England, France,
Poland and so on but, at the same time, "the Jew" was the real power
behind bolshevism which threatened the very existence of those
countries.

From year to year, from month to month, the Nazis ever more
constantly addressed themselves to this theme of Bolshevist-Jewish
danger; while they hoped to win over England and France for the
anti-Russian crusade, the subject of "plutocracy" was held in abeyance:

> Europe's culture . . . shall be protected and strengthened anew.
> Since world bolshevism and Jewry which carries it have proclaimed
> a struggle of destruction against these values, a front against the will

---

[163] Ewald K. B. Mangold, *Frankreich und der Rassengedanke. Eine politische Kernfrage
Europas* (München, Lehmann, 1937, 152 pp.), p. 140.

to destroy is a necessary result of a feeling of responsibility for Europe's culture.[164] This literature took it for granted that bolshevism was simply another name for Judaism. Czarist leaders and writers, like Nikolai Markov or Gregor Bostunitsch-Schwartz, who after 1917 had found refuge in Germany and solace under the wings of Rosenberg, not only had brought with them from Russia the Protocols of the Elders of Zion but also vouched for the fact that bolshevism was imposed upon the 170,000,000 inhabitants of the Soviet Union by the Jews. Even Lenin's and Stalin's non-Jewish origin presented no difficulty since the concept of race could be invoked. A conference of Rosenberg's vast staff was informed by Dr. Georg Leibbrandt, an instructor in Eastern European problems at the Hochschule für Politik:

> At any rate, it must be stated that the leaders of bolshevism, as far as they are not of Jewish origin, racially and mentally are determined as Near-Eastern Oriental.[165]

This Leibbrandt, an intimate of Rosenberg's for years and one of his associates in the struggle against the Bolshevist menace,[166] became closely associated during the war with the murdering of the Jewish population of the Occupied Eastern Territories administered by Rosenberg.

At the staff conference mentioned above twelve speakers analyzed "Europe's Fate in the East." The master-stroke of the Ribbentrop-Molotov pact had not yet been delivered, and Jewish bolshevism was still the paramount topic. Thus, Staatsarchivrat Dr. Wolfgang Kohte of Berlin explained to the audience that "the Eastern Jews act as carriers of [social] diseases,"[167] and Professor Dr. Walther Recke of Danzig, an ardent Nazi of old, stated: "The Jewish proletarian is the real solicitor of bolshevism in Poland."[168] Of that country's population of 34,000,000, he pointed out, at least 3,500,000 were Jews, "and

---

[164] Karl Haushofer und Gustav Fochler-Hauke, Her., *Welt in Gärung. Zeitberichte deutscher Geopolitiker* (Leipzig, Breitkopf und Härtel [1937]). Quoted from the paper by Norbert Gürke, p. 233.

[165] Hans Hagemeyer, Dr. G. Leibbrandt, Dr. G. Payr, Her., *Europas Schicksal im Osten.* 12 Vorträge der vierten Reichsarbeitstagung der Dienststelle für Schrifttumpflege bei dem Beauftragten ... [Rosenberg], 3. Auflage (Breslau, 1939, 208 pp.), p. 25.

[166] Cf. the publishers' preface to Georg Leibbrandt, *Moskaus Aufmarsch gegen Europa* (München, Eher, 1939, 69 pp.): "Reichsleiter Alfred Rosenberg . . . authorized his staff member Dr. Georg Leibbrandt to issue a series of essays on the essence and activities of bolshevism." The cover lists 9 pamphlets in the series. More will have to be said about Leibbrandt in chapters XXVIII and XXXIV.

[167] Hagemeyer, Leibbrandt, Payr, *op. cit.*, p. 151.—Kohte was a pupil of Brackmann's.

[168] *Ibid.*, p. 41.—Cf. also the paper by Dr. Theodor Oberländer, later installed as professor at the University of Prague, in the Haushofer-Fochler-Hauke volume (footnote 164), p. 213: "In Poland ... the bulk of the Jews who partly live on the verge of minimum subsistence always are inclined toward communism."

of these, ninety per cent proletarians of the worst kind." This calculation somehow diverged from the stereotype of Jewish economic domination over Eastern Europe but inconsistency did not disturb the speaker.

As the hour to carry through the Führer's Eastern program drew nearer, a great increase of German interest in Eastern-European Jewry is evident. They knew why: of all Jewish settlements in the world the Eastern-European was the largest in numbers, the most creative culturally, and also biologically the most vital.

A man who played a fatal rôle in familiarizing German scholars and political leaders with Eastern Jewry and, ultimately, in mapping out the "removal" scheme was Dr. Peter-Heinz Seraphim, Professor at the Universities of Königsberg, Breslau and, finally, Greifswald, a gifted and learned descendant of a Baltic German family that had returned to Germany after the first World War. Two Seraphims of the older generation were historians of the Baltic area. Peter-Heinz's father Ernst, then almost an octogenarian, during the present war still contributed anti-Jewish articles to German learned periodicals.[169] A younger brother of Peter-Heinz's, Hans-Jürgen, was a capable economist, particularly interested in Eastern Europe, and for some time was connected with the University of Rostock. Peter-Heinz Seraphim, while still an adolescent, fought in one of the most reactionary military forces that grew up as an aftermath of the first World War, the Baltische Landeswehr. With this background, he embarked upon a scholarly career. To begin, he, like his brother, specialized in economics of Eastern Europe and in 1935 published a thorough study on Poland's economy. From then on, however, he switched to Jewish problems. His book on the Jews in Eastern Europe[170] — be it noted that he, too, uses the term Eastern-European *space*—is a volume of over 700 pages, overstuffed with historical, economic, statistical, and bibliographical material, profusely illustrated and full of maps, charts, and graphs. It was compiled with the help of a well-trained staff of the Osteuropa-Institut (Institute for Eastern Europe) at the University of Königsberg and after extended trips over the whole of Eastern Europe.[171]

---

[169] *Historische Zeitschrift* 161 (1940), 277-308; *Weltkampf* III (1943), 144.

[170] Peter-Heinz Seraphim, *Das Judentum im osteuropäischen Raum* (Essen, Essener Verlagsanstalt, 1938, 736 pp.).

[171] Among other places, Seraphim visited the Yiddish Scientific Institute—Yivo, which until the outbreak of war was located in Vilna, Poland. Provided with strong recommendations by the Polish government, he was shown around and given the information he requested.

A study of the proportions of Seraphim's book evidently could not have been executed without the most liberal support of the Reich Treasury and this support granted at a time of the most rigid supervision over the spending of foreign currency could not have been given by the Nazis merely for research in things Jewish without a very definite "practical" purpose in mind.[172] The files of the Seraphim team in Königsberg would certainly yield quite a few important facts.

The idea underlying Seraphim's presentation is comprised in the following passage of his voluminous book:

> One fact . . . is significant for all anti-Jewish movements of Eastern Europe: there is a lack of a uniformly directed Weltanschauung which conceives of the Jew as of a racially defined group and requires quite a peculiar attitude toward him. Anti-Semitism in Eastern Europe is preponderantly a result of conflicting economic interests, mixed up with emotional and sometimes religious-moral rejection. But goals and sentiments based on nationalism and enmity toward minorities *are no Weltanschauung* and never can have the momentum of such.[173]

As Germany had shown, Seraphim maintained, there was only one solid foundation for anti-Semitism: namely, the racial foundation. This theory was soon to be translated into practice either by the most energetic prodding of the respective states or by the German occupation administration itself. Seraphim personally, with the outbreak of war, was to learn with pleasure that real scholarship did not go unnoticed in his country. He became a member of Rosenberg's circle in the Institut zur Erforschung der Judenfrage (Institute for Research into the Jewish Question) and was privileged to be one of the principal spokesmen at its Frankfort Conference of March, 1941, which will be discussed in detail in chapters XIX-XXI.

A photograph of the entrance to the building of the Yivo is reproduced in his book. There is no doubt that the information gathered by Seraphim in 1936 helped the Germans a great deal in 1941, when a special commission of the Einsatzstab Rosenberg (Rosenberg Task Force) carried away the Yivo library and archives to Frankfort for the Institut zur Erforschung der Judenfrage. Incidentally, Nazi literature showed a good understanding of the rôle of the Yivo in Jewish cultural life. To quote only one sentence from the survey of "Universities and Research Institutions in Poland" by H[ans] J[oachim] Beyer: "…. The Yiddish Scientific Institute Yivo can be considered the secular center of Jewish research activities in Poland; through its publications and numerous branches it influences a large part of the Jewish intelligentsia. . . ." Cf. *Deutsche Kultur im Leben der Völker*. . . . *Deutsche Akademie* XIV (1939), 239.

[172] Be it remarked in passing that at the end of 1937 a number of Jewish publications in Austria and Poland were subscribed to by some German agency with the explicit statement that "the foreign exchange for this purpose has been secured."

[173] P. 673. Italics in original.—A very detailed review of Seraphim's book by Reinhart Maurach appeared in *Weltkampf* I (1941), 113-118. Maurach, an expert on Czarist policies toward the Jews, himself, like Seraphim, was a native of Russia.

Seraphim's idea that Polish anti-Semitism in pre-war days "was based not on racial but rather on economic considerations" was used in the 1943 Gollert memorandum discussed in chapter XXXIII.

XV

WALTER GROSS. THE STAGE SET FOR CONQUEST.
HITLER'S PROPHECY

Together with Grau and Seraphim, Walter Gross, M.D., was to be in the limelight at that Conference in Frankfort. He, too, had had quite a record as a faithful Nazi long before 1933. Neither his youth nor his face, which might be identified as "typically Jewish," prevented him from rising into the Party leadership and, although less than thirty years old at the time, he was one of the speakers (on Politics and the Race Question) at the first Party convention in Nuremberg after the seizure of power. In this speech, he violently attacked the "liberalistic era," whose "mercy and false humaneness" was a sin "against the laws of the Creator himself, for he created the laws of life which in severity and brutality ever again annihilate the sick element as soon as it becomes dangerous to the existence of the race." Then, aiming at the Jews, he paid particular attention to the "soaking-in of foreign-race influences" which is caused by the false teaching that all men were born equal and leads to "the destruction of folk-values by carriers of another spirit of alien racial stock." [174]

With this successful debut Gross, on May 15, 1934, by order of Rudolf Hess was made head of the Rassenpolitisches Amt der NSDAP (Racial-Policy Office of the National Socialist German Workers Party). [175] Its tasks never were clearly defined publicly, but it stands to reason that it was not devoted to talking alone since, if it had been, Rosenberg's training machinery and Goebbels' propaganda machinery could have done the job.

Dr. Gross did not appear in public very frequently, but each appearance was noticed. On March 21, 1935, he was the main speaker at one of the Rosenberg receptions for foreign diplomats and newspapermen. He expounded the population and *Rasse* policies of the new Germany which, a semi-official publication pointed out, "are quite often misunderstood and attacked by the Jewish press with particular hatred." [176] "No threat to our neighbors is involved," Gross stressed. A year later, the *Völkischer Beobachter* conveyed his views

[174] Dr. Wilhelm Ziegler, Her., *Nürnberg 1933* (Berlin, Zentralverlag, 1933, 64 pp.). Gross' address, pp. 59-64.
[175] G. Rühle, *Das Dritte Reich . . . Das zweite Jahr 1934* (Berlin, Hummelverlag, 1935, 498 pp.), p. 334.
[176] Gerd Rühle, *Das Dritte Reich. . . . Das dritte Jahr 1935* (Berlin, Hummelverlag, 1936, 578 pp.), pp. 157-158.

on the essence and function of science in the Third Reich. Both natural and cultural sciences in their traditional form were children of the liberalistic idea, he emphasized, and, therefore, cannot incorporate the racial idea. The National Socialist *Rasse* idea stands as an *undivisible and undivided whole,* above all compartmentalized learning of the former era. Consequently, the idea of race cannot be taught by an old-fashioned specialist, he insisted, but only by a National Socialist who combines knowledge and material of the most different fields into a new insight and on its basis shapes the world picture of a new era.[177]

This rather academic language was peculiar to Gross as long as caution was still in place. But in his discourse on racial thought at the Hochschule für Politik in Berlin on Reich-founding day, January 18, 1939, when the crisis was already in sight, Gross significantly began by saying that the time had come to proclaim many things openly. He then continued:

> A look backward at the development up to this time . . . teaches us that we shall not be spared the final fight with the adversary international powers. . . .
>
> We Germans . . . , to be sure, represent today the truest and most correct thinking [on the rôle of *Rasse* in history] . . . and are not afraid of anyone who may like to conjure a discussion on such things in Germany. . . . Simultaneously however . . . we are prepared, when this play of minds is over, to apply our political will of power. . . . We . . . shall not permit the recurrence of our coming off the losers for ideological reasons in the distribution of the world and in the effectuation of opinions as against the others who had thought more realistically and less spiritually.[178]

Thus the stage was set irrevocably for conquest and the first working conference (Arbeitstagung) of the Wissenschaftliche Akademie (Research Academy) of the National Socialist University Instructors Union, held from July 8 to July 10, 1939, in Munich, proved "that scholarship at German graduate schools had chosen new ways and was in closest contact with the nation (Volksganze)." It was unbearable, Reichsdozentenbundsführer Dr. Walter Schultze stated, pointing to the exertion of all working powers in the whole nation (Volk), "that work be done anywhere for accidental or arbitrary reasons, without regard for the urgency of the task." In the future, he concluded,

---

[177] "Universität und Rassengedanke," *Völkischer Beobachter,* May 12, 1936; cf. *Das Archiv,* 1936, p. 210.

[178] Walter Gross, *Der deutsche Rassengedanke und die Welt* (Berlin, Junker und Dünnhaupt, 1939. 32 pp.), pp. 5, 31. = Schriften der Hochschule für Politik, Heft 42.

all instructors must enhance their efficiency and the general development of research work by planning their activities.[179]

"We . . . live on the eve of a war," a distinguished military writer candidly spoke out [180] at a time when the world at large was still hoping for a miracle. The only unpleasant circumstance was the fact that war, to the average German, could mean not only killing but also being killed. However, applied psychology could take care of this difficulty. The authoritative handbook on military science had advised as early as 1936:

> The first premise of successful propaganda within one's own people is the conviction that the war has been forced upon it. Only the certainty that the passage at arms protects the nation's honor and right to life will make it ready to devote itself fully and completely to the struggle. On this basis the government has to propagate a great idea which as a guiding star shows the way in the light and the darkness of the war.[181]

This precept was executed to the letter by German leadership up to the last moment, both when it screamed to high heaven in the performances of the propaganda machine and when it put to use the subtle language of scholarship. No other single phrase occurred more frequently in the innumerable German publications since September, 1939, down to Hitler's "political testament," than "the war that was forced upon us"; we already encountered it on page 55 in Walter Frank's prefatory notice in the first war-time volume of *Forschungen zur Judenfrage*. This slogan, obviously, could not win the war for Germany; but its success in the indoctrination of the German people is being felt up to this very day.

Into this tense situation on January 30, 1939, burst Hitler's speech before "the first Greater-German Reichstag." It contained the following ominous passages, subsequently quoted and referred to without end:

> . . . Europe cannot be at ease any more until the Jewish question is cleared out (ausgeräumt). And one thing I should like to express now, on this day which perhaps is memorable not only for us Germans. In my life, I often used to be a prophet and for the most part was ridiculed. During my struggle for power it was the Jewish people in the first place who received only with laughter my

---

[179] *Deutsche Kultur im Leben der Völker . . . Deutsche Akademie*, XIV (1939), 255.

[180] Generalleutnant z. V. Horst von Metzsch, *Weltpolitik, Wegweiser und Winke* (Berlin, Hochschule für Politik, 1939, 108 pp.). From the preface.

[181] Gesellschaft für Wehrpolitik und Wehrwissenschaft. Generalmajor a. D. Hermann Franke. Her. *Handbuch der neuzeitlichen Wehrwissenschaften* (Berlin, de Gruyter und Co., 1936-1939, Bd. I-IV), B. I, p. 105: "Geistiger Krieg."

prophecies that some day I would take over in Germany the leadership of the state, and by it that of the whole folk and among many other problems would carry to a solution also the Jewish problem. I believe that the roaring laughter of those days already had stuck in Jewry's throat.

And then he served notice to the world:

> Today I shall again be a prophet: should international finance Jewry in and outside Europe succeed in again throwing the nations into a world war, the outcome is going to be not the Bolshevization of earth and thereby the victory of Jewry but the annihilation of the Jewish race in Europe!

There was everything in this concoction: the most straighforward threat imaginable; Jews and bolshevism in a single hodge-podge with international finance which, in Hitler's lingo, was but another designation for the democratic nations of the West; the inevitable reference to the war's being forced on Germany. To complete the picture, he continued by pointing to the scholarly machinery he could work with:

> The time of propagandistic defenselessness of the non-Jewish peoples is over. National Socialist Germany and Fascist Italy possess those institutions which can, if necessary, enlighten the world about the essence of a question of which many peoples are aware instinctively although it is unclear to them scientifically.[182]

One of those scholars again at hand to enlighten the world about the essence of the Jewish question was Professor Kittel, who since 1933 had greatly advanced in nazism. After he had tried hard, in the first volumes of the *Forschungen zur Judenfrage,* to delve into the problems of race formation he, in his current production,[183] no longer invoked the Christian point of view though he continued to teach Christian theology; instead he praised Hans F. K. Günther who "on the first pages of his *Rassenkunde des jüdischen Volkes* expressed a fundamental truth, which it is well to recall over and over again," namely, that the Jews are not a *Rasse,* but a *Rassengemische* (race mixture). This mixture originated in antiquity; "no less [an expert] than Eugen Fischer" had traced back the racial history of the Hebrews to their origin of the Oriental, Near Eastern, and Mediterranean races.[184] This "racial mixture" was to be removed in order to make way for the German, or Teutonic, race.

---

[182] Gerhard Brendel, *Der Führer über die Juden* (München, Eher, 1943, 84 pp.), p. 82. = Schriften zur weltanschaulichen Schulung der NSDAP. Herausgeber: Der Beauftragte des Führers . . . [Rosenberg].

[183] Cf. footnote 115.

[184] Cf. footnote 59.

The political philosopher Bruno Amann expressed it most vividly:

> The Reich of the Teutonic racial soul rises against the counter-Reich of the Semitic-Bolshevist chaos. The struggle against Versailles and Moscow was the struggle for the *Teutonic* divine reich, for the new world order of the Reich. The clear recognition of the current era permitted conception of all enemies of the National Socialist idea as of one philosophical will, as the will of the Semitic-Jewish world principle. When the Führer called upon the German people to organize for resistance against Jewry, the decisive battle for the Third Reich, for the Teutonic folk reich of the Germans, had set in.

And further:

> In the future, there should be no German university which would not have at least one chair in the Jewish question, which would make accessible the Jew-problem to each student but simultaneously, from the point of view of Weltanschauung, would also be directed against Protestant and Catholic denominationalism in order to achieve uniform attitudes toward the great religious problems of the German folk in the spirit of the National Socialist revolution....
>
> . . . The third phase of the National Socialist victory over world Jewry is before us and [it] culminates in the most tremendous idea of all times, in the *idea of the Third Reich.....* Racial anti-Semitism becomes imperial; it turns into the struggle of the Reich for its political weight (Geltung). . . . Future world history stands under this victorious sign.[185]

---

[185] Bruno Amann, *Das Weltbild des Judentums. Grundlagen des völkischen Antisemitismus* (Wien, Kühne [1939], 363 pp.), pp. 348, 351-352.

Large-Scale Experimenting

XVI

POLISH JEWRY IN GERMAN HANDS. JEWRY=PLUTOCRACY

Barely eight months after Hitler had pronounced his death sentence on European Jewry, the German armies marched and the Campaign of the Eighteen Days was over. The incorporation of western Poland into the Reich and the creation of the "Government General for the Occupied Polish Areas" out of the remainder of the Polish state that had fallen to Germany were carried out too smoothly to have been the product of improvisation; the existence of a plan was obvious even before incontrovertible evidence to this effect was introduced at the Nuremberg trial. What had not been prepared beforehand was swiftly added. Just one small fact may be quoted by way of example in documents now in the possession of the Yivo. On September 30, 1939, when Warsaw had just fallen, the High Command of the Wehrmacht asked the Ministry of Education for suitable personalities who by their scholarship could "support the proof that . . . the recovered (zurückgewonnene) areas belong culturally to the Greater German Reich"; scholars specializing in prehistory should be included; "by this means, . . . Germany's right to this space [should be] proved prehistorically, too." A number of scholars were chosen, the leading positions being assigned to three professors of the University of Breslau, Dagobert Frey, Ernst Petersen and Martin Georg Jahn.[186] Frey, by compiling his book on Cracow mentioned later, certainly did his best. The files of Goebbels' agencies in occupied Poland contain references to prehistorical discoveries which "prove" the Teutonic character of the area.

What is quoted below from a statement signed by two leading history professors applies equally to representatives of all fields of learning at that time:

> The German historians are aware of their duty to provide the historical tools for the central problem of the present war and the

[186] Letter of the High Command of the Wehrmacht no. 1491/39.

84

forthcoming rearrangement of Europe and to envisage and interpret the development of the past from the point of view of the present. By this publication they wish to profess the political character of their science.[187]

Strange as it seems, responsible Germans, in complete misunderstanding of Britain's attitude, seem to have believed that after the dissolution of the Polish state with the support of Russia, the Western powers would accept Hitler's offer and acquiesce in Germany's conquests in the East. When this attempt to buy peace failed, some minor adjustments had to be made in the ideological façade. The Soviet Union, for years played up as but a front of Jewry, was not in the enemy camp. Thus, the Soviet Union had to be complimented for merits previously unnoticed,[188] whereas the attack on the "Western plutocracies" was intensified. Professor Dr. Kleo Pleyer of Tübingen, who previously had fought the "frontier struggle (Grenzkampf)" with sociological studies, turned poet and produced a "Battle Song of the National Socialists": "We are the army of the swastika, / Raise the red banners! . . . . We don't enter into compacts / with Jews and Frenchmen (Welschen) / . . . The task is to put an end / to Europe's great meanness." [189] But scholarship proper did not fail either. Among many other institutions which answered the master's voice the Deutsches Institut für aussenpolitische Forschung (German Institute for Foreign-Policy Research), affiliated with the University of Berlin, came out with thirty-five different papers on "The British Empire and World Politics," and twenty-four papers on "France against Civilization" followed.

Definitely, England was blamed as the major war criminal: "England *wanted* this war because she wanted to prevent by all means the new rise of the German people and to check its way to leadership in Europe"; thus spoke Dr. Wilhelm Ziegler who, though still in charge of the Antisemitische Aktion, with the outbreak of war

---

[187] Dr. Theodor Mayer, professor of the University of Marburg and rector thereof in 1941, and Dr. Walter Platzhoff, professor of the University of Frankfort and rector thereof in 1941, in their preface to *Das Reich und Europa* (Leipzig, Köhler und Amelang, 1941, 141 pp.). The volume contained the transactions of a conference of history professors held at Nuremberg, February 7-8, 1941.—Professor Dr. Paul Ritterbusch, Rector of the University of Kiel, said in the same volume, p. XI: ". . . The war is merely the highest expression of the idea and the will of German folkdom [to achieve] a historical-political totality, which generates a simply elementary power and most concentrated energy."

[188] Karl Haushofer, in his *Zeitschrift für Geopolitik* XVI (1939), 782, explained the about-face of Nazi politics this way: "That's the good thing about hard power struggles with clever minds that they at least see their own advantage and do not stick to ideological prejudices. . . ."

[189] Alfred Rinecker, *Sturm- und Kampflieder für Front und Heimat.* Ausgabe März, 1941 (Berlin, Hochmuth, 1941, 126 pp.), p. 28.

shifted his main interest to the Western democracies.[190] The reason for Britain's defection, it was explained, was the fact that the Jews had seized control over her to the degree of making the British feel and behave like a "chosen people." [191] A statement by Carlyle was quoted to the effect that the Englishman looked like a Teuton but his soul was Jewish.[192] "The English have no understanding whatsoever," Professor Dr. Ernst Schultze of the University of Leipzig remarked, "for the personalities of other peoples, particularly of those with whom they compete. They are the worst psychologists of peoples (in contrast, for instance, to the French)—and they don't even try to be better ones." [193]

As the parenthetical clause shows, France fared better; for a time she was pictured as Britain's victim rather than accomplice[194] except that she, too, had yielded to the Jews who led her into war.[195]

As to the Jews, there was no need of delicacy, no need of even seemingly changing the attitude.

It is important to stop for a moment to examine the number of Jews in German hands at the end of 1939 as given by German statisticians. For Germany proper, the Arbeitswissenschaftliches Institut (Labor Research Institute) of the German Labor Front arrived at the figure of 240,000 Jews within the Greater German Reich, including about 55,000 hybrids. This meant about 185,000 "pure"

[190] Wilhelm Ziegler, *Grossdeutschlands Kampf* (Leipzig, Reclam, 1941, 272 pp.).— With the participation of many hundreds of students mobilized by the Reichsstudentenführung (Reich Student Leadership) "to investigate the history, economy, and culture of all peoples for arguments against England," Dr. Ziegler prepared a large source-book *Dokumentenwerk über die englische Demokratie* (Berlin, Deutscher Verlag, 1940, 336 pp., 4°); cf. *Deutscher Wissenschaftlicher Dienst*, no. 21, November 18, 1940.—Cf. also Professor Dr. Karl Heinz Pfeffer, *Begriff und Wesen der Plutokratie* (Berlin, Junker und Dünnhaupt, 1940, 64 pp.).

[191] Wilhelm Brachmann, *Das auserwählte Volk* (Berlin, Eher, 1940, 79 pp.).

[192] Wolf Meyer-Christian, *Die englisch-jüdische Allianz* (Berlin, Nibelungen-Verlag [1940]. 218 pp.).—Cf. also: Siegbert Dreyer, *England und die Freimaurerei* (Berlin, Junker und Dünnhaupt, 1940, 57 pp.), and Jens Lornsen, *Britannien Hinterland des Weltjudentums* (Berlin, Junker und Dünnhaupt, 1940, 69 pp.), both published by Deutsches Institut für aussenpolitische Forschung; Carl August Weber [Professor at the University of Tübingen], Her., *Die englische Kulturideologie* (Stuttgart, Kohlhammer, 1941. Bd. I, XXIV, 405 pp.), and the pre-war publication, chiefly intended as a handbook for high school teachers: Heinz Krieger, *England und die Judenfrage in Geschichte und Gegenwart* (Frankfurt am Main, Diesterweg, 1938. 115 pp.).

[193] Prof. Dr. Ernst Schultze, *Sorgen des britischen Weltreichs* (Leipzig, Nationale Verlagsgesellschaft, 1940), p. 348.

[194] Professor Dr. Josef Brüch, *Die Anglomanie in Frankreich* (Stuttgart, Kohlhammer, 1941. 102 pp.).

[195] Heinz Ballensiefen, *Juden in Frankreich. Die französische Judenfrage in Geschichte und Gegenwart*. 2. Aufl. (Berlin, Nordland-Verlag, 1941. 188 pp.).—From the jacket: "This book without mercy exposes the forces which governed France and drove her into the war of 1939-1940 which proved so disastrous to the whole country." Cf. also: Reinhard Höhn, ordentlicher öffentlicher Professor an der Universität Berlin, *Frankreichs Demokratie und ihr geistiger Zusammenbruch* (Darmstadt, L. C. Wittich [1940], 76 pp.) (p. 75: "The Jews"; p. 16: "Democracy . . . the organized system which forces the peoples for alien interests into constant wars"); Gerhard Lehmann, *Der Einfluss des Judentums auf das französische Denken der Gegenwart* (Berlin, Junker und Dünnhaupt, 1940, 62 pp.) = Schriften des Deutschen Instituts für aussenpolitische Forschung und des Hamburger Instituts für Auswärtige Politik her. in Gemeinschaft mit dem Deutschen Auslandswissenschaftlichen Institut, Heft 65; Dr. Hans-Joachim Tilse, *Die Wurzeln des Deutschenhasses in Frankreich* (Stuttgart, Kohlhammer, 1941. 106 pp.).

Jews, as against 499,000 "pure" Jews in 1933. Naturally, the inventory was considered satisfactory. It was even more pleasant when the age distribution was compared: the number of children had fallen from 18 to 10 per cent in the male group, from 15 to 7 per cent in the female, while the proportion of old people had increased correspondingly. A paper on this investigation added: "The old people quietly may await their end here. As far as *Rasse* and folk are concerned, they are dead already and don't need any particular surveillance any more." [196] Before long, the author probably had to atone for this false humaneness, evidently a psychological remnant of the liberalistic era.

The Jews on territories acquired by "peaceful" means after Munich were not included in this survey but, as a jurist of standing associated with Walter Frank and contributor to *Deutsche Justiz* put it,

> . . . Fate had decided upon these Jews the very moment the territory became part of the Greater German Reich. The execution of the de-Judaization was only a matter of time.[197]

Nor did the figures quoted include the Jews, nearly a million in number, who lived in the western and northern Polish areas incorporated into the Reich after the conquest of Poland. Of these, according to Peter-Heinz Seraphim, about 333,000 were indiscriminately dumped into the Government General.[198] This latter area, according to Seraphim again, on January 1, 1940, possessed a Jewish population of 1,269,000.[199]

The sum total of Jews in Greater Germany on January 1, 1940, consequently, can be estimated as follows: [200]

Old Reich	185,000
Austria	50,000
Sudeten, Protectorate	85,000
Incorporated Polish Territories.....	630,000
Government General	1,270,000
	2,220,000

[196] *Der Weltkampf*, XVII, 195 (März, 1940), 62.

[197] Dr. Sievert Lorentzen, *Die Juden und die Justiz* (Hamburg, Hanseatische Verlagsanstalt, 1942. 200 pp.), p. 189 = Schriften des Reichsinstituts für Geschichte des neuen Deutschlands.

[198] *Die Burg*, I (1940), 56-63. Repeated in: Peter-Heinz Seraphim, *Das Judentum, Seine Rolle und Bedeutung in Vergangenheit und Gegenwart* (München, Deutscher Volksverlag [1942], 72 pp.), p. 49. In the incomparable language of detached research, Seraphim called this deportation: ". . . Einsiedlung ins Generalgouvernement aus den vom Reich rückgegliederten deutschen Ostgebieten . . ." ("bringing into the Government General for settlement from the recovered German Eastern areas").

[199] Peter-Heinz Seraphim, *Das Judentum. Seine Rolle . . .*, p. 68.—Six hundred thousand Jews more were added after June 22, 1941, when Eastern Galicia, too, fell into German hands and, renamed District of Lemberg, was made part of the Government General.

[200] Without giving any reason, Seraphim, *Das Judentum. Seine Rolle . . .* lists for the Old Reich, Austria, and the Sudeten region and the Protectorate, respectively, the following figures: 500,000; 191,000; 118,000. These figures, accurate as they were for pre-Hitler days, obviously were highly exaggerated as of January 1, 1940; forcible emigration and deportation had brought about the changes.

Seraphim therefore was right in stressing that the Greater German Reich had become the third largest Jewish settlement in the world after the United States and the USSR. If we add, as we must, the countries occupied during the war and the satellite states,[201] Germany at the peak of her power had the greatest Jewish population ever concentrated under one government, i.e., eight and a quarter million.

Germany certainly did not let the opportunity pass unused.

Before Britain firmly said her "no" to Germany's overtures after the defeat of Poland, some half-wit in Hitler's entourage might have believed in earnest that the omnipotent Jews in the plutocratic countries would call off the war against Germany, in order to save the millions of Jews in German hands. When this failed to happen, the time had come to execute the Nazi anti-Jewish program. In the Government General, this could be done with even less restraint than in Germany proper. Hans Frank, the Minister of Justice and President of the Akademie für deutsches Recht, who was appointed Governor General for the Occupied Polish Territories,[202] certainly could be relied upon. There seems to be no doubt that the Germans moved into Poland not only with the general goal of subjugating the nation but also with the decision to "solve" the Jewish question, though high-level discussions concerning details must have continued. The triumphant article in *Der Weltkampf* under the heading: "The Crushing of the Eastern Ghettos. The Largest Ghetto of the World under German Control" speaks for itself:

> World Jewry is in essence derived from two sources: Morocco-Spain and Poland-Western Russia-Rumania. Today the former plays only an insignificant part in reinforcing world Jewry.... It is quite different with the Eastern Jew.... Today Jewry worries about its fostering source. England's demand to reconstitute the old Polish state is nothing else than the wish of world Jewry not to permit the application in Poland of the inexorable fundamental National Socialist conceptions that have already begun to work for the benefit of entire Aryan humanity. Germany, which by its recognition of the racial question and of the value of each folkdom awakens one people after the other, which, after crushing all Jewish fortresses so nicely constructed in Central Europe, today holds in its

---

[201] Seraphim, *op. cit.,* p. 68 gives the following estimates as of January 1, 1940: European part of the Soviet Union in pre-1939 boundaries, 2,860,000; Soviet-occupied former Polish territory, 1,214,000; Soviet-occupied former Rumanian territory, 285,000; Baltic states, 365,000; Hungary, 370,000; Rumania, 397,000; France, 200,000; Slovakia, 137,000; Holland, 112,000; Greece, 75,000; Yugoslavia, 68,400; Belgium, 50,000; Bulgaria, 50,000; Italy, 48,000.

[202] With the gains in western Europe firmly consolidated and the war seemingly nearing its victorious end, the time had come for the Germans to efface the last reminiscence of the name of Poland. On October 2, 1940, the name of Frank's satrapy was changed to "Government General" pure and simple, to be considered a *Nebenland* (by-country) of the Reich.

hands the decision over the being or not being of Jewish world domination, must [so the Jews think] be destroyed for all eternity in order that the eternal Jew regain peace. We know the aim of the Jew and we shall act accordingly. As the Führer put it: "A new world war will mean the end of Jewry!" [203]

Two months later Walter Buch, supreme judge of the NSDAP, in other words, one of the highest Nazi dignitaries, in a lengthy New Year's message in the official organ of his agency said in part:

> . . . For what else did we struggle, take upon us want and deprivation, for what else did the courageous men of the SA and the SS, the boys of the Hitler Youth fall, if not for the possibility that one day the German people might start its struggle for liberation against its Jewish oppressors? In this struggle we are now involved.... Neither Jew nor freemason will finish the war with treaties that bear in them new mischief. Victory will be attained by Adolf Hitler and he will bring Europe the peace that forever takes away from the Jewish sub-man the opportunity to decompose men and peoples and play them off against each other. [204]

XVII

THE GHETTO IN SCHOLARLY THEORY AND IN PRACTICE

In October, 1939, an order was issued in Warsaw (which at that time had about 400,000 Jews, roughly a third of the whole city population) restricting the Jews to certain quarters. [205] The decided opposition of the Jewish community caused the Germans to abstain from their plan in Warsaw for a whole year, [206] but they began introducing ghettos in minor places, where less resistance could be expected. [207] The way the job was done is made clear in the following technical report on the city of Radom, which at the outbreak of the war had over 25,000 Jews:

> Before the Campaign of the Eighteen Days the present district capital Radom had a population of about 80,000.... The influx of

[203] Der Weltkampf, XVI, 91 (November, 1939), 457-461.

[204] Der Parteirichter. Amtliches Mitteilungsblatt des Obersten Parteigerichts der NSDAP (München), 2. Januar 1940, p. 2.—The same Walter Buch in a paper "The Honor and Defense of Honor of the National Socialist Man" published in the time-honored Deutsche Justiz, 100, 2 (1938), 1660, had declared: "The National Socialist has recognized: the Jew is not a human being (kein Mensch). He is a phenomenon of putrefaction."

[205] A photostatic copy of this rare document is in the Yivo archives.

[206] Cf. S. Mendelsohn, The Polish Jews behind the Nazi Ghetto Walls (New York, Yiddish Scientific Institute, 1942, 32 pp.).

[207] Dr. Max Freiherr DuPrel, Her., Das General-Gouvernement, Im Auftrage und mit einem Vorwort des Generalgouverneurs Reichsminister Dr. Frank. 2. Aufl. (Würzburg, Triltsch, 1942, 404 pp.), p. 357: "The former district of Lowicz was the first in the Government General which installed living quarters (Wohngebiete) for Jews. As early as May, 1940, about 15,000 Jews of the old part of the district were placed in compact living quarters in five different localities."

[German occupation] authorities and the aggregation of business firms in the district center caused a great lack of apartments which had to be remedied quickly.... Some elbow space was created by transferring Jewish tenants of spacious dwellings in the city center into the Radom Jewish quarter. This, however, also constituted only a temporary solution apart from the fact that the swaggering of the Jewish element on the main streets of the district seat could not be tolerated as a matter of principle. In further pursuance of a solution of the housing problem, especially since the Jewish quarter cannot take in any more people, from September 3rd to 5th about two thousand Jews were moved into rural areas.... With the further development of economic life in Radom ... new measures for eliminating the Jewish element may be expected.[208]

Within a year, Frank's administration felt sufficiently strong to act in Warsaw, and in the second half of October, 1940, all Jews in Warsaw were segregated in a ghetto.[209] Then the Germans had all Jews at hand for their more radical further measures.

In the meantime, the plan of a Jewish reservation in the district of Lublin had been launched in October, 1939, and abandoned after uncounted thousands of Austrian and German Jews had perished there.[210] It should be noted that at the beginning the Germans, as in many other cases, cunningly chose to present the forcible separation of the Jews as the re-establishment of the natural order of things that had been upset through the false emancipation of 1789. The first edition of the above mentioned semi-official German handbook by Du Prel, issued in Cracow at the beginning of 1940, spoke in detail about the Jewish Councils (Judenräte) which were generously granted the Jewish population, of the workshops organized at the initiative of SS Brigadeführer Globocnik, and then went on to say:

Social welfare is the important task of the Judenrat (Jewish Council). The German administration deems it important that the Rat takes measures in all fields of welfare it considers important without interference. In a report of the Lublin Judenrat the many fields in which social welfare is being offered are listed.

It is urgently recommended that the foreign newspaper agitators who so often babble about alleged barbaric persecutions of Jews in the German Eastern Space convince themselves on the spot of the wide margin which the German administration leaves to the Jews in the conduct of their autonomous life. In organizational set-ups of their own, with internal Jewish forces, a kind of self-administrative

---

[208] *Der Weltkampf*, XVIII, 105 (January, 1941), 36.
[209] Mendelsohn, *op. cit.*, pp. 3-4.
[210] Cf. *Yivo Bleter*, Journal of the Yiddish Scientific Institute, XV (1940), 154-157.

system was constructed which secures the interests of Jewry within the realm of possibility.[211]

Hermann Erich Seifert in a book written in Lublin apparently at the end of 1940 struck the same note, though his recklessness in defining "the realm of possibility" is more conspicuous:

The individual Jew does not exist for the German authorities in occupied territory. There are in principle no negotiations with an individual Jew or with a *mishpokhe*,[212] but exclusively with the Jewish Ältestenräte (Councils of Elders) that, comparably to the Polish self-government, represent a similar self-governing body for the affairs of the Jews under German guidance. With the help of their Ältestenrat the Jews can arrange fully for themselves and among themselves their internal affairs, including the affairs of their religious communities, but on the other hand they have to execute in full responsibility the tasks and requirements of the German administration. The members of the Ältestenrat, in most cases the richest and most distinguished, are personally responsible for this execution. No doubt this Ältestenrat is remotely reminiscent of the Kahals of which the [Czarist] Russian Jew-policy made use, but with one great difference: Jewish rights were given to and defended by kahals; Jewish duties are received and distributed by the Ältestenräte in the Government General.... There is no discussion of or argument against the German orders.

The last page of the book speaks about the prospects:

All these [measures] are of course only preparations for the solution of the Jewish question. It is too early to speak today about what this solution will ultimately resemble. Once there was some talk of a Jewish settlement area in the district of Lublin, a kind of reservation for the Jews . . . but this would not be a definitive solution either....

The definitive solution, Seifert felt, should consist in removing the Jew into the dwelling areas of the colored races.

But there is no need for us to go into this question today. For the time being, the war sets us its tasks and the victory will put before the German people new tasks, even greater ones, most of which will be more important than the problem of the Jewish reservation. The last word has not yet been spoken, but it will be spoken in due time from authoritative lips....[213]

---

[211] Dr. Max Freiherr DuPrel, Her., *Das deutsche Generalgouvernement Polen. Ein Überblick über Gestaltung und Geschichte* (Krakau, Buchverlag Ost, 1940, 344 pp.), pp. 142-143.

[212] The Yiddish term for "family" which is used also in other languages when the strength of family ties among the Jews is alluded to.—As an example of the ruthlessness with which the Germans applied the principle: "The individual Jew does not exist ...," the following detail may be quoted. During 1940 and part of 1941, the Jews in the ghetto of Lódź (renamed Litzmannstadt by the Germans) were still allowed to send postal cards abroad but only under the condition that in all cases *Der Älteste der Juden in Litzmannstadt Ch. Rumkowski* (Ch. Rumkowski, Elder of the Jews in Litzmannstadt) be indicated as the sender. Specimens of such postal cards are in the archives of the Yivo.

[213] Hermann Erich Seifert, *Der Jude an der Ostgrenze* (Berlin, Eher, 1940, 88 pp.), pp. 82, 88.—Another book by Seifert, *Der Jude zwischen den Fronten* (Berlin, Eher, 1942,

Those high up, however, did not see any need for constraint, and Hans Frank, speaking in his capacity as Nazi Gauleiter at a Party function in Cracow on August 15, 1940, concealed nothing:

> Here we are in this land and as Germans we shall never leave this land. The swastika will continue to stream over this land into the farthest future. And the Polish people, as they were once seven hundred years ago, are again under the patronage of the German nation. The Vistula is from now on Germany's river and shall remain Germany's eastern river....

With regard to the Jews, it was unnecessary even to observe common propriety of language:

> We must see to it that particularly this German city of Cracow be completely deprived of its Jewish character and I have decreed, as you know, that until today the Jews have voluntarily [sic] to depart. Whoever, being a Jew, after this midnight remains in the city, tomorrow will be liable to forced labor. It is an impossible situation that the representation of Adolf Hitler's Greater German Reich establish itself here in a city which swarms with Jews to the degree that a decent man simply cannot walk the streets.

He ended his speech in words which at that time were not yet frequently heard:

> And it is clear that hereby a serious signal is given: the Jews must disappear from the whole of Europe.[214]

Out of lack of insight and historical knowledge responsible circles in the democratic countries fell into the Nazi trap of mixing the different loose meanings of the term *ghetto*. When the Nazi writer quoted on page 88 rejoiced over Hitler's "crushing the Eastern ghettos" and bringing "the largest ghetto of the world under German control" he spoke, disparagingly of course, of the concentration of many million Jews on the territory of Central-Eastern Europe. This Eastern Jewry for long had been the chosen object of anti-Jewish hatred because it represented Jewry at is fullest. Walter Frank, in his swan song on May 18, 1940, had stressed the peculiar character of this Eastern Jew, who, indeed, was different from his Western-European brother. In its traditional variant, Eastern Jewry had created a way of life that has been second to none in its ethical and moral standards. During the last century, it created modern Yiddish and Hebrew literature. It essentially contributed

---

183 pp.), particularly stresses the part of research institutions and scholarly literature in the struggle against the Jews.

[214] From a facsimile of the *Krakauer Zeitung* reproduced in *The Jewish Bulletin* (London), no. 45, May, 1945. The report had a large two-column headline: "Die Juden müssen aus Europa verschwinden" ("The Jews Must Disappear from Europe").

to the upbuilding of the American Jewish community and virtually alone built up the present-day Jewish community of Palestine. Within two generations, it gave the world at large many brilliant representatives of literature, art, and scholarship. It actively participated in the struggle for liberty in all countries of Eastern Europe. All this was achieved under conditions of poverty which even the covetous Nazi writers were compelled to acknowledge. Even Seraphim's comprehensive book published on the eve of the war, biased as it was, could not distort the picture completely. The experience of the war years again showed the unusual vitality of the group and thus, in a sense, confirmed the reason for the hatred by the Nazis: under the inhuman conditions of the German occupation, in the city ghettos and in the slave-labor camps, large-scale cultural activities were carried on and, finally, Eastern Jewry produced the fighters in the memorable battles of the ghettos.[215]

The second confusion concerning the term ghetto which the Nazis introduced on purpose refers to the Jewish living quarters of pre-emancipation days. For many months, the Germans wanted the world to believe that the ghettos established by them in the present war were a return to the ghetto of old and, strangely enough, the world did believe them. But even the judgment that the Germans had "revived the worst institution of the Middle Ages" was a gross injustice to the Middle Ages and was utterly false and misleading. The term *ghetto* to the Jew is one of those learned words acquired from non-Jewish sources; the original Yiddish designation is merely *yidishe gas*, "the Jewish street." Thus, Seifert's statement that the Kahals of old represented a right whereas the Jewish Councils of Elders were imposed as a duty may more properly be restated this way: the Jewish quarters up to the seventeenth and eighteenth centuries were living quarters; the German-imposed ghettos of the twentieth century were intended for putting their inhabitants to death. The fundamental difference between the two institutions was openly acknowledged by no less an expert than Seraphim at the official occasion of the opening of the Frankfort Conference, to which we shall come in the next chapter. At that time the Nazi plans had progressed farther, so they could afford to speak:

[215] Cf. Abraham Joshua Heschel, "The Eastern European Period in Jewish History," *Yivo Studies*, Vol. I (New York, Yiddish Scientific Institute, 1946); *Underground Cultural Work in the Jewish Ghettos of Poland. A Report sent from Warsaw on May 20, 1944* (New York, Yiddish Scientific Institute, 1945, 6 pp.); the *Geto-Yedies* ("Ghetto News") published in the ghetto of Vilna in 1943, cf. *Yivo Bleter*, Journal of the Yiddish Scientific Institute XXV (1945), 133-142; and the two papers by S. Mendelsohn listed in footnotes 206 and 362.

Sometimes it is pointed out that this solution [the isolation of the Jews from the non-Jews] is indicated by history since in the Middle Ages the Jewish settlement area, the ghetto, was in existence. This historical argumentation appears inappropriate. The ghetto of the Middle Ages was to a much greater extent rather the *right* of the Jews than a forced measure.... The ghetto of the Middle Ages was in essence a voluntary community of dwelling in addition to which it by no means excluded business contacts between Jews and non-Jews. . . . Consequently the ghetto of today, if it makes sense, should be different from the medieval ghetto, without contact or possibility of contact with non-Jews.[216]

There is extant in German scholarly literature of the period a description of the situation which the Germans had created for the Jews in Poland—a description which in its cynicism can hardly be surpassed though the wording, in accordance with good tradition, was duly restrained. Dr. Herbert Morgen, a man of Haushofer's school, had made a trip through "The New German Eastern Areas." After stating that the Poles "are to be considered a typical hybrid race (Mischrasse)" and that "externally the Poles are submissive though their inner attitude frequently may be different," he reported as follows:

Jewry constitutes a particularly sad chapter in the racial composition of the population. In 1921, over ten per cent of the total population were Jews massed in the urban settlements (up to eighty per cent in the small towns!).... The Jews everywhere are being employed for clearing and reconstruction work, and under guard they seem to achieve some working results. In some fields of labor, for instance as tailors and cobblers, the Jews are said to show dexterity. Jewish adaptability is sufficiently known and this also explains that most Jews are able to make themselves understood in several languages: German, Polish, and Russian.

The chronicling went on and the expected *racial* conclusion was arrived at:

As an external sign of belonging to their tribe the Jews carry—dependent upon the directive of the Landrat—a yellow star of David or a yellow triangle or a yellow disk or something like it on their breasts and backs. The general impression one receives of this human mass is appalling. And one quickly arrives at the conclusion that one deals here with a completely degenerated, inferior part of human society.[217]

---

[216] Peter-Heinz Seraphim, "Bevölkerungs- und wirtschaftspolitische Probleme einer europäischen Gesamtlösung der Judenfrage," *Weltkampf*, I (1941), 43-51.—Cf. T. Oelsner, "The Jewish Ghetto of the Past," *Yivo Studies*, Vol. I (1946).

[217] *Zeitschrift für Geopolitik*, XVIII (März, 1941), 139.

XVIII

HANS FRANK'S INSTITUT FÜR DEUTSCHE OSTARBEIT (INSTITUTE FOR GERMAN WORK IN THE EAST)

By decree of the Governor General Dr. Hans Frank of April 19, 1940, the Institut für deutsche Ostarbeit (Institute for German Work in the East) was founded and solemnly inaugurated the following day in the rooms of the former University in Cracow. Paragraph 3 of the decree reads as follows:

> It is the task of the Institut für deutsche Ostarbeit scientifically to clear all fundamental questions of the Eastern Space as far as they concern the Government General and to disseminate the results of the researches. In accomplishing this task, the Institut für deutsche Ostarbeit will collaborate with other institutions of similar aims.

The *Völkischer Beobachter* of April 21 stressed the presence of "high representatives of the Wehrmacht, the SS, and the Police" at the inauguration ceremonies and quoted Governor General Dr. Frank as saying that the Institut was to become "the spiritual bulwark of Germandom in the East." The opening of the Institut, it was emphasized, had been set for April 20, Hitler's birthday, "so as to present the Führer with a gift of a particular nature."

The Institut was to be considered an institution of public law and the Governor General was to be its president. In addition to books, it published a quarterly *Die Burg* and a monthly *Das General-gouvernement;* subsequently, a periodical *Deutsche Forschung im Osten* was added. The creation of a large library and archives was contemplated.[218]

The first issue of *Die Burg,* a splendid quarto-size review on peacetime paper and generously illustrated, carried a large study by Peter-Heinz Seraphim on "The Jewish Question in the Government General as a Population Problem" (cf. p. 87) and one by Josef Sommerfeldt on "The Development of Jewish Historiography in Poland." The apparent dispassionateness of the writers and the skill they displayed emphasized the viciousness of their purpose.

Seraphim's connection with the Cracow institute was of a more casual nature, limited to articles in the publications and to occasional

---

[218] *Verordnungsblatt des Generalgouverneurs für die besetzten polnischen Gebiete,* I, April 20, 1940, no. 30.—*Dokumente der deutschen Politik. Der Kampf gegen den Westen.* Teil 2, Bearb. von Dr. Hans Volz (Berlin, Junker und Dünnhaupt, 1943, 904 pp.).

lectures. Josef Sommerfeldt was attached to the institute from its inception as a division head (Referent) on the Jewish question. He was a pupil of Professor Manfred Laubert's and at his teacher's suggestion had written his doctoral dissertation on "The Jewish Question as an Administrative Problem in South Prussia." His scientific interests ranged from "The Jews in Polish Proverbs" to "Galicia in the First Immigration Waves of Russian Jews to America (1881-1883)." He also contributed to *Weltkampf*, the anti-Jewish research periodical of the Frankfort Institut.

The Institut für deutsche Ostarbeit was headed by Dr. Wilhelm Coblitz, who had been connected with Hans Frank in legal studies in the years preceding the war and had been taken by Frank to Cracow when the German armies moved eastward. A jurist by education who had received his doctoral degree at the University of Erlangen in 1932, Coblitz had been, for example, managing editor of a bulky volume on German administrative law[219] published by Frank in 1937. On the eve of the war, he was editor-in-chief of a monthly of legal bibliography, published by the Central Publishing House of the National Socialist Party.[220]

In a conference of the Institut für deutsche Ostarbeit held in Cracow from March 27 to 29, 1941, Professor Dr. Peter-Heinz Seraphim participated as a guest. Dr. Coblitz, as director, spoke of building German scholarship in the East upon the best German tradition. The main tasks of the institute were to supply the factual material for the political aims and for the formulation of the goals of German statesmanship in the East. It was contemplated to open branches of the institute in Warsaw, Radom, and Lublin, Dr. Coblitz announced. As to the question of Eastern Jewry which also entered the field of the institute, he said, it was to be studied and elucidated in a very close contact with the Frankfort institute which just had held its Conference. He added that this problem "requires a basic scientific treatment in order to prepare the final all-European solution of the question by the Führer after the war." [221] It should be stressed that a

---

[219] Cf. footnote 75.

[220] *Das deutsche Rechtsschrifttum. Monatliches Verzeichnis der juristischen Buch- und Zeitschriftenliteratur* (München, Eher).

[221] *Weltkampf*, I (1941), 176.—A paper written by Dr. Coblitz a little bit earlier informed readers that "at present 11 sections function [at the Institut, among them a section for]... the study of *Rasse* and folkdom, with divisions (Referate) on anthropology, ethnology and Jew-research." Cf. *Deutsche Kultur im Leben der Völker ... Deutsche Akademie*, XVI (1941), 449-452. Two more papers on the Cracow Institute, not accessible to the present writer, were published in *Der Deutsche im Osten*, IV (1941), 89-91, and *Deutsche Forschung im Osten*, November, 1941, pp. 29-35.

report by the same Dr. Coblitz, published a year or so later, though defining the place of the Jewish problem in his institute in very similar terms ("The Jew-research at the institute is being carried on in the closest connection with the central organs of the Party and the State in the sense of totally clearing up (Gesamtbereinigung) the European Jewish problem")[222] made one ominous change: the time at which the Jewish problem would have to be "solved" was no longer postponed until after the war. The decision on disposal of the Jews as it was actually done was taken between these two reports.

No wonder that the Cracow institute in things Jewish leaned heavily on the Frankfort giant-brother. There could be no thought of competing.

XIX

THE INAUGURATION OF ROSENBERG'S INSTITUT ZUR ERFORSCHUNG DER JUDENFRAGE (INSTITUTE FOR RESEARCH INTO THE JEWISH QUESTION) IN FRANKFORT ON-THE-MAIN

In June, 1939, the convention of German librarians heard a paper by Volkmar Eichstädt, a staff member of the famous Prussian State Library in Berlin, about the large-scale anti-Jewish library that was about to be officially opened in Munich as part of Walter Frank's Reichsinstitut. The unique arrangement of the library was outlined and its efficiency praised.[223] About a year later Günter Schlichting, of the staff of that library, reported in detail[224] about the institution which he considered "first and singular" among the libraries devoted to the Jewish question. It was to be not a library on Jews in general, but explicitly "on the Jewish question," i.e., "in accordance with the principles of the National Socialist movement." In May, 1937, the library had no more than 300 volumes whereas in the summer of 1940 it had reached 20,000 volumes and was still growing. Cross-reference catalogues were being prepared and each author was scrutinized "through a genealogical project of the Reichsinstitut" as to his Jewish origin or relations.

The splendor, however, was but short-lived. Meanwhile a new development had taken place which spelled Frank's doom. On

---

[222] DuPrel, Das General-Gouvernement (cf. footnote 207), p. 187.

[223] The convention was held May 30-June 3, 1939, in Graz, Austria. The paper was published in full in the leading German library publication Zentralblatt für Bibliothekswesen 57, 1/2 (1940), 67 sq. and reprinted, "in changed and enlarged form," in Forschungen zur Judenfrage, VI (1941), 253-264.

[224] Historische Zeitschrift, 162 (1940), 567-572.

April 15, 1939, Alfred Rosenberg founded the Institut der NSDAP zur Erforschung der Judenfrage (Institute of the National Socialist German Workers Party for Research into the Jewish Question).[225] At that time the fact was hardly noticed and it was not until March, 1941, that the Institut made its debut. But at this time, in concurrence with Rosenberg's sense for the grandiose, it already represented Nazi dream planning at its highest. The Führer himself, it was stated, had conceived the idea of erecting at the Chiemsee, the largest and most beautiful Bavarian lake about thirty miles from Berchtesgaden, an institution that would make the whole world wonder. It would be known as the Hohe Schule (High School) and would constitute "the central place for National Socialist research, teaching, and training." This plan had not yet materialized but it gave Rosenberg the opportunity of winning the race in establishing the leading anti-Jewish institute of the epoch.

Whether personal jealousy or principles were involved, Rosenberg was not completely happy about the way Frank was conducting anti-Jewish research. Rosenberg's *Nationalsozialistische Monatshefte,* to quote an instance, complained about Kittel's study in Frank's *Forschungen zur Judenfrage,* vol. I (cf. p. 82), that it was "not entirely free of denominational theological reminiscences" and about the whole of volumes I-III the reviewer found that "the particular papers sometimes make a rather diversified impression as far as Weltanschauung is concerned," since they did not sufficiently stress the racial viewpoint.[226] Naturally, at a time when the war had already been decided upon and preparations were under way to put through Hitler's threat of January, 1939, against the Jews, neither Hess' protégé, the industrious theorist Walter Frank, nor talkative Goebbels could compete with Rosenberg, who had proved to be the man of both Weltanschauung and action. Thus Frank's attempts to transfer to Munich the Judaica and Hebraica treasures of the Frankfort Municipal Library were bound to fail. The 40,000 volumes of this collection (mostly donated by Jews, as the Nazis themselves repeatedly stressed) certainly were worth striving for. But Grau, who after his rift with Frank luckily found shelter under Rosenberg's roof, was only too glad to support the claim of the Frankfort Nazi dignitaries, Gauleiter Sprenger and Oberbürgermeister Staatsrat Krebs, that their city be

---

[225] Alfred Himstedt, *Das Programm der NSDAP wird erfüllt* (München, n. d. [after 1940], 79 pp.), p. 25, gives this name and date.

[226] Cf. the September issue of 1939. The review was by [Dr.] Curt Tiltack, later a contributor to the *Weltkampf* published by Rosenberg's Frankfort Institut.

given preference. It was therefore decided in the first place that the Jewish collections of the Frankfort Municipal Library be turned over to Rosenberg's institute, then (1939) still in its embryonic state. After that, Rosenberg was able to convince the Führer that, though the Hohe Schule was still wishful thinking, branches (Aussenstellen) of the prospective super-institute could be called into being already, and as the first Aussenstelle of the Hohe Schule the Institut zur Erforschung der Judenfrage (Institute for Research into the Jewish Question) was opened in Frankfort on-the-Main. The name finally chosen for the institution was: Institut zur Erforschung der Judenfrage, Aussenstelle der Hohen Schule der NSDAP (Institute for Research into the Jewish Question, Branch of the High School of the NSDAP). It was provided with a large double house at Bockenheimer Landstrasse 68-70.

The inauguration was celebrated with the usual ostentation of the Nazi state functions at a three-day Conference (Tagung), March 26-28, 1941, in Frankfort in the Bürgersaal of the city hall.[227] Among the "guests of honor" were four gauleiters (Sprenger, Sauckel, Florian, Eggeling); Lieutenant General Reinecke as the representative of General Keitel, Chief of the Army Supreme Command, "whose presence," as was stressed in the opening address, "particularly expresses the interest of the Wehrmacht in the Weltanschauung problems of the National Socialist movement"; high representatives of the Reich treasurer of the Party [Schwarz], of the chief of staff of the SA [Lutze], of Himmler, of the university student leader, and of several Reich ministries and Party departments, among them Ministerialdirektor Ehrensberger of the Ministry of Interior; and the entire Party instructors' personnel. Needless to say, apart from the speakers to whom we shall soon return "there appeared as representatives of

---

[227] All papers read at the Conference were published in *Weltkampf*, the organ of the Institut, no. 1/2 (April-September), 1941: Rosenberg, pp. 3-6 and 64-72; Grau, pp. 7-15 and 16-21; Wirsing, pp. 22-29; Schickert, pp. 30-42; Seraphim, pp. 43-51; Gross, pp. 52-63; the representatives of different nations, pp. 73-99. The whole issue, the editorial informed the readers, "according to the wish of the Rumanian government," was republished in Rumanian. The main papers were issued, in pamphlet form, in Hungarian translation. A general report on the Conference appeared in the same issue of the *Weltkampf*, pp. 106-112; some details have been added here from the reports in the *Völkischer Beobachter* of the time written by Rosenberg's press representative Karlheinz Rüdiger; we had no access to his article on the Conference in *Rheinische Blätter* 18 (1941), 193-196, which may contain some more particulars.—The papers by Grau (two), Gross, and Seraphim were republished in pamphlet form, in 1943 by the Hoheneichen-Verlag, Munich, in its series "Kleine Weltkampf-Bücherei." Rosenberg's first address was republished in pamphlet form by the Eher house. It is worth mentioning in this connection that the Hoheneichen-Verlag, previously an enterprise of the Rosenberg circle, according to *Nationalsozialistische Monatshefte* 10 (1939), 50 by "an arrangement between the Reichsleiters Rosenberg and Amann, the latter representing the Eher Verlag" (see footnote 12), was to be "developed into the NSDAP publishing house in the domain of Weltanschauung and scholarship. The *Weltkampf*, I (1941), calls the Hoheneichen-Verlag the publishing house of the Hohe Schule.

scholarship a great number of rectors of German universities and illustrious representatives of German mental life," among whom particular mention is made of Eugen Fischer and Hans F. K. Günther. In addition, "worthy representatives" of nine countries were present, among them Quisling from Norway and Mussert from the Netherlands. To stress the international character of the gathering, the flags of the nine nations represented were displayed in a wreath surrounding two swastika banners.

It was Alfred Rosenberg's long waited-for triumph and, as could be expected, it was Rosenberg who sounded the keynote of the Conference. He opened it with a speech which, naturally enough, was hailed as "directive" and "was received with storms of enthusiastic applause." [228] He also closed the Conference with a second address that was broadcast over all German stations. As he was developing his ideas with the self-assurance that was appropriate to the victories Germany's armed might had achieved and with a definite foretaste of greater victories to come, he felt free to show the broader implications of the "Jewish question." He started in the sublime spheres of broad historic generalizations:

> . . . The day will come when the struggle of the democracies against racial cognition will be evaluated on the same level as the struggle of the era of the inquisition against the awakening national cultures and the personality self-awareness of the European peoples.

He attacked the United States, which dared to stand in Germany's way, though it was a nation without culture:

> Roosevelt's speech in Hollywood only can confirm us [in our resolution] to defend ourselves against this mental degeneration of the white race and of all cultural races of the world. By the way, in speaking today of American culture, there is one thing more to be said: the whole of America up to the present does not possess any state opera. Metropolitan Opera is being maintained by a group of stock-jobbers. In Chicago, too, there is a similar arrangement. While in allegedly barbarian Germany almost each middle-size city endeavors to maintain a good dramatic and a good opera theater, this most gigantic country of the world has not succeeded in creating even real *foundations* for a *forthcoming* cultural development. This fact is paralleled by the lack of great thinkers, sculptors, and poets. Instead, the world is being swamped with the sweetest and most mendacious trash productions, with ludicrous stagings which consume millions upon millions; but while glittering musicals perhaps can pass for freedom and culture with the people's medley

---

228 Cf. *Die Judenfrage*, January 15, 1943

of Broadway, each man of real culture sees in them only symptoms of an infantile decay.[229]

Rosenberg then proudly reviewed Germany's victories in the West:

> The year 1940, therefore, in this great folk revolution will always be called a decisive year in which the troops of the Rothschild republic were beaten and in which the German armies now stand as immovably at the Channel and the Atlantic Ocean as they have placed under their protection and care the entire Northern Space.

Emphasizing the "biological world revolution" going on he, finally, boldly looked into the future:

> In this housecleaning of ours, Mr. Roosevelt with his Baruchs and his film-Jews, too, will be unable to interfere . . . and the strongest military instrument that history has ever known, the Wehrmacht of Adolf Hitler, will see to it that this last furious attempt once more to put the white race on the march against Europe for the sake of Jewish-finance domination is terminated forever. . . . We believe that this great war is also a cleansing biological world revolution and that those peoples that today still are aligned against us at the end of the war will recognize that Germany's cause today is the cause of the entire European continent, the cause of the entire white race but also the cause of all the other civilized races on this globe that struggle for a secured cultural and state life conforming with their species (arteigen).[230]

XX

THE STAFF, THE LIBRARY, AND THE ORGAN OF THE FRANKFORT INSTITUTE

At this Frankfort Conference, after some years of obscurity, Grau re-emerged as Director of the Institut (Leiter der Aussenstelle). His vengeance was thorough: Walter Frank, the man who had tartly dismissed him and then scolded him in print, had dropped out of the picture completely. When Grau, at the opening of his Institut, spoke of establishing research connections, he referred to Coblitz's Institut in Cracow and Grundmann's in Jena, but no mention was made of the Reichsinstitut in Munich. Neither Frank nor any of his men were appointed corresponding members of the Aussenstelle.[231]

---

[229] *Weltkampf*, I (1941), 69.—Italics in original.
The lack of "Kultur" in America had been stressed in Nazi literature long before. Cf. Johannes Stoye, *Die U. S. A. lernt um!* (Leipzig, Goldmann, 1935, 301 pp.), p. 38: "The American provides the curious spectacle of a European with the manners of a Negro and the soul of the Indian . . . Anglo-Saxon civilization . . . the most primitive and shallow of European civilizations."

[230] *Ibid.*, p. 72.

[231] The appointment by Grau on Rosenberg's authorization of four corresponding members was announced in *Weltkampf* I, 3 (1941), 182: Dr. Wilhelm Coblitz, Cracow; Friedrich

But otherwise, Rosenberg had mustered the best men available. When, in the very first paragraphs of his inauguration speech, he expressed his certainty that there would be "close and loyal collaboration with the German universities" [232] he meant what he said. Likewise, it was no trifle to his subordinate Grau that he could point to the fact that the archives of the institution would be administered by "trained staff members," just as "a sufficient number of research librarians of the higher and middle service" would handle the library "according to the most modern principles." Even more was he pleased to be able to announce that the research department would employ on a full-time basis a number of "highly qualified younger and older German scholars." [233] If we wish to understand the phenomenon we are dealing with, we must see that the alliance between "science" and politics was being taken seriously. Not that these appeals to scholarship could induce us to assess the products and producers of this school with any more forbearance than we show when confronted with the "practitioners" of the Himmler-Streicher type; but while we realize that the learned ones in a sense were more dangerous, we must recognize the difference between the two. The Graus and Seraphims, who had succeeded in winning Rosenberg's favors, like the Franks and Kittels, who failed in this respect, not only displayed the regalia of research, such as quotations, footnotes, charts, and maps, but also appealed, and were entitled to do so, to the perennial traditions of German scholarship. [234]

Peter-Heinz Seraphim, the best expert on Eastern-European Jewry, was prominent among the men whom Rosenberg had attracted. He had been won for the editorship of the *Weltkampf,* the journal of the institute; later, this place was taken by another capable staff member, Dr. Klaus Schickert, author of the comprehensive book on the

Kienzl, producing director of the Tobis Filmkunst Corporation, Berlin; Professor Dr. Peter-Heinz Seraphim; and Dr. Josef Vogt, Professor [of Ancient History] at the University of Tübingen.

[232] *Weltkampf,* I (1941), 4.

[233] *Ibid.,* p. 19.—No complete list of the staff members of the Institut seems to have ever been published; of those identified the following may be mentioned apart from persons who have appeared before: Dr. Friedrich Cornelius, Dr. Otto Paul, Dr. Johann[es] Pohl, Dr. Fritz Zschaeck.

In addition, the *Weltkampf* had regular contributors, such as the famous bibliographer Joris Vorstius of the Prussian State Library in Berlin.

[234] Cf. p. 8.—In connection with an exhibition, "German Scholarship in the Struggle for the Reich and Living Space," which opened in Berlin exactly on the day of the Pearl Harbor attack, Ritterbusch declared: "Scholarship is indispensable for any historical life struggle. A folk that does not simultaneously recognize these tasks of its scholarship cannot be a folk that makes world history and defines historical epochs. . . . Alongside the best soldier in the world there must stand the best scholar in the world." Cf. *Deutscher Wissenschaftlicher Dienst,* no. 69, December 8, 1941, pp. 1-2.

Jews in Hungary. This journal, incidentally, was characteristic of the long upward way that German "Jew-knowledge" had traveled.

When Rosenberg in 1924 founded in Munich *Der Weltkampf*, with the subtitle *Monatsschrift für die Judenfrage aller Länder* (Monthly Devoted to the Jewish Question in All Countries), it was a fighting sheet of the cheapest quality. To the outsider, it seemed to harp maniacally upon the same limited number of topics on Jewish aspirations to world domination. Accuracy in reporting facts was not even attempted. For instance, the existence of two historically defined cultural groupings in present-day Jewry, the so-called Sephardim (Spanish Jews and their descendants, *Sefarad* being the medieval Hebrew name for the Iberian peninsula), and the Ashkenazim (Central and Eastern European Jews and their descendants, *Ashkenaz* being the traditional Hebrew name for Germany), was presented to the readers of *Der Weltkampf* in connection with the 1932 American presidential campaign the following way: there were among the Jews themselves civilized people, the so-called Sephardim, but those were opposed by the Ashkenazim, "the Jewish Bolsheviks"; and Roosevelt, it was stated, was the candidate of the B'nai B'rith, *that is* the Ashkenazim.

As Rosenberg's state and party duties multiplied, the direction of *Der Weltkampf* passed to Hans Hauptmann and subsequently to Ludwig Deyerling. Under the latter, the subtitle read: *Monatsschrift für Weltpolitik, völkische Kultur und die Judenfrage in aller Welt* (Monthly for World Politics, [German] Folk Culture and the Jewish Question the World Over), but no substantial change in contents occurred. Nor was any appreciable step taken toward even elementary accuracy in reporting or more reticence in language. But then the great change took place. In its issue no. 207 of March, 1941, the Munich *Der Weltkampf* announced that it was being promoted: it was passing from the Deutscher Volksverlag into the Hoheneichen-Verlag affiliated with the Party Central Publishing House and would from that time on serve as the organ of the Institut zur Erforschung der Judenfrage in Frankfort on-the-Main. The editors then asserted:

> . . . If we today put the editorship into other hands, we do it with the satisfaction that *Der Weltkampf* continues to fulfill a task which underscores its importance as an anti-Jewish organ.

The former workers might have been a little hurt that they themselves had not been found equal to the job ahead. But all feelings of this kind must have turned into legitimate pride when they saw the degree of distinction their grown-up child had attained. It was no more a homely thin sheet in small-octavo size but an issue of hundred pages or more of double size. Most of the contributors were professors or doctors, and magnificent reproductions illustrated the text. And despite this new found elegance, the journal did not renounce its past, the title being changed only slightly to *Weltkampf*. The subtitle presently read: *Die Judenfrage in Geschichte und Gegenwart* (The Jewish Question in History and in Our Time).

Grau's editorial introducing the first issue called attention to the fact that "the political activity of the [National Socialist] Movement in the meantime had been joined by scholarship as an ally" and then outlined the task of the journal as follows:

> [*Weltkampf*] is going to be the mouthpiece of German and European scholarship.... Scholarship, too, today more than at any other time, looks upon this [anti-Jewish] work as upon a "world struggle (Weltkampf)," as upon a war which is inevitable for the peoples that are aware of their peculiarities (Eigenart).[235]

Even a less vain person than Grau would have boasted of his achievements. He had only to look back at his humble beginnings and the cool reception of his proposals at the 1936 conference of historians in Karlsruhe. In 1941 he had succeeded. The Hebraica and Judaica departments of the Frankfort Municipal Library were in his hands. Many German Jewish libraries, public and private, had been confiscated even before the outbreak of war, particularly after the "tide of popular anger" had swept over Germany in November, 1938. Among the collections were those of the Berlin Jewish Gemeinde, of the Breslau Rabbiner-Seminar, and of the Vienna Jewish Gemeinde and Rabbinical Seminary. In his report Grau publicly acknowledged, moreover, that during the crucial year of 1940 Alfred Rosenberg had ordered for delivery to the Institut new important book collections, public and private. We know that the libraries of the Alliance Israélite Universelle and the École Rabbinique in Paris, the Rosenthaliana in Amsterdam, and many others from Eastern Europe (see document on next page) were among them.

The lavishness with which the Institut was equipped can be gauged from the fact that the city of Frankfort had granted an amount of 160,000 marks exclusively for the acquisition of reference books. Rosenberg in his opening address voiced his particular thanks

---

[235] *Weltkampf*, I (1941), 1. The German compound *Eigenart* contains the biological term *Art* "species."

Der Reichsstatthalter
Reichspropagandaamt
Zweigstelle Litzmannstadt
—

Aktenzeichen: G1./Le.
in der Antwort anzugeben

Litzmannstadt, den 24. April 1941
König-Heinrich-Str.
Fernsprecher: Sammel-Nr.

2 6. APR. 1941

R

An das
Reichsministerium für
Volksaufklärung und Propaganda

B e r l i n W 8
Wilhelmplatz 8-9.

Betrifft: Erlass vom 16. April 1941, gez. Dr. Hillake.
Az. R 1432/7.4.41/268-1,1.

Ich nehme Bezug auf mein Schreiben vom 11. April 1941
und teile mit, daß die Bestände zwar äußerst umfangreich
sind, ein grosser Teil jedoch sich nach entsprechender Sichtung ausscheiden lässt, als Altpapier. Die Sichtung ist
augenblicklich im Gange. Soweit es sich um polnische Lite-
ratur handelt, kann sie dem Generaltreuhänder zur Verfügung
gestellt werden, sofern nicht das Ministerium daran interes-
siert ist. Eine Übersicht ist erst dann möglich, wenn die
Sichtung beendet ist.

Bezüglich des jüdischen Schrifttums besteht die Absicht,
es dem Institut zur Erforschung der Ostjudenfrage zu sichern
und zwar geschieht dies im Auftrag des Reichsleiters Alfred
Rosenberg und des Gauleiters des Reichsgaues Wartheland.
Ich bitte meinen Bericht, der nach Beendigung der Ordnung
und Sichtung des Materials an das Ministerium gegeben wird,
abzuwarten. Über endgültige Verfügung kann erst dann entschieden werden, Die Sichtung dürfte noch einige Monate
in Anspruch nehmen.

Heil Hitler!

A branch of Rosenberg's Frankfort institute was established in Lódź under
the direction of Adolf Wendel according to a JTA report datelined Stockholm,
August 7, 1942, quoting as its source *Litzmannstädter Zeitung* "reaching here
today." Nothing, however, has become known about the activities of this branch.

to Reichsleiter [Xaver] Schwarz, treasurer of the Party, "who in the most liberal way had interested himself in the entire financing and entire administering of the forthcoming Hohe Schule and its branches." The library and the archives of the Institut were proclaimed to be the largest in the world in their field, and it was obviously in anticipating the imminent beginning of the Eastern campaign that Rosenberg promised the library "would be enlarged in the years to come in quite a decisive way." [236]

No wonder then that Grau felt justified in saying:

> There comes into being here, created by the greatest political anti-Jewish force in existence in Europe, namely, by the NSDAP, a mental powerhouse whose task it is to lay out the great safeguarding lines for the future and mentally to maintain the positions now. [237]

XXI

THE FRANKFORT CONFERENCE OF MARCH, 1941. SCHOLARLY BACKING FOR THE "UNIVERSAL EUROPEAN SOLUTION OF THE JEWISH QUESTION"

The high points of Rosenberg's speeches at the Conference of Frankfort regarding its immediate topic, the Jews, were as follows:

> The Nuremberg Laws are to revolutionize history.
>
> The struggle has made us sufficiently hard to continue this once established fighting policy without any weakness.
>
> For Germany, the Jewish question will be solved only when the last Jew will have left the Greater German space.... We may say, I believe, for all Europeans as well: for Europe the Jewish question will be solved only when the last Jew will have left the European continent. [238]

The five papers read at the business meetings of the Conference, naturally enough, developed the same theme. Among them, three deserve our most careful attention:

---

[236] As a matter of fact, the "Rosenberg Task Force" most industriously took over the Jewish cultural treasures in the territories of former Poland, the Baltic countries, and the Soviet Union proper, which the German armies overran in 1941. Cf. footnote 171. As if to veil that pillage, the *Deutscher Wissenschaftlicher Dienst*, no. 9, of August 26, 1940, supplied the German press with an essay by Professor Dr. Paul Lehmann of the University of Munich: "The Sacking of German Libraries" ("Plünderungen deutscher Bibliotheken"). The author started with the events of the thirty-years war and wound up his survey with the following paragraph, unmindful of the saying *qui s'excuse, s'accuse*: "In 1939/40 our Wehrmacht saw to it that Germany should not be subjected to such sacking any more. For this protection we have to thank the Führer and the army over and over again. Should, however, the *German* anew be represented as the *barbarian*, one ought to point to the historical facts only alluded to above [which prove] that the French who are so proud of their civilization without scruple robbed and sacked German culture and art treasures."

[237] *Weltkampf*, I, 1/2 (1941), 19.

[238] *Ibid.*, pp. 66-71.

Dr. Wilhelm Grau: "Attempts to Solve the Jewish Question in Past History."

Dr. Peter-Heinz Seraphim: "Problems of Economic and Population Policies Regarding a Universal European Solution of the Jewish Question."

Dr. Walter Gross: "The Racial-Political Premises of Solving the Jewish Question."

Dr. Giselher Wirsing's paper on "The Jewish Question in the Near East" can here be dispensed with as not belonging directly to our subject; Schickert's address: "Jewish Emancipation in Southeastern Europe and Its End" will be more conveniently discussed together with the impact of German anti-Jewish policies on other countries.

Let us recall that the Frankfort Conference took place at the very end of March, 1941, at a time when Hitler already had taken "the hardest decision of his life" to attack the Soviet Union, but the preparations were still veiled in the greatest secrecy. Grau, in following Rosenberg's lead, stated that "the ideological and political situation today makes possible great decisions in the Jewish problem,"[239] and Rosenberg's accessory Rüdiger in his front-page article in the *Völkischer Beobachter*[240] confidently declared: "We shall see to it that never again a Jewish 'renaissance' takes place." It has been a hard struggle but "now through research work the ways can be looked for to cleanse the [European] space from the decomposing elements in a planned manner."[241]

Forgotten were presently the protestations that the Nuremberg Laws had "solved the Jewish question." Scholarship now was able to prove that even pressing the Jews into ghettos was no solution. Of course, the suffering inflicted upon the Jews was immaterial, but the formation of ghettos within the cities, it had turned out, created inconveniences for the non-Jewish population as well. Besides, Seraphim showed in his paper that complete segregation simply could not be maintained.

> . . . In practice this [complete segregation] means not only the erection of a ghetto wall but also permanent police surveillance over the entire ghetto border, the prohibition for non-Jews to enter the ghetto or to approach it. This ghetto comes closer to the type of the Jewish isolation zone as for instance (but explicitly as a

[239] *Ibid.*, p. 21.
[240] Berlin edition, March 25, 1941.
[241] *Ibid.*, March 26, 1941.

transitory solution) the attempt to form a ghetto for the Jews in Litzmannstadt.[242]

Seraphim went on:

> Inasmuch as such a strictly closed ghetto is not created but only a wall erected (as at the beginning in Warsaw) and a number of important government offices still are located in the district declared as the ghetto, main thoroughfares pass through the ghetto and thus entrance to it cannot be prohibited. The ghetto is in a large measure ineffective in practice....

To achieve real distancing, the whole life of the cities would have to be disrupted:

> Creating the city ghetto is in practice quite difficult. Cities are organic units: lines of communication, buses, trolleys are installed and serve the whole city area. Highways cross or cut the ghetto. The supply of water, gas, electricity is uniform; the consumption must be metered; repairs must be made. It is impossible simply to cut out of the communal body such a significant part of the area of the community (up to one-third of the inhabited area). If this is done, the rest remains a torso! In many other respects, too, the ghetto as a district within a city constitutes a danger. The spread of epidemics is possible even in spite of a wall! Finally, the constant police surveillance in the ghetto requires disproportionately large forces. Decreasing them, on the other hand, would mean increasing the danger of trespassing beyond the ghetto border in practice.

Seraphim's thorough economic studies were not wasted:

> One more argument against the closed city ghetto is derived from economic considerations: the city ghetto cannot supply itself with either manufactured goods or raw materials and fuel or with food.
>
> Consequently, the entire demand would have to be imported. These importations could be small per capita of the ghetto inhabitants and not exceed the subsistence minimum and yet in their totality they represent a constant notable import burden and practically would mean that the Jews would be fed and supported by

[242] The situation in this ghetto of Lódź in its "normal" conditions, before the actual extermination started, is illustrated by the following items taken from secret German police reports:

"October 7, 1940.... In the ghetto of Litzmannstadt [Lódź] the situation grows ever more critical. Because of insufficient food supply, there again occurred riots and manifestations. In nineteen cases, shooting weapons were made use of; two Jews were killed and four wounded. The number of infectuous diseases in the ghetto did not decrease."

"December 4, 1940 .... For guarding the ghetto [in Lódź] there are still needed four hundred police sergeants (Polizei-Wachtmeister). In attempting to leave the ghetto without justification one Jew was shot and one wounded. The number of cases of contagious diseases like dysentery, typhus, tuberculosis, typhoid fever, diphtheria, scarlet fever, etc., did not decrease."

Cf. Der Chef der Ordnungspolizei, O.-Kdo. g 2 (01), no. 6, XVIII/40 (g) and O.-Kdo. g 2 (01), no. 233/40 (g); documents in the possession of the Yivo. Cf. also "Deutsche Polizei im Osten," special issue of *Die deutsche Polizei*, 1. Februar, 1941; Zirpins, "Das Ghetto in Litzmannstadt, kriminalpolitisch gesehen." *Die deutsche Polizei* 9 (1941, November, Dezember), 379-380, 394-395, 409-412.

the non-Jews. It goes without saying, however, that feeding the ghetto is unthinkable without an economic return by the ghetto. A possibility of return exists only in the use of Jewish manpower. It contradicts the principle of the closed ghetto and of the elimination (Ausgliederung) of the Jews to apply this manpower outside the ghetto. Applying it in the ghetto, however, is possible only if machines and raw materials are delivered to the ghetto, if a compulsory labor service is introduced and its execution is watched over, in short, if external surveillance over the ghetto is supplemented by a sufficient internal surveillance, organization, and supervision, certainly by no small number of non-Jewish superintending personnel. The economic result still remains dubious because the manpower made use of is put in motion exclusively by external force. The result of forced labor always remains economically unsatisfactory.

The next paragraph in this cool deliberation suddenly revealed that the author was no longer concerned with former Poland alone. The time had come—it is March, 1941—when Germany had recognized her responsibility for the whole of the continent:

> For most cities of Central, West, South, and East Europe, where the number of Jews is scantier, ghettoization of the Jews is out of the question because the number of the Jews is much too small for the establishment of such communities. If one wishes to pass over this stage of the political, social, economic dissimilation, it may be practicable to concentrate the Jews in several places away from their previous living areas. Unlike Eastern Europe, one would naturally not choose any cities in existence, but living places supplied *ad hoc*. There would, however, be only a small difference in principle between such forced Jewish residence and the Eastern Jewish forced ghettos.[243]

The suggestion arose, therefore, Seraphim proceeded to argue, that the above-mentioned difficulties might be met by assigning to the Jews a certain larger territory.

> It is known that in following up these plans, it was frequently contemplated to form such a "Jewish reservation" in the eastern part of the present Government General in the district of Lublin which could hold the Jews of the Greater German Reich and the rest of the Government General and in due course also the Jews of the rest of Europe.

This plan, Seraphim conceded, looked fascinating at first glance, but there were also difficulties to be reckoned with. The territory could not be made self-supporting. Furthermore, 5,000,000 Jews would have to be moved into this reservation and 2,700,000 non-

243 *Weltkampf*, I (1941), 48-49.

Jews would have to be removed. But in Europe there is no place for them. "This means," he exclaimed indignantly, "that non-Jews would have to be made to emigrate from Europe in order to settle Jews in Europe." Guarding the outer frontiers of such a giant ghetto would involve, moreover, colossal expenditures. Seraphim, therefore, emphasized:

> Through legislation and administrative measures, the Jews in the cities are to be replaced by non-Jews to the degree in which qualified non-Jews are available for this substitution.... There remains as the highest maxim: the Jew must yield wherever an equally qualified non-Jew is available.[244]

The other speakers at the Conference, too, maintained that the time had come, as Grau put it,

> . . . to give this problem on European soil a definite solution once and for all in this century. There must be no doubt: the twentieth century, which at its beginning saw the Jew at the summit of his power, will at its end not see Israel any more because the Jew will have disappeared from Europe.[245]

Seraphim in his capacity of demographer and geo-politician considered the question more in detail by pointing to the difficulties of providing shipping space and money for removing the Jews from Europe, but believed that the obstacles were not insurmountable; he felt that the Jews themselves would have to cooperate. This point seems to have impressed the audience because Rüdiger stressed it in his report to the *Völkischer Beobachter.* Exactly half a year later, the Reich law depriving all German Jews abroad of their citizenship and ordering the confiscation of their property (*Reichsgesetzblatt* I, 722) took up the hint in providing: "The forfeited property shall be used for furthering all aims connected with the solution of the Jewish question."

Gross, as could be expected, attacked the problem from the point of view of "racial science":

> The concept of race . . . through the modern development of genetics, biology, and anthropology has come to assume solid and definite shape.... The physical and mental-psychical characteristics of human groups are in disposition (in der Anlage) of a hereditary nature.... A race is a group of people who by common possession of hereditary dispositions of physical as well as of mental-psychical kind differ from other human groups.... The two basic

[244] *Ibid.,* p. 50.
[245] *Ibid.,* p. 15.

components of the Jewish race-mixture . . . science calls the Near-Eastern and the Oriental race....

The Jew, being "racially alien" to all European peoples, has no place in Europe. In choice of the classes of persons to be eliminated a "uniform definition of the concept 'Jew'" should be agreed upon by all European nations. German experience shows that only "racial" criteria are consistent, religion or the degree of rootedness (Bodenständigkeit) or citizenship being irrelevant. "Hybrids (Mischlinge) of the first degree, so-called half-Jews, fundamentally are to be treated entirely as Jews. The increase in progeny of hybrids of the second degree, as far as they remain within the European peoples, is to be kept as low as possible."

That the Jews were a "race mixture" and not Orientals or Near Easterners by race was duly stressed in the interest of a Germany at war:

This fact is important. Otherwise it could occur to us to ascribe the peculiarities of Jewry which to us seem so bad and hostile to the Near-Eastern or the Oriental race as such. That would be a great mistake. On the contrary, it turns out that these races, too, where they have appeared as relatively pure, strike the European, it is true, as alien and different in species (andersartig) but in their own living space and within the cultural patterns created by them they present quite esteemable and agreeable traits. Let me remind only of the Arab tribes and peoples whose racial foundation is fairly purely Oriental.... *And it would be well for the sake of clarity if the European world in its struggle against the Jews always remained aware of this context and did not call the struggle, as hitherto, anti-Semitism.*[246] Because it is directed not against peoples of Semitic tongue but against the unharmonious Near Eastern-Oriental-Mediterranean Jew-people which is being so passionately rejected also by the purely or preponderantly Oriental, Semitic tribes and peoples.[247]

---

[246] Italics in original.

[247] *Ibid.,* p. 57.

The latest issue of the *Weltkampf* in the library of the Yivo, and probably its last issue in general (1944, 3, September-December), on p. 168 reproduced an exchange of letters, "which took place some time ago" and was to explain "why we don't use any more the concept of *anti-Semitism.*" The Iraqi Prime Minister Rashid Ali el Gailani (deposed in 1941, but still recognized by Germany as if nothing had happened) inquired of Professor Dr. Walter Gross as the Director of the Racial-Policy Office of the Nazi party whether Germany really considered the Arabs, like the Jews, as racially inferior. "As Prime Minister of Iraq I too well know my countrymen, and the Arabs in general, not to know that they don't believe that statement because in their struggle for their freedom and their rights they had so much recognition and support from the Germans that they are convinced of their respect and amity. But since the enemy propaganda constantly repeats that lie I feel it would be useful if Germany officially opposed it by presenting the truth about the German attitude toward the Arab race."

Gross' reply, dated October 17, 1942, confirmed that the Jews, as a "disharmonious race mixture," were to be strictly distinguished from the people of Near Eastern and Oriental race; that the expression *anti-Semitism* was wrong; that "the Semitic-Arab peoples, languages, and cultures always were the object of affectionate interest on the part of German scholarship" and

As to the prospects of getting rid of the Jews, Gross was most cheerful:

> We look upon Jewry as quite a realistic phenomenon which was exceptionally clever in matters of earthly life but which likewise is subject to historical death. And as far as the historical phenomenon of the Jew in Europe is concerned, we believe that this hour of death has come irrevocably.[248]

As this program unfolded in the presence of the highest Reich authorities and representatives of German science, it is obvious that it was not merely a proposal submitted for discussion but a course of action already decided upon. Eugen Fischer and Hans F. K. Günther, who attended as guests of honor, must have enjoyed listening to the decisions on complete elimination of the Jews, based on and justified by their teachings on the Near-Eastern and Oriental racial composition of the Jews. What nobler and fuller satisfaction can a scholar hope for than to see his theoretical findings materialize in state policies?

Before the German archives disgorge their contents it remains debatable whether the talk on forcibly evacuating the Jews from Europe to some dark continent, obviously used as a camouflage for the extermination program that soon was to be put into effect, was meant seriously by some participants. The minor performers at the Frankfort Conference perhaps really thought how pleasant it would be to "evacuate" the Jews to some undefined place in so convenient a manner and to force the Jews of the democratic countries into subsidizing the grandiose migration scheme. Some cunning fellow even might have figured that Germany could make some money on the deal, just as she had on the expulsion of the Jews from Germany in the pre-war years by stripping them of the last bit of property and pushing them over the frontier with ten marks in their pockets. But this benefit of the doubt cannot be given to Rosenberg and the

---

"that the racial theory recently changed nothing." "No responsible person or institution in Germany," Gross concluded, "ever said that the Arabs were racially inferior or stood on an unfavorable place in the rank order of human races. On the contrary, National Socialist racial theory considers the Arabs members of a high-value race that looks back upon a glorious and heroic history. That is why, too, the struggle of the Arabs for political liberation against the Jewish usurpation of Palestine has always been observed and supported by Germany with particular sympathy." As to the evaluation of the Near-Eastern and Oriental rates by national socialism, Gross, of course, for political reasons diverged from the truth, and even after his letter was written, a colleague of his, Professor Dr. [Karl] Metzger in an official publication in which Gross, too, was represented, said explicitly: "In administrative enforcement of race protection some are to be considered as alien in species (Artfremde), with whom any miscegenation is prohibited, particularly all Jews, gypsies, and colored persons as well as their hybrids to definitely fixed degrees, and likewise the members of the Near-Eastern and Oriental races, with the exception of European Turkey." Cf. the publication mentioned in footnote 380, p. 53.

[248] *Weltkampf*, I (1941), 52.

leading men around him at the time of the Frankfort Conference. As established at the Nuremberg trial, the attack on the Soviet Union, which started on June 22, 1941, had been decided upon as early as September, 1940. It is evident, then, that the plans for disposing of the Jews in the conquered Eastern territories much more radically than by "evacuating" them from Europe must have been ready by the end of March, 1941; otherwise, those plans would not have worked as smoothly as they did when the actual *Ausmerze* began on the territories over which Rosenberg was soon to exercise almost sovereign power. At that time, at any rate, there was no difficulty whatever in interpreting Rosenberg's Frankfort speech of 1941 the right way; its essence was summarized by a responsible writer of Rosenberg's staff in the following sentence: "The world will not gain rest until this fungus of decomposition is extirpated." [249]

XXII

SECRETS OF THE ANTI-JEWISH PROPAGANDA. THE REPRESENTATIVES OF THE CONQUERED AND SATELLITE COUNTRIES AT THE FRANKFORT CONFERENCE

In order properly to understand the appearance of the foreign guests at the Frankfurt Conference, we have to look backward. That German actions and research on the "Jewish question" could but have international repercussions was evident even at a time when the Nazis themselves were anxious to deny that their philosophy was for export. Even then, to be sure, Goebbels' agencies were putting out their smooth tentacles but they did so under the cover of "private" institutions like the Deutsche Akademie or through *ad hoc* organizations. One of these, which concededly also engaged in anti-Jewish propaganda, was the Gesamtverband deutscher antikommunistischer Vereinigungen (General Association of German anti-Communist Societies), founded in 1933 by Dr. Eberhard Taubert, high official in Goebbels' ministry. Taubert, in a secret memorandum of February 7, 1934, outlined his aims in the following way:

> Any anti-Bolshevist propaganda is directly in our favor, especially if conducted along these lines: (1) bolshevism is the gravest danger menacing the world's security and culture; (2) we have saved the world from this danger; (3) our defense action against

communism had to be directed against Jewry too, because they are
allied (which is to be proved, cf. the book by Fehst);[250] ... (6)
we are the pioneers of a real understanding of peoples on the basis
of mutual respect of the nations. (How this proposition comes in
in this context, will be shown below.)

If this propaganda be consistently carried through, one must
come to understand the new Germany abroad, particularly the
authoritarian regime, the concentration camps, the regulation of
the Jewish question....

In order to carry on this propaganda [Dr. Taubert continued],
in each country to be sure, I consolidated the German private associations which were engaged in combating communism, particularly
the church and scientific ones, into one General Association of
German anti-Communist Societies. The aim is particularly this:
The Russian Communists carry on their anti-German propaganda
"privately," i.e., according to the above mentioned fiction not
through the state but through agencies of the Communist party.
To avoid difficulties for the German state from the Russians, I here
so to speak turned the tables and likewise carry the anti-Communist
propaganda not on behalf of the state but through this private
General Association, *which in reality is secretly subordinated to
me.*

In November, 1936, the Anti-Comintern called the first confidential international anti-Communist conference at Feldafing near
Munich, where the anti-Jewish issues were not overlooked either.
The conference moved to consider itself the nucleus of a forthcoming world anti-Communist congress; [251] this organizing committee was
led by Goebbels' agent, the Swedish journalist Nils von Bahr, but
"secretly was steered as a German government agency," as Dr. Taubert
admitted in a report covering his activities down to the end of 1944.
In the same document, Taubert gave as the immovable goal of his
organization:

In Germany: unflinching continuation of the anti-Bolshevist and
anti-Jewish propaganda, creation of political literature in these fields.
This has been done particularly with the help of the Nibelungen-
Verlag (Nibelungen Publishing House), also an establishment of

[250] Hermann Fehst, Dozent an der deutschen Hochschule für Politik, *Bolschewismus und
Judentum* (Berlin, Eckart-Kampf Verlag, 1934, 167 pp.). The book was published jointly by
the Institut zum Studium der Judenfrage and the Anti-Comintern.

[251] The report had the following title page (the copy now in the Yivo library bears
no. 67): Streng vertraulich! *Protokoll der ersten Vertraulichen Internationalen Antikom-
munistischen Konferenz in Feldafing bei München vom 4. bis 10. November 1936* (n. p.,
n. d., 100 pp.). It is certainly no trifle that the conference was attended not only by
representatives of Germany, Italy, Spain, etc., but also by two Polish delegates, prelate Kwiat-
kowski and an official of the Ministry of the Interior Szymborski, and that expressions of
homage were telegraphed also to Marshal Rydz-Smigły of Poland.

Dr. Taubert's . . . Abroad: creation of friendly organizations in every country of the world. . . .[252]

In 1937, a full confession was made by Goebbels' associate and disciple, Wilhelm Ziegler, the man who was in charge of the Institut zum Studium der Judenfrage:

> . . . The impetus for what we now observe as the Jewish question in the world came from Adolf Hitler's Germany in the Jewish legislation of the year 1933 and the following years. It is from here that a spiritual movement was kindled which more and more spreads over other countries.[253]

When the war started and Germany's might began rising to unseen heights, the insistence of Germany in imposing its views on and policies toward the Jews upon the conquered and satellite countries kept increasing.

German scholarship in this respect too can boast of an appreciable record. We have already mentioned Seraphim's contention expressed in the end of his voluminous book, that anti-Semitism would never assume proper shape and proportions in Eastern Europe unless it based itself on the concept of *Rasse*. He stressed the same point in a special paper,[254] and other scholars came to the same conclusion concerning other countries. German scholarship obligingly did its best to help the neighbors to overcome the ignorance of "Race." The *Welt-Dienst* (World Service) news agency, Taubert's "Anti-Comintern," and many other agencies of Goebbels' Propaganda Ministry provided for translations of the Protocols of the Elders of Zion and other tracts of this kind into almost every European language. But true to the rule that propaganda in order to succeed must also have in mind the intellectuals who look for scientific "proof," and in order to act more directly and effectively later on, the Germans stimulated a series of studies which were to show the detrimental part the Jews had played in the neighboring countries. Karl Alexander von Müller, who, as we have seen, had supervised the education of Walter

[252] Copies of the two memoranda by Dr. Taubert are in the possession of the Yivo. The second document was particularly sarcastic about unintentional supporters of nazism: "With the help of the charitable action, in which the participating clergymen of the two denominations were permitted to be used as puppets of our propaganda . . ."; "the Archbishop of Canterbury later recognized for whom he had worked and stated in deep regret that he had permitted to be used 'as a fig leaf of the Propaganda Ministry'"; "it has always been one of the unforgettable stories of the Anti-Comintern that the little parsons (Pfäfflein) of Saarbrücken never knew whose business they had been doing"; Ewald Ammende, the agile and amiable secretary general of the International Congress for Minority Questions is revealed as a Nazi agent. Italics in the above quotation in original.

[253] Wilhelm Ziegler, Oberregierungsrat im Reichsministerium für Volksaufklärung und Propaganda, Dozent an der Deutschen Hochschule für Politik und an der Universität Berlin, *Die Judenfrage in der modernen Welt* (Berlin, Junker und Dünnhaupt, 1937, 32 pp.), p. 12.

[254] Peter-Heinz Seraphim, "Der Antisemitismus in Osteuropa," *Osteuropa* 14 (Februar, 1939), pp. 332-346.

Frank and paved the way for Wilhelm Grau, also inspired the doctoral dissertation of Klaus Schickert on the Jews in Hungary. Schickert, in the summary and conclusions (Zusammenfassung) of his book, clearly pointed to Germany's part in bringing Hungary to the realization of the essence of the Jewish question:

> . . . Hungary is ready to cooperate within the framework of the European community of nations when the expulsion of the Jews from Europe will start. . . . Racial thinking is no German requirement, it has become a *European requirement*. . . . Europe eliminates the Jews and with them capitalism. Europe seeks the new order—and finds it: in the fighting community of its peoples which is a guarantee of the peace to come.[255]

Similarly, a thorough-going study by Hans Schuster on "The Jewish Question in Rumania," accepted as a doctoral dissertation by the University of Leipzig and published by one of the most respectable publishing houses, expressed its confidence that

> with the growth of the [Jewish] menace simultaneously . . . will grow the recognition of the importance of German racial legislation.[256]

In the spring of 1941, this hope had materialized. Sextil Puscariu, the foremost linguist of Rumania, Professor at the Universities of Cluj and Berlin, wrote the following statement for the organ of the Nazi Deutsche Akademie:

> New Rumania, following in its orientation the course of the Danube up stream, goes from the Black Sea to the Black Forest. With her whole will and the greatest confidence she aligns herself with the new order of Europe. . . .[257]

Thus, connections with "cognate" movements and governments abroad were firmly established. It was, therefore, a shrewd move to invite to the Frankfort Conference of March, 1941, "not only Germans but also a number of worthy representatives of many European countries," as Grau put it in telling of "personal conferences" he had held with them.[258] Among these guests were: Vidkun Quisling (Nor-

[255] Klaus Schickert, *Die Juden in Ungarn* [1. Auflage, 1937], 2. Auflage (Essen, Essener Verlagsanstalt, 1942, 317 pp.), p. 288. In the preface to the second edition, the author expressed his gratitude to the Antijüdische Aktion for its assistance.—The quotations are from the second edition; the first did not contain the concluding chapter.

[256] Hans Schuster, *Die Judenfrage in Rumänien* (Leipzig, Meiner, 1939, 244 pp.), p. 239. = Abhandlungen des Instituts für Politik, ausländisches öffentliches Recht und Völkerrecht an der Universität Leipzig, N. F., Heft 5. The reviewer of Haushofer's *Zeitschrift für Geopolitik*, XVII (November, 1940), 567, commented: "A book that is comprehensive and for the time being probably not repeatable in its kind."

[257] Sextil Puscariu, in: *Deutsche Kultur im Leben der Völker . . . Deutsche Akademie* XVI (1941), p. 98.

[258] *Weltkampf*, I (1941), 16, 21.

way); Robert van Genechten, Prosecutor General, and Anton A. Mussert, recognized leader of the NSB, the Dutch National Socialist organization (the Netherlands); Professor Alexander Cuza, "past master of European anti-Semitism," as an official reporter put it,[259] and Professor George Cuza (as representatives of the government of Rumania); state secretary director general Alajos Kovács and section chief Kultsar (as representatives of the government of Hungary); Dr. Peter Schischkoff, member of Parliament (Bulgaria); Erling Hallas, Stabsgruppenleiter (Denmark); René Lambrichts, lawyer (Flanders); Sano Mach, Minister of the Interior (Slovakia); Professor Veszo (Italy).[260]

All guest speakers, as was to be expected, extolled Adolf Hitler and his policies against the Jews; some of them are worth quoting.

From Vidkun Quisling's address:

> According to the last [Norwegian] census of 1930, 1359 persons belonged to the Mosaic creed. According to common estimates, we at that time had in Norway about 3,000 full Jews, [but] Norwegian history of the last generation is a rapidly increasing Judaization of all strata of society, a development which with elementary force could but lead to the national catastrophe which took place on April 9, 1940, when the attempt was made to involve Norway in the Anglo-Jewish war against Germany.... Over 10,000 Norwegians, and the most influential at that, through freemasonry had become artificial Jews.... A new Norway arises on the firm ground of national socialism and the Nordic racial principle.

From van Genechten's address:

> Germany would do the Netherlands a great service if she shipped to the area she has reserved for the Jews in Poland also those Jews whom we got as a present for instance from Germany after August, 1914, and who amount to a score or so of thousands.... We trust that the Führer in solving the European Jewish question will not forget the Netherlands and we promise on our part to do everything to facilitate this solution.

From Schischkoff's address:

> As is known, the Bulgarian people are pro-German through and through and cling to the old brotherhood of arms [established in World War I]. But all the Jews in Bulgaria even today are still on England's side and that's why all of them have been placed under police surveillance.

[259] *Ibid.,* p. 106.
[260] The last two names did not appear in the report of the *Weltkampf.* Mach, however, was mentioned as present by the *Völkischer Beobachter* of March 27 and Veszo (otherwise unindentifiable) by the *Frankfurter Zeitung* of March 27, 1941.

From Lambrichts' address:

> There are among us about 100,000 Jews who have to be re-
> moved. The predominant part of the Flemish and Walloon peoples
> still keep aloof from our struggle.... We who profess the concept
> of manly honor as the main point for the person of Teutonic blood
> are proud of having been the first in our country who without
> reservations joined the cause of Adolf Hitler.

Here also belongs Dr. Klaus Schickert's paper. He, though himself a German scholar, was pleading the cause of Southeastern
Europe when he told the audience:

> The revolution of national socialism gave the Southeast Euro-
> pean space a new direction, in fact inaugurated for it a new era.
> The solution which Germany has found for her Jewish question
> works as an example and has had repercussions in all those coun-
> tries.... All governments hope for the great emigration to come,
> and some explicitly declared their willingness to further it. Trans-
> lating the thought into deeds transcends the power of any single
> state. For this purpose a master plan is needed, and so our dis-
> cussion terminates in the idea that the Jewish question in South-
> eastern Europe can be solved finally only along uniform lines and
> in cooperation with the German Reich.

As one may deduce from the tenor of these speeches and also
from a sentence of Quisling's ("since the Jewish question cannot be
solved simply by exterminating or sterilizing the Jews"), at least some
of the "worthy guests" from abroad might have believed that ghettoization or expulsion to another continent constituted the highest aim
of the Nazi politics. Rosenberg himself refused to discuss the details.[261] But August Schirmer, the representative of Germany—though
a whale among the minnows, Germany also had sent a delegation
in order to preserve the appearances of a truly international gathering—was more outspoken. He emphasized the intimate connection
between the Nazi's quest for power and their anti-Jewish policy:

> A day on which the burdens which the brutal destructive *Diktat*
> of Versailles had imposed upon the German people could be re-
> moved could come only after all possibilities for sabotaging Ger-
> many's recovery from within had been eliminated. For this purpose,
> in the first place the influence and dominating position of the Jews
> had to be broken.... The rise of the new Germany, whose re-
> invigoration is substantially tied up with the elimination of
> Jewry. . . .

Schirmer explained that it took some time to make the Jewish
problem an international one:

---

[261] *Weltkampf*, I, 1/2 (1941, 70: "There is no need to treat the question [of where
and when] now. Its solution will be reserved for a forthcoming [international] agreement."

At the start, it could not be the task of the National Socialist movement to unroll this question outside the frontiers of the Reich.

He repeated the formula about the war forced upon Germany:

And today, after Jewry has succeeded in unleashing through England, France and Poland the war for which it had striven for so long a time....

He was fully cognizant of the disaster brought upon the Jews by the war:

With the annihilation of Poland and the liberation of Rumania, it [Jewry] has lost its biological cradle.

And Schirmer concluded by repeating Hitler's somber prophecy of January, 1939:

The last part of this European task is still before us. England, whose plutocratic élite (Führerschicht) is so keen about giving itself the air of stemming from the ten lost tribes of Israel, faces her annihilation. She has identified herself with Jewry, she went the road of Jewry—she shall go down to the bitter end. At the end of this great contest which was forced upon us there is going to materialize the prophetic word of the Führer which he uttered on January 30, 1939: "Should international finance Jewry in and outside Europe succeed in again throwing the nations into a world war, the outcome would be not the victory of Jewry but the annihilation of the Jewish race in Europe." [262]

XXIII

BETWEEN THE FALL OF FRANCE AND THE ATTACK ON THE SOVIET UNION. THE CONCEPT OF GREATER SPACE

That England's refusal to give up and Hitler's inability to invade Britain had as early as the autumn of 1940 created a new world situation, became evident only much later. To the participants and onlookers at the Frankfort Conference things appeared quite rosy. The newspapers which featured the Conference also displayed lengthy reports on Matsuoka's visit to Berlin, in the course of which Ribbentrop had announced: "The fate of England already has been decided." [263] A "well-known commentator on problems of economic policies," as the publisher introduced him, thus opened his analysis of the European situation before the attack on Soviet Russia:

---

[262] *Ibid.*, pp. 73-77. Incidentally, Schirmer was not quite accurate in quoting the Führer. He had said, according to the official text, "wird das Ergebnis . . . sein (the outcome is going to be)," while Schirmer transformed it into "würde . . . sein (would be)."
[263] *Völkischer Beobachter*, Berlin edition, March 29, 1941.

With the crushing of France and the heaviest collapse of British influence in the European west, in the Scandinavian countries and in the Balkans, the road has been cleared for the rearrangement of Europe.... Since 1940, the new Europe with the leadership position of the Axis is sure of that deployment of power which is necessary to prepare a large area for common peaceful collaboration.[264]

Germany's fight is Europe's fight, we learn from Haushofer in a book review:

[The author] with noble ardor out of a wide world outlook tells the German why he, under the tremendous pressure of gigantic greater-economy spaces, must struggle on his very own behalf until he has achieved the equality that had been denied him, against the art of strangulation and intimidation of the Anglo-American gold power and space force.[265]

Greater Space (Grossraum) became the watchword in endless articles and books:

Present and future are under the domination of the Greater Space. The power of a folk is being valued according to its race value and the force of its blood stream. The task of the Reich, in conformity with its position in Central Europe, lies on this continent. It must attempt to collect and to keep its blood in one single bloc in order to maintain its middle position and to be able to fulfill its task. The soil belongs only to him who tills it, not to him who dominates it [sic]. This can be accomplished only according to the eternal laws of blood and soil, folk and space.[266]

Haushofer's pet idea (here expressed by a pupil of his), that eastern colonization comes before overseas colonies, had definitely received the official sanction. True, Hitler had reiterated his claim for the former German colonies but he did not insist. As to the "regained areas in the East," he had not lost a single minute. On October 7, 1939, a decree (Erlass) of the Führer and Reich Chancellor was issued which, by the way, seems to have constituted the "legal" basis for the eviction of non-Germans from their places of settlement and for the subsequent ghettoization of the Jews before their ultimate extermination. In confidentially communicating this decree "concerning the solidification of German folkdom" to the Reich ministries, Dr. [Hans Heinz] Lammers, Reich Minister and Chief of the Reich Chancellery, added: "It is not desirable that the decree, which for the time being is not going to be promulgated, should

---

[264] Alfred Oesterheld, *Wirtschaftsraum Europa* (Oldenburg-Berlin, Stalling, 1942, 472 pp.), p. 9.

[265] *Zeitschrift für Geopolitik*, XVIII (May, 1941), 305. Review of Lorenz Fritsch, *Deutschland erkämpft die Freiheit Europas* (Heidelberg, Hüthig und Co., 1940, 110 pp.).

[266] Hans-Joachim Voigt, "Geopolitische Betrachtungen zum Weichselgebiet," *Zeitschrift für Geopolitik*, XVIII (January, 1941), 12.

become known in its text to broader circles." The decree started with the following paragraph:

> The effects of Versailles in Europe are done with. Thereby the Greater German Reich has the possibility of receiving and settling within its space German people who hitherto had to live abroad, and within its boundaries of interest [267] to shape the settlement of folk groups in such a way as to achieve better lines of demarcation between them. The accomplishment of these tasks I entrust to the Reichsführer SS along the following lines:
>
> I . . . no. 2. The elimination of the detrimental influence of such population elements alien to the [German] folk that constitute a danger for the Reich and the German folk community.... In fulfillment of the task indicated in paragraph I, no. 2, the Reichsführer SS can assign the population elements in question definite living quarters.[268]

Thus started Himmler's fatal activity in a new direction, namely, in his capacity as the Reichskommissar für die Festigung deutschen Volkstums (Reich Commissar for the Solidification of German Folkdom). Hitler's tremendous population transfers of 1939-1940, which meant the uprooting of hundreds of thousands of Germans in the Baltic countries, Bessarabia, Bucovina, the South Tyrol, etc., can be properly understood only in the light of these new tasks assigned to Himmler. They meant reckless Germanization of the territories annexed from Poland. "Through bringing back those Reich and Folk Germans who were to be considered for ultimate home-coming into the Reich the folk loss is being rectified which had been caused by the planless individualistic emigrations of bygone centuries." [269]

Scientists, naturally, were quickly at hand to support and interpret the administrative measures. Dr. Walter Geisler, university professor of geography, at Himmler's request started a series of monographs on the new opportunities. The first issue of the series, written by Geisler himself under the title: "German, the East Calls You!", contained a preface by Dr. Winkler, the newly appointed mayor (Bürgermeister) of Posen [Poznań], in which the following passage occurred:

> German weapons again have brought back the German East to the Reich. By the Führer's will here is to rise German heartland (Kernland); German people are to find a new home.[270]

[267] This was the term used in the German-Soviet agreement of September 17, 1939, concerning the partition of Poland.

[268] A copy of this confidential document is in the archives of the Yivo.

[269] *Lehrplan für die weltanschauliche Erziehung in der SS und Polizei.* Erarbeitet und herausgegeben vom SS-Hauptamt (Berlin [1944], 88 pp.), p. 17.

[270] Walter Geisler, *Deutscher, der Osten ruft dich!* (Berlin, Volk und Reich Verlag,

In commenting on the techniques of producing German "heart-land," Professor Dr. Otto Hummel of the newly founded Reich University of Posen said: "It was an inevitable political necessity and a measure of war economy immediately and comprehensively to *relieve* (Ablösung) the Polish and Jewish employers." [271] This drawing upon the rich resources of the German language by German scholars was certainly touching: if they called expropriation "relieving," deportation "cleansing (Säuberung)" or "resettling (einsiedeln)," the deported "Jews eager to emigrate (auswanderungslustige Juden)" and the very killing "deportation (Aussiedlung)," then the action itself did not appear so black as it was, and the dignity of scholarship was preserved. With the passage of time, as techniques progressed, German semantics developed, too: instead of "liquidieren," the euphemism "to treat in a particular manner (sonderbehandeln)" appeared even in official documents to designate mass murder, and in 1944 a linguistic scholar treated himself to the beautiful expression "extinguishment of eternally inimical forces (Auslöschen ewig feindlicher Elemente)." Whether the questionnaires on soldier language prepared in 1936-37 by German linguists for a new emergency were concerned also with these turns of speech has not been disclosed. At any rate, a study of this field will be important to anybody who tries to understand the working of the German mind.

But to revert to Himmler's policy and its apologists. There was a flaw in the texture in that the Poles could not be removed from this "German heartland" as promptly and as radically as the Jews, but this disadvantage, Professor Geisler believed, had an advantage, too, provided the proper attitude was taken:

> Anyway, one sees that the German in the present-day eastern space is going to find Poles, too.... The elements fit for organized work no doubt will be able to do usable work in the reconstruction work.... This way the working capacity of the German folk members will be freed for higher tasks.... It goes without saying that

1941, 104 pp.). — Die wirtschaftlichen Möglichkeiten in den eingegliederten Ostgebieten des Deutschen Reiches. Im Auftrage der Haupttreuhandstelle Ost und des Reichsführers SS, Reichskommissar für die Festigung deutschen Volkstums, her. von Dr. Walter Geisler, o[rdentlichem] Professor der Geographie an der Reichsuniversität Posen, Band I.—Professor Dr. Heinrich Wiepking-Jürgensmann of the University of Berlin wrote in a paper on "Space Arrangement and Shaping of the Landscape, Concerning the Creative Forces of the German Folk," in *Raumforschung und Raumordnung* 5 (1941), XX: "The new Reich areas in the East have been terribly deforested and, what is the same [*sic*], de-Nordified. In order to create here a truly new and final German homeland, the countryside that has been deprived of its shape must be fundamentally reshaped."

[271] Professor Dr. Otto Hummel of the University of Posen (Poznań), in *Osteuropäische Wirtschaftsfragen, Vorträge gehalten auf der Tagung des Vereins deutscher Wirtschaftswissenschaftler* (Weimar, 1942, 125 pp.), p. 85 = Schriftenreihe des Zentralforschungsinstituts für nationale Wirtschaftsordnung und Grossraumwirtschaft.—Italics in original.

all leaders are supplied exclusively by the Germans and even in the smallest businesses Poles are being subordinated to Germans.[272]

In bygone days, when outside powers used to interfere with things that were none of their concern, this state of affairs might have led to some repercussions. But now Germany, and Germany only, was to decide. A courteous writer, in complete control of his language, in the following manner expounded Germany's self-restraint and the unfairness of her opponents:

> Through resettlement within the Polish territory . . . in the Danzig Gau and Warthegau [273] a purely German space was created, which became part of the Reich, whereas the parts [of Poland] settled by Poles will become, in the form of a German Government General, the scene of the future Polish life of own (Eigenleben), within which also the problem of Eastern Jewry is going to become regulated.

> By thus establishing order in German Middle-Europe, the Führer took the position that no power belonging to this Lebensraum is entitled to interfere with these conditions. But simultaneously he once more offered England and France the possibility, after having recognized the situation created in Middle Europe, to settle the further questions of European common living at a conference of the European major powers from a high vantage-point and with a broad outlook. In his Reichstag speech of October 6, 1939, at a time when among the three major powers the arms hardly had spoken despite the state of war which already prevailed, he unfolded the foundations of such an understanding (Verständigung), in which he, to begin with, again pointed to the necessity of limiting armaments as an essential premise of the lasting peace longed for; besides, he merely announced for Germany—incidentally, in no ultimatum form but as a demand which is just both politically and economically—her claim for the return of her colonies.

This magnanimous proposal, the writer complained, was turned down:

> The European peoples would have been spared many losses in blood and goods if the two Western-European democracies had seized the hand of peace extended to them and shown willingness to organize a Europe built upon a real sense of responsibility.

> But the opposite was the case. Neither England nor France was prepared to abstain from their aim: to destroy Greater Germany

[272] Geisler, op. cit., p. 58.
[273] The gau (province) Danzig-Westpreussen included the former Polish Corridor with the cities Gdynia (renamed by the Germans: Gotenhafen), Bydgoszcz (in German, Bromberg), Grudziądz (in German, Graudenz), Toruń (in German, Thorn); the westernmost section of former East Prussia; and the districts of Rypin (renamed Rippin) and Lipno (renamed Leipe), which before the first world war had belonged to Russian Poland. The gau Wartheland included the area of Poznań (Posen), Inowrocław (Hohensalza), and Łódź (renamed Litzmannstadt); at least half of it before the first world war had belonged to Russian Poland.

and to remove her hegemonic position in Middle Europe, which balked their own predominance.[274]

The stubbornness of the western Allies was due to the fact that their views of international law, tainted by Jewish influence, had become obsolete. In reality

a declaration like the one by Adolf Hitler, on February 20, 1938, that the Reich takes upon itself the protective power regarding the German folk groups of alien citizenship created genuine international law (Völkerrecht) of a new kind. Thus, the drawing up and execution of the principles valid within a greater space (Middle and Eastern Europe) does not belong to powers alien to the space and to their law conceptions (which, under Jewish impact, have completely emptied and dissolved the notion of state and soil) but to the state and folk powers carrying this space, that is [sic], the German Reich.[275]

Carl Schmitt, who had been among the first to proclaim this law-creating power of the Reich, in a' new treatise on the Reich and Europe again played the same tune:

The development leads to a new greater-space arrangement of the earth. New powers and new energies carry the new space revolution, and this time it is the German people to whom leadership is due.[276]

The complete unanimity of German scholarship as to the war was stressed in a volume by German university professors, the preface to which was signed by August Faust, Breslau, and dated May, 1941. The contributors were asked only the general question: how the war is conceived of in German legal thinking, in German historiography, in German poetry and, last but not least, in German philosophy. No further uniformity as to size or documentation was required.

All the more remarkable is the essential agreement in contents which occurred quite spontaneously. The result shows the deep relationship between our Weltanschauung and the philosophical root in it and all the fields of the humanities which deal with the problem of war. Moreover, the essential agreement of the historical studies of the present work perhaps serves as some evidence that in German thought there were always ready powers which we National Socialists today feel to be particularly in conformity with our species (artgemäss) and timely, though they previously never

[274] Paul Herre, *Deutschland und die europäische Ordnung* (Berlin, Deutscher Verlag, 1941, 212 pp.), p. 174.—The book was cordially reviewed in *Nationalsozialistische Monatshefte*, July, 1941, p. 635.

[275] Dr. habil. Josef März, Dozent an der Deutschen Karls-Universität Prag, in: *Zeitschrift für Geopolitik*, XVII (November, 1940), 564.

[276] Carl Schmitt, *Das Reich und Europa* (Leipzig, Köhler und Amelang, 1941), p. 105.

could function completely because in previous history the pooling of all powers of Greater Germany, which we owe only to the Führer, was absent.[277]

In January, 1941, the Society for European Economic Planning and Greater Space Economy was founded. There was no board any more but a Leaders' Circle (Führerring) presided over by Werner Daitz, envoy and former prominent staff member in Rosenberg's Foreign Affairs Office; among the "leaders" were high Reich officials. Besides, a Research Council (wissenschaftlicher Beirat) was created, of which Professor Dr. Theodor Vahlen, President of the Prussian Academy of Sciences, was chairman; Professor Dr. Carl Schmitt, member of the Academy of German Law, and Professor Dr. Fritz Rörig, Director of the Seminar of History at the Berlin University, were listed among the members.

Werner Daitz, in his introductory words to the first publication of the institution, declared:

> Now that the Führer by the sharpness of the German sword has freed Europe from her outdated universalistic ties, the European family of peoples can reaccommodate itself according to the natural weight of its peoples into a more productive, crisis-proof *unforced* order.[278]

Admittedly, the rearrangement of spaces meant not only the exclusion of "alien" powers but also some realignments among those states that were lucky enough to belong to the "European family":

> True, the concept of responsibility which characterizes the German leadership opposes some previous notions of the nations' lives of their own. [Previously] even the smallest folkdom splinters embedded in the living space of great nations could claim independence and in the era of liberalism the claim was recognized by international law. Henceforth, such a right to unlimited separate

---

[277] *Das Bild des Krieges im deutschen Denken,* her. von August Faust, Erster Band (Stuttgart, Kohlhammer, 1941, 409 pp.).
    Cf. also Georg Leibbrandt and Egmont Zechlin, "Weltpolitik und Wissenschaft," *National-sozialistische Monatshefte,* no. 129, December, 1940, pp. 747-753: "After the German folk found its form in national socialism and the war has paved the way for the reshaping of Europe, it [scholarship] shall help to create the spiritual foundations for the approaching contest with the rest of the world as well."
[278] *Das neue Europa. Beiträge zur nationalen Wirtschaftsordnung und Grossraumwirtschaft.* Her. von der Gesellschaft für europäische Wirtschaftsplanung und Grossraumwirtschaft (Berlin, Meinhold, 1941, 375 pp.), p. [12]. Italics in original. Vahlen in his letter to "dear Party comrade Daitz," dated January 14, 1941, and ending in "Heil Hitler," congratulated Daitz on the founding of the society.—In 1942, Daitz wrote: "The coming order-principle of the world, therefore, will consist in the proclamation of biological Monroe doctrines." Cf. "Echte und unechte Grossräume," *Reich - Volksordnung - Lebensraum Zeitschrift für völkische Verfassung und Verwaltung* II (1942), 86.—Two years later, Daitz published a book on "The Rebirth of Europe through European Socialism," in which he developed the idea that only under Adolf Hitler's guidance Europe would be freed from plutocracy, bolshevism, and Judaism. In the preface, the author told that the book was written for the most part "in air-raid shelters and under the bombing attacks of Anglo-American terror fliers." Werner Daitz, *Wiedergeburt Europas durch europäischen Sozialismus. Europa-Charta* (Amsterdam, De Amsterdamsche Keurkamer [1944], 160 pp.).

existence, degenerated into oddness and self-exclusion, will not be able to stand before European responsibility. In the same sense, a solution of the Jewish question for the whole of Europe is needed.[279]

But there was nothing to argue about.

The thing to do today is to overcome the mental and physical principles of the last two millennia, to revolutionize the European continent as a Teutonic-German continent and to strengthen and complete it as the bulwark of the new idea of national socialism.[280]

XXIV

SCHOLARLY BACKING FOR THE ASSAULT ON THE EASTERN SPACE

The blitz advance into the "Eastern space" after June 22, 1941, opened before the German people new vistas of a truly global nature.... "Unusual distances [are to be covered] which cannot by any means be compared with Middle-European concepts," a Party publication declared.[281]

When this war began, it appeared to many Germans in essence, to begin with, as a struggle for the Greater-German order. But already one year later, after the die in Northern Europe had been cast and the West succumbed to German arms, Europe came up before us as the great obligation. The struggle for the self-affirmation of this continent against powers and ideologies alien in space (raumfremde) became the great watchword. Now, a year later, the task has expanded still more.[282]

Indeed, the tempo and the possibilities had become breath-taking:

Already on August 1, 1941, on which Galicia, the country around Lemberg, was included in the Government General and, consequently, in the Reich, the center of Northern Germany, from the state point of view, was in Posen [Poznań]. For this capital of our Reichsgau Wartheland is approximately as distant from Hamburg as it is from Lemberg, from the North Sea as from the new Reich frontier toward Rumania. If, however, the imperial castle in Posen, from the state point of view was, or is, the center of Northern Germany—Frankfort on-the-Oder lies in West Germany.

What superlatives then could be adequate to the occasion when the German Wehrmacht stood at the Volga and in the Caucasus?

---

[279] Herre, *op. cit.*, p. 185.

[280] Friedrich Schmidt, *Das Reich als Aufgabe* (Berlin, Nordland-Verlag, 1940, 80 pp.).

[281] *Schulungsbrief der NSDAP*, 1943, 1/2, p. 13.

[282] Karlheinz Rüdiger, in: *Nationalsozialistische Monatshefte*, no. 137, August, 1941, pp. 648.

At that time, the allegory of the frog who wanted to become a bull entered no German mind.

We are entitled to leadership in the new spaces by virtue of our large number (we are the largest people of Europe proper), by virtue of our position (we are placed in the heart of our continent, we are the "country between countries" and the "country between seas"), by virtue of the creative ability of German blood (who counts and names the great Germans!) and, finally, by virtue of our greatest sacrifices for saving the European space from bolshevism in the East and plutocracy in the West.[283]

For those Germans who could not stand such fast riding there were at least three cues with which to silence their gnawing anxiety.

First: this acquisition of territory (Landnahme)—again one of those beautiful euphemisms—is no conquest; it is a return of the Germans to once familiar areas. Russia is essentially a geographical concept, not a historical one, a Munich university professor discovered.[284]

It is not true that space forcibly defines people. No, to a far greater extent man defines the space according to the laws of his blood which over and over again leads his thinking. That is evidenced by German development to everybody who wants to see it.... The living space of the German people, which our Führer Adolf Hitler opened with our Wehrmacht and defends against attackers alien to this space (raumfremd), largely corresponds to the struggling and working space of our forefathers, i.e., not as novices do we come into this space but in continuing an old mandate that has been handed over from generation to generation. Old home space is involved, and it is the task of the nearest future to secure it and to start feeling at home in it again.[285]

Second: the "Eastern person" readily will obey his new masters, provided the orders are supported by convincing acts:

Once the artificial stiffness of Communist conviction in the Eastern person (Ostmensch) is broken and he possibly is shaken up externally, the old insecurity comes up again and he who gives

[283] Dr. Friedrich Lange, *Deutsche Volksgeschichte. Deutsches Raumdenken* (Berlin, Eher, 1943, 128 pp.), pp. 5, 126.

[284] Professor Dr. Heinrich Bechtel in the book mentioned in footnote 271, p. 43: "We do know a geographical concept Russia but no historical one; therefore, there is no Russian economic history either, but only an economic history of the Eastern space."

[285] Lange, *op. cit.*, pp. 6-7.—A professor at the University of Leipzig and director of the Race and Ethnology Museum of that city, in a paper on the racial composition of the Western Slavs, i.e., the Poles and Czechs, arrived at the conclusion that their leaders, racially, always had been Germans: "Since leadership remained in Teutonic hands, there probably never was a real Slav period in the Eastern Teutonic space, that is [there never was] a time of actual Slav domination." Dr. Otto Reche, "Stärke und Herkunft des Anteils nordischer Rasse bei den West-Slawen," *Deutsche Ostforschung* I (Leipzig, Hirzel, 1942, 596 pp.), p. 89.

him a clear watchword and presses him into iron forms can dominate him.[286]

Third: the Soviet Union wanted to engulf Germany in war; even the date had been set and the Führer merely forestalled the attack by delivering the first blow. Everything had seemed so well arranged:

> . . . In the spring of 1941, the space seemed to have been staked off in which, from the point of view of economics and colonization (siedlungsmässig), in other words, on one hand from the point of view of state and greater space, on the other from the point of view of folkdom, we, our children and children's children could have been satisfied, to live strongly and freely and still to contribute to the further development of Europe. We Germans, our allies and friends needed only one thing for it: peace. And it was disturbed this time not only by England but from two sides and this way the internal European rearrangement has been widened into a new world war.

The new danger in the critical hour came from the East and in essence was only an old danger.

> Again and again, ever since the times when the Huns invaded the Reich of our Goths, real swarms of peoples rose from the wide planes near the Black Sea and the Caspian which invaded and sacked the fields and gardens of the civilized peoples of the middle. . . . Against this formlessness, against this quicksand and human flood of the steppes of the East again and again rose the Nordically defined Teutonic person. . . . While the Reich in 1941 defended Europe against the British "brigands of the sea," in the East the "brigands of the Steppes" under Stalin, the Jenghiz Khan of our century, had armed their 180 million to the utmost. The great assault on Germany and Europe was intended for August, 1941. To evade this new danger was impossible any more. Thus our Führer in a difficult decision—as he confessed, the most difficult of his life—in time ordered the counterthrust. It started in the midsummer night, on the ever-memorable June 22, 1941.[287]

The materialization of the midsummer night's dream had been well prepared in advance. "Might and culture define the fate of a people. But might comes from culture"[288] — this German maxim

---

[286] Professor Dr. Erik v. Sivers of the University of Posen (Poznań) in the book mentioned in footnote 271, p. 15.

[287] Lange, *op. cit.*, p. 109.

[288] From a speech by Ludwig Siebert, President of the Deutsche Akademie, in Munich on November 5, 1941. Cf. *Deutsche Kultur im Leben der Völker . . . Deutsche Akademie*, XVI (1941), 488.—"To possess a space ultimately, it must be won spiritually," Hanns Streit, *ibid.*, XVII (1942), p. 114. For this purpose among other institutions, a new university at Posen (Poznań) was founded, of which Streit was Gaudozentenführer, or Party whip. "The Reich University in Posen," he declared (p. 115), "together with the old eastern universities in Königsberg and Breslau shall form a consolidated Eastwall of German spirit which forever watchfully prevents any Slav inroads." Streit in his article (p. 117) announced the founding at the Posen University of an "Institute for the Study of the History and Language of Jewry" but nothing has become known of its activities, if any.

applied to the eastern phase of the Hitler adventure as well. In July, 1941, with this new development in view, the theoretical Party organ, though always 'exacting in its totalitarian demands, had nothing but praise for the efforts of the German scholars:

> German scholarship, it can be justly stated, successfully placed itself at the service of the tasks of the present. It not only actively participated in the spiritual rearrangement through activating numerous forces of German spiritual life but also has re-examined the great political and economic revolution which today concerns the whole world as to its historical and traditional foundations and presented the new evaluations resulting from the re-examination.[289]

As to the "tasks of the present" there was no dissenting voice: ". . . The Eastern territories occupied in 1941-42, as far as non-cognate peoples are concerned, are territories for the economic utilization by Germany and by the European greater-space economy," [290] and enough scholars had been trained betimes for the tasks ahead. Let us mention just a few names by way of illustration. Dr. Werner Essen in 1938 had published a book on Northeastern Europe as a greater area.[291] In 1941, the same Essen appeared as Director of the Space Department (Leiter der Abteilung II Raum) in the Reich Commissariat Ostland in Riga. Dr. Erwin Koschmieder, professor of Slavonics at the University of Munich and head of the Department for German Eastern Relations (Abteilung für deutsche Ostbeziehungen) of the Deutsche Akademie, in 1942 was engaged in compiling handbooks "for every German who works in the East." [292] Koschmieder had started his academic career at the University of Breslau, then for a number of years, well into the Hitler era, had changed into a patriotic Pole and become professor in Poland, and finally had gone back to serve National Socialist Germany as best he could.

And now a third example. The Reich Commissar for the Solidification of German Folkdom, that is Heinrich Himmler (see p. 121), was concerned not merely with the "German heartland" appropriated

---

[289] *Nationalsozialistische Monatshefte*, Juli, 1941.—The official editor of the central German university catalogue, Professor Dr. M[ax] Clara of the University of Leipzig, in his prefatory note to the 1941/42 edition stated: "In the last peace years many a wrong judgment was expressed about scholarly work and the carriers of this work. It was overlooked that not to a small extent the self-denying, quiet but arduous work of the universities had created the foundations which, on their part, made possible the materialization of the four years' plan, the harnessing of the question of raw materials, the rearmament of the Wehrmacht, etc.; today we can proudly state that scholarship contributed its share to the success of the Führer's great plans. . . ." Cf. *Deutsches Hochschulverzeichnis, 120. Ausgabe, 1941/1942* (Leipzig, 1942, 345 pp.), p. IV.

[290] Professor Dr. Karl Theisinger of the University of Frankfort on-the-Main, in the book mentioned in footnote 271, p. 108.

[291] Dr. Werner Essen, *Nordosteuropa, Völker und Staaten einer Grosslandschaft* (Leipzig, Teubner, 1938, 54 pp.)

[292] *Deutsche Kultur im Leben der Völker . . . Deutsche Akademie*, XVII, 2 (1942), 338.

in western Poland. He did not even limit himself to extensive colonizing plans in 'the Government General;[293] he had under under him a
"Main Department: Planning and Soil" which, from its headquarters in Berlin-Dahlem, inquired into the colonization opportunities in the territories recently snatched from the Soviets. It is
no surprise to find the confidential "exploratory surveys" of this "Main
Department" [294] excellently executed and provided with hundreds of
first-class special maps; for the man in charge was Dr. Franz Doubek,
the foremost German expert on ethnic boundaries in the East. A
native of Graz, Austria, he for a time was instructor in German
philology at the University of Vilna, Poland, and then was picked
up by research institutions in the Reich; on the eve of the war he
was a permanent contributor to the splendid scholarly · periodical on
Baltic-Scandinavian problems *Jomsburg* which, it turns out, was one
of the many enterprises of Goebbels' ministry.

While Doubek's exploratory surveys intended "to give the peruser
quick and preliminary information about the settling space in question" remaining, however, within the realm of facts, Himmler himself
proclaimed:

> It is our task not to Germanize the East in the old sense, i.e.,
> to impart to people dwelling there German language and German
> laws but to see to it that in the East dwell solely people of real
> German, Teutonic blood.[295]

With this aim in view, a memorandum by the Labor Research
Institute of the German Labor Front (Arbeitswissenschaftliches Institut der Deutschen Arbeitsfront) went much farther than Doubek's
"Main Department." In dead earnestness, the memorandum discussed
the number of German settlers who would be able to go to the East
each year and then said in so many words:

> Within approximately a hundred years the territory up to the
> Urals would be compactly settled by Germans in the density of
> present-day Soviet settlement—insofar as one bases one's estimates
> on the current German birth-rate and insofar as it will be con-
> sidered at all politically expedient 'to push back the former Soviet

---

[293] Cf. p. 180 sq.

[294] Der Reichskommissar für die Festigung deutschen Volkstums. Stabshauptamt. Hauptabteilung Planung und Boden. Nur für den Dienstgebrauch. *Vorläufige Angaben über West-
litauen. Berichtsstand: April 1942* (Berlin-Dahlem, Podbielski-Allee 25/27, 23 pp., 36 maps).—
The Yivo also possesses memoranda of the "Main Office" on the Crimea, White Russia,
and the Białystok district. All of them were prepared by Doubek with the assistance of Dr.
H. Kabermann.

[295] *Sicherung Europas.* Erarbeitung und Herausgabe: Der Reichsführer SS, SS-Hauptamt.
Schriften für die weltanschauliche Schulung der Ordnungspolizei, Jahrgang 1943, Heft 1 und 3
(Berlin, 1943, 86 pp.), p. 86.

population to the territories east of the Urals, which are no less fertile and rich in treasures of the soil than the European part of the USSR.[296]

Obviously, the alternative to "pushing back" was the outright extinction of "the former Soviet population."

XXV

PREPARING FOR THE EXTINCTION OF THE JEWS

A considerable part of the mission that history had entrusted to the German folk, we now know, was the utter extermination of the Jews on the territories under their domination, which in 1941-42, for all intents and purposes, meant the whole of continental Europe. The grandiose scheme developed gradually and took more definite shape with each successive Nazi victory. To recapitulate the events, the Nuremberg Laws of September 15, 1935, marked the end of a period, in which the Jews were promised a safe, if restricted, life of their own (Eigenleben). The indifference of the world permitted the program of forced emigration of the Jews from Germany, and at the time the Greater German Reich had become a reality through the annexation of Austria and the Sudeten area, this program had been perfected into compulsory emigration without any property. In discussing the population movements in Europe caused by recent developments, Haushofer's *Zeitschrift* in 1941 used this "scientific" language:

> Somehow, as far as their deportation is concerned, the cleansing actions regarding the Jews, too, belong in this context... On the whole, about 400,000 Jews left the Reich borders and will not see Germany any more. Thank God, we have eliminated those foreign bodies.... In days to come the Germans will not be any more a people for others[297] but will all serve the greatness and eternity of the Reich.[298]

The outbreak of war brought with it further reprisals against the Jews in the Reich. On the newly occupied Polish territories, they

---

[296] Geheim! *Die Durchdringung des Ostens in Rohstoff und Landwirtschaft.* Herausgeber: Arbeitswissenschaftliches Institut der Deutschen Arbeitsfront (Berlin, Dezember, 1941, 32 pp.). The copies were numbered; the copy in the possession of the Yivo bears the number 231.

[297] The expression was borrowed from the book by Dr. E. Quentin, *Die Deutschen als Volk für andere,* 2. Auflage (Leipzig, Weicher, 1938, 192 pp.), where the contributions of German immigrants to the civilization of many countries were extolled.

[298] Alfred Thoss, Sturmbannführer SS, "Die Umsiedlungen und Optionen im Rahmen der Neuordnung Europas," *Zeitschrift für Geopolitik,* XVIII (March, 1941), 125-136. On the attempts of satellite Slovakia to "evacuate the Jews on a large scale" this disciple of Haushofer's commented: "In the summer of 1940, one could see on the Danube many ships occupied by Jews eager to emigrate [*sic*], often comprising four hundred and more persons. They chiefly came from Slovakia and currently on the Danube were left to themselves; several such ships did not have even then permission to leave the Danube estuary."

were "marked as aliens" by the introduction of the Star of David,[299] but this measure was soon deemed insufficient and as the "Lublinization" idea for Austrian and German Jews turned out to be unrealistic, ghettoization came to the fore. "For the Germans, the Polish-Jewish problem was and is only a problem of organization," the author who was just quoted[300] declared, and organize they did indeed. But even in March, 1941, that is, at the time of the Frankfort Conference, this spokesman of the Propaganda Ministry announced, and perhaps what he said was true on his own level: "What shape the fate of the Jews in Warsaw and in the Government General as a whole is going to assume in the more remote future, we don't know."[301] Meanwhile, the German army had reached the Atlantic from the Arctic to the Pyrenees and had got hold of the Jews in the western countries as well. Finally, when "the greatest hour of all," as Haushofer termed it, had struck and the Eastern Space was included in the sphere of German "organization," the time for the "radical solution" had come. In the Reich proper, it too had been prepared by endless restrictions and reprisals accompanied by screaming denunciations of Jewish aggressiveness.

But if there is as yet no conclusive proof that a definite plan about murdering all Jews had been adopted before 1941, there is certainly sufficient evidence that the idea had been both contemplated and proclaimed while Europe was still at peace, well in advance of Hitler's prophecy. At least one pronouncement to this effect was made by an Austrian Nazi intellectual even before the Anschluss in unmistakable, if involved language; note his taking up the cue of the war's being forced upon Germany—by the Jews, of course:

> [Should the Jews start a new world conflagration, they] should not forget: he who approaches the hard things which they [the Jews] have thus created for themselves this way, out of moral and pure necessity of self-preservation and out of the feeling of responsibility towards Germany and the fate of Europe and solely from this point of view does what is to be done and not one hairsbreadth more or less—he can pass the test of his conscience and of history. The only thing is that no mote of inferior instincts should blemish the severe action. Let it be hard, clean, polished like the sword and the duty to undertake this action. Thus the

---

[299] *Die Judenfrage,* August 1, 1940.   [300] "Dr. J. L." = Dr. Johann von Leers?

[301] *Die Judenfrage,* March 10, 1941, p. 35. On September 10, 1941, Dr. A. Dresler in *Die Judenfrage,* giving the number of the Jews in the Government General on July 1, 1940, as one million seven hundred thousand, declared: "It has remained for the National Socialist state leadership presently to carry to a final settlement, for the benefit of the Polish nation, the Jewish question which had remained unsolved under the Polish kings." This was said in a review of a German translation of a Polish anti-Semitic tract of 1618.

account will be settled here on earth and no blot falls on the right cause.[302]

But since January 30, 1939, the day Hitler had uttered his threat in a most solemn Reichstag speech, the theme about the forthcoming annihilation of the Jewish race became fashionable in Nazi circles. In March, 1939, in anticipation of the war which was to be launched soon, a prominent staff member of the Institut zum Studium der Judenfrage declared:

> If the signs do not deceive, the solution of the Jewish question in the eastern space which is coming along will result in the necessity of solving the world Jewish question.[303]

On September 1, 1939, Hitler repeated his threat before the Reichstag.

Immediately after the invasion of Poland, Dr. E. Taubert of Goebbels' ministry—the man who introduced himself as the wire-puller behind the scene of the Anti-Comintern—conceived the idea of a colossal film that would once and for all unmask "The Eternal Jew." [304] From Jewish sources we know of the recklessness with which the Nazis forced the Jews in the ghettos to pose for their cameramen; they even went so far as to distribute food among the hungry people, only to grab it away again as soon as the filming was over. The picture was ready for presentation in November, 1940, and on November 28 a special issue of *Die Judenfrage* devoted to the film was issued. Dr. L. F. Gengler summarized the content of the picture:

> . . . the savage-looking celebration in the synagogue, where during the action and the service the Jews in the rear continue their haggling business because their God loves haggling.... [Toward the end] we hear the Reichstag speech of 1939 in which the forthcoming war is named as the last Jewish attempt at inciting the nations and as its result the *"annihilation of the Jewish people in Europe"* [305] is announced. True, a world incited by the Jew shrieked at that time; today, the events have shown that the materialization of the Führer's word is near.

On January 30, 1941, Hitler again announced in the Berlin Sportspalast:

---

[302] Franz Schattenfroh, *Wille und Rasse*. 3. Auflage (Berlin, Stubenrauch, 1943, 444 pp.), p. 370. Preface to the first edition dated March, 1938.

[303] Hans Georg Trurnit, in: *Mitteilungen über die Judenfrage*, March 21, 1939.

[304] This, "Der ewige Jude," was the name of the picture.—An exhibition under the same name, shown in several cities, was prepared by the famous German historian of journalism, Professor Dr. Karl d'Ester of the University of Munich. Cf. *Deutscher Wissenschaftlicher Dienst*, no. 69, December 8, 1941, p. 8. The exhibition was first shown in December, 1937, in Munich.

[305] Italics in original.

And I should not like to forget the hint which I already made once on September 1, 1939, in the German Reichstag, namely, the hint that should the other world be thrown by Jewry into a general war, the entire Jewry would have finished playing its part in Europe. Let them laugh at this even today just as they laughed at my prophecies before. The coming months and years will prove that here, too, I saw correctly.[306]

From then on, as the actual annihilation set in, the accompaniment of verbal threats became more and more audible. A leading article in the *Judenfrage* of October 1, 1941,[307] closed with a repetition of Hitler's prophecy of January, 1939, which was both italicized and underscored.

It is in the light of these pronouncements "from authoritative lips," as Seifert had put it, that the realities behind the Frankfort Conference must be evaluated and the question of premeditation in the mass murder of the Jewish people decided upon before direct evidence is discovered.

XXVI

ANTI-JEWISH RESEARCH INSTITUTIONS ON GERMAN MODELS IN ITALY, FRANCE, LITHUANIA, CROATIA, HUNGARY, AND DENMARK

We may interrupt here for a moment to examine further Germany's part in enlightening and prodding the satellite and subjugated countries as to the essentials of the "Jewish question." It has been shown already (pp. 116-119) what German scholarship had contributed directly and how highly the "worthy representatives of many European countries" at the Frankfort Conference had spoken of Germany's policies. There were, however, two more fields in which the influence of Germany made itself felt. As those countries became more and more tied to Germany, the screw of anti-Jewish legislation and administrative practice was turned more and more tightly. Moreover, anti-Jewish research work on the spot was strongly stimulated by German models.

As far as the first aspect is concerned, we shall quote from the highly scholarly publication, *Europa*, published by the German Insti-

---

[306] Prominently displayed on the front page of *Die Judenfrage*, February 10, 1941.

[307] Signed *Gö*, probably G. Löffler.

In discussing the premeditation of the German rulers in the extermination of the Jewish people, we should not overlook the following statement by Professor Dr. Wilhelm Ziegler in *Grossdeutschlands Kampf*, 1941 (see footnote 190) on Hore-Belisha: "Through him speaks the typical blinded optimism of his race that walks with open eyes into the yawning abyss (aus ihm spricht der typische verblendete Optimismus seiner Rasse, die mit offenen Augen in den gähnenden Abgrund wandelt)."

tute for Research in Foreign Affairs.[308] Ribbentrop himself had put the official stamp on this cooperative project of Axis political science which, according to the editorial note, was in essence concluded in the spring of 1942.

The authors referred to a semi-official Rumanian memorandum on rural sociology and then went on:

> The Rumanian memorandum just quoted contains a sentence in another passage: "The example of Adolf Hitler's totalitarian National Socialist state was the best spur for the Rumanian people to free itself from the yoke of Western Jewry and from freemasonry supported by it and again to turn to its original convictions by the help of which it was able to overcome even the hardest obstacles in the past." This applies not only to the Rumanian people; today it applies almost to the whole European continent: Europe is about to lock out *Jewry and freemasonry* totally from its national life. The fundamental cultural significance of this fact does not need much arguing. Europe has set out to recognize and to solve the Jewish question as a question of common European fate. Today there can be no more doubt that there is an inner connection between the common front of the peoples of Europe against Jewry and the spontaneous comradeship of arms of almost the whole continent in the struggle against bolshevism. In bolshevism Jewry has tried to secure its European vanguard. The settlement of Europe's account with bolshevism is therefore simultaneously the closing act of the total European solution of the Jewish problem.
>
> The political measures of the European countries against the Jews make it clear that the legislator's pen is directed not by blind racial hatred, but by sober considerations about population, economy, and of course also about race and character.

A survey of particular countries followed:

> . . . *Hungary* . . . owing to the purposeful policy of her government has already proceeded so far as to prohibit in principle marriages between Jews and Aryans (August 8, 1941).
>
> *Rumania,* to be sure, has not made up her mind either to adopt a pure racial concept of the Jew but in a series started on August 9, 1940, and today amounting to many more than fifty laws and

---

[308] Deutsches Institut für Aussenpolitische Forschung, Her., *Europa. Handbuch der politischen, wissenschaftlichen und kulturellen Entwicklung des neuen Europa.* Mit einem Geleitwort von Joachim von Ribbentrop, Reichsminister des Auswärtigen. 2. Auflage (Leipzig, Helingsche Verlagsanstalt, 1943, 320+80 pp., 4°). The advertisement on the book, defined as a "handbook of the political, economic, and cultural development of the new Europe," in *Börsenblatt für den Deutschen Buchhandel,* 110 (1943), no. 76, read in part: "The first edition (first to twelfth thousand) has been completely exhausted through subscription (advertisement in the *Börsenblatt,* October 7, 1941) and other advance orders. The second edition (thirteenth to twenty-fourth thousand) serves export purposes exclusively. Only orders for foreign currency can from now on be executed."

directives has practically deprived Jewry of the possibility of further expansion.[309]

There is no need to continue the survey with the same completeness, since we may assume as known corresponding measures in *Bulgaria, Croatia,* and *Slovakia.* In this respect, *Slovakia* proceeded particularly energetically with her Jew-code of September 10, 1941.

In *Denmark, Holland,* and *Belgium* the anti-Semitic currents are on the increase.

France, since October 3, 1940, when the first statute against the Jews was promulgated, has from month to month intensified her policy against Jewry, both in the definition of the Jew and in the economic defense measures. Simultaneously there appear in Vichy the *Documents Maçonniques* which try to prepare a similar policy against French freemasonry. If we add the *Axis Powers* whose anti-Jewish policy needs no discussion here, the front against Jewry in Europe is, apart from a few minor gaps, already closed today.[310]

Care was taken, however, to avoid the impression that this development had taken place under German pressure. If at all, Germany influenced other countries only by her example; contrary to British practice, she never imposed her ideas by force:

> In Europe this war did not supplant one relation of cultural domination by a new one, but formally took the cultural life of the peoples out of the struggles for power and domination and reestablished it in its natural—spatial, racial, and historical—order of relation. This *natural* field of cultural unfolding differs from the *artificial* one in that the influences of one nation upon the other do not assume the form of *propaganda,* but result in the fertilization of one's own.[311]

The same independence of the countries dominated by Germany was alleged also with respect to the anti-Jewish research institutions which came into existence there. Whether anybody, in or outside Germany, believed in these pretenses is another matter. Even if nothing else had been known, the wording of the announcements about those institutions would have betrayed their origin.

Let us summarize the scattered information about them. In order not to revert to the subject, we shall present all data available, which extend to the end of 1944.

---

[309] A small book on Rumania published a year later was able to announce considerable progress: "The decisive blow . . . was dealt by the Antonescu government which proceeded to apply strong measures, the only ones that promised success. Collecting the Jews in one Jewish pool (Transnistria) serves to purify the country from Jewish interspersion, and radical measures broke their economic preponderance. The promulgation of racial laws which correspond to the Nuremberg Laws on the Jews align Rumania with the front of modern European anti-Semitism." Cf. Dr. Alfred Malaschowsky, *Rumänien* (Berlin, Junker und Dünnhaupt, 1943, 95 pp.), p. 44.

[310] *Europa,* pp. 154-155.

[311] *Ibid.,* p. 153. Italics in original.

ITALY

A semi-monthly *La Difesa della Razza* (The Defence of the Race) had been established in Rome as early as August, 1938.

In the beginning of 1942, "Study Centers for the Jew-Problem" were founded in Milan and Florence, "which are under the supervision of the Italian Minister of Popular Culture and are to spread enlightenment in the anti-Jewish sense." [312]

On June 29, 1942, an "Office for Studying the Jewish Question" was founded in Trieste under the supervision of the Racial Office of the Ministry of Education; Ettore Martinoli was put in charge. [313]

In the first half of 1943, an "Institute to Study the Jewish Question," under the directorship of Dr. Mario Tirelli, was opened at Bologna. Mastroianni, a staff member of the Institute at that time in the army, published a documentary work on the responsibility of world Jewry for the war, under the title: "Mars and Israel. What Do We Fight for?" [314]

FRANCE

In the spring of 1941, the founding of a society for the study of the Jewish problem under the name of Centre d'Action et Documentation was reported. "Its aim is to put information on the Jewish and freemason question at the disposal of all organizations, newspapers, departments, and trade unions. The society already has published pamphlets and educational treatises." [315] At a later date, the name of the director of the Centre was given as [Henri] Coston. [316]

On May 11, 1941, the opening session of the Institut d'Études des Questions Juives (Institute for the Study of Jewish Questions) took place. Headed by C. Serpeille de Gobineau, it pledged allegiance to Marshal Pétain's order "to rejuvenate France." It proceeded from the theory that the Jewish problem was a racial problem and intended to study the following fields: legislation, press, scholarship, health,

---

[312] *Die Judenfrage*, March 15, 1942, p. 55.—The pamphlet *Gli Ebrei hanno voluto la guerra* (The Jews Wanted the War) (Firenze, Vallecchi, 1942, 45 pp.) seems to have emanated from the Florence Study Center. It contained the following contributions: A. Luchini, "The Sages of Zion"; G. C. A. Evola, "Western Civilization and the Jewish Mind"; M. Scaligero, "Judaism against Rome"; P. Pellicano, "The Essence of Jewry"; G. Preziosi, "Jewry Wanted this War."

[313] *Die Judenfrage*, July 15, 1942, p. 152; *Weltkampf*, II (1942), 314, where reference is made to *Regime Fascista*, no. 155, of June 30 and *Tevere*, no. 209, of July 1 [1942].

[314] *Die Judenfrage*, June 1, 1943, p. 189.

[315] *Die Judenfrage*, May 5, 1941, p. 71.

[316] *Europäischer Wissenschafts-Dienst*, III, 7 (July, 1943), 16.

industry, commerce, agriculture, propaganda (theater, moving pictures, radio).[317] On September 5, 1941, the Institut sponsored an exhibition "The Jew and France," which, among others, purported to show the Jewish origin of Marat and Gambetta.[318] "The said Institut," we are informed at the same time, "propagates a new Europe and combats treacherous England which has been identified as the stronghold of international, anti-European Jewry."[319] In spite of this record, a remodeling of the Institut was deemed advisable. Some time in the spring of 1943, the Institut d'Études des Questions Juives et Ethno-Raciales (Institute to Study Jewish and Ethno-Racial Questions) was opened in Paris, 21 rue la Boëtie. "For the first time, French scholarship and research with state support places itself at the service of the anti-Jewish struggle. The Institut was founded already two years ago but at that time it did lack adequate personnel. It is only through the efforts of the well-known race student Dr. Georges Montandon... The 1943 catalogue ... envisages seven courses ... [to be given by] Gérard Mauger, Armand Bernardini, Jean Héritier, Charles Laville, André Chaumet, Pierre Villemain. ... Educational writing and books [also will be prepared]."[320]

A bi-weekly *La Question Juive en France et dans le Monde* made is appearance in 1942.

By government decree of November 6, 1942, a chair in Jewish history was established at the Sorbonne and entrusted to Professor Henri Labroue.[321]

LITHUANIA

At the end of 1941, a "Studien-Büro/Studiju Biuras" was founded in Kaunas (renamed Kauen by the Germans) which at the end of 1942 was moved to Vilna. Until the end of 1943, it published at least three volumes of *Lietuviu Archivas* (Lithuanian Archives) and, in German, *Bulletin für die Erforschung des Bolschewismus und Judentums,* which came out as a rule every two weeks, intended apparently as copy for the German and neutral press.[322]

---

[317] *Die Judenfrage,* June 16, 1941, p. 107.

[318] *Ibid.,* September 10, 1941, p. 168.—The question of the origin of these two personalities seems to have been a matter of considerable concern; the *Archiv für Judenfragen* 2 (Berlin, 1943) carried an article about Gambetta's being a pure Aryan, which was duly registered by Eugen Engelhardt. *Jüdische Weltmachtpläne,* 2. ed. (Berlin, 1943), p. 21.— The Yivo archives possess over fifty original photographs of the exhibition: "Le Juif en France."

[319] *Die Judenfrage,* September 25, 1941, p. 190.—See also *Weltkampf* II (1942), 61.

[320] *Die Judenfrage,* May 1, 1943, p. 152.

[321] *Europäischer Wissenschafts-Dienst,* III, 7 (July, 1943), pp. 15-16.

[322] *Die Judenfrage,* November 1, 1943, p. 340.—The library of the Yivo possesses the

CROATIA

The opening in Zagreb of an Institute to Study Jewry, Free-masonry, and Bolshevism was announced in the fall of 1942.[323]

HUNGARY

"On January 1 [1943], an Institute for Research into the Jewish Question was opened.... [It tends to create] the foundations for a scientific study of the Jewish question in Hungary... moreover [it will develop] an educational and propaganda activity in the field.... The German model is the guide in the organizational structure of the institute.... [It intends] to establish and maintain . . . close relations with similar institutions . . . in the Greater German Reich, Italy, France, and elsewhere." Zoltán Bosnyák, a well-known anti-Semitic writer, was appointed director. In November, 1943, the German press carried an article by Bosnyák on his institution. However, its official inauguration by Ladislas Endre, State Secretary in the Ministry of Interior, took place as late as May 11, 1944. On May 20, 1944, the first issue of the weekly *Harc* (Struggle) edited by Bosnyák for the institute, made its appearance.[324]

DENMARK

The Dansk Antijödisk Liga (Danish anti-Jewish League), led by Aage H. Andersen, in 1944 changed its name into Dansk Liga til Fremme af Racebevidstheden (Danish League for the Furtherance of Race Consciousness).[325]

The *Weltkampf* of the Frankfort Institut, which continued until the end of 1944, considered itself the organ of this international anti-Jewish research. It carefully listed anti-Jewish publications in all languages and to some of the foreign writers considered particularly competent, like Georges Montandon, Jean Héritier, Gueydan de Roussel, Jean Drault, Jacques Meurgey, etc., it opened its own columns.

following issues of the *Bulletin*: 29 (Kauen, August 25, 1942), 30-32, 33 (Vilna, December 21, 1942), 34-44, 46-49, 51-54 (the latest issue is dated Vilna, February 28, 1944).
[323] *Die Judenfrage*, October 15, 1942, p. 223.
[324] *Die Judenfrage*, January 15, 1943, p. 24, *Europäischer Wissenschafts-Dienst* 3, 11 (November, 1943), pp. 10-14; *Weltkampf*, IV (1944), 209.—The Yivo library possesses some issues of *Harc*.
[325] *Welt-Dienst*, XI, 15/16 (August, 1944), 13.

XXVII

THE EXTINCTION OF THE JEWS IN THE EASTERN TERRITORIES BEGINS. SCHOLARLY THEORIES REAPPEARING IN WEHRMACHT ORDERS

The assumption is sometimes advanced that in spite of the threats dealt with in the previous chapters, the extermination of the Jews actually was ordered by the Germans in reply to the entry of the United States into the war. This assumption is unfounded. The new course regarding the Jews must have been the object of deliberations at the same time the attack upon the Soviet Union was contemplated. At any rate, when the columns of the Wehrmacht blasted into the "Eastern Space," in June 22, 1941, the hour of the Jews had struck, too. "It would be a mistake to overlook the intensification of Germany's anti-Jewish attitude brought about by the events of the last weeks," a Danish language newsletter published in Berlin informed its readers.[326] "Attitude" here meant action. On the basis of incontrovertible evidence which we are now going to present it can be said that the slaughter of Jews began in the "Eastern Space," i.e., in the Baltic countries, White Russia, and the Ukraine, as soon as the German armies moved in, i.e., in the summer of 1941, and that the "final solution" was premeditated before Pearl Harbor.

The Yivo possesses about a hundred secret original German documents pertaining to the extermination of the Jews in the Ostland; of course, they have been made available to the United States prosecutor at the Nuremberg trial. Though all of them may be published in the course of time, as their contents undoubtedly warrant, only a few can be quoted in the present context, still fewer can be reproduced in extenso. But they ought to be referred to in connection with some facts and accounts that have become known from other sources as they have a direct bearing on our subject. Particular attention should be paid to the language the official documents use and the reasons they adduce; "by their fruits you shall recognize them" may be safely said about the scholars who had prepared the ground.

During the first weeks of the blitz, Himmler's SS (Schutzstaffel, Elite Guard) and SD (Sicherheits-Dienst, police force) took the lead, supported by Lithuanian and Lettish "patriots," respectively,

---

[326] *Dansk Berliner Korrespondance*, Udgivet og redigeret af Hans Lützhöft, Dänisches Pressbüro, Berlin, no. 94, July 8, 1941, p. 8.

who thought their hour had come to re-establish their nations according to Nazi pattern.[327] A letter by a German soldier from this period deserves to be quoted extensively; it was reproduced in a booklet of letters from the front issued under the auspices and with a preface by Dr. Goebbels:

THE END OF JEWISH DOMINATION

Lance-corporal Heinrich Sachs in a signal corps in the East to Obergemeinschaftsleiter Friedrich, in Gross-Strehlitz:

Dear Party member Friedrich:

Through radio, newsreel, and newspapers you will have a small picture of the events in the East in word, picture, and lively description. But all these well-intentioned commentaries to a happening of unparalleled force fade as compared with the brutal reality.... A chapter in itself is the fact that presently the Jewish question is being solved with imposing thoroughness amid enthusiastic cheers of the native (einheimische) population. As the Führer put it in one of his speeches shortly before the outbreak of war: "Should Jewry succeed in inciting the European nations to a senseless war, this will mean the end of this race in Europe!" The Jew ought to have known that the Führer is accustomed to take his word seriously, and now he has to bear the consequences. They are inexorably hard but necessary if ultimately quiet and peace are to reign among nations.[328]

The verbatim quotation from the Führer's speech and the general adherence to the formulae we have met so many times ("the Jewish question is being solved with imposing thoroughness," "inexorably hard but necessary") may, to a mind not accustomed to regimentation, raise the question of authenticity. But this question is immaterial; the facts are depicted adequately and what counts is that the letter was intended by the editors to make the impression of authenticity. We are not surprised to find in another letter in the same booklet

---

[327] Both in Latvia and Lithuania, local volunteer detachments from the very beginning substantially supported the Germans in the extermination of the Jews. They proved so successful that the Germans began to employ them for the same purpose outside their own countries, as far away as Minsk (see pp. 152, 155) and the ghetto of Warsaw. One of Goebbels' organs, *Die Aktion, Kampfblatt für das neue Europa* 4 (September, 1943), 360, gave the following picture: "Pretty soon [after the invasion] the German administration started drawing up *Lettish protective detachments* (Schutzmannschaften). The crowd of volunteers was large. By preference, officers and soldiers of the former Latvian army applied. Thus it became possible to employ battalions of the protective detachments not only for safeguarding the country which had been pacified and freed of bands but also for actively fighting the bands in Lithuania, White Russia, and the Ukraine as well as in the Rear Army Area of the Northern front. The experience was good." A top secret ("Geheime Reichssache") report to Dr. Goebbels of September 17, 1942, now in the Yivo archives, speaks of "legions of about 10,000 to 30,000 men per [Baltic] state and corresponding protective detachments up to 60,000 men for internal security."

[328] Feldpostbriefe aus dem Osten. *Deutsche Soldaten sehen die Sowjet-Union,* Eingeleitet und herausgegeben von Wolfgang Diewerge (Berlin, Wilhelm Limpert [1941], 63 pp.), pp. 38, 45.

(p. 45) the sentence: "In murdering, burning, and slaughtering the Jew is a master indeed."

About the time this collection of letters was published, Goebbels' ministry issued a secret *Propaganda-Parole* requesting newspapermen not to use the terms "liquidation" and "to liquidate" in reports from the Eastern Space unless referring to actions of Soviet rulers.[329]

It will be noted that the letter from the front does not specify the SS and SD as the perpetrators of the deeds the writer praises, and in this it undoubtedly was correct. The SS and SD were simply, as in many other respects, the vanguard. There was no exaggeration in the boast of the official SS publication (see footnote 269) that the SD was "the infallible conscience of National Socialist Weltanschauung" and as such stood without a rival in the whole world "both as to lightning-quick striking power and exactness of scientific research"; in some cases, Wehrmacht members are said to have been shocked by what they saw; but as a whole, the Wehrmacht concurred. General Keitel personally on September 12, 1941, from the Führer's headquarters issued a directive concerning "Jews in the occupied eastern territories" which said in part:

> The fight against bolshevism demands in the first place also reckless and energetic action against the Jews, the main carriers of bolshevism.[330]

We therefore are not astonished to read at that time in *Die Judenfrage,* the organ of Ziegler's institute now renamed "Antisemitische Aktion":

> In the occupied parts of Russia . . . signs of a terrific settlement of accounts [with the Jews] appear.... The world will have to thank German mind and German courage for causing to perish forever the most extreme product of Jewish anti-mind (Ungeist) and hatred at the gates of Europe.[331]

Another ominous Wehrmacht directive now divulged was issued on October 10, 1941, by Field Marshall von Reichenau to the sixth army. The man, we shall recall, had been chosen by War Minister von Blomberg to represent the Ministry at the opening of Walter Frank's anti-Jewish institute. The way of reasoning in the document he issued is as significant as the order itself:

---

[329] Document in the possession of the Yivo.

[330] From the document marked: High Command of the Wehrmacht W. F. St./Abt. L (IV/Q), Nr. 02041/ geh.—The *geh.,* or *g.,* in all German documents published here meant "geheim (secret)."

[331] Issue of September 10, 1941.

Anl. 2 zu "Richtlinien für die militärische Sicherung und für die
Aufrechterhaltung der Ruhe und Ordnung im Ostland"
zu W Bfhu In Nr.705/41 geh.v.25.9.41
A u s z u g

Oberkommando der Wehrmacht   ...., den 12. 9. 1941.

W.F.St./Abt. L(IV/Qu)
Nr. 02041/41 geh.

Betr.: Juden in den neu besetzten Ostgebieten.

pp.

Der Kampf gegen den Bolschewismus verlangt ein rück-
sichtsloses und energisches Durchgreifen vor allem auch
gegen die Juden, die als Träger des Bolschewismus.

Es hat daher jegliche Zusammenarbeit der Wehrmacht
mit der jüdischen Bevölkerung, die offen oder versteckt
in ihrer Einstellung deutschfeindlich ist, und die Verwendung von einzelnen Juden zu irgend welchen bevorzug-
ten Hilfsdiensten für die Wehrmacht zu unterbleiben.
Ausweise, die den Juden ihre Verwendung für Zwecke der
Wehrmacht bestätigen, sind durch militärische Dienststellen keinesfalls auszustellen.

Hiervon ausgenommen ist lediglich die Verwendung
von Juden in besonders zusammengefaßten Arbeitskolonnen,
die nur unter deutscher Aufsicht einzusetzen sind.
pp.

      Der Chef des Oberkommandos der Wehrmacht

        gez. K e i t e l

Verteiler:

pp.

      Für die Richtigkeit des Auszuges:

           Hauptmann

There are still many obscure conceptions about the conduct of the military regarding the Bolshevist system.

The essential aim of the campaign against the Jewish Bolshevist system is the complete crushing of the power and extermination of the Asiatic influence in the European culture area.

In this way tasks originate also for the military which exceed the traditional one-sided conception of the soldier. In the Eastern Space the soldier is not only a fighter according to the rules of military art, but also a carrier of the inexorable folk-idea and the avenger of all bestialities committed against German and cognate (artverwandt) folkdom.

The soldier must therefore fully understand the necessity of hard but just expiation on the part of Jewish subhumanity. He further aims to nip in the bud revolts behind the front of the Wehrmacht which, according to experience, are always instigated by Jews....

The immediate duties of the soldiers then were defined as follows:

Apart from all political considerations of the future, the soldier has a twofold task to fulfill:

1. To destroy completely the Bolshevist heresy, the Soviet state and its army.

2. To exterminate mercilessly the malice and cruelty of alien species (artfremd) and thus to secure the life of the German Wehrmacht in Russia.

Only in this way will we be equal to the historical task to free the German people once and for all from the Asiatic Jewish danger.[332]

A covering letter dated November 13, 1941, and bearing the stamp "Secret" indicated that the directive had been approved by the Führer himself and ordered to be brought to the attention of other commanders in the field.

Coincidental with the issuance of this document, the wearing of the Star of David was made compulsory for all Jews within the Reich and a widely publicized article by Goebbels on November 16 under the headline: "The Jews Are Guilty" provided the following reasons for the enforcement of the measure:

In this historical contest each Jew is our enemy, regardless of whether he vegetates in a Polish ghetto or still leads a parasitic life in Berlin or in Hamburg, or whether he blows the war trumpet in New York or Washington. All Jews by virtue of their birth and race belong to an international conspiracy against National

---

[332] Reproduced in facsimile in the Russian collection Документы обвиняют [Documenty obvinyayut, "The Documents Accuse"], vol. I ([Moscow], 1943, 253 pp.), pp. 92-93.

Socialist Germany. They wish her defeat and do whatever in their power to assist in this.... Each German soldier who falls in this war goes to the debt account of the Jews. He is on their conscience and they, therefore, must pay for it.[333]

XXVIII

THE EXTINCTION PROCEDURE UNTIL THE END OF 1941. THE CLASH BETWEEN ECONOMIC INTEREST AND POLITICAL GOALS

As the Wehrmacht cut deep into the Soviet Union and the unstable demarcation line of 1939 remained far behind the battle fronts, a civil administration of the occupied territories was established. It was entrusted to the Ministerium für die besetzten Ostgebiete (Ministry for the Occupied Eastern Territories) headed by Rosenberg, who here saw the coronation of his life work. Under Rosenberg, the conquered areas ultimately were divided into Reichskommissariat Ostland, with Reich Commissar Hinrich Lohse, and Reichskommissariat Ukraine, with Reich Commissar Erich Koch. The facts we possess mainly refer to the Ostland, i.e., the northern part of Rosenberg's realm.

The first steps of the civil administration seemed rather moderate if measured by Nazi standards. An official panegyrist told about the first trip of Reich Commissar Lohse through his dominations[334] that over 5,000 Jews were found in so small a town as Slutsk. Of Vilna one learns that there were "many" Jews and of Kaunas we are told that on August 15 the establishment of the ghetto in the suburb of Viliampole was completed. "The laws and customs of their own, under which Jewry lives there [in the ghettos], do not interest us," we are advised in language strikingly resembling that which had been used to describe the German attitude in the Government General. "To us it is sufficient that they have forever finished their rôle in the Ostland."

The more lenient style of warfare—and lenient it was if compared with outright killing—also is exemplified by the outlines for press censorship in the Occupied Eastern Territories, issued by Rosenberg's ministry:

[No. 14]. In historical essays, frequently the invasion of Asiatic

---

[333] *Die Judenfrage*, January 1, 1943, p. 15.

[334] E. Frotscher, *Ostland kehrt nach Europa zurück. Notizen von einer Reise des Reichskommissars Hinrich Lohse durch Litauen und Weissruthenien* (Riga, 1941, 42 pp.), pp. 14, 23.

hordes is spoken of to designate the Hun and Mongol storms in the East. Such a general designation is to be avoided.

[No. 80]. Topics on England's economic exploitation policies, on one hand, and Germany's correct behavior are recommended. It should, however, be borne in mind that English methods in Estonia, Latvia, and Lithuania were so clever [sic] that these peoples hardly noticed their dependence on England. It is therefore not practicable to speak of "merciless exploitation."

[No. 178] . . . Instead of Peter the Great, the name Peter I is preferable.

[No. 357]. Historical essays on the impact of German romanticism and enlightenment upon the growth of national feeling among the Eastern peoples are undesirable....

[No. 363]. The designation Russia for the Moscow-dominated area is to be avoided even in historical discussion....

[No. 425]. Subhumanity (Untermenschentum). This term, adequate for the Bolshevist wire-pullers, the Jewish officials, and the bandit leaders, is to be avoided with reference to the population of the Soviet Union and the Occupied Eastern Territories as well as to the Soviet soldiers.

Some passages devoted completely to Jews show that only by accident "Jewish officials" were singled out in the preceding paragraph. There was to the authors of the instructions no difference between Jew and Jew.

[No. 103]. In articles on the enemy powers the fraternization between the Jewish-plutocratic and the Jewish-Bolshevist world must be emphasized. This world has only one aim, the establishment of world Jewish domination, and it hates everything that blocks its way in the attainment of its aim.

[No. 132] . . . Articles on the destructive rôle of the Jews in the history of the East are desirable.

[No. 183]. Of course, constant reference is to be made to the Jews as alien exploiters and oppressors of the peoples of the Soviet Union. Naturally, it is not allowed to take into consideration in any form the Bolshevist [sic] concept of the Jew as a member of an ethnic minority (nationale Minderheit). Reference should be made particularly to the rôle of international Jewry as instigators of wars, war profiteers, etc., who incited to war for the purpose of profiteering and dominating the world. As often as feasible, one should point to the kinship between Jews and leading non-Jewish Bolshevists.[335]

---

335 Geheim! *Richtlinien für die Pressezensur in den besetzten Ostgebieten.* Herausgeber: Pressechef für die besetzten Ostgebiete (([Riga], n. d., 175 pp.). From the preface: "The contents of this publication are a state secret." The copy in the possession of the Yivo bears the number 044. A later publication of this kind, dated Berlin, May 11, 1942, contained the following instruction: "It is requested not to introduce the *Rasse* concept (*Rasse* struggle, *Rasse* treachery, etc.) in connection with the Eastern Asiatic war."

It would be erroneous, however, to think of the civil administration under Rosenberg's aegis as representing a fundamentally different policy with regard to the Jews in the eastern territories the German army had overrun. Just as Keitel and Reichenau were at one with Himmler, so were Rosenberg and his staff. On November 27, 1941, Regierungsrat [Karl Friedrich] Trampedach, a high official of Rosenberg's civil government, prepared a memorandum concerning the expansion of the Department II-a (Political Department) of the Reich Commissariat Ostland. "Division 8: Jewry," Trampedach informed, with Ordensjunker [Günther] Maskow in charge, dealt with the following subjects: (a) Definition and seizure;[336] (b) Hybrids; (c) Interim treatment; (d) Participation in forced labor; (e) Final solution. What "final solution" meant in this context is perfectly clear. Thus, although we shall for some time encounter directives emanating from the civil government which aimed at mitigating the zeal of Himmler's élite army, the statement is warranted that the disagreements were only as to procedure; the aim was the same.

In order rightly to evaluate the relationship between the three carriers of power, Wehrmacht, SS and SD, and civil administration, we must bear in mind that the SS and SD still were very much present. In name they had been subordinated, after the creation of the civil government, to the Reich Commissar Ostland and, on the lower levels, to the three Commissars General in Riga, Kaunas, and Minsk. But actually, Himmler's agency remained omnipotent and was pressing for complete *Ausmerze* of the Jews while it did its best through partial and casual "actions." In one case, in the city of Liepaja, the "action" was so outrageous that the civil authorities interfered. The Himmlerites promptly complained to Berlin, and on October 31, 1941, the Ministry for the Occupied Eastern Territories requested Reich Commissar Lohse to report immediately whether he actually had prohibited "executions of Jews in Libau [the German name of Liepaja]." This inquiry was signed by Dr. [Georg] Leibbrandt, the man who, in Rosenberg's immediate entourage, had been active for many years in writing, editing, and stimulating anti-Jewish research.[337]

The original of this letter is in the possession of the Yivo, as is the draft of the reply, dated November 15, 1941. It was written by Regierungsrat Trampedach but corrected and initialed by

---

[336] The German term used is *Erfassung*, which can mean both 'seizure' and 'accounting for'.—The document (no. 296/41 g.) is in possession of the Yivo.

[337] The letter bears the number 2591/41.

Der Reichsminister
für die besetzten Ostgebiete

Berlin W 35, den   31. Oktober 1941
Rauchstraße 17/18
Fernsprecher: 21 95 13 und 39 50 46
Drahtanschrift: Reichsministerost

Nr. I / 2591 /41
Es wird gebeten, dieses Geschäftszeichen und den
Gegenstand bei weiterer Schreiben anzugeben.

An den
Reichskommissar Ostland

in R i g a
Hermann Göring Str. 26

      Von seiten des Reichs- und Sicherheitshaupt-
amtes wird Beschwerde darüber geführt, dass der Reichskommissar Ostland Judenexekutionen in Libau untersagt
habe. Ich ersuche in der betreffenden Angelegenheit
um umgehenden Bericht.

      Im Auftrag
      gez. Dr. Leibbrandt

Beglaubigt
Regierungsinspektor

Reich Commissar Lohse himself. The reference to the "brown file" in the last paragraph of the reply is not clear. From the Soviet publication "The Documents Accuse" [338] we know of the existence of a "green file," a set of secret advance directives issued by Goering in June, 1941, on the economic exploitation of the areas to be occupied in the East; apparently, an analogous secret document had been issued by Rosenberg to his subordinates. But while this particular remains to be investigated, the letter as a whole speaks a highly eloquent language:

Secret

The Minister for the Occupied Eastern Territories
Berlin.

Re: Executions of Jews.
I forbade the wild executions of Jews in Libau because in the form they were conducted they could not be justified.

Please inform me whether your inquiry of October 31 is to be understood as a directive in the sense that all Jews in the Ostland are to be liquidated? Is this to take place without regard for age and sex and economic considerations (for instance, those of the Wehrmacht for skilled workers in military establishments)? It goes without saying that cleaning the Ostland of Jews is an urgent problem; but its solution is to be brought into accord with the necessities of war economy.

Neither from the directives on the Jewish question contained in the "brown file" nor from other decrees could I to this time gather such an instruction.

Without, of course, any knowledge of this correspondence the local Wehrmacht commander in the Ostland, Braemer, had appealed to Reich Commissar Lohse. He did not take issue with anything the SS had committed or Keitel and Reichenau had ordered; most certainly, he would have subscribed to Lohse's statement: "It goes without saying that cleaning the Ostland of Jews is an urgent problem" as he, too, stressed the preponderant part of the Jewish population in anti-German propaganda, resistance, and sabotage in White Russia. But Braemer had responsibilities of a practical nature and he was satisfied that "the bringing in of [new] Jews" would interfere with the discharge of his duties. His letter, dated November 20, 1941, contained the following passage:

The bringing in (Antransport) of Jews, in my opinion, for the time being is quite impossible in view of the strained transporta-

[338] P. 10.

tion situation. The Central Army Group (Heeresgruppe Mitte) has asked me to stop the transports of Jews because the railroad is needed for increased supplies. I have forwarded this request to the chief of transportation. Moreover, the preparation of winter quarters, the bringing up of building material, glass, coal, etc., is so urgent in addition to other supply problems that transports of Jews ought to be postponed for this reason alone.[339]

Another reason that temporarily seemed to work in favor of part of the Jews was the necessity of saving a great number of skilled workers. As long as the theory was expounded, both in previous years and currently, it was said to be notorious that the Jews were parasites, unable and unwilling to adapt themselves to any useful work; the disciple of Haushofer's who reported on the Jews in Poland (p. 94) seemed to know only from hearsay that they showed some dexterity as tailors and cobblers. But on November 7, 1941, the Reich Commissar for the Ostland wired the following message to the District Commissar (Gebietskommissar) of the city of Vilna, where wholesale executions of Jews seized at random had been taking place:

> I request [you] to prevent by all means depriving the Wehrmacht of Jewish manpower that is irreplaceable for tasks of war economy.[340]

And on December 3 the Reich Commissar issued a general order to all his subordinates based on General Braemer's appeal:

> The Chief Commissar, Wehrmacht Commander Ostland, complains that the Wehrmacht by liquidation is being deprived of Jewish skilled workers in military establishments and repair shops, for whom there is at present no substitute.
>
> I urgently request [you] not to allow the liquidation of Jews who are employed by the Wehrmacht as skilled workers in military establishments and repair workshops and at present cannot be replaced by natives [Einheimische].... The training of native substitutes fit for skilled work is to be cared for speedily.[341]

No particular attention, however, was paid to reasons of this kind and, as new transports of Jews from the west continued to be dumped into the Ostland, the liquidation went on. The letter which follows shows that the Wehrmacht by no means was unanimous in opposing the annihilation even from the point of view of expediency.

[339] Letter of the Wehrmachtsbefehlshaber Ostland. 1 c 82/41 geh. H. Qu., November 30, 1941, to the Reich Commissar of the Ostland (document in the possession of the Yivo).

[340] The letter, in Trampedach's original handwriting, in the possession of the Yivo.

[341] The Reich Commissar in Riga to the Höhere SS und Polizeiführer in Riga and the District Commissars in Reval [Tallinn], Riga, Kauen [Kaunas], and Minsk, no. 220/41 g. (in the possession of the Yivo).

II a   Tgb.Nr.220/41 g.

Geheim

An
den Reichskommissar f.d.Ostland
- Höherer SS- und Polizeiführer-

in R i g a

die Herren Generalkommissare
in R e v a l
R i g a
K a u e n
M i n s k

Nachrichtlich an den Wehrmachtbefehlshaber Ostland

in R i g a

Der Chefintendant beim Wehrmachtbefehlshaber Ostland
beschwert sich darüber, dass der Wehrmacht in Rüstungsbetrieben
und Reparaturwerkstätten jüdische Facharbeiter durch Liquidation entzogen würden, die dort zur Zeit nicht zu ersetzen
sind.

Ich ersuche nachdrücklichst die Liquidation von Juden zu
verhindern, die in Rüstungsbetrieben und Reparaturwerkstätten der Wehrmacht als Fachkräfte tätig und zur Zeit durch
Einheimische nicht zu ersetzen sind. Das Einvernehmen darüber,
wer zu den unersetzlichen jüdischen Arbeitskräften gehört,
ist mit den Gebietskommissaren (Abtlg. Soziale Verwaltung)
zu erzielen.

Für Schulung geeigneten einheimischen Nachwuchses als
Facharbeiter ist beschleunigt Sorge zu tragen.

Das gleiche gilt für jüdische Fachkräfte in Betrieben,
die nicht unmittelbar den Zwecken der Wehrmacht dienen, aber
wichtige Aufgaben im Rahmen der Kriegswirtschaft zu erfüllen
haben.

This personal letter Commissar General Wilhelm Kube in Minsk wrote to his chief, Reich Commissar for the Ostland Hinrich Lohse in Riga. To grasp the full significance of this top secret document one has to consider that both men were gauleiters and personal friends, that Kube as early as 1912, while a student, had been active in the anti-Semitic movement [342] and that in Hitler's time he was counted among the most ruthless representatives of the Party and the regime. He no doubt was quite sincere when he complimented himself as being "hard and ready to help solve the Jewish question"; no doubt he, too, was interested in bringing about "the necessary effect," as he termed it, i.e., the annihilation of the Jews. He did not even contemplate giving any vaccines to the Jews threatened by epidemics: "vaccines are not available for them," and at that it stood. But even this obdurate man wavered for a while at the sight of what was going on. He flinched from the idea of entrusting the "slaughtering"—his own word—to his Lithuanian and Lettish mercenaries who in the summer of 1941 had proved so efficient in killing Jews in their own homelands that they were put to the same use all over Eastern Europe. [343] Thus Kube, in order to save at least one group of Jews, tried to appeal to cultural reasons, to economic reasons, to reasons of health with regard to the Wehrmacht:

Minsk, December 16, 1941.

Reich Commissar for the Ostland
Gauleiter Hinrich Lohse
Riga.

Secret Reich Matter

Secret State Matter

My dear Hinrich:

I ask you personally for an official instruction as to the attitude of the civil administration toward the Jews who were deported from Germany to White Russia. Among these Jews there are front fighters [of the first world war] with iron crosses of the first and second class, [first world] war casualties, half Aryans, even one three-quarters Aryan. Of the 25,000 announced Jews for the time being only 6-7,000 arrived. It is not known to me where the remainder are. During repeated official visits at the [Minsk] ghetto I found out that there were among these Jews, who also by their

---

[342] Cf. Willi Buch, *50 Jahre antisemitische Bewegung* (München, Deutscher Volksverlag [1937], 104 pp.), p. 27.

[343] Cf. *Die Judenfrage*, March 15, 1942, p. 52: "Today, battalions of Lithuanian volunteers side by side with the soldiers of the other European peoples and under the leadership of Germany fight against the Jewish-Bolshevist world enemy...."

Minsk, 16.Dezember 1941

Herrn

Reichskommissar für das Ostland
Gauleiter Hinrich L o h s e ,

R i g a

Geheime Reichssache

Geheime Staatssache!

Mein lieber Hinrich!

Ich bitte Dich persönlich um eine dienstliche Anweisung
für das Verhalten der Zivilverwaltung gegenüber den Juden,
die aus Deutschland nach Weißruthenien deportiert worden
sind. Unter diesen Juden befinden sich Frontkämpfer mit dem
Eisernen Kreuz erster und zweiter Klasse, Kriegsverletzte,
Halbarier, ja sogar ein Dreiviertelarier. Bis jetzt sind
hier von den 25.000 angekündigten Juden nur 6 - 7.000 gekommen. Wo die anderen geblieben sind, entzieht sich meiner
Kenntnis. Bei wiederholten dienstlichen Besuchen im Ghetto
habe ich festgestellt, daß unter diesen Juden, die sich auch
durch persönliche Sauberkeit gegenüber russischen Juden un-
terscheiden, auch Facharbeiter sind, die etwa die fünffache
Tagesleistung von dem leisten, was russische Juden vermögen.

Die Juden selbst werden in den nächsten Wochen wahrschein-
lich erfrieren oder verhungern. Sie bilden für uns eine unge-
heure Seuchengefahr, da sie naturgemäß den Ansteckungen der
22 Epidemien, die im gesamten Weißruthenien herrschen, genau
so ausgesetzt sind, wie wir Reichsdeutsche. Impfstoffe stehen
für sie nicht zur Verfügung.

Auf eigene Verantwortung gebe ich dem SD eine Anweisung
über Behandlung dieser Menschen nicht, obwohl gewisse Forma-
tionen der Wehrmacht und der Polizei schon jetzt scharf auf
den Besitz der Juden aus dem Reiche sind. Der SD hat bereits -
ohne zu fragen - einfach 400 Matratzen den Juden aus dem Reiche
abgenommen und auch sonst allerhand beschlagnahmt. Ich bin
gewiß hart und bereit, die Judenfrage mit lösen zu helfen,
aber Menschen, die aus unserem Kulturkreis kommen, sind doch

b.w.

153

etwas anderes, als die bodenständigen vertierten Horden.
Soll man die Litauer und Letten, die hier auch von der Bevölkerung abgelehnt werden, mit der Abschlachtung beauftra-
gen? Ich könnte es nicht. Ich bitte Dich, mit Rücksicht
auf das Ansehen unseres Reiches und unserer Partei hier
eindeutige Anweisungen zu geben, die in der menschlichsten
Form das Nötige veranlassen.
Mit herzlichem Gruß und

Heil Hitler!
Dein

Wilhelm Kube

personal cleanliness differ from Russian Jews, skilled workers as well whose efficiency per day is five times as large as that of Russian Jews.

The Jews themselves within the next few weeks will probably perish from cold or hunger. They constitute a tremendous danger of epidemics for us because naturally they are exposed to infection by the twenty-two epidemics spread in the whole of White Russia just as are we Germans from the Reich. Vaccines are not available for them.

On my own responsibility, I am not going to give the SD [Sicherheits-Dienst] instruction about dealing with these people, although some formations of the Wehrmacht and police are already eager to obtain the Jews from the Reich. The SD already—without inquiring—simply took away 400 mattresses from the Jews from the Reich and also confiscated all kinds of things. I certainly am hard and ready to help solve the Jewish question but people who come from our cultural sphere are quite different, I submit, from the native brutish hordes. Is the slaughtering to be entrusted to the Lithuanians and Letts who here are looked askance at by the population, too? I shouldn't be able to do so. I ask you, in consideration for the respect for our Reich and our Party, to issue in this matter unequivocal instructions which will bring about the necessary effect in the most humane form.

Heil Hitler!

Yours,

WILHELM KUBE.

There is no need for us to sift the facts which Kube presented from distortions and falsehoods. Suffice it to say that his intervention failed. In the meantime, Lohse had received a categorical reply to his inquiry from his chiefs in Rosenberg's ministry in Berlin; the letter, marked Secret Reich Matter (Geheime Reichssache) No I/1 157/41 geh. Reichssache and dated December 18, 1941, stated:

Re: Jewish question

Your letter of November 15, 1941.

It is assumed that in the meantime there has been achieved clarity on the Jewish question through oral conferences. As a matter of principle, economic interests shall not be considered in regulating the problem. For the rest, it is requested to regulate any questions that may occur directly with the Chief of SS and SD (Höhere SS und Polizeiführer).

At that time, on December 1, 1941, the Deutsche Akademie in Munich, the research institution to which so many celebrities belonged, held a function which elicited great interest in German intellectual

**Der Reichsminister
für die besetzten Ostgebiete**

24

Berlin W 35, den 18.Dezember 1941
Rauchstraße 17/18
Fernsprecher: 21 95 15 und 39 50 46
Drahtanschrift: Reichsministerost

Nr. I/1 / *157* / 41 geh.Reichssache

Es wird gebeten, dieses Geschäftszeichen und den
Gegenstand bei weiteren Schreiben anzugeben.

Tgb. Nr. 394/41 *g R s*

Geheime Reichssache

1.)

An den
Herrn Reichskommissar für das Ostland
R i g a / Leitort Tilsit
Adolf Hitler Strasse

Betrifft: Judenfrage
Auf das Schreiben vom 15.11.1941

In der Judenfrage dürfte inzwischen durch mündliche
Besprechungen Klarheit geschaffen sein. Wirtschaftliche
Belange sollen bei der Regelung des Problems grundsätz-
lich unberücksichtigt bleiben. Im übrigen wird gebeten,
auftauchende Fragen unmittelbar mit dem höheren SS - und
Polizeiführer zu regeln.

Im Auftrag

156

circles. The Akademie, to recall the facts, early had become linked with the Nazi system and was generously supported from state funds until by a decree of the Führer of November 15, 1941 (*Reichsgesetzblatt I*, p. 717), it was declared a corporation of public law. This step, taken as it was "in consistent development of far-looking plans . . . during the most difficult military contests in the East," was duly interpreted as an acknowledgment that "the cultural work in the domain of language abroad [was] . . . emphatically important for the war." [344] No secret was made in the charter (Article 6) of the fact that the Akademie was subordinated to the Minister of Public Enlightenment and Propaganda; [345] as far as activity abroad was concerned the Foreign Ministry was authorized to issue directives.

To celebrate the elevation of the Deutsche Akademie to the rank of an overt state agency, a public meeting was held with the participation of Goebbels, guardian angel of the institution. On this occasion, the president of the Akademie said in part:

> In the bold advance of the young nations a new world was born. Our incomparable soldiers stand on the front, finally to throw to the ground and to crush forever the formidable power of the last enemy of Europe on the continent who at the command of international Jewry, freemasonry, and the plutocratic powers of the West has assaulted culture.

Goebbels' own address was summarized by the official reporter as follows:

> He, among others, discussed information policies during the war; they, too, may be a war instrument which even may influence battles. Furthermore, he discussed the danger of the East with its bolshevism annihilating culture and the strife of Western imperialism for domination. Dr. Goebbels particularly stressed the fact that the final solution of the Jewish question would constitute a decisive factor. [346]

[344] *Jahrbuch der Deutschen Sprache.* Im Auftrag der Deutschen Akademie her. von Erich Gierach, Bd. II (Leipzig, 1944, 240 pp.), pp. 135, 138. Director of the Akademie from its inception was Dr. Franz Thierfelder, who after the outbreak of war was employed on special missions in the Balkans and published several books about the Balkan countries. He was supplanted by Dr. phil. habil. Dr. Gustav Fochler-Hauke, with Regierungsrat Dr. Bäuml as deputy. In 1943, the Akademie (see *Jahrbuch* . . . II) "maintained [abroad] over one hundred lectorates [permanent courses of German language and culture for foreigners] with about two hundred instructors."

[345] Through its Abteilung Ausland (Foreign Department); see *Nachrichtenblatt* of the Ministry, no. 26, of September 27, 1941.

[346] *Deutsche Kultur im Leben der Völker* . . . *Deutsche Akademie*, XVI (1941, December), 372, 374.—It should not pass unnoticed that the solemn session of the Deutsche Akademie in Vienna on June 29, 1942, saw among its "guests of honor," together with the rectors of three universities, Professor Dr. [Wilhelm] Ziegler, etc., also the SD chief, Höhere Polizeiführer SS-Obergruppenführer [Ernst] Kaltenbrunner. *Ibid.*, XVII (1942, November), 330.— On December 7, 1943, by decree of the Führer, Dr. Arthur Seyss-Inquart was appointed President of the Deutsche Akademie. *Ibid.*, XVIII (1943), 103.

XXIX

NEW TASKS FOR GERMAN SCHOLARSHIP AFTER PEARL HARBOR: JEWRY THE LINK BETWEEN PLUTOCRACY AND BOLSHEVISM

At this juncture Japan attacked Pearl Harbor and Hitler declared war on the United States. It was no pleasant news to the German people in the third winter of a war which they had expected to end in a matter of weeks. Thus it was time again to apply the old rule of blaming the adversary for starting the fight. A. Sanders, an author on foreign affairs held in high esteem by the regime, thus explained "Europe's War against the USA":

> The struggle of today is fought between Europe and the over-seas powers, i.e., between Europe and those international circles which up to this time have executed world domination and did not want to permit the strengthening of Europe in order not to be disturbed and hampered in their plans for absolute world domination. The regeneration movement in Italy and in Germany was considered by those circles an attempt against their domination system.... Owing to the penetration of national socialism into German interests of their own species (arteigene deutsche Belange) and of fascism into the interests of the Italian people, both of them arrived at common-European and total-European ties and obligations....
>
> . . . In the middle of 1941 there stood against Europe a front which reached from the Arctic to the Black Sea and from the Caucasus to Egypt and Tobruk. The community of fate of the European nations is nowhere as clear as in the deployment of Germany, Italy, Spain, France, Hungary, Rumania, Croatia, Slovakia, Finland, Norway, Denmark, Holland, Belgium for the common struggle against bolshevism....
>
> With the disruption of the ring around Europe there started the liberation of the European nations from the power overseas and from bolshevism.
>
> In this duel between overseas and Europe, Japan too saw the right moment to interfere in the great controversy in order to provide for a new arrangement of East Asia on the basis of a system of her own.[347]

But who incited the overseas powers? Of course, the Jews.

> . . . From the point of view of attempts at absolute world domination there is harmony (Zusammenklang) between puritanism, freemasonry, and Judaism.... In those we have to see the powers which resist rising Europe and under the leadership of

---

[347] A. Sanders, *Die Stunde der Entscheidung. Kampf um Europa.* 2. Auflage (München, Hoheneichen-Verlag, 1943, 314 pp.), pp. 193-195.

Jewry have proclaimed war on Germany, the most powerful representative of European concentration.[348]

Another author, more disposed toward the use of philosophical language, put the case this way:

> With the debacle that North America is going to experience through this lost war, it inevitably will return to what it always has been: a colonial land. In this war, organic connection will conquer decay and atomization, the inflation of all values. It is the victory of healthy peoples and people-families over race chaos, the victory of the biological world view, of national socialism defined by blood over all internationalisms, over the children of liberalism, over capitalistic democracy (plutocracy), the victory of personality in organic unity of tension [sic] with the community against the mass, of culture against pleasure-technique and dullness. Simultaneously [it is] the victory of obligation toward the soil and of peasantry over exhausting the soil, devastation and nomadism (farmer), the victory of Nordic fate attitude which perishes upright and unbendingly bears its fate as opposed to the "happy end" of the American trash film.
>
> Germany in this war defends the old culture of Europe not by safeguarding the gates of the museums but by rejuvenating this culture. She defends it in the East against the threat of bolshevism just as in the West against the threat of Americanism, against the world domination of the inferior average. In other words, in effect, she fights against the annihilation of all culture values by destructive Jewry.[349]

A third writer, Professor Dr. Karl Heinz Pfeffer of the University of Berlin and a recognized German authority on the Anglo-Saxon countries, was willing to concede non-Jewish elements in American culture but, politically, arrived at the same conclusion:

> . . . England . . . has become "Judaized (verjudet)" in that its existence serves Jewish interests. . . . America even much less than England can afford to heed to *Volk* and *Rasse* because, should this happen, her melting pot would break asunder and the peoples absorbed by the "American nation (Amerikanertum)" would go back to themselves. . . . The foundations of Americanism are certainly not of Jewish origin; they are a mixture of British Puritan tradition and the peculiar situation of a young colonial country; but they serve the Jews splendidly. . . . Thus, the war against plutocracy is a victory over Judah. . . ."[350]

---

[348] *Ibid.*, p. 44.

[349] From the concluding paragraph in: Franz Otto Wrede, *Nord-Amerika Wirklich* (München, Eher, 1943, 52 pp.). Nur für den Dienstgebrauch. Schriftenreihe zur weltanschaulichen Schulungsarbeit [der NSDAP], Heft 10, Der Beauftragte . . . [Rosenberg].

[350] Professor Dr. Karl Heinz Pfeffer, *Der englische Krieg auch ein jüdischer Krieg* (München, Eher, 1943, 16 pp.), p. 16. Nur für den Dienstgebrauch. Schriftenreihe zur weltanschaulichen Schulungsarbeit der NSDAP, Heft 29, Der Beauftragte . . . [Rosenberg].

Nor was this theme limited to analyses of a general nature. Many a study was made on quite specific subjects. For instance, a paper was devoted to the question of why Wendell Willkie's ancestors left Germany. The evidence presented from German archives was rather inconclusive, but it was no surprise to learn that it was a Jew who forced them to emigrate.

> And here once more the tragedy of emigrated German blood comes up. Willkie, whose grandfather was deprived by a Jew of his parental property and his home, today fights for the interests of Jewry and against national socialism, whose aim it is to liberate the German man from Jewry.[351]

On November 11, 1941, Hitler, in addressing his old guard, stressed that the Third Reich for the first time was using methodical scholarship as a means of combating "the international Jew." With America's entrance into the war, all masks had been torn away. The Jews, in their perennial hatred for Germany, had prevailed upon Roosevelt to attack her. On January 30, 1942, Hitler reiterated before his Sportpalast audience:

> We are fully aware that this war can end only either in the extermination of the Teutonic peoples or in the disappearance of Jewry from Europe. I said it already in the German Reichstag on September 1, 1939—and I am on my guard as to rash prophecies— that this war will not terminate as the Jews imagine, namely, in the extermination of the European Aryan peoples, but that the outcome of this war will be the annihilation of Jewry.[352]

Be it noted that there was nothing new whatsoever in this plain statement as compared with Hitler's pre-Pearl Harbor enunciations on the subject: he had made up his mind before. But his scholars and propagandists got hold of a convenient thesis, which he himself later took up, too: the Jews, who from the outset had inspired Russian bolshevism, now formed the link between the USSR, whom they had incited against Germany first, and Anglo-American plutocracy. The idea was shelved for several years, but it had been voiced previously. As early as in 1937 Professor Dr. Rudolf Craemer of the University of Königsberg had not hesitated to propose the following research project, nor did the leading German historical review hesitate to publish his suggestion:

> . . . It would be worthwhile investigating how Zionist thinking constitutes, so to speak, the connecting link between Wilson's demo-

---

[351] Hermann Goebke, "Warum wanderten Wendell Wilkies deutsche Vorfahren aus?", *Weltkampf*, I (1941), 169-174.
[352] Gerhard Brendel, *Der Führer über die Juden* (see footnote 182), p. 80.

cratic ideals and the promises of bolshevism to make peoples happy.[353]

After Pearl Harbor this fixed idea, endlessly varying and still remaining substantially the same, became the leitmotif of German reasoning, speaking, and yelling. Monotonous as this talk on Jewry as the embodiment of bolshevism and plutocracy is, we have no right to ignore it: it was to its accompaniment that millions of Jews were murdered by millions of Germans after scores of thousands had been murdered, between June 22 and December 7, 1941, as alleged representatives of bolshevism pure and simple.

In vain an English-writing author at the beginning of the war had found ". . . comfort in misery at least that the German Jews cannot be held responsible even by the Nazis for the outbreak or for the conduct and outcome of the present conflict." [354] Just the opposite, the German Jew, any Jew, whether encountered in the face of the Wehrmacht's advance or resident in the Reich, was individually responsible for anything that displeased Germany's rulers. Goebbels recently had re-coined the formula: "The Jews are guilty," and so it went. An Austrian writer who before the Anschluss had warned the Jews that "whatever does not conform, whatever is not fit, *perishes*" and had underscored the last word of the sentence lest no doubt remain, in the preface to the third edition of his book, dated August, 1942, was in a position bluntly to confirm what he had predicted several years earlier.

The Jews have decided upon a path that is extremely dangerous for them. They have unleashed a new world conflagration by starting to instigate England and France against Germany after they had Bolshevized Russia. And if the guilt is not yet quite visible to the naked eyes of the masses, the unveiled frankness with which America entered the war at Jewish behest and under Jewish steering did not permit even the appearance of another interpretation. Thus the great controversy between the authoritarian and the so-called democratic states is nothing else than a duel between the Aryan and the Jewish systems of thinking.... Let the German appeal to Europe broaden into an appeal of Europe to the non-Jewish world; then the decision will have been taken in correspondence with the severity and the tremendous sacrifices of this juncture in history. At the threshold of this period has stood and stands one will—that of Adolf Hitler.[355]

[353] *Historische Zeitschrift,* 157 (1937/1938), 553.
[354] Karl Loewenstein, *Hitler's Germany,* new edition (New York, Macmillan, 1940, 230 pp.), p. 157.
[355] Schattenfroh, *op. cit.,* p. 371.

Hitler himself on September 30, 1942, again proclaimed that "after this war had been forced on us no power of arms nor time will beat us down" and that not "the Aryan peoples of Europe are going to be exterminated but Jewry." His New Year's message of 1943 contained this passage:

> [I said some years ago that] the hope of international Jewry to be able to destroy through a new world war the German or other European peoples would be the gravest error of Jewry for millennia, that at any rate it would destroy not the German people but itself. There is today no doubt about this....

He then elaborated:

> ... That this [Jewish] race is the main cause of this war can best be proved by the ' fact that the seemingly extremest contrasts have allied in the struggle against the European folk-states (Nationalstaaten). The alliance of the arch-capitalist states of the West, or even more so of America, with the mendacious mock-socialist regime of bolshevism is conceivable only because leadership in both of the cases lies in the hands of international Jewry, even if the personalities visible from without seem to contradict this thesis.[356]

And Goebbels on the same day protested:

> ... Don't forget, it is the Jew who fights against us. One has only once to have made the acquaintance of the Jew with his Old-Testament hate in order to know what's going to happen to us if the Jew could take revenge from us. What do you think, what is going to happen to your wives, to your fiancees, to your daughters? ...[357]

---

[356] *Deutschland im Kampf,* her. von Ministerialdirektor A. I. Berndt, Reichspropaganda-Ministerium, Oberst von Wedel, Oberkommando der Wehrmacht (Berlin, Stollberg, 1943, Januar-Lieferung, no. 81/82 der Gesamtlieferung), p. 44.
[357] *Ibid.,* p. 90.

Execution of the Program

XXX

JEWRY—THE ONLY FRONT ON WHICH VICTORY COULD BE WON.
EXTINCTION OF THE JEWS IN THE GOVERNMENT GENERAL

Let us conceive of the situation as it presented itself in the minds
of the Germans ever since the Allied landings in North Africa, and
particularly since the intensification of the Anglo-American air attacks, which coincided with the German disaster of Stalingrad. The
multifront war, feared above anything else since Bismarck's times
and frequently dismissed by Hitler as a dread he would never allow
to materialize, had become a reality. From the South and the East
and the West the enemies were moving ever closer to Germany's
sacred frontiers, and in spite of all sacrifices, of all delaying movements, nothing essentially could be done about the advance of the
Allied forces.

> It is . . . shameful to see that the state which in the past did
> quite a bit for European power and culture committed the worst
> treason against Europe in the decisive hour: Great Britain. . . .
> There is in Northern Germany a village by the name of York, in
> England a county by the same name and in North America the
> real capital today is called New York. From this one word one
> may read the origin, the development and the decay of the large
> migrations of peoples and if one is to hate his adversaries today
> this hatred of ours is coupled with a feeling of contempt and
> disgust.

Alfred Rosenberg — it is he whose philippic we are quoting —
then went on:

> There is lacking in the manner in which our enemies fight
> under their leadership that measure of chivalry which even in the
> hardest war of the past frequently lent some historical splendor
> even to the bitterest struggles. Today this seems to have been lost
> and forgotten. The dirty flood of the Jewish press, the insults
> thrown at our state heads and leaders for years, all this today cul-
> minates in the infernal warfare which was consciously started by
> British fliers on orders of Jewish international capitalism and today

endeavors to lay in ruins the highest monuments of human creativity.

. . . The present war of our enemies is a struggle against the foundations of all European nations. A flier sent out by political gangsters who lets down his bombs on the most beautiful cultural places of Europe does not know what he does, he has not the slightest idea of what culture is altogether. And when the USA lately goes so far as to put Negroes on its bombers, this shows how this country, once founded by Europeans, has fallen....

The bridges behind the people of Europe are burned. In the struggle in which all of us are involved there are no two or even three ways, but only one way of struggle and war. . . .[358]

But even the powerful Alfred Rosenberg could do the RAF and AAF but little harm by thundering on them denunciations like the above. There was, however, one enemy front that could be attacked incessantly and on which conspicuous victories had already been won since 1933. It was the Jewish front. After all that had happened to them since that year, the Jews had nothing to expect from Germany; every Jew could be presumed to be anti-German. So in 1941, instead of annihilating the Red Army which refused to be annihilated and continued fighting, one could kill helpless Jews, and we saw that this substituting began as soon as the war with the Soviet Union was started. Instead of driving away the Anglo-American fliers, one again could kill Jews: after the first RAF bombardment of Cologne, 258 Jews in Berlin were lined up in the Gross-Lichterfelde barracks and shot "in reprisal." [359] In other words, while the actual fighting foes were out of reach, Germany could kill, as savages do, the images of the foes, the Jews. But in this case the images, too, were people of flesh and blood.

On a rational plane, nothing could be attained for Germany by killing these people. On the contrary, from the economic point of view the adult Jewish population could be put to work for Germany. Actually, while reason still prevailed to a degree, the ghettos of Warsaw, Lódź and Lublin were converted into tremendous workshops under German slave drivers, and we recall that even at the beginning of the Ostland occupation persons high in the Party and Wehrmacht hierarchy tried to halt the killings and to save the workers very badly needed at that time. But after tens of thousands of Jews in Vilna,

---

[358] Quoted in: *Das Gesicht des Bolschewismus* (Berlin, Eher [n. d.], 79 pp.). Aus der Schriftenreihe zur weltanschaulichen und politischen Schulung der Wehrmacht. Her. von der Dienststelle des Reichsleiters Alfred Rosenberg.

[359] Cf. the New York newspapers of the time, e.g., *PM* of December 9, 1942.

Kaunas, Riga, Minsk and countless towns of the area[360] had been disposed of, it was decided that no economic reasons were to be taken into consideration and soon new transports were moved in to share the fate of the earlier victims.

On January 15, 1942, at a meeting convened in Berlin by Heydrich at the suggestion of Goering,[361] the decision is said to have been taken to dispose of all Jews in the way that had proved so successful on the Eastern testing-grounds. The total was no trifle as the number of the Jews in the Government General alone after the incorporation of Eastern Galicia (district of Lemberg) in the late summer of 1941 had amounted to over a million and three quarters and millions more had to be accounted for all over Europe. But German ingenuity had mastered more difficult tasks than this German-Jewish war, in which a nation armed to its teeth contested a people practically deprived of weapons and emaciated by being jailed for years in gigantic concentration camps. Both Jewish survivors and secret German documents now unearthed show for certain that the battle of the Warsaw ghetto in April-May, 1943,[362] was but the climax of many acts of Jewish resistance in the ghettos of Nieśwież, Białystok, Vilna, Krynki, Będzin, etc.; even the prison camps of Poniatów, Trawniki, and Janów, even the death factories of Treblinka and Oświęcim witnessed rebellion. Historians and artists will deal with the subject in years to come. Essentially, however, the German-Jewish war could but be a one-sided affair.

We followed its first stages, preceding Pearl Harbor, in the Ostland. As to the Ukraine, where the course of events was substantially the same, there is still lack of detailed accounts. Only one summarizing survey has fallen into our hands. It is a secret report by Dr. Hans-Joachim Kausch, of the Propaganda Ministry, on his trip to the Ukraine and Crimea, June 3-22, 1943. Only a few sentences in the 20-page document[363] concern the Jews, but they convey the message:

---

[360] Isolated cases of wholesale executions in 1941 are known also from the territory of the Government General. Cf. *Dos naye lebn*, a Yiddish weekly issued in Lódź, no. 20, of November 4. 1945, p. 6: "In Kazimierz, 16 km. from Konin, twenty mass graves were discovered. In these graves are buried over twenty thousand Jews of the area around Konin, Zagórowo, Pleszewo, Pulinkowo, and other Jewish communities of the district of Konin. The extermination took place as early as 1941. The Jews were expelled from their homes in groups and forced to dig their graves. Then they were driven into the ditches and machine-gunned. On the 6th of last month [October, 1945] the Jewish survivors of Konin erected a monument reading: 'The Jewish suvivors of Konin to their murdered brethren,' "

[361] Cf. *New York Times*, November 22, 1945.

[362] Cf. S. Mendelsohn, *The Battle of the Warsaw Ghetto* (New York, Yiddish Scientific Institute, 1944, 28 pp.).

[363] It is dated June 26, 1943, and bears the number 500/43 g (now in the Yivo archives).

On the Jewish question we hear quite unequivocal and clear-cut statements. There were 1.1 million Jews among the 16 million inhabitants of the territory of the Ukrainian civil administration. They have been liquidated without remainder. As a matter of fact, during our entire trip, we saw only four Jews; they worked as tailors in a penal camp of the SD. As the last group the Jewish artisans were liquidated. During some executions Hungarian or Slovak officers took photographs which afterwards found their way to America. This was considered particularly unpleasant....

Much more can now be said, on the basis of German reports compiled with usual accuracy, on the events in the Government General. The SS and SD had shown their efficiency in Rosenberg's domains and therefore could be entrusted with the task of solving the Jewish question in this area, too. By decree of the Führer of May 7, 1942,[364] a State Security Secretariat (Sekretariat für das Sicherheitswesen) was created in the Government General, and the Höhere SS und Polizeiführer (Chief of the SS and SD) was given the rank of state secretary. In matters concerning security and the solidification of German folkdom he was to receive instructions directly from the Reichsführer SS, i.e., Himmler.

The actions of Himmler's agency in the Government General are reflected in the following reports addressed by the Governor of Warsaw to his superiors in Cracow and by Goebbels' representatives to the Propaganda Ministry, respectively.

On August 15, 1942, the Governor of Warsaw Fischer wrote:

[p. 7] Situation in the Jewish settlement area (Wohnbezirk).
On July 21 the SS and Polizeiführer informed that on July 22, 1942, the deportation (Aussiedlung) of the Jews from Warsaw would begin. Until the end of the reporting period [July 31, 1942] about 59,000 persons have been deported from the Jewish settlement area in Warsaw. All measures related to this [action] were in the competence of the SS and Polizeiführer.... After the resettlement (Umsiedlung) decree was announced the previous chairman (Obmann) of the Judenrat [Czerniakow] committed suicide.... The food supply of the Jewish settlement area . . . for the time being . . . is secured, hence the resettlement action can be carried on without obstacle.[365]

The report of October 15, 1942, listed much greater battle successes:

---

[364] *Reichsgesetzblatt*, I, 293. Cf. *Deutscher Beamtenkalender 1943 . . . Fachschaft Reichs- und Länderverwaltungsbeamte* (Berlin, Verlag Beamtenpresse, 300 pp.), p. 71.
[365] Geheim. Der Gouverneur des Distrikts Warschau. An die Regierung des General-gouvernements (document in the Yivo archives).

[pp. 3-4] . . . The evacuation of the Jews from the district of Warsaw. . . . During the reporting period [August-September, 1942, they] have been deported except small remaining parts. . . . The Jewish settlement area is essentially empty. . . . It is not yet possible at this moment to say what are going to be the economic effects of the decrease of the population of the city of Warsaw by about 400,000 people. . . . The tense food situation [will be] alleviated. . . . On the other hand, there is at present a shortage of about 100,000 workers. . . . Furthermore, it should not be overlooked that numerous enterprises and properties suffered colossal losses. . . . These economic disadvantages, however, must be accepted because the extinction (Ausmerzung) of Jewry is unconditionally required for political reasons.[366]

Goebbels' representative in his survey for the month of October added some touches to the picture:

Warsaw. The Jewish Question. The largest part of the Jews in the Jewish settlement area in Warsaw during the months of July, August, and September, 1942, were deported. Out of a total of 380,000 Jews who lived in Warsaw there are now about 30,000 who work in direct military enterprises (clothing and shoe production). These are being kept in barracks (kaserniert) in the Jewish settlement area.[367]

There was again a report by Fischer dated Warsaw, December 10, 1942. It is not clear whether it refers to the forthcoming extermination of the remainder of the Jews or to measures contemplated with regard to Poles; anyway, the appearance of the Space Arrangement Office and the Commissariat for the Solidification of German Folkdom is significant in that it leads us back to the root sources of the system:

[p. 18] Space Arrangement Office. . . . Plannings for the forthcoming resettlement were agreed upon with the SS and Polizeiführer in the District of Warsaw in his capacity of Commissar for the Security and Solidification of German Folkdom.[368]

The reports of Goebbels' agency also contained two communications from Lemberg which show that the "radical solution" started simultaneously in the whole of the Government General. Under the date of August 29, 1942, the following was transmitted:

The fundamental question whether in removing (Beseitigung) the Jews political considerations are to be put before reasons of war economy, apparently in the highest place has been de-

366 Same title as in previous footnote.
367 Streng vertraulich. Hauptabteilung Propaganda. Wochenberichte der Distrikte vom Monat Oktober 1942, p. 15 (document in the Yivo archives).
368 Title of the document as in footnote 365.

cided in favor of the political point of view. The decrease in economic efficiency in the areas affected must be condoned. I beg to say in anticipation that the effects in Galicia probably will be very appreciable.[369]

Again, Lemberg came in six weeks later. At first we are amazed that even Goebbels' agent voiced some indignation at the manner the "resettlement" was being carried out and even uses the term "liquidation" explicitly discarded by his chief. But soon it turns out that he differed only in matters of etiquette. Incidentally, the question of what is "worthy of a cultural people" reappears in a document concerning the extinction of the *Polish* people which we shall discuss later.

> Lemberg, October 16, 1942. The resettlement of Jews, which partly assumes forms not worthy of a cultural people, directly provokes a comparison of the methods of the Gestapo with those of the GPU.
>
> The transports are said to be in such a bad state that it is impossible to prevent Jews from breaking out. The result is that on intermediary stations there occur wild shootings and regular manhunts. It is also reported that corpses of shot-down Jews for days lie on the streets.
>
> Although the Reich German as well as the alien population is convinced of the necessity of liquidating all Jews, it still would be more appropriate to carry this through in a manner that causes less sensation and offense.[370]

The skillful author already quoted once (pp. 127-128) was able to present the same matter in a language that sounded quite different:

> A commendable achievement is also the far-reaching elimination of the Jews. If for instance Lublin, Lemberg and Reichshof [Rzeszów] during the last decades owing to the spread of the Jewish plague belonged to the most disgusting places of Middle Europe, now each of these cities, after the Jewish crust has been removed, is freed in its individuality and thus has again become congenial to the German. Lemberg with its great German-folk past today even can be again considered a positively beautiful city.[371]

But regardless of divergences of opinion as to etiquette, Hitler in his proclamation of February 24, 1943, was able to speak in more definite terms than usual. He repeated: "This struggle . . . will not end . . . in the annihilation of Aryan mankind but in the extermination of Jewry in Europe," but then he added a statement of fact:

---

[369] Streng vertraulich. Hauptabteilung Propaganda. Wochenberichte der Distrikte vom 15. September 1942, p. 9 (document in the Yivo archives).

[370] P. 19 of the document mentioned in footnote 367.

[371] Lange, *op. cit.*, p. 117.

The German people ... is about to finish off the Jewish internal enemy definitively....[372]

And while *Die Judenfrage* of March 1, 1943, mockingly spoke of "indefinite fantastic rumors" put out by British and American Jews about " 'new dangers' allegedly threatening the Jews in Europe ... just now," Hitler took the platform again on March 21:

A war without compassion and mercy has been forced upon us by eternal Jewry.... And I repeat my previous prophecy that at the end of this war....[373]

On November 9, 1943, he called the Jews, of whom millions already had been murdered, "these criminals" and promised that they would be dealt with. "Let people have no doubts or delusions about that," he shouted.[374]

The war progressed. The chances of victory became ever smaller. But the extermination of the Jews was being speeded up. Did not the German leaders fear the retaliation that might befall their own people? Most certainly not, because they knew quite well that no matter how complete Germany's defeat, no one on earth would be ruthless enough to make German men, women, and children pay in kind for what Germany had done to Jewish men, women, and children, to the Jewish people as a whole. Instead, while they still hoped against hope, it might have appeared to the leaders that if one could forge the German people from a community of fate into a community of crime this would enhance their power of fanatical resistance. As time went on and even the hope of survival for the regime gradually faded away, one more consideration could have entered the minds of the doomed Germans: that it might be a good thing to remove from Germany's opponents in a prospective World War III a group which obviously would side against Germany. That thoughts about the next war were ever present, is proved by German general population and depopulation policies in Eastern Europe. Justice Robert H. Jackson, in his opening speech at the Nuremberg trial, too, expressed this idea:

---

[372] "... endgültig zu erledigen im Begriffe ist...."

[373] Prominently displayed in *Die Judenfrage*, April 1, 1943.

[374] Fittingly, the Central Training Office of the Nazi party at that time produced a sheet on "Three Thousand Years of Jewish Hatred" : *3000 Jahre jüdischer Hass*. Herausgeber: Der Reichsorganisationsleiter der NSDAP., Hauptschulungsamt (München, 1943, 7 pp.) = Schulungsunterlage [Sonderheft], No. 13.—Incidentally, a secret Nazi document, now in the Yivo archives, reveals an amazingly small Jewish criminality in Germany during the war years. Cf. Josef Guttman in *Yivo Bleter*, Journal of the Yiddish Scientific Institute, XXVI (1945), 210-217.

The Nazi purpose was to leave Germany's neighbors so weak-
ened that even if she should eventually lose the war, she would still
be the most powerful nation in Europe.[375]

And so, in the midst of the severest labor shortage and the tie-
up of road and rail transport in the vast areas of the East and in
Germany proper, thousands of badly needed railroad cars came to
be used to deport millions of starving and nearly dead Jews from as
far as the Netherlands and Southern France and Greece into the
death factories established in Poland; and to run the gas chambers
and crematories thousands of engineers, physicians, and biologists
were employed who certainly could have better served the Nazi war
machine had rational considerations prevailed. But matters of the
highest order were at stake; Europe was to become "a free continent
which under German guidance . . . develops its culture free from
Jewish influences." Thus spoke Otto Kriegk, a distinguished writer,
a former member of Hugenberg's staff who had gone over to the
Nazis. As opposed to the Jewish war aims consisting in enslavement
and annihilation, Germany, Kriegk said, aimed at creating an order
in which "the person of the highest achievements, of purity of soul,
of mental clarity, of moral cleanness would ultimately prevail."[376]

XXXI

NEW DEVELOPMENTS IN RACIAL SCIENCE: REFOLKING VS.
PURITY OF BLOOD

Himmler did his very best to achieve for the German people this
purity of soul, mental clarity, and moral cleanness. He had become
the executioner's sword—a function for which he had longed—to an
undreamed-of extent. But the race problem was now no longer a
problem of the Jews. It had grown infinitely more complex with the
occupation of the Eastern Space and the transfer of at least ten
million foreign slave laborers into the Reich. How were the biological standards proclaimed by the Third Reich to be maintained
even after the Jews would have been disposed of?

The problem was not entirely new to German thinkers. On the
eve of the war Alfred Pudelko, a man attached to Rosenberg's offices
and prominent among Nazi Germany's educators, had written warn-
ingly in anticipating the conquest of vast territories:

[375] Professor Dr. Kleo Pleyer, as quoted by Friedrich Burgdörfer, *Volksdeutsche Zukunft*
(Berlin, Junker und Dünnhaupt, 1938, 39 pp.), p. 39: "The decisive fundamental power of
the frontier struggle is biological potency." See p. 85.
[376] Otto Kriegk, *Die Geburt Europas* (Berlin, Scherl, 1943, 395 pp.).

Mixing of different races is undesirable from any point of view. . . . To keep one's own racial powers healthy and pure through organized eugenics and genetics (Erb- und Rassenpflege) is a premise of dominating the space. . . . To employ alien racial forces for one's own aims is dangerous. They require careful direction and supervision. Employing people of our blood in alien spaces and among other peoples very easily leads to folk destruction.[377]

In 1943, the danger was at the very doorstep. It was vividly described by Dr. Walter Gross of the Racial-Policy Office of the NSDAP in a preface to a small book which one of his staff members, Egon Leuschner, wrote for the Wehrmacht on "National Socialist Policies toward Foreign Folks."[378] "For understandable reasons not all pertinent questions have been comprehensively and exhaustively dealt with," Gross apologized; only matters that appeared immediately applicable were discussed. But the dilemma was presented clearly and warrants extensive quotation:

> The bitter injustice and pain which the infamous Versailles Treaty caused us in the East is for all time compensated for by the crushing of Poland and the incorporation of the Eastern areas into the German Reich. Such an extensive territorial gain, however, puts before the leadership of state and folk tremendous tasks which ought to be tackled only with the greatest circumspection and well considered planning, if an organic absorption of the new parts of the country into the mother country is to be guaranteed. The same National Socialist state which in its eastern re-arrangement and policy has to take into consideration not only frontier-posts, the structure of the country, industrial and economic conditions but, because of racial consciousness, has to turn its attention in the first place to the human stock of this space, is confronted with problems which ought not to be solved in the ways of old.

Before racial science came into being, conquerors had been naive:

> Former wars used to end in that the conquertiong state appropriated the area of the conquered people, larger or smaller, and thus simultaneously made the inhabitants resident in this area its own citizens. Whether these people were able to fit into one's own

[377] Alfred Pudelko, *Rasse und Raum als geschichtsbestimmende Kräfte* (Berlin, Eher [1939], 52 pp.), p. 50. On pp. 48-49, the author wrote: "The importance of race mixture is evidenced also by examples of individual personalities who operated in history as typical hybrids (Mischlinge) . . . In German history, Otto III presents the best example of a racial hybrid. This man from the Saxon imperial house, whose mother was the Greek woman Theophano, brought unutterable mischief upon the entire German Eastern policy in the raving year 1000 by founding the archbishopric of Gnesen [Gniezno]. He hereby withdrew large areas from the influence of the German archbishops and sustained the rise of a national, cultural-political center of the Polish nation (Polentum) which was forming at that time."

[378] Egon Leuschner, Reichsschulungsbeauftragter des Rassenpolitischen Amtes der NSDAP, *National-Sozialistische Fremdvolk-Politik: Der deutsche Mensch und die Fremdvölkischen.* Nur für den Gebrauch innerhalb der Wehrmacht. Tornisterschrift des Oberkommandos der Wehrmacht, Allgemeines Wehrmachtamt Abt. Inland, Heft 82 (1943, 48 pp.).—The pamphlet also refers to Tornisterschrift no. 29, *Deutsche Rassenpflege,* by Professor Dr. Staemmler.

folk according to their extractional origin, according to their social substance, was not thought of, in ignorance of the essence of racial processes. One was content with the fact that the people involved were prepared to change their nationality and to promise to become law-abiding, tax-paying citizens.

History frequently avenged very bitterly this grave lack of insight, inasmuch as the momentary gain of people and space offered a fertile soil for later phenomena of decomposition and dissolution and the neighborly relations of the peoples contained the seed of new complications.... All folk-policy work in the long run has meaning only if it is racially defined; all racial political work is successful and reasonable only if it recognizes in its aims political expediencies and the possibility of political materialization as a reality.[379]

In another volume, also emanating from very high quarters, Gross elaborated at some length on the essence of racial processes, of which Nazi Germany was no longer ignorant. His first paragraph appeared remarkably sound:

An attempt to evaluate mixed marriages according to the racial distribution of the particular peoples cannot be carried through: designating peoples as Nordic, Slavonic, or preponderantly Nordic, and so on, does not say anything about the racial classification and the hereditary biological value of the individual who by chance may be a Jewish hybrid or otherwise different from the average type of his people. On the other hand, it is politically unbearable in view of the war to group the European peoples as biologically desirable and biologically undesirable, since in many cases racial and political classifications diametrically oppose each other (e.g., Norway, Italy). Finally, even the correct racial diagnosis of the individual spouse, as possibilities of observation now stand, almost invariably depends upon the bodily appearance; thus such diagnosis can not or can only incompletely comprehend the quality of psyche and character and since documentation as to the species (Art) is mostly lacking, the diagnosis cannot give a sufficiently reliable picture of the actual hereditary biological value.

But then Gross pointed out:

Mixed marriages with non-Germans, therefore, in most cases will bring into one's own people undesirable inheritance, in almost all cases inheritance that is not known for certain. Consequently, they constitute from the point of view of hereditary biology the danger which in case such unions assume greater proportions must become historically fateful.

Scruples from the point of view of folk are to be added: each generation will only to a limited extent be able really to Germanize

[379] From the preface to Leuschner, *op. cit.*, p. 4.

(Eindeutschung) even good racial elements, since this presents a great educational task. Each mixed marriage between different peoples poses hard psychological problems to each spouse, in regard to educating the children and so on. The less time the German spouse can devote to the personal element of the family, the more complicated are these problems. They are, therefore, as a rule disastrous for the war and the postwar period.

Inference: refutation of any marriage with non-Germans as a matter of principle. Any attempt to break this directive and to judge differently in a particular case . . . is dangerous and irresponsible.[380]

As will be seen easily, this was the set of ideas the Germans had become accustomed to through the efforts of their scholars who kept insisting:

Racial science (Rassenkunde) is not a National Socialist invention, but a recognized international science.... Races originate as a result of natural or artificial breeding selections. For this purpose the breeder makes use of the means of rigid selection, of isolation, and inconsiderate extinction (Ausmerze) of all descendants who do not fit into the breeding goal....[381]

Consequently, even the publications of the Reichsführer SS intended for the rank and file continued in orthodox vein:

The Nordic race defines the character of the German folk constituting as it does its greatest part (50-60 per cent). Almost every German is a carrier of Nordic blood which at some time and somewhere entered his ancestry.... An animal out of its instincts carries its life, maintains its species. How could it be otherwise with man? [382]

But while racial science was praised louder than ever, Himmler already had embarked upon quite a new policy. These were his words to a selected circle, as revealed by Justice Jackson at the Nuremberg trial:

[380] Prof. Dr. [Walter] Gross, in: *Der Kampf um unsere Weltanschauung. Gedankenführungen zu weltanschaulichpolitischen Vorträgen zur Partei- und Wehrmachtschulung.* Her. im Einvernehmen mit dem Amt Wehrmachtschulung der Dienststelle des Reichsleiters Rosenberg. Nur für den Dienstgebrauch (Stein/Oberkrain, der Gauvertreter des Reichsleiters Rosenberg in Kärnten, n. d. [1943 or later], 148 pp.), pp. 51-52.

[381] Prof. Dr. [Karl] Metzger [of the Technische Hochschule, Dresden], *ibid.,* p. 53. Professor Dr. Ernst Rüdin of Munich (see chapter V), in reviewing the sterilization laws of the Third Reich in *Deutscher Wissenschaftlicher Dienst,* no. 5, of July 29, 1940, came to the following conclusion: "Scruples and nagging of a political and philosophical nature against the [1934] law have almost ceased in view of the continuing onward march of National Socialist ideas and achievements. On the contrary! Not only at home but abroad as well, voices are heard which congratulate the German Reich on having found the leading man with his assisting staff who dares to break also with racial-hygienic measures the terror of the inferior kind of people."

[382] Der Reichsführer SS, SS-Hauptamt, Her., *Rassenpolitik* (Berlin [1943], 72 pp.), pp. 19, 47.

Either we win over any good blood that we can use for ourselves and give it a place in our people or, gentlemen—you may
call this cruel, but nature is cruel—we destroy this blood....[383]

To us, it is a shock to read this light-hearted matter-of-fact appeal
to cruelty, but to the German students of race who for years had
taught that the lower folks were to be kept at a distance the first
part of the passage was a much harder blow. "To win over [alien]
good blood that we can use for ourselves and give it a place in our
people" certainly was an idea that deviated radically from the previous
holy concept of racial purity.

To measure the distance racial science had traveled while still
being advertised as the sole hope for salvation, the following two
quotations from equally official publications may be confronted. One
stated:

> The dominant principle to be applied is not to introduce into
> the German folk body any drop of foreign blood that might de-
> compose and impair its uniform cohesiveness but in turn, not to
> cede a drop of valuable German blood to an alien folkdom."

The second read:

> People who on the basis of their character attitude vow their
> allegiance to us, thereby prove that they possess Nordic qualities
> even if externally they do not entirely correspond to the Nordic
> ideal. The upright vow of allegiance to the Reich by a European
> [non-German] volunteer, therefore, is not only a political factor
> but also the expression of a biological attachment (Zuordnung).[384]

It was only natural, therefore, for Professor Dr. Walter Gross
as the responsible head of the Racial-Policy Office of the Nazi
party to explain the new development. In a paper of confidential
nature which was called to the particular attention of Party leaders
and circularized among high officials, Gross drew a line between
racial science and racial politics, the latter to be conceived of as
"political application of scientific cognitions." Besides science and
politics, however, a third element is involved, Gross went on to say:
no racial politics is possible without a certain conception of history.
The racial history-picture is a direct result not of scientific cognitions
but of the intuition of "individual geniuses," among whom Rosenberg
was named. The method of racial politics

---

[383] Quoted by Justice Jackson in his opening address at Nuremberg.
[384] The first quotation from: Ulrich Greifelt, "Festigung deutschen Volkstums im deutschen
Ostraum." *Raumforschung und Raumordnung* 5 (1941), 3. The author was a brigade leader
in the SS and director of the [Berlin] Office of the Reichsführer SS in his capacity as the
Reich Commissar for the Solidification of German Folkdom.—The second quotation from:
Lehrplan für die weltanschauliche Erziehung in der SS und Polizei...(see footnote 269), p. 77.

within one's own folk amounts to differential steering of propaga-
tion but particularly in times of strong population movements and
migrations of peoples such as we observe at present, it reaches far
beyond the boundaries of our folkdom and thus comes into closest
relation with considerations of economic and foreign policy....

"It is obvious," Gross added, "that about this essential racial-
political practice there can be no talking or teaching in public." [385]

But while Gross could temporarily put his administrative duties
above his task of a race student, German scholarship as a whole could
not stop functioning. "It is the job of science at all times," an ambitious writer declared, "to see to it that the power whose interpreter
it [science] is not only unconsciously fulfills its mandate but also
puts [the mandate] into ideas and executes [it] in full consciousness
of its task." [386] Scholars possessing such a live feeling of duty never
would sacrifice principles to expediency. Thus, in order to bridge the
gap, the principles themselves had to be refashioned.

Here the concept of "refolking" came in to reinforce the scientific
foundations of the solidification of German folkdom in its new,
broadened sense.

The concept had not sprung into being out of nothing. An
extremely able group of scholars connected with the Deutsches Aus-
landsinstitut (Institute on Germans Abroad) in Stuttgart (Dr. Heinz
Kloss, Dr. Hans-Joachim Beyer, Dr. Otto Albrecht Isbert, and others)
were publishing the periodical *Volksforschung* (Folk Research) sev-
eral years before the outbreak of the war; they had initially called it
Auslandsdeutsche Volksforschung (Research concerning German Folk
Abroad), but soon widened its scope. Now another group, concen-
trated in the Institut für Grenz- und Auslandstudien (Institute for
Frontier and Foreign Studies) obeyed the call. Headed by Professor
Dr. Carl von Loesch and characterized by such scholars as Professor
Dr. Max Hildebert Boehm, the Institut before the outbreak of war

---

[385] Walter Gross, "Rassenpolitik," published in *Deutschlands Erneuerung* (August, 1942)
and reprinted in *Informationsdienst, Rassenpolitisches Amt der NSDAP, Reichsleitung,* October
20, 1942, no. 130.—A year later, Professor Gross, in heartily commenting upon a new volume
on biology, Gerhard Heberer, *Die Evolution der Organismen, Sammelwerk* (Jena, Fischer,
1943, 774 pp.), confessed before his inner circle: "During the last years, there were recurrent
controversies in public on questions of biology and the discussion sometimes was so utterly
beside the point that for the sake of respect to German scholarship and in order to avoid
further confusion in the ranks of our own folk further discussion outside the professional
periodicals finally was stopped. As is known, I for the same reason also prohibited detailed
treatment of questions of this kind in [Nazi party] training." Cf. *Informationsdienst, Rassenpolitisches Amt der NSDAP, Reichsleitung,* August 20, 1943, no. 140, p. 499.

[386] Otto Westphal, *Das Reich. Aufgang und Vollendung.* Erster Band, 2. und 3. Auflage
(Stuttgart, Kohlhammer, 1943, 668 pp.), p. VIII. The author then continued: "And the idea
into which the current German mandate is to be put is this: for the first time in the history
of the German people, the National Socialist revolution has imposed upon it the duty to let
a new world order rise out of the ideas awakened in it to life. For that duty has never yet
been imposed upon any German greatness and therefore never has been accomplished."

specialized in German minority rights abroad and, since the advent of Hitler, as a matter of course justified each of his territorial demands and acquisitions. The German assault on the East brought studies on ethnic conditions in the Slav countries and on the German contribution to the development of those areas. But in 1943 an interesting and significant volume concerning specific problems of refolking made its appearance.[387]

It seems that this revolutionary theory nowhere was more clearly expounded than in the above-mentioned Wehrmacht publication by Egon Leuschner. In seeming conformity with everything a faithful racialist would profess, he chose the following point of departure:

> A National Socialist policy concerning foreign folk, while recognizing all exigencies of economics, must consider as its supreme principle to do nothing and refrain from everything that can weaken or jeopardize the biological stock of a folk.

He then carefully defined the general folk concepts at which German biological and social sciences had arrived and several of which we have already encountered such as "belonging to foreign folks (fremdvölkisch)," "related in species (artverwandt)," "of like stem—of alien stem (stammesgleich—stammesfremd)," "of German blood (deutschblütig)," "of German stem (deutschstämmig)," "of German folk (volksdeutsch)," "mixed marriage (Mischehe)," and, finally, "assimilation (Assimilation)" and "refolking (Umvolkung)." National socialism, the reader was instructed, always had been utterly opposed to assimilation, meaning as it does a "non-genuine entrance into the foreign folk." There was, however, a definite possibility of amalgamating alien elements "without a danger to race."

> Growing mentally and psychically into another folk, being innerly absorbed by a new folkdom, we describe by the concept "refolking (Umvolkung)". . . . Refolking can take place voluntarily (the Huguenots), if the portion to be refolked brings with it the readiness to refolk, but it can also be imposed and that is what happened as a rule until today through events of power politics, through drawing new frontiers after wars.

[387] *Volkwerdung und Volkstumswandel.* Her. von Carl C. von Loesch (Leipzig, Schwarzhaupter-Verlag [1943], 216 pp.). — Volkstumskundliche Untersuchungen des Instituts für Grenz- und Auslandstudien zum europäischen Problem, 2. Folge.—Some of the subjects, circumspectly investigated and presented as comparative material, were: "The *Blakkede.* An Attempt at Explaining the Interstitial Stratum in Northern Schleswig" (Ernst Schröder); "The Dynamics of Language Change in Schleswig" (Paul Selk); "The Foundations of Scotch Nationalism" (Dr. Gerhard von Tevenar); "The Frisians in the Netherlands" (Hans Peterleitner); "The Estonian-Russian Ethnic Border in South-Eastern Estonia between 1922 and 1934" (Dr. Gerhard Teich); "The Immigration of Croats into the German Reich" (Dr. Lujo Tončić Edler von Sorinj); "The Copts" (Dr. Johann Gottfried Ivo Theiss); "Psychological Problems of Refolking (Professor Dr. Max Hildebert Boehm); "Refolking and Becoming a Folk" (Dr. Wilhelm E. Mühlmann).

Two new terms appear for the first time on page 40: "umvolkungs-fähig (capable of refolking)" and "umvolkungswürdig (worthy of refolking)."

A decision as to which member of the foreign folk ought to be admitted into the blood stream of the German folk is dependent upon his capability of refolking. Thus decision depends in the first place upon what folk he stems from, since it can be of like stem, of alien stem, or of alien race. With members of folks of like stem refolking in general is to be approved of; with folks of alien stem it can be approved of in exceptional cases so long as the individual does not possess traces of alien races (Jewish, Negroid, Asiatic, etc.); as to alien races, refolking is to be denied by principle. Establishing the capability of refolking is not sufficient for passing a judgment and there is need of a complementary test that is no less important. We know that people of each folk, in spite of most far-reaching racial similarity, still are very different as to their mental capacity, achievement, character and so on.... Unfortunately, this point of view is frequently but little taken into consideration when questions of Germanization are discussed.... We have to put up a demand that each member of an alien folk who is to be considered for Germanization must not only be refolkable but worthy of refolking. By his achievement and character he must promise to become the type of a valuable German man.

XXXII

REFOLKING THE LETTS AND THE POLES

In close touch with and upon the instructions of the Reichsführer SS in his capacity as Reich Commissar for the Solidification of German Folkdom, specialists set out to look for "refolkable" groups that would also be "worthy of revolking." The earliest suggestion of this kind we know of was contained in a secret memorandum of October, 1941, by Dr. [Wilhelm] Lenz of the University of Posen, who worked for Rosenberg's civil administration in Riga. The document, entitled "The Racial Composition of the Letts and German Influence upon Them" reached its climax in the conclusion:

The present-day situation of the Lettish people offers the opportunity to carry through the final Germanization (Eindeutschung) of this tribe (Volksstamm) which is related to us in species (artverwandt) and close to us in respect to culture.[388]

---

[388] *Die rassische Zusammensetzung der Letten und ihre Beeinflussung durch die Deutschen.* Copy in the Yivo archives. — Trampedach, head of the Political Department, in handing over this memorandum to Reich Commissar Lohse, added: "Dr. Lenz wrote this report at my personal request. He was a Studienrat [high-school teacher with full academic education] in Mitau [the German name of Jelgava, Latvia] and is now engaged in research work in Posen."

The highest authority of the Ostland, Reich Commissar Lohse, was so well pleased with the idea that he added in red pencil "Excellent."

About a year later Dr. Lüdemann reported to the Propaganda Ministry from Cracow under November 3, 1942:

> There is evidently [in the Government General] the intention to drain the élite (Führerschicht) from the Ukrainian people and also from certain Polish groups and to put it to the use of the Reich through Germanization (Eindeutschung).[389]

Hesitancy as to the Poles is apparent in these few lines. It so happened, however, that the refolking of the Poles especially assumed the proportions of a large-scale problem. Reference to it is found in the following paragraph of Leuschner's book discussed above:

> In certain regions of the old Reich during the last months Polish families were settled as farm workers who do not fall under the restrictive regulations concerning Poles and shall remain settled there permanently. This measure decided upon by the Reich Commissar for the Solidification of German folkdom often was received with surprise and with a feeling of uneasiness out of ignorance of racial biology.

To alleviate the anguish of people who for years had been imbued with orthodox racial teaching, the explanation was offered that, originally, these people had been Germans; consequently they merely had to be brought back into the German folk community. There were two groups among the newcomers, Leuschner suggested. One consisted of persons whose German origin was obvious:

> In spite of their professing to think and to feel in a Polish way they quite ostensibly differ in their whole way of life from the Polish population surrounding them. Cleanliness, sense of order, self-sureness, honesty, straightforwardness, and frankness—these are their characteristics of which the opposite is typical for the Polish folk-character. It would be biologically shortsighted and politically stupid to leave to the Polish folk to make usable for itself these people who after all have in common with the Poles only [sic] their professing Polishness (Polentum) and therefore the Polonized people of German stem have to be regained and Germanized. On the basis of a special selective process, the circle of people of German stem is being tested as to their value by the offices of the Reichsführer SS in his capacity as Reich Commissar for the Solidification of German Folkdom together with the Racial - Policy Office of the

---

Through a bibliographical reference we know of a book by Dr. Lenz on refolking processes in feudal Livonia: *Umvolkungsvorgänge in der ständischen Ordnung Livlands* (Posen, 1941).

[389] Document in the possession of the Yivo.

NSDAP....[390] In order to facilitate this process of their infolking (Einvolkung) they cannot remain among the Polish population since this [association] perhaps could even jeopardize the process of Germanization....

But the other group, whose German origin could not be proved, was not to be rejected either, Leuschner insisted. For racial science teaches that

> refolking of members of peoples of alien stem is possible if the persons to be received into the folk (einzuvolkend) correspond with the racial composition of the German folk, i.e., people who are preponderantly defined as Nordic Faelic. There is no doubt that the Polish folk, if only to a very small extent, does possess folk members who meet these requirements. With the help of a carefully weighted racial sampling, the desettled (abgesiedelte) Polish peasants whose farms were taken over by resettlers (Germans from Volhynia, Bessarabia, etc.) were tested as to their racial capability. In this, the Nordic physical appearance is not valued one-sidedly but in observations extending over weeks the mental, psychical attitude is examined and also evidence about achievements which is important for evaluation is referred to. Judgment is not passed upon the evaluation of the individual person but all individual members of a family or kin (Sippe) are examined and on the basis of the sum total of the established values the decision about the average value of a family is reached.

Should any adherent of racial science still hesitate from motives of conscience, his scruples could be removed by asserting that if a man was good he probably was of German stock anyway:

> The observations and experiences gained in these investigations, from the point of view of character, mind, and psyche, justify the assumption that most of these Polish families still somehow are of German origin, i.e., ultimately only Polonized people of German stem but that the process of Polonizing for them lies so far back that today no documentation like a former German name, baptism, and marriage documents indicate German origin.[391]

XXXIII

SPLITTING UP THE POLES: REFOLKING, ENSLAVEMENT, EXTINCTION

The reasons for giving the Poles precedence in the program of refolking were of a political nature. Several million of them lived

---

[390] Gross' language in the book quoted in footnote 380 was even more direct: "... The Reich Commissar for the Solidification of German Folkdom ... is to establish the circles of such persons according to origin and number and to place them at the disposal of the German people."

[391] Leuschner, *op. cit.*, pp. 41-42.—Note the addition to Third Reich semantics in the preceding quotation: *desettled* for "expropriated."

within the new Reich frontiers on the territories incorporated into the Reich in 1939. Then, fifteen million more were, according to German estimates, in the Government General, i.e., in the immediate vicinity of the Reich. The future of this territory, after three and a half years of German domination, was still undecided; its designation as a by-country (Nebenland) of the Reich was no solution except in that it constituted a new addition to the German vocabulary. As to the fate of the Poles within the Reich, there was no question but that they had to disappear as Poles. With regard to the Government General, Germany's rulers came to the conclusion that about half of its Polish population would qualify for refolking or, to put it flatly, for Germanization.

The problem with all its implications was outlined in a memorandum to the Propaganda Ministry written in the beginning of 1943 and signed by Dr. Gollert. In a decision upon the fate of the Government General and the fate of the Polish people in it, the possibility of a Polish state must be ruled out to begin with, the document stated. Whoever thinks of restituting Polish independence must be ruthlessly extinguished (ausgemerzt) as an enemy of the [German] state. A protectorate likewise would be undesirable as representing some form of Polish self-government. Even the formula of the Governor General Dr. Frank that the Government General is to become "a home (Heimstätte)" of the Poles is utterly inadmissible; the fifteen million Poles now in the area with the passage of time could increase to twenty or twenty-five millions and become dangerous to the Reich. "Only if the entire Vistula space, including the Government General, during the next years and decades ultimately is transformed into a German space, may the Polish danger be considered as removed."

A somewhat earlier report of a high official in the Propaganda Ministry [392] had pointed out that "the Reichsführer SS in his capacity as Reich Commissar for the Solidification of German folkdom follows a policy which, the Governor General feels, can be considered only for peace time and for ultimate settlement planning." Himmler's agencies had no such scruples, as they believed they had the situation well in hand. They therefore went ahead with their plan to balk the Government General "by drawing a 'protective strip' through colonizing 30,000 German peasant families" in the district of Lublin. The

---

[392] Report to Dr. Goebbels by Dr. [Hans] Schmidt-Leonhard, Ministerial-Dirigent in the Propaganda Ministry and Professor at the University of Berlin, on his trip to the Government General, dated November 11, 1942, no. R1621 (Yivo archives).

beginning was made in the Zamość region. Several thousand Poles were rounded up, confined in camps, and later sent away to Germany for forced labor, while their wives and children were loaded into freight cars and deported to various towns in the district of Warsaw. The settlers who moved in were German peasants from Croatia and Bosnia.

But let us come back to the Gollert memorandum. Transformation of the Government General into a German space (or, as another passage bluntly puts it: incorporation into the Reich) presupposed a decision about the population, the document advised. Three possible choices presented themselves.

(a) To Germanize all the fifteen million Poles. But apart from the difficulties, the Germanization of fifteen million aliens (Fremdvölkische) was undesirable in the light of refolking experiences.

> (b) A second solution would consist in extinguishing (auszumerzen) those fifteen million by a radical cure. This solution, too, is to be dismissed. Certainly it can be justified before history sometimes to apply such radical measures for biological reasons, as it has been necessary, for instance, with the Jews. But it is unworthy of a cultural nation simply *this* way to remove an alien folkdom of fifteen millions. The plan of an American to sterilize the male population of the German Reich justly was branded by the entire German press as a disgrace to culture. We Germans also should feel too strong to solve the Polish problem in such a way.[393]

(c) A third solution could be found in evacuating all the Poles from the Vistula space. This was possible technically but undesirable again: it would create the danger of an irredenta, especially if the Poles be removed to the east.

(d) Hence the Poles, it was suggested, should be split up into three categories:

1. Those who can be Germanized as time goes on.
2. Those who are valuable as laborers (arbeitspolitisch) and therefore may remain in the Vistula space.
3. Those who are out of question for German interests and therefore are to be removed from the Vistula space.

---

[393] Be it stated, to make the text entirely clear, that everything set up in smaller type constitutes verbatim quotations; other portions of the documents are related in a language as close as possible to the original.—The Yivo possesses two drafts of the Gollert memorandum. The first, from which the quotation is taken, was dated Warsaw, March 29, 1943; the second, after the words "for instance, with the Jews," continued: "but such a solution seems unworthy of the tradition of the German people with regard to a people large portions of which still live within the Reich borders. The plan of that Jewish American to sterilize . . ."

In deciding who is Germanizable, one could afford to be liberal because millions of Poles are valuable

> not only because of their racial appearance but also because of their capabilities in general. Naturally, in testing this mass of people we should have to free ourselves from our views on the "Nordic man." We may do so calmly if we consider that nearly all Germans east of the Elbe have some Slav touch (cf. the cheekbones of the German population east of the Elbe). After all, "Prussiandom," which no doubt has been of the greatest importance for the state and folk development of our Reich, is a mixture to a large extent of Teutonic and Slav elements. This combination— in the light of centuries—has turned out to be favorable; hence, a renewed blood mixture of valuable Slav Poles with the German population is not to be condemned. It may be estimated that, even if more rigorous standards be adopted, seven to eight million Poles may score as Germanizable.

Into the second group might be classified four to six million Poles who could be used "without danger" as laborers.

Finally, there remained two to three million

> who are without any value to us Germans. Here belong not only the Polish fanatics who naturally are to be extinguished (ausgemerzt) without remainder but, moreover, all asocial elements, all sick persons and other persons who are out of the question for our interests as laborers as well.

"As to this third category," the document signed by Dr. Gollert concluded, "which in numbers is considerably smaller than the other two, radical measures cannot be avoided (werden Radikalmittel nicht zu vermeiden sein)."

Rumors to the effect that the Poles ultimately would fare no better than the Jews had been current among the Polish population ever since the mass extinction had begun. A "strictly confidential" report by a representative of Goebbels' ministry in the Government General (now in the possession of the Yivo) informed his chiefs about a particularly brutal German police raid in Lublin, which took place on October 1, 1942: "All Poles, men and women, who could not prove that they had work were carried away and brought to a camp. Their children under fifteen years of age were turned over to an orphanage." The propaganda official then proceeded to say:

> . . . The whole city is furious over the action. Many Poles say: "Were we not right that the deportation over the Bug [to the east] is coming. It came earlier than expected. It began promptly on October 1 in the morning." The fact that the people were registered according to age and sex is considered a proof of deporta-

tion over the Bug. Furthermore it is maintained that the evacuated are allowed to take with them no more than 25 kg. [56 pounds] of baggage. This is alleged to be a proof that an action like that against the Jews is envisaged. The Poles [people say] now are about to be used for soap production just like the Jews.

The anonymous official showed no excitement over the allegation that Germany was producing soap from the fats of the slaughtered Jews. Nor did he refute the accusation as groundless.

The above mentioned Propaganda Ministry memorandum written on February 23, and also a previous draft of February 15, 1943, related that rumors about the intended splitting-up of the Poles, with the prospective fate of each class clearly indicated, had become particularly intense in the days immediately following "the blow of Stalingrad," i.e., at the beginning of 1943. No other proof is needed to show that Dr. Gollert's plan was by no means a brain-child of his own but rather a set of ideas current among the German administration of the Government General. "The resistance movement answered with the statement that the Poles, consequently, are to share the fate of the Jews and that they now practically are confronted with nothingness." Another report, dated February 15, 1943, and also in the possession of the Yivo, put it this way: . . . "The rumor spreads among the Polish population that the Poles are threatened with the same fate as the Jews, about whose treatment each Pole in the Government General is most accurately informed." Why the wholesale murder of the Polish people did not actually occur is a matter of guess. Certainly suspicions about humane considerations are out of place when one recalls Hitler's order given on the eve of the war and revealed at the Nuremberg trial: "Have no pity. Have a brutal attitude . . . kill without pity all men, women and children of the Polish race or language." [394]

It may be assumed that the two to three million Poles "who are without any value to us Germans" were saved by the turn of military fortune and the beginning decline in Germany's might. The annihilation of the remaining Jews, it is true, continued with increasing momentum, but there was not enough energy left to embark upon another even bigger enterprise of this kind. Had German successes on the battlefields continued some years longer not only some millions of Poles might have shared the fate of the Jews but also other peoples might have undergone "splitting-up" and annihilation. Even the

[394] *New York Times*, November 24, 1945.

Ukrainians, of whom very many had supported Hitlerism from the outset, were slated for the same fate. Dr. Taubert's 1944 report (see page 114) boasted, rightly or wrongly, that only the interference of the Propaganda Ministry had prevented "the total extermination (Ausrottung) of the Ukrainian intelligentsia."

As matters stood, only one part of the program, refolking, took place, and to no small degree. We now understand better whence came part of the "displaced persons" whom the armies of the Western Allies discovered in Germany. Whether their claim to have been brought to Germany against their wish is justified in all cases does not concern us here; certainly, serious doubts of unwillingness are justified at least the case of the Lettish or Estonian SS and their following.

XXXIV

CONTINUING EXTINCTION OF THE JEWS: REVISION IN THEORY, CONSISTENCY IN PRACTICE

On the "Jewish question" too, German science had arrived at some fundamental revision in doctrine. "Aryan," as we have seen, was discarded first, though Hitler himself relapsed into the old habit of using the term. Then, "Semitic" and, by inference, "anti-Semitic" were cast away. The Jewish *Rasse* turned out to be a myth. In trying to get himself out of the scrape, an SS writer in a book drawing heavily from such scholars as Kühn-Staemmler-Burgdörfer, Erwin Baur, Hans F. K. Günther, Arthur Gütt, Ernst Rüdin, and others, declared: "The Jews are not to be called a race but they do represent a psychically uniform racial type." [395] Several years of strenuous efforts by scientists were needed again to reach the conclusion that this "counter-race" in effect represented a race mixture, i.e., was no different from any other "racial" group. But it *had* to be fundamentally different, so it had to be proved that the Jews were a *specific* mixture, "no organic mixture," whatever an "organic" mixture may be. And why did not the Jewish race come out from the melting pot according to the general laws of racial blending? Because, said the race students, of the particular historical circumstances, in which the Jews had lived several thousand years. But historical circumstances, according to German science itself, create folks, ethnic groups, out of divergent racial ingredients. If so, are not the Jews, after all, an ethnic group or, in

[395] P. 41 in the publication mentioned in footnote 67.

Nazi usage, a *folk?* No, they *cannot* possibly be a folk because the scientific basis for the *Ausmerze* would fall into ruins, and German mentality had taken such a shape during the nineteenth century that a scientific foundation had to be provided for any actual policy. So the Jews were, for a time, promoted into a "counter-folk (Gegenvolk)," whatever that means, until Dr. Gerhard Teich arrived at a concept that was even better suited to demonstrate *quod erat demonstrandum,* namely that the Jews were to be wiped out. The Jews, it was currently maintained, were a "sham folk (Scheinvolk)" and Walter Gross was so eager to make this new discovery accessible to his disciples that he reprinted the paper and released it through his highly official information service:

> The fate of and compulsion on Jewry is, independent of its will, an assault on human society [Dr. Teich declared]. This unequivocal stand explains why it is impossible to solve the Jew-problem.... A right understanding of Jewry must require its complete annihilation.[396]

But, although theory had to be overhauled, practice provoked and justified by it went on. Or, to use Walter Gross' conceptual framework, while "racial science" was reformulating its tenets, "racial politics" with regard to the Jews continued in full gear.

We have already summarized above what had happened in the Government General from the fateful summer of 1942 through the battle of the Warsaw ghetto, which began on April 18, 1943. For 1944, only one scarce item can be quoted; it is found in an article by Ernst Kundt, Governor of the District of Radom, in one of the showy periodicals of the Cracow Institut für deutsche Ostarbeit. Note the sober academic language depicting the extermination of at least a million and three-quarters human beings:

> The Jew and half-Jew in the non-German sphere, too, was less and less admitted to participation until he was completely isolated and partly was deported (ausgesiedelt), partly harnessed for aggregate [397] useful work under German supervision.... It can be stated here that for the Government General the Jewish question has been solved without remainder within a short time....[398]

---

[396] Dr. G[erhard] Teich "Scheinvolklichkeit des Judentums," *Volk und Rasse* (May, 1942). Reprinted in *Informationsdienst, Rassenpolitisches Amt der NSDAP, Reichsleitung,* August 20, 1943, no. 140, pp. 491-498. The terminological development in this passage, too, merits attention. To Teich, "solution" meant according the Jews some form of existence; he therefore preferred to put the dot on the i.—Another paper on the Jews as a sham folk was published in *Volk und Rasse* (January, 1943, pp. 16-17) by Hermann Stölting.

[397] 'Aggregate (geschlossen)" was meant to signify forced labor in working squads.

[398] Ernst Kundt, Unterstaatssekretär, Gouverneur des Distrikts Radom, "Enstehung, Probleme, Grundsätze und Form der Verwaltung des Generalgouvernements," *Die Burg,* V (April, 1944), 47-67. The quotation is from p. 53.

As to the Ostland, where the large-scale "actions" had started a year earlier in a somewhat improvised manner, the beginning of 1942 saw the application of more careful advance planning. *Die Judenfrage* of February 1, 1942, contained the following passage:

> ... The task has been from the very beginning to render harmless this element which is radically hostile to German nature and German order.... The Jewish question of the Ostland now under German leadership comes into the sphere of fundamental, systematic, and disciplined solutions....

A group of German journalists taken on an information tour through the Ostland in the summer of 1942 unanimously reported very definite progress:

> Where there are still Jews in the country, they have been collected in ghettos behind barbed wire, they are being used in groups for clearance work or function as artisans where there are no native artisans, as mostly is the case in the East. In cities like Dünaburg [Daugavpils, Dvinsk], which had eighty per cent Jews, Minsk which had fifty per cent, Vilna, which had thirty per cent Jews among the population, a clear atmosphere has been created through the elimination of Jewry.[399]

"In the streets [of the towns of Latgale, the easternmost province of Latvia]," the writer remarked in another passage, "war prisoners and Jewish columns are engaged in clearance and repair work." That was all he had to say about the Jews. Another reporter, who went into more details about the city of Vilna, wrote:

> In 1939, Vilna had a population of about 250,000. Of them, sixty per cent were Poles, thirty per cent Jews.... The Jewish question, through the creation of ghettos and deportation (Aussiedlung) essentially has been solved....

The German administration obviously was doing a thorough job. We shall recall the momentary remorse of Commissar General Kube in Minsk as exemplified by his letter of December 16, 1941, and how he was rebuked by his superiors. Within six months, Kube himself had changed completely: every tinge of sentiment was gone and there remained only the unwillingness to be bothered with new transports of Jews. On July 10, 1942, Kube explained to his subordinates[400] that "the economic value of the Jewish skilled workers as regards their numbers is quite out of proportion to the disadvantages which Jewish support of the partisans involves." He therefore urged a reexamination, "applying the strictest standards," of the necessity of

---

[399] *Auf Informationsfahrt im Ostland. Reiseeindrücke deutscher Schriftleiter* (Riga, 1944, 307 pp.), pp. 54, 66, 116.

[400] Document in the possession of the Yivo.

keeping the previous numbers of Jewish skilled workers, and a segregation (aussondern) of those who economically were not absolutely necessary. As to those Jewish skilled workers who "even then will temporarily be needed," they have to be "strictly confined to barracks, and the principle of absolute separation of the sexes is to be applied."

The full meaning of this order was revealed in the report which Kube wrote to his superior in Riga three weeks later, on July 31, 1942:

> In all clashes with partisans in White Russia it turned out that both in the former Polish and in the former Soviet parts of the District General, Jewry together with the Polish resistance movement in the West[401] and the Red Army men in the East is the main carrier of the partisan movement. Therefore, the treatment of Jewry in White Russia in view of the menace to the entire economy is an eminently political matter which therefore should be solved, too, not from the economic but from the political point of view. In detailed conferences with SS brigade leader Zenner and the eminently able director of the SD, SS Obersturmbannführer Dr. jur. Strauch, we in the last ten weeks in White Russia liquidated about 55,000 Jews. In the rural region of Minsk Jewry has been completely extinguished (ausgemerzt) without jeopardizing the manpower supply. In the predominantly Polish region of Lida 16,000 Jews were liquidated, in Slonim 8,000 Jews, etc. By an encroachment of the Rear Army Region of which report to you already has been made, the preparations made by us for liquidating the Jews in the region of Głębokie were disturbed. The Rear Army Region, without getting in touch with me, liquidated 10,000 Jews whose systematic extinction (Ausmerzung) had been planned by us anyway. In the city of Minsk on July 28th and 29th about 10,000 Jews were liquidated, among them 6,500 Russian Jews—predominantly old people, women and children—the rest consisted of Jews unable to work (nichteinsatzfähige) who in November last by the Führer's order were sent to Minsk from Vienna, Brünn [Brno], Bremen, and Berlin.
>
> The region of Slutsk, too, has been relieved (erleichtert) of several thousand Jews. The same applies to Nowogródek and Wilejka. Radical measures are still in store for Baranowicze and Hancewicze. In Baranowicze in the town itself still live about 10,000 Jews, of whom 9,000 will be liquidated next month.
>
> In the city of Minsk there have remained 2,600 Jews from Germany. In addition, all the 6,000 Russian Jews and Jewesses are still alive who during the action remained as manpower with the units that employ them. Minsk in the future, too, will retain the largest number of Jews (Judeneinsatz) since this is for the

---

[401] By mistake, the original has the word *Osten* (East) twice.

Geheim!

Abt. IIa Nr. 2407/428

Minsk, am 31. Juli 1942

Der Generalkommissar
für Weissruthenien

Abtlg. Gauleiter/G.- 507/429.
(Bei Beantwortung unbedingt anzugeben!)

Der Reichskommissar für das Ostland
Tgb. Nr. _____ 1122/42 g.

Geheime Reichssache!
.-.-.-.-.-.-.-.-.-.-.-.-.-.-.-.

Herrn

Reichskommissar für das Ostland
Gauleiter Hinrich L o h s e ,

R i g a

V. 118.

> **Reichskommissar
> Ostland
> 7. VIII. 1942
> Hauptabt**

Betreff: Partisanenbekämpfung und Judenaktion
im Generalbezirk Weißruthenien.

       Bei allen Zusammenstößen mit Partisanen in Weißruthenien
hat es sich herausgestellt, daß das Judentum sowohl im ehemals
polnischen wie auch im ehemals sowjetischen Teil des Generalbezirks
zusammen mit der polnischen Widerstandsbewegung im Osten und den
Roten armisten Moskaus im Osten Hauptträger der Partisanenbewegung
ist. Infolgedessen ist die Behandlung des Judentums in Weißrutheni-
en angesichts der Gefährdung der gesamten Wirtschaft eine hervorragend politische Angelegenheit, die infolgedessen auch nicht nach
wirtschaftlichen, sondern nach politischen Gesichtspunkten gelöst
werden müßte. In eingehenden Besprechungen mit dem SS-Brigadeführ-
rer Zenner und dem hervorragend tüchtigen Leiter des SD, SS-
Obersturmbannführer Dr.jur. Strauch, haben wir in Weißruthenien in
den letzten 10 Wochen rund 55.000 Juden liquidiert. Im Gebiet
Minsk-Land ist das Judentum völlig ausgemerzt, ohne daß der Arbeitseinsatz dadurch gefährdet worden ist. In dem überwiegend polnischen
Gebiet Lida sind 16.000 Juden, in Slonim 8.000 Juden usw. liquidiert
worden. Durch einen dorthin bereits berichteten Übergriff des Rück-
wärtigen Heeresgebietes sind die von uns getroffenen Vorbereitun-
gen für die Liquidierung der Juden im Gebiet Glebokie gestört worden. Das Rückwärtige Heeresgebiet hat, ohne Fühlung mit mir zu nehmen, 10.000 Juden liquidiert, deren systematische Ausmerzung von
uns sowieso vorgesehen war. In Minsk-Stadt sind am 28. und 29.Juli
rund 10.000 Juden liquidiert worden, davon 6.500 russische Juden -
überwiegend Alte, Frauen und Kinder - der Rest bestand aus nicht-
einsatzfähigen Juden, die überwiegend aus Wien, Brünn, Bremen und

                                   b.w.

188

Berlin im November des v.J. nach Minsk auf den Befehl des Führers
geschickt worden sind.

Auch das Gebiet Sluzk ist um mehrere tausend Juden erleichtert
worden. Das Gleiche gilt für Nowogrodek und Wilejka. Radikale Maßnahmen stehen noch für Baranowitschi und Hanzewitschi bevor. In
Baranowitschi leben allein in der Stadt noch rund 10.000 Juden,
von denen 9.000 Juden im nächsten Monat liquidiert werden.

In Minsk-Stadt sind 2.600 Juden aus Deutschland übrig geblieben.
Außerdem sind noch sämtliche 6.000 russische Juden und Jüdinnen am
Leben, die als Arbeitseinsatz während der Aktion bei den sie be-
schäftigenden Einheiten verblieben sind. Minsk wird auch in Zukunft
noch immer den stärksten Judeneinsatz behalten, da die Zusammen-
ballung der Rüstungsbetriebe und die Aufgaben der Eisenbahn das
vorläufig notwendig macht. In sämtlichen übrigen Gebieten wird die
Zahl der zum Arbeitseinsatz kommenden Juden vom SD und mir auf
höchstens 800, nach Möglichkeit aber auf 500, festgesetzt, sodaß
wir nach Beendigung der noch angekündigten Aktionen in Minsk 8.600
und in den 10 übrigen Gebieten, einschließlich des judenfreien Ge-
bietes Minsk-Land, etwa 7000 Juden übrig behalten. Die Gefahr, daß
die Partisanen sich in Zukunft noch wesentlich auf das Judentum
stützen können, besteht dann nicht mehr. Mir und dem SD wäre es
natürlich das liebste, nach Wegfall der wirtschaftlichen Ansprüche
der Wehrmacht, das Judentum im Generalbezirk Weißruthenien endgültig zu beseitigen. Vorläufig werden die notwendigen Ansprüche der
Wehrmacht, die in der Hauptsache Arbeitgeber des Judentums ist, be-
rücksichtigt.

Zu dieser eindeutigen Einstellung dem Judentum gegenüber kommt
noch die schwere Aufgabe für den SD in Weißruthenien, immer wieder
neue Judentransporte aus dem Reich ihrer Bestimmung zuzuführen.
Das nimmt die materiellen und seelischen Kräfte der Männer des SD
über Gebühr in Anspruch und entzieht sie ihren Aufgaben, die im
Raume Weißrutheniens selbst liegen.

Ich wäre daher dankbar, wenn der Herr Reichskommissar es

- 2 -

Geheim!

ermöglichen könnte, weitere Judentransporte nach Minsk wenigstens
solange zu stoppen, bis die Partisanengefahr endgültig überwunden
worden ist. Ich brauche den SD im hundertprozentigen Einsatz gegen
die Partisanen und gegen die polnische Widerstandsbewegung, die
beide alle Kräfte der nicht überwiegend starken SD-Einheiten in Anspruch nehmen.

Nach Beendigung der Minsker Judenaktion meldet mir heute
Nacht mit gerechter Empörung SS-Obersturmbannführer Dr. Strauch,
daß plötzlich ohne Weisung des Reichsführers SS und ohne Benachrich-
tigung des Generalkommissars ein Transport von 1.000 Juden aus
Warschau für den hiesigen Luftgau eingetroffen sind.

Ich bitte den Herrn Reichskommissar (bereits durch Fern-
schreiben vorbereitet), derartige Transporte als höchster Hoheits-
träger im Ostland zu unterbinden. Der polnische Jude ist genau wie
der russische Jude ein Feind des Deutschtums. Er stellt ein poli-
tisch gefährliches Element dar, dessen politische Gefahr weit das
übertrifft, was er als Facharbeiter wert ist. Unter keinen Umständen
können in einem Gebiet der Zivilverwaltung Wehrmachtsdienststellen
des Heeres oder der Luftwaffe ohne Genehmigung des Herrn Reichskommissars aus dem Generalgouvernement oder anderswoher Juden hier
einführen, die die gesamte politische Arbeit und die Sicherung des
Generalbezirks gefährden. Ich bin mit dem Kommandeur des SD in
Weißruthenien darin völlig einig, daß wir jeden Judentransport,
der nicht von unseren vorgesetzten Dienststellen befohlen oder ange-
kündigt ist, liquidieren, um weitere Beunruhigungen in Weißruthenien
zu verhindern.

Der Generalkommissar für
Weißruthenien.

190

time being necessitated by the clustering of military enterprises and by the tasks of the railroad. In the rest of the regions the number of Jews employed as manpower is being fixed by the SD and myself at a maximum of 800, but as far as possible at 500; we shall thus retain, after the termination of the anticipated actions, about 8,600 Jews in Minsk and in the ten other regions, including the rural region of Minsk, which is free of Jews. There will then not be any more the danger that the partisans materially rely on Jewry. Naturally, both I and the SD would much prefer, after the economic demands of the Wehrmacht cease to exist, finally to get rid of (beseitigen) Jewry in the District General of White Russia. For the time being the necessity demands of the Wehrmacht, which in the main is the employer of Jewry, are taken into consideration.

This unequivocal attitude toward Jewry is augmented by the hard task of the SD in White Russia again and again to dispose of (ihrer Bestimmung zuzuführen) new transports of Jews from the Reich. This immoderately taxes the material and psychical power of the SD men and takes them away from their tasks lying in the space of White Russia itself.

I should therefore appreciate it if the Reich Commissar could make it possible to stop further transports of Jews to Minsk at least until the partisans menace is ultimately overcome. I need the SD 100 per cent against the partisans and against the Polish resistance movement, both of whom tax all the power of the not too strong SD.

After the end of the Jewish action in Minsk SS Obersturmbann-führer Dr. Strauch today informs me with just indignation that suddenly, without an order by the Reichsführer SS and without warning to the Commissar General, a transport of 1,000 Jews for the air force command (Luftgau) here has arrived.

I ask the Reich Commissar (as already suggested by telegram) in his capacity as the highest carrier of sovereignty in the Ostland to stop transports of this kind. The Polish Jew like the Russian Jew is an enemy of Germandom. He represents a politically dangerous element whose political dangerousness far surpasses what he is worth as a skilled worker. Under no circumstances can Wehrmacht units of the Army or the Luftwaffe in a civil government area import here, without the permission of the Reich Commissar, Jews from the Government General or from anywhere else who jeopardize the entire political work and the security of the District General. I am completely in agreement with the SD commander in White Russia in that we liquidate every transport of Jews that had not been ordered or announced by our superior organs so as to prevent further disturbances in White Russia.

The Commissar General
for White Russia KUBE

Now Kube had shown himself equal to the task he had been entrusted with and he could look his superiors straight into their faces when an inquiry from Rosenberg's ministry arrived signed by [Dr. Georg] Leibbrandt, the political scientist who had proved to be a very efficient executive as well:

Berlin, October 23, 1942.

Re: Jewish question.

Please inform on the state of the Jewish question in the District General of White Russia, particularly about whether Jews are still employed by German administrative agencies, be it as interpreters, artisans, etc. Please report speedily since I intend to bring about a solution of the Jewish question as soon as possible.

The penciled question mark on the margin of the document referring to the words "as soon as possible" may be in Kube's own hand. The job of "solving" had been almost accomplished even before explicit orders had been issued. With the air of a person who had done his duty, Kube replied:

November 23, 1942.

Re: Jewish question.

With regard to your decree of October 23, 1942.

Jewry in the District General of Minsk during the first year of the civil government has been reduced to the number of about 30,000 in the whole District General. The rural areas may be said to have been cleansed of Jews. Jewish ghettos are in existence exclusively in a number of larger towns of the District General. The inmates (Insassen) of the ghettos are under strong surveillance and consist solely of absolutely necessary skilled workers and labor that for the time being cannot be supplanted by native workers. Not a single Jew any more is employed in White Russia in the capacity of an interpreter. Only artisans and skilled workers still serve German authorities and military units. In agreement with the Sicherheits-Dienst, the possibilities of further pushing back (Zurückdrängung) Jewry are constantly examined and made use of....

All this went on behind an iron curtain. The German press was instructed not to report on details of the extinction activities, lest the newspapers fall into the hands of foreigners who might not accept unconditionally Hitler's formula: "If I lead into war and death hundreds of thousands of worthiest German youth, shall I refrain from extinguishing the worst enemies of Germany?" [402] In periodicals issued

    402 Secret. Press Department, Reich Government Division Head (Referent) for the Press of the Eastern space. Confidential Information no. 3/42, Berlin, February 10, 1942 (copy in the Yivo archives): " ... On the Jewish question ... in the occupied Eastern territories, ... the press within the Reich territory does not report."—Cf. the circular letter of the Propaganda Ministry, dated July 24, 1943, no. 194/43 g (7)—S 8240/R 1485 (copy in the Yivo

in the occupied East the blackout was sometimes lifted by a matter-of-fact communication of a line or two to the effect that Jews had not been counted in the Lithuanian census of 1942 or the Latvian census of 1943.[403] Or a regulation was issued that Jews working in forced labor squads were not to receive any payment themselves and that compensation for their work was to be paid to the treasury of the respective Gebiet commissariat.[404] But from some time in 1942 no mention at all is made any more of the Jews in the law gazettes or in economic and statistical surveys. Professor Dr. Dagobert Frey of the University of Breslau, the prominent historian of art who at the very beginning of the war had been called in to serve the occupation government, as early as 1941 had contrived to publish a magnificently illustrated book on Cracow without even once mentioning the Jews who had formed part of the city for over half a thousand years, and in a 1942 guide to Lublin — also one of the oldest Jewish communities in Poland with forty thousand Jews in 1939—the word Jew is mentioned only once, in passing, in the historical survey.[405] Splendidly illustrated official monthlies like *Ostland* contained essays on "Classicism and Romanticism in the Painting of the Ostland" and reported that Commissar Hingst in Vilna—a man directly responsible for the death of tens of thousands of Jews—had accepted chairmanship in the newly founded Vilna Kulturring (Culture Circle), a society for music, literature, and art appreciation consisting of both Germans and Lithuanians. The Jews were not even worthy of having their disappearance recorded. They had been handed over to Kaltenbrunner's Sicherheits-Dienst and, as opportunity offered, they were killed secretly or, in another neologism which occurs in the secret reports of the SD, they were "treated in a special manner (sonderbehandelt)." The

---

archives): "By order of the Führer henceforth the export of printed material is not to take place in all cases in which utilization against the Greater German Reich must be envisaged. This regulation applies to all products of press and printing, official printed matter, business advertising matter, address books and directories, lists of firms, industrial reports, etc. Since such a utilization of printed material is possible not only in the case of export, all data that somehow could be useful to the enemy should be kept out of printed materials, as far as they are available to the public, by way of censorship before printing."

[403] Cf. *Ostland*, 1942, p. 22, on the preliminary returns of the Lithuanian census of May, 1942.—Cf. *Statistische Berichte für den Generalbezirk Lettland*, Jahresheft 1943 (Riga, 1943, 211 pp.), p. 133; *Statistische Berichte für das Ostland*, January-April, 1944, p. 5. These reports were compiled by the well-known statistician and demographer Dr. Eugen Stieda, Director of the Central Statistical Division in the Reich Commissariat for the Ostland.

[404] Directive on Compensation for Jewish Labor in the District General of Latvia, *Amtsblatt des Generalkomissars in Riga*, 2, 1 (1942), 149.

[405] Cf. p. 84. Frey even refused to identify Cracow as a *Polish* city. Dagobert Frey, *Krakau* (Berlin, Deutscher Kunstverlag [1941], 48 pp., 96 ill.), p. 45: "There may be [sic] Slav traits, only with difficulty conceivable as to details. But as a whole what results here from the interpretation of a Northern and Southern culture sphere is an admirably grown unity which has its strongest and most prolific roots in German soil." In 1939, Cracow had a population of about 240,000, among them about 60,000 Jews.—Fritz Schiller and Max Otto Vandrey, *Führer durch die Stadt Lublin* (Krakau, Buchverlag Deutscher Osten, 1942, 27 pp.).

Anordnung
über die Entschädigung jüdischer Arbeitskräfte im Generalbezirk Lettland.
Vom 19. März 1942.

Zur Regelung der Entschädigung jüdischer Arbeitskräfte im Generalbezirk Lettland wird folgendes angeordnet:

§ 1

Juden erhalten selbst keinen Lohn.

§ 2

(1) Wer jüdische Arbeitskräfte beschäftigt, hat eine Entschädigung an die Finanzkasse des zuständigen Gebietskommissars zu zahlen, die sich in ihrer Höhe nach den in der „Allgemeinen Anordnung für die einheimischen Arbeiter im öffentlichen Dienste und in der Wirtschaft" des Reichskommissars für das Ostland vom 21. November 1941 (VBl. S. 45) festgelegten Lohnsätzen richtet. Die Gebietskommissare erlassen für die Einzahlung besondere Bestimmungen.

(2) Für Mehr-, Sonn-, Feiertags- und Nachtarbeit, die nur mit Zustimmung des zuständigen Gebietskommissars — Arbeitsamt — gefordert werden kann, ist ein Zuschlag nicht zu zahlen.

§ 3

Wer gegen diese Anordnung verstösst, kann mit Haft, Geldstrafe oder beiden Strafen bestraft werden.

§ 4

(1) Diese Anordnung tritt mit der Veröffentlichung in Kraft.

(2) Frühere entgegenstehende Vereinbarungen und Anordnungen gelten damit als aufgehoben.

Riga, den 19. März 1942.

Der Generalkommissar in Riga
Im Auftrage:
D o r r

(Veröffentlicht in der DZ im Ostland Nr. 90 31. 3. 1942)

context suggests that, in the Ostland, this term meant wholesale shooting.

XXXV
THE SCIENTIFIC ASPECTS OF THE DEATH FACTORIES

When the death factory at Oświęcim was established—in comparison with its output the Ostland liquidations looked like a mallet against a sledge-hammer—its managers, too, termed their activity *sonderbehandeln;* in writing, as a time-saving device, the abbreviation *SB* was adopted. Apparently, linguistic creativity has its limits. Whether the operators of the movable gas-wagons, whether the managers of Majdanek, Treblinka, Dachau, Buchenwald, Belsen-Bergen, and all the minor death factories were more inventive as to terminology perhaps will be told some day.

Because of their research work, the death factories, too, form part of our subject. Himmler expressed his vivid interest in the plants by personal visits, and direction was in the hands of the chief of the Sicherheits-Dienst Ernst Kaltenbrunner. But "production" could not have been started and kept going except for the participation of high-grade construction engineers; scientific management was applied; and at least at Dachau and Oświęcim research in biology and medicine was an integral part of the system. While the Renaissance had raised the problem of using corpses for scientific purposes, twentieth-century rejuvenated Germany had progressed to a stage where there was no lack of living human beings for all kinds of experimentation. Very little, to be sure, will ever be known about the places as compared with the countless tragedies which they witnessed; the victims of the experiments, even if they could be subpoenaed, only in very few cases could be expected to give the names of the experimenters or to define exactly what scientific supposition or theory they were privileged to have tested on them for the benefit of mankind. But it so happens that at least some picture as to the scientific aspects of the two death camps have become available.

The defendants in the Dachau trial comprised five physicians, among them Dr. Fritz Hintermeyer and Dr. Klaus Schilling. The latter was sentenced to death by hanging for killing hundreds of inmates by experimenting on them with malaria germs. Other scientists at Dachau used to freeze prisoners by immersing them in ice-cold water and then tried on them different methods of reviving. The experiments are said to have been suggested by medical higher-ups as far back as May, 1942, and started by order of Goering in May, 1942.[406]

Much more intimate details can now be presented on the research activities at the Oświęcim camp owing to a small book in Polish published in Warsaw in the second half of 1945 by Dr. Filip Friedman.[407] In spite of their efforts, the Germans could not manage to burn all the files as they had to leave, under the onslaught of the Red Army, on January 27, 1945. Friedman's study is based on an analysis of those original files and on the testimony of some trustworthy survivors from among the inmates, chiefly medical men.

Oświęcim is a Polish town west of Cracow.[408] On an experimental scale, gassing started here on September 15, 1941, when Germany seemed to have brought the entire world to its knees. In 1942, the firm of I. A. Toff und Söhne in Erfurt undertook to build two up-to-date crematories in nearby Brzezinki, called by the Germans Birkenau and also known as Oświęcim II. Later two more crematories, even more modern ones, were added. Besides, uncounted numbers of inmates died of starvation or were killed by other means than gassing and cremating. Production ceased by order of Berlin on September 2, 1944. According to rather conservative estimates, during the three years roughly five million people — predominantly, but not exclusively Jews—were delivered to the place which extended over an area of sixteen square miles; only tens of thousands came out alive, very few of them Jews. The SS man knew quite well what he spoke about when he warned the incoming victims ominously, pointing in the direction of the crematories: "Don't try to escape; there is only one way out of here—by the chimney."

When measured with the yardstick of a profit-making private enterprise, Oświęcim certainly was guilty of a good deal of waste. But judging it that way would mean applying improper standards. Primarily, it was established for annihilating people; everything else, including research, was incidental. Viewed from that angle, Oświęcim was a masterpiece of construction and management, appallingly effi-

---

[406] Cf. *New York Times*, November 17 and 18, 1945; *New York Herald Tribune*, December 16, 1945.

[407] Friedman, Dr. Filip, *To jest Oświęcim!* [This Is Oświęcim] (Warszawa, Państwowe Wydawnictwo Literatury Politycznej, 1945. 109 pp.), pp. 19, 21, 31, 38, 42, 53-54, 55, 56, 57, 58, 61-62, 81, 83, 84, 100. The author, a noted historian in pre-war Poland affiliated with the Yiddish Scientific Institute, survived underground and is now director of the Central Jewish Historical Committee in Poland.

Cf. also: *Souvenirs de la Maison des Morts. Le Massacre des Juifs. Documents inédits sur les camps d'exterminations* (Paris, L. Simon, 1945, 78 pp.).

[408] Sometimes it is referred to under the German name of Auschwitz.

cient for its purpose. It is almost beyond comprehension that, under the very eyes of their torturers, the *morituri* carried on underground activities and that at least once, on November 25, 1943, even an open rebellion of about seventeen hundred Warsaw Jews took place; of course, it was doomed in advance.

As befits far-sighted planning, research work was provided for from the outset. There was a Wissenschaftliche Abteilung (Scientific Department) in block 10 of Camp Oświęcim I where experiments on women were carried on. Professor Schumann[409] was interested in sterilization by X-rays and surgical operations; he was assisted in his work by Dr. Wirths, and Dr. Bruno Weber is also mentioned in this connection. Experiments in sterilization by the use of chemicals were conducted by Dr. Carl Clauberg, professor of gynecology at the University of Königsberg, author of several books and over fifty research papers, who had taken a leave of absence from the university[410] to continue his studies under infinitely more favorable conditions than at the University's Women's Hospital in which he previously had been chief physician. His assistant was Dr. Goebel. Other scholars were engaged in mass experiments on artificial impregnation. Still another group of women were experimented upon through the transplantation of cancer tissue into the uterus. The "Statistical Survey of Number and Dislocation of Women Prisoners according to Different Categories" contained a permanent heading: "Prisoners Assigned to Different Experiments." From May 15 to July 30, 1944, 1,508 women were listed under that heading. Experiments in sterilizing and castrating men were conducted, too. Dr. Fritz Klein carried on experiments in subcutaneous injections of petroleum, etc.; cut-out parts of the skin and tissues were sent to Breslau for histologic investigations. Experiments on malaria were conducted here, too.

Among the physicians who used to select the incoming victims and to send a considerable part of them directly to the gas chambers were Dr. Helmerson, Dr. Thiele, Dr. Koenig, Dr. Mengele. Some of them had also scientific ambitions. Dr. Koenig, an aspiring surgeon, was fond of amputations and used to cut off limbs which could have healed without surgery within a week or two; then the patients were SB'ed. Koenig, furthermore, engaged in mass experiments on the

[409] No details about this professor are available.
[410] Clauberg is listed as being on leave of absence both in the central university catalogue *Deutsches Hochschulverzeichnis* for 1941-1942 and in the Königsberg University catalogue of summer, 1944.

effect of electric current on the human brain and this way, too, disposed of many inmates. Dr. Thiele, together with a Dr. Fischer, without looking much for indications, conducted operations of hernia. Dr. Endress, as soon as an inmate complained of pain in the stomach, carried out a so-called gastroenterostomy. Most of the operated upon died on the operation table; if not, they were gassed afterwards.

Dr. Joseph Mengele, assistant at the Institute of Hereditary Biology and Race Research founded in 1934 in Frankfort by Professor Dr. Otmar Freiherr von Verschuer (see p. 27),[411] was known to be particularly severe and sometimes used to send whole transports to the gas chambers immediately on their arrival. But he was a scholar in his field and even while serving Führer and Reich he did not forget his studies in twins. Prisoners who worked at the reception tracks sometimes managed to whisper to the new arrivals about Dr. Mengele's racial-biological research. In no time children who somewhat resembled each other were brought together and taught new names, and then they introduced themselves to the Germans with the formula: "We are twins." Usually they were put aside for Dr. Mengele's studies and part of them have survived. How many real twins there were among the alleged two hundred children whom Mengele selected nobody knows. "At any rate," Dr. Friedman grimly observes, "racial science in this case did not build upon very firm foundations."

Another Oświęcim scholar, unfortunately not mentioned by name, was tempted to investigate the extent of biological difference between Eastern and Western European Jews; "racial science" at times had hinted at differences among the Jews themselves (Sephardim and Ashkenazim). Therefore, two groups were given typhus injections. The westerners really turned out to be much less resistant than the control group of Eastern-European Jews and nearly all of them died within ten days.

German pharmaceutical firms, we are told, sent their new preparations to the camp for trying them on inmates. From several blocks, experiments are reported about whose nature there are few particulars.

Three and a half miles from Oświęcim, in Rajsko, there was another research institution, the so-called Institute of Hygiene, in which about fifty researchers from among the prisoners were put to work.

---

[411] Dr. Mengele is mentioned in the University of Frankfort catalogue of 1943.

A certain Le Motte from Liége, Belgium, was in charge. The work seems to have centered around experiments in typhus.

The physician in charge of Oświęcim as a whole (leitender Arzt) was SS Hauptsturmführer Dr. Endress; for some time, a Dr. Roman Zenktellier seems to have occupied that position. As to management, an elaborate system was devised which augured well for the development of greater-space economy under German leadership in days to come. Operations were standardized. Cooperation of the workers, though certain anyway, was enhanced by such thoughtful inscriptions on the barrack walls as: "Be honest!", "Respect your superiors!" [412] Supply of manpower was plentiful, in fact, overabundant. The thirty or more industrial and agricultural enterprises started in the vicinity used to hire slave labor, among them the Bunawerke of the I. G. Farben at Monowice, which place also was known as Oświęcim III. This labor, true, was not very efficient, as Professor Seraphim had foreseen in describing the disadvantages of a ghetto (see page 109), but it did not cost much, was easy to handle, and conveniently replaceable.

There was no waste on those put to death either. Before being sent to the gas chambers, the inmates were thoroughly shaved; sometimes they had to wait for that procedure many hours, standing naked in the open air regardless of season and weather, men and women on a completely equal footing. The hair then was sorted, packed in bags of 20 kg. (44 pounds) and shipped to Germany for the production of felt, blankets and mattresses. On March 7, 1945, 293 bags of women's hair, which the Germans had not managed to ship home, were discovered in one of the warehouses. The bags weighed 7,000 kg. (15,400 pounds) and the experts of the Investigation Commission estimated that it had belonged to 140,000 women.

Bones at the beginning were pounded, ground and thrown into the river. Then, in 1943, it dawned upon the managers that they could put the product to more effective use; so they started selling the bones for processing into fertilizers. In the files found at the camp administration there were letters showing that 112.6 tons of bones were sold to the Strem plants for that purpose. Most of the ashes was carried from the crematories directly to the farms in the vicinity for fertilizing. Part of the material, however, was used also for commercial purposes. Families of murdered persons received letters

[412] The anteroom to the gas chamber at Oświęcim was adorned with inscriptions like: "Observe cleanliness!", "Don't forget soap and towel!" Cf. Friedman, op. cit., p. 67.

reading as follows: "Your . . . Mr. . . . died in Oświęcim from . . . We shall forward the urn with his [her] ashes to you after receiving the expenses in the amount of . . ." Many persons paid the money and cases are known where the ashes were solemnly buried in cemeteries. Behind this trade there was common fraud: corpses never were cremated individually and the ashes gathered into the urns simply used to be taken from the piles.

Whether soap from human fats also was produced at Oświęcim is uncertain. Rumors to that effect were current, though so far as the existence of such a factory was confirmed only in Danzig (Gdańsk),[413] and we find this production explicitly mentioned in a secret German document (p. 183) without any indignant comment. Many people in Poland, we are told by Dr. Friedman, in fear of this "Beilis soap" (*bejlisowe mydło* in Polish)[414] during the German occupation refrained from using the soap cakes which the German authorities distributed from time to time among the population.

We should not overlook the six carloads of gold which, according to the files discovered by the Investigation Commission, were sent to Germany to bolster Reich economy; how much gold and valuables was appropriated by the personnel before it found its way into the Movable Properties Chamber (Effektenkammer), we, of course, shall never know.

Nor should the trains of other effects moved from Oświęcim into Germany be forgotten. In thirty-five stockrooms the belongings of the murdered inmates were sorted and packed. Twenty-nine of them were set on fire by the Germans before they left; but the six that remained told the story. There were found: 348,820 items of men's apparel; 836,255 items of women's wear, etc. Between December 1, 1944, and January 15, 1945, i.e., already in the Twilight-of-the-Gods period, Oberscharführer SS Reichenbach, the files disclosed, was able to ship to Germany 514,843 items of linen. Explicit orders from institutions and private persons to the SS were found requesting

---

[413] Cf. *New York Herald Tribune*, December 9, 1945: "Nazis Used Human Bodies in Soap. Warsaw, Dec. 8 (AP).—Colonel Edward J. York, of San Antonio, Tex., described here today a German concentration camp he saw in the center of Gdańsk (Danzig) where the Nazis made soap out of human bodies. York said that in a group of buildings behind five-foot-high brick walls were long rows of aluminum vats which held 400 gallons of liquid under steam pressure. He said that alongside each cooker were recipes in German on the walls describing how long parts of human flesh should be cooked and how to extract fats for soap making. He asserted some vats still contained torsos and arms and legs. York said Polish investigators determined that the scheme to make soap and other products from human bodies was conceived by two German doctors."—See also Friedman, *op. cit.*, p. 84.

[414] Friedman, *ibid.*

specified items such as baby-carriages, trunks, etc.[415] Two carloads of eye-glasses were collected. As if to emphasize the complicity of the European Jews with the perpetrators of the Anglo-Saxon air attacks, two hundred and forty carloads of clothes were shipped to Germany as "Love's presents (Liebesgaben)" to the population of the bombed-out cities. Ten cars with the most exquisite women's wear were forwarded to Gotha, to the central stores for SS fiancées (SS-Bräute-Ausstattungslager).

It would be exaggerated to assume that the recipients of all those gifts, bridal and otherwise, thought that in the East these nice little things were growing on the trees. Large parts of the German population must have been aware of what was going on after "Aryanization" had been kept going for many years in broad daylight in Germany proper, and then in Austria, in the Protectorate, and so on, to the delight of many more persons than those who profited directly. As for the Ostland, we shall recall that at one time Goebbels even was eager to publicize first-hand information concerning the behavior of German soldiery toward the Jews.[416] On the death factories, reports were not published but letters from the eastern front did come in, and besides, the hosts of soldiers and officers on furlough certainly did not move around with their lips sealed. In addition, Dachau, as evidence at Nuremberg showed, frequently was visited by excursions of students, professional men, SS men, party leaders, and business men, and the inmates of the death camps worked side by side with free German civilians in factories and farms.

The crimes were of such a widespread nature that the German public could not have avoided knowledge of them. But the precious things had belonged to Jews, or else to some other subhumans, so what did it matter? Whether the Jews were a *counter-folk* or a *sham folk,* their belongings were really useful. Only for tedious statistics indulged in by the group around Dr. Hjalmar Schacht and Dr. Walther Funk, could it be of any importance whether the grand total of the property taken from the Jews was more or less than the estimated eight billion dollars. For all practical purposes, the iron curtain had fallen before the Jews not to rise any more.

[415] Friedman, *ibid.,* p. 82. In Majdanek, according to Friedman, a letter was found ordering a certain number of suitcases "out of the known action (aus der bekannten Aktion)." *Dokumenty obvinyayut,* p. 55 contains the facsimile of a letter found on a German soldier, in which a Berlin woman wrote: "This is my foot size! [the outline of the foot was drawn on the paper.] The high boots just arrived, [they are] first class. Tell me, could you not procure women's boots, lined inside? At any rate, within the next days an old shoe will be forwarded [to you]."

[416] See p. 141.

XXXVI

THE JEW AS A DEMON. BELIEF IN DEMONS AND
PLAIN DECEIT. RITUAL MURDER

This descent of the curtain does not mean, however, that things Jewish at that time disappeared as topics from German general or research literature. As a matter of fact, hardly a subject was brought up more consistently or discussed more passionately. But we observe a peculiar way of writing. Not only do we search in vain for any chronicling of the subsequents stages of the extinction process. Even on actual conditions of the few remaining Jews practically nothing is said overtly in books or periodicals and many issues of even so specialized a publication as *Die Judenfrage* have to be scrutinized before short statements like these are found:

> Regardless of how long the present war is going to last, the position of Jewry in Europe is annihilated (Issue of January 15, 1943).

> The Jewish quarters of the East which are still in existence are only a transitional measure necessitated by the times; the final goal before us is complete spatial separation, *the extinction* (Ausmerzung) *of the Jews from Europe* (Issue of April 15, 1943).

> . . . The course of the present war has inequivocally and sufficiently proved that Jewish losses cannot be called inconsiderable (unbeträchtlich) either and that further losses, as the war becomes protracted and its severity increases, will still rise tremendously. That irresponsible agitation against Germany[417] at bottom unleashed this world struggle and thus also gave the signal for the annihilation of the Jewish nation (Nation) in Europe (Issue of May 15, 1943).

> . . . A recovery of the nations is . . . possible only through the final solution of the Eastern-European Jewish question, which solution after preliminary dissimilation of the Eastern Jews can consist only in their total deportation (Aussiedlung) (Issue of July 1, 1943).[418]

Whatever reference was made to Jews in that last period of Nazi domination did not apply to human beings, living or put to death or desperately fighting for their lives. It was a struggle with a demon.

At the beginning, it all had seemed very serviceable and worked very smoothly. For years, the Jew had been made the object of limitless hatred; during the war, he had been driven, like game, from

---

[417] The article dealt with the "Stop Hitler Now" meeting held in New York on March 1, 1943.

[418] "Eastern Jewry—Reservoir of World Jewry" by Horst Seemann. The author gratefully acknowledged his indebtedness to Peter-Heinz Seraphim for his research work on Eastern Jewry.

cover under the hunter's fire; finally, he had been killed. But the killers discovered, to their horror, that the struggle was not yet over. The victim had reappeared as the incarnation of a demon who, conquered and downtrodden, continued to ply his evil and daring devices and was all the more dangerous since he was unseizable. In a frantic effort to stave off inevitable defeat, the German leaders again and again repeated their adjurations and incantations:

> . . . Germany in this war chose the position which, after warding off the enemies' onslaughts, guarantees ultimate victory. The solid construction and the undestructible power of the German fighting position could be achieved only because—contrary to the first world war!—the germs of internal decomposition and the bacillus carriers of defeatism had been extinguished (ausgemerzt) in time and energetically. In this respect, the *clear solution of the Jewish question* in National Socialist Germany turned out to be one of the *most important premises* of the successful conduct of the war.[419]

Or:

> The first world war and Versailles could not choke Germany's life power. Therefore, the Jews unleashed the second world war in which the Judeocracies (Judokratien) fight the young aspiring (aufstrebend) peoples in order finally to secure Jewish world domination....[420]

The following is a quotation from Goebbels himself, one of the most capable, most educated and most formidable evil-doers in Nazi Germany:

> The Jews . . . are the incarnation of that destructive drive which in these terrible years rages in the enemies' warfare against everything that we consider noble, beautiful and worth preserving.... Since it is impossible for the Jews, because of their extinction (Ausmerzung) from the German folk body, to shake this equilibrium from within, they lead the peoples misled by them to the struggle from without.... Who drives Russians, Englishmen and Americans into the fire and offers hecatombs of other people's lives in a struggle without prospects against the German people? The Jews! ... The Jews at the end of this war are going to experience their Cannae. Not Europe but they themselves are going to perish....[421]

Only in terms of demonology can this catching at shadows be understood. Of course, there were also those who made a business

---

[419] Dr. L. F. Gengler, in *Die Judenfrage*, November 1, 1943, p. 329. Italics in original.
[420] Horst Seemann, *ibid.*, p. 323.
[421] From an article in *Das Reich* reprinted, among others, in *Frankfurter Generalanzeiger*, January 17, 145.

of other people's obsessions, and sometimes it is difficult to tell one from the other. Where, for instance, should we place a scholarly essay on "Conduct of the War and Ethics. Thoughts on the Terroristic Methods of Our Adversaries," which on May 16, 1944, was circularized by one of Goebbels' agencies as "working material for press and writing on current topics" ?

> Time and again we pointed to the fact that our adversaries by their war conduct have unmasked themselves. It is the thousand-years-old hatred by Jewry and the plutocratic-Bolshevist world directed by it which not only operates in the war conduct but also—if it could be victorious—would define the essence of the peace.... *To strive after noble humaneness is decidedly a personality trait of the Germans....* In the Middle Ages ... man stood in the center of economic interests as well.... *"And it was this solidly compacted world,"* Werner Sombart writes in his book *The Jews and Modern Capitalism, "that the Jews assaulted!"* Jewry puts itself in opposition to the high conception of man as it is rooted in the German people....
>
> Thus we Germans are particularly prone to give even the conduct of war *a humane form....* He who for instance knows the statements of the Prussian general [Clausewitz] ... will understand the current events on the Eastern Front. According to Clausewitz, breaking of the adversary's will to resistance is decisive in war. It is achieved through the annihilation of the enemy fighting force. He does not contemplate terrorizing the civil population.[422]

Perhaps, regardless of one's attitude toward the contents of that tract, one should reserve judgment as to the sincerity of its writer. But then again we come across writings in which deceit seems obvious. Take, for instance, the release *Deutscher Wochendienst* classified "Strictly confidential. Not for publication," in which another team of Goebbels' disciples presented "Topics of the Time" to speakers and writers. Each topic, carefully prepared, consisted of at least four sections: Why timely? ; Pointers; Working material; Bibliography. The issues of the end of 1944 and the beginning of 1945 do not confine themselves to Jewish subjects, but these are definitely preponderant. Thus, the issue 281/150 of September 22, 1944, starts with a paper entitled: "Judah's Struggle for Financial and Economic Domination." The answer to the question: "Why timely?" reads:

> In the European nations occupied by the Anglo-Americans, Jews as well as economists and financiers subservient to the Jews seize

---

[422] *Politischer Dienst, Arbeitsmaterial für Presse und Publizistik,* Ausgabe A, no. 218, May 16, 1944 (mimeographed; copy in the Yivo archives). Italics in original.

the entire economic life in order to carry through also from this side their plans of dominating the world.

The "Pointers (Ausrichtung)" to the Topics of the Time always offered two paragraphs: "Stress (Betonen)" and "Avoid (Vermeiden)." With regard to the particular topic under discussion, the writer or speaker was expected to *stress* . . . "Judah's guilt in the economic collapse, now recognizable, of the states occupied by the Anglo-Americans (examples Italy and France)," but for easily understandable reasons he was instructed:

> *Avoid* comparing the Jewish methods in taking economic possession of the occupied nations with German economic and financial policies in the areas formerly occupied by us.[423]

Another issue of the *Deutscher Wochendienst*[424] suggested as a Topic of the Time: "Who Rules in the United States?" The subject was timely because

> both Germany and foreign countries must recognize that the corrupt Roosevelt group, half and three-quarter Bolshevist, in view of its moral inferiority is incapable of arranging the world.—The entrenchment of the Americans in Europe must be presented to the European peoples as the deepest shame, their being dominated by the Roosevelt group as a burning disgrace.

The "Pointers" listed under *Stress*:

> The Roosevelt group is the old Wilson group re-enforced by new Jews and profiteers, to a large extent already strongly marked by bolshevism.—USA democracy by its very essence always will bring to the fore corruptionists, speculators, war-hawks,[425] and agitation profiteers.—The fact of the USA's being dominated and penetrated by Jews must be sturdily emphasized.

But the *Avoid* was even more outspoken:

> *Avoid*: using general slogans.—[Avoid] indulging in false objectivity and in treating the democratic speculators at the head of the USA as statesmen.—[Avoid] openly expressing the hatred against the people of the USA (disgusting as the Yankees are to us, the point for us is to drive a wedge between them and the Roosevelt group in order to divide leadership and people over there).—[Avoid] insulting the population of the USA as a whole.[426]

---

[423] We may recall the instruction to the press censorship (see p. 146) which read: "English methods in Estonia, Latvia, and Lithuania were so clever that these peoples hardly noticed their dependence on England."

[424] 288/154. Ausgabe, 28. Oktober, 1944.

[425] This English expression is used in the original and then rendered by "Kriegshetzer."

[426] The literature recommended comprised books by Giselher Wirsing, Johann von Leers, and Friedrich Schönemann.

The issue of February 19, 1945,[427] in dwelling upon "the Struggle of the Jews for England" prescribed: "*Avoid* ... discussing the achievements of Jews who emigrated from Germany for English scholarship and for the war. However, mention may be made of the extensive appearance of emigrated Jewish physicians in London and other cities, which repeatedly has been disapprovingly stressed by the English physicians as well." Finally, the last issue in our hands analyzed the topic: "World Jewry as Prolonger of the War," declared timely for the following reasons: "The Yalta decisions, entirely unacceptable to the German people, show that the leading statesmen [428] in the enemy camp, on instructions of Jewry, wish to make any real peace impossible and to prolong the war indefinitely." The "Pointers" suggested that the writer or speaker *stress* that "Jewry in the whole world decided to provoke the new war [World War II] not because in Germany it was subjected to a number of restrictions which at the beginning were very insignificant but because it had gained so many successes in World War I that it wanted a second world war to carry through its maximum program, bolshevism, and wished to prevent the anti-Bolshevist forces from growing stronger." But again the instruction as to what ought to be *avoided* in the discussion was even more impressive:

> *Avoid* averting the look [of the people] from Jewry through discussing other causes for the length of the war.—[Avoid] disparaging other peoples, be they friendly, neutral or indifferent to us, in order not to jeopardize the aim of presenting Jewry as the common enemy of all [of them] and as the systematic prolonger of the war.[429]

To appraise the degree to which the assault on Jewry was intensified during this last period, the reintroduction of the subject of the Jews' using Christian blood for ritual purposes may be pointed to. It never was completely absent from the Nazi arsenal but, whatever the reasons for such restraint, it was for years definitely held in abeyance. A Nazi bibliography on the Jewish question compiled during the war [430] listed only two Party publications on Jewish ritual murder, issued one in 1933 and one in 1937,[431] in addition to a third

---

[427] 302/171. Ausgabe.

[428] So they were worthy of being called statesmen, after all!

[429] 308/177. Ausgabe, 31. März, 1945.

[430] [Joachim Menzel] *Schrifttum zur Judenfrage, Eine Auswahl* (München, Eher, n. d. [1940], 32 pp.).

[431] The second was written by Gerhard Utikal, whom we shall meet again as an official of Rosenberg's among the organizers of the international anti-Jewish congress in 1944.

treatise written by a sympathetic outsider. But simultaneously with the spread of the massacres and while the super-crematories at Oświęcim were being built, the subject did come up again. As far as can be ascertained, it reappeared for the first time in *Die Judenfrage* of the Berlin Antijüdische Aktion. An article in that periodical by Dr. Hellmut Schlamm was preceded by this editorial note:

> The question of Jewish ritual murder for centuries consciously was held by Jewry in darkness. We therefore asked Dr. Hellmut Schlamm, who has studied this question in detail and soon is going to publish a book on Jewish ritual murder, to express himself on this topic.[432]

Dr. Schlamm did not hesitate to state quite unequivocally that Jewish ritual murder was as old as Jewry itself and therefore inferred:

> For our generation which currently is engaged in the severest struggle with this world pest in view of the Jewish ritual murders which ultimately ought to represent symbolically the annihilation of the non-Jewish world, there is only one possible conclusion: spiritual and physical annihilation of the hereditary Jewish criminality.[433]

When Schlamm's book appeared a short while afterwards—an impressive illustrated volume of nearly five hundred pages,[434]—*Die Judenfrage* felt that it "will render valuable service . . . in the struggle against the Jewish world enemy."[435] After this sanction, the trend was sharply accelerated. A later publication on the subject, after adducing all the "proofs," and supplying illustrations of Jewish ritual murders beginning with a "case" of 1282, culminated in a paragraph based on contemporaneous considerations:

> Today the part of the Jews with us has been played out after their last attempt to instigate the peoples of Europe to mass murder against each other. The Jew still believes he has the last trump in his hand since he succeeded in making subservient to his interests Jewish bolshevism coupled with the no less Jewish capitalism of the English and Americans. But the last trump too will be torn from his hand and the war unleashed by the Jews will end in the radical destruction of Jewry.[436]

[432] *Die Judenfrage*, November 15, 1942, pp. 247-248.
[433] *Ibid.*
[434] Hellmut Schlamm, *Der jüdische Ritualmord. Eine historische Untersuchung* (Berlin, Theodor Fritsch Verlag, 1943, 475 pp.).
[435] Issue of December 15, 1942.
[436] Frederik to Gaste, *Die Wahrheit über die jüdischen Ritualmorde* (Berlin, Paul Hochmuth [1944], 48 pp.).—Also issued in a Polish translation (copy in the Yivo library).

XXVII

THE INDOCTRINATION LITERATURE OF THE WEHRMACHT
AND OF THE FOREIGN MINISTRY

The scope of this survey prevents us from analyzing the intimate connection between the anti-Jewish research literature and the curriculum of elementary and secondary schools as established under the Nazis. It can only be mentioned that the numerous handbooks for teachers on the treatment of the Jewish question contained ample references to the authorities whom we encountered in our discussion, such as Baur-Fischer-Lenz, Grau, Günther, Kittel, Seraphim, etc.

But among the government sponsored literature of the late Hitler era one kind deserves more than passing notice: the indoctrination literature of the Wehrmacht bearing the endorsement of the highest military authorities. That Field Marshal Keitel was personally interested in the contribution of anti-Jewish research "to the spiritual conduct of the war" in 1941, that Commanding General von Reichenau had represented the Reich War Ministry at the inauguration of a leading anti-Jewish research institution as early as 1936, has been pointed to previously (pp. 48, 51). Three War Ministry representatives were permanent members of the Reichsinstitut für Geschichte des neuen Deutschlands (see p. 47). Some excerpts from the "thought guides (Gedankenführungen)," as the official educational tracts for the Wehrmacht were sometimes called, will show us better than anything else what stuff the German armed forces were fed as long as their weight could resist Allied steel and how accurately this literature reflected the ideas set into the world by the anthropologists, historians, and political scientists. Be it emphasized that the excerpts are not from SS or Nazi party publications but exclusively from those which were authorized by the Keitels and the Jodls and for the most part are classified "for use in the Wehrmacht only."

> Europe can be saved from bolshevism and the dollar imperialism of the USA only through German victory. Europe's fate is in our hands.[437]

The author then proceeded diligently to restate what he had learned from the scholars:

> . . . On one side Anglo-Americanism and bolshevism, on the other Japanism and Greater-German national socialism. American-

---

[437] *Der Kampf um unsere Weltanschauung* . . . (full title in footnote 380), p. 23.

ism and bolshevism arise from breadth of space; national socialism and Japanism from narrowness of space.

The two peoples of breadth of space refute the identification with the concept of race.

The two peoples of narrowness of space identify themselves with the concept of blood and soil.

The two peoples of breadth of space teach the negation of race.

The two peoples of narrowness of space profess species and the preservation of species (Art und Arterhaltung).

The negation of race leads to disengagement from the concept of family and kin (Sippe).

The negation of race also leads to the formation of teachings which stem from the ideology of liberalism.... Americanism is measureless imperialism (the American century), [and] bolshevism looks for the bolshevization of the world (the International); the two peoples which identify themselves with space and race require living space adequate to their species (Art).

The highest values, "honor," "community of folk," "[national] socialism," are identified with the genuine concept of race and have no validity for the powers of breadth of space.[438]

The following is from an official pamphlet of the Army Supreme Command; note again the striking resemblance to earlier statements of the scholars:

For us, the Jewish question is a race question, though world Jewry represents not a uniform race but a race mixture. It consists of Near-Eastern and Oriental race ingredients, intermingled with Negro strains and the blood of different host-peoples.

It is no exaggeration to say: "Capitalism is practical Mosaism" (W. Sombart)....

With regard to other races of alien kind (artfremd), among whom there are some of very high standing too, such as the Japanese, National Socialist race cultivation merely stresses the difference in species (Artverschiedenheit). Since blood mixture offends the racial fundamental order desired by Providence and the sound racial sense of both parts strives against it, marriages with persons of foreign blood shall not be entered into....

Since in the Greater German struggle for liberation world Jewry openly sided with our adversaries, he [the Jew] was made recognizable by the Jewish star lest, under the mask of an honest man, he carry on inflammatory work inimical to the folk. The removal (Entfernung) of all Jews from the Reich will finally solve the Jewish question in the field of internal politics....[439]

---

[438] *Ibid.*, p. 41. The quotations are from a paper by Fritz Sotke.

[439] OKH / Oberkommando des Heeres [Supreme Army Command], Generalinspekteur für den Führernachwuchs des Heeres. *Nationalsozialistische Führung. Heft 8: Die Judenfrage und ihre Bedeutung für das deutsche Volk* (Frankfurt a/Main, Diesterweg, n. d., 12 pp.), pp. 3, 6, 10-11.

This was written before Germany's attack on the Soviet Union. Obviously, as time passed, the stress put upon this idea could but grow in intensity, and a Wehrmacht publication of 1944, when comparatively little remained still to be done, bluntly repeated Hitler's prophecy:

> . . . We National Socialists believe the Führer when he says that the struggle unleashed by the Jewish world parasite against us who are his strongest adversary will terminate in the annihilation of Jewry in Europe....[440]

The book, "What We Are Fighting For," adorned by a three-page facsimile endorsement which the Führer himself issued in his headquarters on January 8, 1944, was particularly important. It brought in something novel in that it reverted to the subject of masonry and classified nations and personalities according to the exigencies of the moment:

> Today almost all heads of state and government members of the enemy powers are freemasons, and chiefly high-grade freemasons: Churchill, Eden, the King of England (high-grade freemason), Roosevelt (high-grade freemason), just as are all heads of state in the South American republics (except Argentina). The policies of the enemy powers can be rightly understood only if one is constantly aware of the fact that world Jewry, represented by freemasonry, is the motive-power. The King of Italy and the traitor-general [Badoglio] were freemasons.

Apart from this labored argument, the tune sounds rather familiar, but still the following paragraph is illuminating in its conciseness:

> Why Jewry's Struggle against Us?
>
> Because Adolf Hitler's Germany does not wish to put herself under a Jewish world order.... The Jew is the antagonist (Gegenpol) of the Nordic man, the arch-enemy of any free people in general. The creative, constructive philosophy of national socialism with its idealistic goals is opposed by the Jewish philosophy of materialism and individualism as expressed in bolshevism and in the liberalism of the Anglo-Saxon democracies.... In our struggle it is irrelevant whether Stalin puts his comrades Roosevelt and Churchill before the carriage of his Bolshevist policies or whether Roosevelt and Churchill make the Soviet Union serve their Jewish-plutocratic aims. For us, there is only one decision: to fight bolshevism and to fight the plutocracies. Our victory over both of them means the annihilation of Jewry and thereby the pacification of the nations and the guaranty of a new world order.[441]

[440] NS-Führungsstab der Wehrmacht, *Der Jude als Weltparasit*. Richthefte des Oberkommandos der Wehrmacht, Heft 7 (n. p., 1944, 48+32 pp.), pp. 2-3.
[441] *Wofür kämpfen wir?* Herausgegeben vom Personalamt des Heeres (n. p., January, 1944, 144 pp.), p. 17.—In stressing again the paramount importance of the *Rasse* issue,

Again a pamphlet taken over by the Wehrmacht from Rosenberg's Commissionership and abounding in quotations from Goethe and Schiller, professed:

> For the German man, every struggle is degraded if it is not born out of and carried by the decision to lead a real idea to victory. Where man struggles for ignoble goals, he supports the element inimical to life, he annihilates culture, he sins against the laws of life. We have examples of that in the activities of Jewry, in the activities of communism, and in the tenets of some denominational conceptions....
>
> .... We must endure the struggle in this war which was forced upon us by the Jewish and plutocratic powers. They envied us everything that we had acquired laboriously through our Weltanschauung in constant struggle and ceaseless work of the individual and the folk as a whole: our National Socialist folk community, our socialism, our labor achievement, the discoveries of our invigorated economy, our high national income, our national health, our youth, our military strength, in short, everything that we had created for ourselves under the most adverse conditions through our own strength.[442]

The latest specimen of this indoctrination literature that has come to our knowledge—and the most outspoken—is a book of instructions for the Wehrmacht concluded September 1, 1944. That year, a new tide of educational efforts had set in to have the last officer and soldier grasp the paramount importance of race, species, and other concepts processed by the scholars for the greater glory of the Reich. No. 3 of the series "Political Discussion" contains, for example, topic 7, "To Know the Jews Means to Understand the Sense of the War," and topic 8, "Americanism Would Mean the End of Europe."[443]

"There are still light-minded people," the anonymous author wrote, "who think it wouldn't be so bad if the Americans came." The reader was therefore referred to topic 4, "The System of the Plutocracies," and in addition informed that the USA entered the war to enslave Europe economically, to suppress it socially, to destroy European culture. "The German soldier risks his life conscious of his close

---

another Wehrmacht publication (concluded April 15, 1944) wrote as follows: "National Socialist Reich leadership courageously tackled this historical task. Scholarship, in the fields of race cultivation and genetics, had provided the legislator with the cognitions which he now applied conscious of his high responsibility." *Stoffsammlung. Führungsunterlagen Folge 1.* Herausgeber: Nationalsozialistischer Führungsstab des Oberkommandos der Wehrmacht (n. p., 56 pp.), p. 29.

[442] *Der Kampf als Lebensgesetz,* Bearbeiter: H. Griesdorf und H. Lichtnau, Richthefte des NS-Führungsstabes des Oberkommandos der Wehrmacht, Heft 5 (1944, 47 pp.), pp. 6, 10.

[443] *Politische Aussprache. Führungsunterlagen Folge 3.* Herausgeber: Nationalsozialistischer Führungsstab der Wehrmacht (n. p., [September, 1944], pp. 49-80).

association with folk and home—the American bombardier flies for the dollar pay," [444] his aim being to Americanize all of Europe.

There are still today within our people persons who in their hearts are not quite positive when we speak of the extermination (Ausrottung) of the Jews in our living space. In our midst there was needed the character, strength, and energy of the greatest man in our folk for thousand years to tear from our eyes the Jewish delusion....

JEWISH PLUTOCRACY AND JEWISH COMMUNISM ARE CHASING THE GERMAN PEOPLE THAT ESCAPED THEIR SLAVERY.

The Jew wishes to force us into a life of slaves in order that he may live with us as a parasite and exploit us. The sound life-form of our people stands against the parasitic life-form of the Jew.

Who in this struggle can still speak of mercy, love of one's neighbor, and so on? Who believes in the possibility of improving the parasite (for instance, the louse)? Who believes that there is a way of compromise with a parasite? We have only the choice of being devoured by the parasite or of destroying him.

THE JEW MUST BE ANNIHILATED WHEREVER WE MEET HIM!

By this we do not commit a crime against life but we serve its law of struggle, a law which always stands up against everything that is hostile to healthy life. Thus our struggle serves the preservation of life.

THE GERMAN VICTORY—THE VICTORY OF THE ORDER OF CREATION. [445]

It is but little known that the German authorities, through a Central Leading Staff (zentraler Führungsstab), presided over by Reich Foreign Minister Ribbentrop, tried their best to indoctrinate the prisoners of war in Germany, too, with the guiding ideas of the Nazi regime. A document now in the Yivo archives, [446] intended to frustrate the efforts of the Propaganda Ministry to take over the "educational" work among war prisoners, gives a number of particulars. Of personalities who participated in the Leading Staff Theodor Abetz, fifth columnist and subsequently ambassador to Vichy, and Dr. Colin Ross, specialist for United States problems and Wehrmacht propagandist, may be mentioned. The foremost aim of the propaganda among the war prisoners was described in the following paragraph:

---

[444] *Ibid.,* p. 61.
[445] *Ibid.,* pp. 55-56.
[446] Abschrift zu Rk. 3314E. *Aufzeichnung über Gliederung und Tätigkeit der Kriegsgefangenenorganisation des Auswärtigen Amtes,* 15 typewritten pages. The document was signed by Envoy Schmidt and dated April 17, 1944.

To advise the [P.W.] camp commanders concerning the right psychological treatment of the prisoners in order to increase their desire to work, to win over the prisoners for active propaganda in the anti-Bolshevist and anti-Jewish direction, and in general to influence the prisoners as carriers of German propaganda after their return home.

The work had been done since the beginning of the war through cooperation of the OKW (Supreme Army Command) and the Foreign Ministry on special orders of the Führer. Each national group of prisoners was treated in a specific way. Among the twelve pamphlets distributed in 1943 among the British prisoners, then numbering 65,000, there were:

John Amery, *England and the Continent,*
Jews in the American Administration,
Jew in the British Administration,
Jews Must Live (*Reports on the Political Machinations of the Jews* [by Samuel Roth].

At the beginning of 1944, 20,000 copies of the pamphlet *How Odd of God* [447] were distributed among the [British] prisoners of war, which pamphlet the Führer called the best written, most effective anti-Jewish material.

Books, too, were made accessible to the British prisoners of war.

Many thousand books of anti-Jewish and pro-German (für Deutschland werbend) content were sold to the war prisoners through the W. P. Organization. (Experience in the war prisoner camps has led to the conclusion that the Englishman is little interested in literature distributed free of charge, rejecting it as propaganda. Therefore, for some time books and pamphlets have been sold for low prices, or they [English prisoners] have been given the opportunity to acquire this literature illegally....)

Some issues of books in English translation ordered by the Foreign Ministry, among them *Mein Kampf* and Peter Aldag's *The Influence of the Jews in England,*[448] were burned in Allied air raids. Many more, however, could be distributed and probably did not remain without effect. Two separate camps, one each for British officers and enlisted men, were instituted for the purpose of particularly intensive propaganda, and at the beginning of 1944 a twenty-man nucleus of a "British Legion" was formed which was to start its recruiting work at the end of April.

[447] This title was mentioned in English in the document; the previous ones have been re-translated from German.
[448] Apparently, a translation of: Peter Aldag, *Juden beherrschen England,* 2. Auflage (Berlin, Nordland-Verlag, 1939, 390 pp.).

The American war prisoners were entrusted to the care of Professor Otto Koischwitz, who provided for the distribution of the above mentioned English pamphlets "as far as they were suitable for the American mentality" and also published special material, such as a newspaper *O. K.* (Overseas Kid), and several pamphlets.[449]

XXXVIII

ANTI-JEWISH RESEARCH LITERATURE IN THE TWILIGHT-OF-THE-GODS PERIOD

While the products of theoretical scholarship thus were put to practical use and thereby affirmed that research was not a mere luxury or an extraneous activity, anti-Jewish research proper had not stopped. The ninth and last volume of Walter Frank's *Forschungen zur Judenfrage* was ready in 1944. The *Weltkampf* of Rosenberg's institute,, under Schickert's assiduous editorship, continued until the end of 1944, i.e., as long as any organized intellectual life in Germany was possible,[450] and had attracted about sixty different contributors, among them at least thirteen professors and an additional twenty-six Doctors of Philosophy, a count which does not include contributors from abroad. Then the Antijüdische Aktion maintained by Goebbels' ministry (see pp. 58-62), in addition to its more popular *Die Judenfrage*, in 1943 launched a research periodical *Archiv für Judenfragen, Schriften zur geistigen Überwindung des Judentums* (Archives for Jewish Questions, Publications for Overcoming Jewry Mentally). Finally, several general research institutions, such as the German Academy of Sciences in Prague, considered the Jewish subject important enough to issue monographs on some of its aspects.[451] In a forthcoming chapter we shall hear a student given to thought explain why this intense study was needed though the enemy seemingly had been crushed; here let us state the fact that the problem of training

[449] The document contains the following passage: "The entire broadcasting action to England and America (Professor Koischwitz), known to the Führer, in which greetings by prisoners are delivered, prisoners themselves speak, communications about dead, wounded, etc., are transmitted, has been built on the care of war prisoners by the Foreign Ministry." Koischwitz until 1939 was an Assistant Professor of German at Hunter College of the City of New York.

Other persons, except Koischwitz, in charge of American war prisoners, as mentioned in the document, were: consuls general Gyssling and Draeger, LR. Pawelke, and WHA. Schmölder.

[450] The last issue in the library of the Yivo is Heft 3, September-December, 1944. It is a safe guess that nothing more was published.

[451] [Professor Dr.] Theodor Hopfner, *Die Judenfrage bei Griechen und Römern* (Prag. 1943, 84 pp.). — Abhandlungen der Deutschen Akademie der Wissenschaften in Prag, Philosophisch-Historische Klasse, Heft 8.

a younger generation of scholars in the field was not neglected. A prominent bibliographer with wide international connections, deploring that formerly only Jewish students chose Jewish subjects for their doctoral dissertations, was able to boast:

> . . . The German universities, too, have recognized their duty to contribute building stones for the study of Jewry and today such papers are written only by Germans.... From 1939-1942, i.e., during the war, no less than thirty-two dissertations treating the Jewish question [were written].[452]

> . . . The German universities more and more recognized the new way the problem has been posed and contributed to its solution through university studies suitable for the purpose. They are chiefly conducted by young historians, but also by jurists, economists, Germanists, students in journalism, as well as by medical and race students.[453]

To this younger generation belonged Otto Paul, of Grau's research staff in Frankfort, who flatly denied any Jewish contribution to world civilization.[454] Significantly, his paper was printed in a periodical dealing with the Eastern Space; and Leibbrandt, Lohse, Trampedach, Strauch, and Kube, who did their utmost to put an end to Jewry's false pretenses, might have enjoyed reading it.

There is no need to epitomize the contents of this research literature which kept growing; instead, let us speak of some of its typical representatives.

We have already met Professor Dr. Gerhard Kittel, of Tübingen and then of Vienna. At the advent of Hitler he had "proved" that the Talmud considered every non-Jew a stranger which, read in reverse, was to justify the disfranchisement of the Jews in Germany in 1933. In his 1939 book he insisted that the Jews were irreconcilable opponents of Germany's greatness and invoked Adolf Hitler's name to hint at what was in store. Then in 1942, when the German state machinery was well advanced in "solving the Jewish question" and seemingly no further theory was needed, Kittel, with the air of "You know what I mean," declared that, again in the Talmud,

---

[452] Dr. Hans Praesent, prominent staff member of the Deutsche Bücherei in Leipzig. in: *Die Judenfrage*, November 15, 1943, 351-353.

[453] Idem, in: *Weltkampf*, IV (1944), 103-105. Cf. also: *Hochschul-Schrifttum. Verzeichnis von Dissertationen und Habilitationsschriften.* Ausgewählt von der Parteiamtlichen Prüfungskommission zum Schutze des NS-Schrifttums (München, Eher, 1942, 94 pp.). = 4. Beiheft der Nationalsozialistischen Bibliographie.

[454] Otto Paul, "Der Anspruch des Judentums, kulturschöpferische Leistungen vollbracht zu haben," *Volk im Osten* 4 (1943), 63-71.

... killing the Gentile ... explicitly and by principle is declared non-punishable (straffrei).[455]

He developed the theme a little later in the new scientific periodical, *Archiv für Judenfragen,* which set out to study not only the Jewish people or the Jewish race but "in general everything that is Jewish or is allied or connected with this Jewish element." In the first issue of this *Archiv* the very first article is Kittel's on "The Treatment of the Stranger according to the Talmud," and the idea of the paper appeared in a seemingly academic statement in the last paragraph:

> At the beginning of the second century the Jews in North Africa and Cyprus once thought their hour had come and broke into a rebellion (Dio Cassius, *Hist.* 68, 32). In Cyprus alone they then put to death a quarter of a million people, in Cyrenaica no less, partly slaughtering people in the most cruel way.

"The problem of right or wrong does not exist for Talmudic thinking in the case of political murder of non-Jews; the question can only be one of expediency, whether it is going to lead to success,"[456] declared the theological scholar who—not in the second century but in the twentieth—had discussed the annihilation of the Jews from the point of view of mere expediency[457] and soon had seen the goal achieved.

Together with Kittel, Eugen Fischer, one of the foremost German scholars, in 1943 published a large-size book of almost 250 pages on World Jewry in Antiquity.[458] While Kittel produced a profusely documented list of Jewish settlements in the Roman Empire, running into the hundreds, Fischer devoted himself to an analysis of ancient portraits which he conceived of as Jewish. Quite a subject for a *Rasse* student and only a little too idyllic for the period in which the study was made! But do not suspect the co-authors of escapism; the preface to the volume showed that they made every effort to keep in accord with the spirit of the times:

> ... Always the aim [of the Jews] is: world domination, whether the Jewish slave girl, with authentic or forged letters, is the go-between in the relations of the empress and the Jew-princess; whether the Egyptian tax-collecting Jew and high financier becomes

---

[455] Gerhard Kittel, "Das talmudische Denken und das Judentum," *Die Judenfrage,* October 1, 1942, pp. 208-209.

[456] Gerhard Kittel, "Die Behandlung des Nichtjuden nach dem Talmud," *Archiv für Judenfragen,* Gruppe A1, Heft 1 (1943), 7-17.

[457] See p. 42.

[458] Eugen Fischer, Gerhard Kittel, *Das antike Weltjudentum. Tatsachen, Texte, Bilder* (Hamburg, Hanseatische Verlagsanstalt, 1943, 236 pp.). = Forschungen zur Judenfrage, Band 7.

the "friend" of the emperor and personal banker of the empress; whether the Jewish legation from Alexandria by way of the empress gains the favors of the emperor and aims at the execution of the anti-Jewish leaders—or when, if opportunity offers, because the emperor is busy elsewhere, the Jewries of Egypt and Cyrene and Cyprus in their savage rebellions slaughter hundreds of thousands of non-Jews. Or, in the ritual reading on the feast of Purim, and through the wall pictures in their synagogues they recall to memory the bloody stories of Esther and Mordecai and get intoxicated about how in days to come the peoples of the world will fall on their faces, deliver all treasures and become their slaves. Always, at all times, in the first century as in the twentieth, world Jewry is the dream of exclusive world domination on earth and in the hereafter! ..."[450]

In a short paper founded on the larger study just referred to, Fischer remarked:

> . . . It is interesting from the point of view of racial science that already at that time [in Alexandria, Egypt, in the first and second century of our era] both of the known types, that of the Eastern Jew (Ashkenazim) and that of the Western Jew (Sephardim) are discernible;

and Fischer concluded his presentation largely addressed to scholarly audiences in the neutral countries with a broad hint:

> World Jewry of old has been proved; we know its expansion, its power, its appearance. It ruled and flourished. But, as intimated, it was crushed when the Teutons after the era of the migration of peoples established their reichs.[460]

To appreciate the speed with which the products of anti-Jewish scholarly research found their way into "applied science," it is instructive to look into an article "Jews as Soldiers" which appeared in the *Deutscher Wochendienst* of November 10, 1944.[461] With his thoughts obviously directed to the numerous acts of Jewish resistance which had started in 1943 and could not have failed to impress even the regimented German minds, Goebbels' anonymous adjunct declared:

> The conception that the Jews always are afraid of the naked sword or of battle stems from a presentation which *prettifies the Jew*. Brutal violence even is not rare with Jews. What the Jews lack is the soldierly sense of chivalry.

---

[450] *Ibid.*, pp. 10-11.
[460] Professor Dr. Eugen Fischer, Freiburg i. Br. "Judenporträts in der Antike," *Europäischer Wissenschafts-Dienst* III, 9 (September, 1943), 8-9.
[461] 288./157. Ausgabe.

We may recall that lack of chivalry was also one of the faults Alfred Rosenberg had found with the British and Americans; thus, to the doleful German reader, one more trait revealed itself that the Jews had in common with the plutocracies.

Then the "abominable cruelties of the Old Testament" were quoted—rather a standing feature of German anti-Jewish literature since 1933—and finally "the frightful things" recorded by Dio Cassius "on the Jew-rebellion in Cyrene" were retold; this new idea, evidently suggested by the recent study of Professors Kittel and Fischer, stressed again the conformity between government enunciation and the scholars' performance. As expected, the conclusion of the article limited itself by no means to antiquity:

> That's why the Jews, even where they fought tenaciously, no-where were considered truly honest adversaries. Emperor Titus, therefore, after the conquest of Jerusalem refused the title "Judaicus."

And then came the sentence which showed what was in the writer's mind:

> Captive Jews were not executed by the sword (they, in the Roman sense, had no *caput,* i.e., no honor, and therefore could not be deprived of what they did not possess), but they suffered the slave death of crucifixion.

Would the writers of those papers and the originators of those ideas admit that they needed to pass a purgatory after the inferno they prepared for others? Oh, no. Even after the war is over they most certainly feel that "no blot falls on the right cause," as one of them quoted above has put it. And should the prosecution insist on indicting them, their alibi, in their own opinion, would be complete. Did they soil their hands in blood? No Dudley Roberts test would discover any traces. Did they administer the poison? By no means; they only wrote the prescription. When Professor Dr. Walter Frank, at that time the standard bearer of anti-Jewish research in 1941, was received in audience by Field Marshal Keitel, the communiqué stressed the contribution "to the spiritual conduct of the war." Professor Dr. Walter Grundmann defined the aims of his institute as developing certain "scientific conclusions." Professor Dr. Karl Clauberg at Oświęcim also was interested solely in developing new ways in medicine and nobody probably would be rude enough to suggest to scholars of such intentions that they introduce cancer tissue into the uteri of their own wives and sisters first. Thus anyone will have to admit that while German scholarship advocated and backed "the extinguishment of eternally hostile forces," which had forced the war upon Germany, they had emphasized, as the Führer did, the primacy of spiritual values. As the linguist Dr. Walter Kunze, a leading man in the Deutsche Akademie, put it in 1944:

> The current constantly widening struggle of peoples must be interpreted in the sense that it is a world-creating contest in which alongside the sword also spiritual weapons are needed. Not only new frontier delimitations and reasonable economic forms are involved, not only extinguishment (Auslöschen) of eternally hostile forces, but in the first place a new spiritual Europe, a new world image, mutual understanding of the peoples and true friendship. The Führer himself over and over again stressed the spiritual touch of our struggle alongside the struggle proper.[462]

XXXIX

AN INTERNATIONAL ANTI-JEWISH CONGRESS IN 1944

In February, 1944, about the time Kunze was writing as above about "the spiritual touch of our struggle," Alfred Rosenberg received the Führer's permission to convoke an international anti-Jewish congress on a scale considerably larger than the Frankfort Conference of 1941.[463] It may sound strange that such an idea should have come up at a time when Germany's chances had crumbled beyond repair: the Russians stood at the Vistula and the invasion of Western Europe was imminent. But the Nazi mind worked differently. Governor General Hans Frank, who immediately became enthusiastic about the idea, gave the reasons for the enterprise as follows:

> The time for such an anti-Jewish demonstration is particularly advantageous because it underscores at this juncture of the war the unbroken fighting will of Germany, which does not even for a moment think of giving in as to an essential point of her war-waging.

The first preliminary meeting was called for February 16 by Hans Hagemeyer, the man whom we have met already on the eve of the war as a co-editor of the volume on "Europe's Fate in the East" (p. 76),

---

[462] Quoted from a paper by Dr. Walter Kunze, leading man in the Deutsche Akademie, in a 1944 yearbook of that institution, to which the outstanding German linguists contributed (cf. footnote 344), p. 135.

[463] The whole matter of this congress, to our knowledge, never was discussed in a German or another publication. Our presentation is based on a file entitled "Geheim. Gesch[äfts]. Z[ahl] No. 222/44 g (1) Pr. 2203. Internationaler antijüdischer Kongress," which consists of over one hundred sheets. It was found in the ruins of the Goebbels' Ministry of Popular Enlightenment and Propaganda in Berlin and is now in the possession of the Yivo.

2. Das Auswärtige Amt schlägt vor, eine wissenschaftliche Stelle
als Veranstalter zu wählen. Hier wurde das Institut zur Erforschung der Judenfrage ohne die Bezeichnung "Aussenstelle der Hohen
Schule der NSDAP." hinzuzusetzen, vorgeschlagen. Ferner wurde die
Möglichkeit erwogen, dass die Einladung nur von einigen bekannten
deutschen Wissenschaftlern und bekannten Persönlichkeiten des
Auslandes unterzeichnet wird. Hier würde es darauf ankommen, dass
nicht nur Ausländer gewonnen werden aus dem befreundeten Ausland,
sondern z.B. auch aus den neutralen wie Schweden, Spanien und der
Schweiz.

Es wurde darauf hingewiesen, dass auf jeden Fall erreicht werden
muss, durch diesen Kongress so viel Material in die Hand zu bekom-
men, dass im nächsten Jahr sowohl vom Auswärtigen Amt als vom Pro-
pagandaministerium als von der Dienststelle Rosenberg ein Großein-
satz auf dem Gebiet der Judenbekämpfung erfolgen kann. Es kommen
zur Teilnahme nicht nur Rasseforscher, sondern auch Sozial- und
Wirtschaftswissenschaftler in Frage, Vertreter aller Gebiete, auf
denen das Judentum eine Rolle gespielt hat und spielt. Der Kreis
der Teilnehmer soll so weit wie möglich gezogen werden, die Anzahl
dagegen durch eine gute Auswahl der Persönlichkeiten beschränkt
bleiben.

Um die Teilnehmer der nichtkriegführenden Länder nicht bedenklich
zu machen, sollen die Namen der prominentesten Redner u.U. gar
nicht auf dem Programm erscheinen. Vom Auswärtigen Amt wurde darauf
hingewiesen, dass man den Kongress nicht zu sehr tendenziös ver-
schärfen dürfe, um nicht an Resonanz im Auslande zu verlieren.
Durch eine Häufung von bedeutenden politischen Persönlichkeiten würde die indirekte Wirksamkeit vielleicht herabgesetzt. Dem wurde
entgegengehalten, dass durch die Auftragserteilung an Reichsleiter
Rosenberg durch den Führer das politische Übergewicht für den Kongress gegeben sei. Es muss selbstverständlich versucht werden, den
grösstmöglichen Erfolg zu erzielen. Wir haben den Auftrag, mit
diesem Kongress an die Bildungsschicht der europäischen Völker
heranzukommen, die bisher mit der einfachen antijüdischen Propaganda nicht erfasst werden konnte.

Berlin, den 23. Februar 1944   gez. Hans Hagemeyer
                                        Dienstleiter

and at that meeting the general aim of the congress was openly defined in these words:

> We are instructed to reach by this congress the intellectual stratum (Bildungsschicht) of the European peoples who up to now could not be won (erfasst) by simple anti-Jewish propaganda.

In his capacity of head of the "Main Office on supra-State Powers" in Rosenberg's Training Commissionership, Hagemeyer invited representatives of several Party and Reich departments for a discussion of the following agenda: (1) Place of the congress (Pressburg [Bratislava], Prague, Paris); (2) Official host: Institut zur Erforschung der Judenfrage, Aussenstelle der Hohen Schule in Frankfort on-the-Main, or a special executive committee; (3) Time of the congress; (4) Program: (a) Topics; (b) By-program; (5) Distribution of organizational work; (6) Honorary board; (7) List of guests to be invited; (8) Formation of the working committee.

The meeting at Hagemeyer's office in the Berlin suburb of Lichterfelde-West was attended by a representative of the Foreign Ministry, three members of Hagemeyer's staff in addition to himself, including Gerhard Utikal, placed in charge of the preparatory work; and three men of the anti-Jewish news service *Welt-Dienst* in Frankfort on-the-Main, among them Dr. Johann Pohl, staff member of Rosenberg's Frankfort Institut zur Erforschung der Judenfrage. Representatives of Himmler's Reichssicherheitshauptamt (Reich Main Security Office) and the Propaganda Ministry were prevented from coming by an air-raid on the capital which had just taken place. The conversations, therefore, were considered of a preliminary nature. As to the choice of place, the wish of the Führer was referred to that the danger of air attacks be eliminated as far as possible. For reasons of foreign policy, it was deemed desirable not to hold the congress in Germany. Paris was dismissed "both because of the invasion to be expected and of the insecure political situation in general"; Bratislava, it was indicated, would involve the necessity of procuring foreign exchange, Slovakia having its own currency. In view of the importance of the problem, the Rosenberg office was advised to take up the matter again with the Foreign Ministry.

With respect to the signers of the invitation, the Foreign Ministry representative felt that the call should emanate from a scholarly institution. It was suggested that the Institut zur Erforschung der Judenfrage be chosen, but without adding the further identification: "Aussenstelle der Hohen Schule der NSDAP" (Branch of the High

School of the National Socialist German Workers Party). Another suggestion was to have the invitation signed "by some known German scholars and known personalities from abroad." It was stressed that not only foreigners from friendly countries but also from neutral ones should be induced to come, "as, for instance, Sweden, Spain, and Switzerland." The significance of the congress was thus summed up:

> . . . At any rate the result should be to get through the congress so much material that within the next year [1945] the Foreign Ministry, the Propaganda Ministry, and the Rosenberg Office will be able to undertake a large-scale attack (Grosseinsatz) in the field of fighting the Jews (Judenbekämpfung). Invitations are contemplated [for issue] not only to race students but also to scholars in the social sciences and in economics, representatives of all fields in which Jewry has played and still plays a part. The range of persons should be as wide as possible but the number should be limited through a good choice of personalities.

Caution was recommended as a matter of principle:

> In order not to make the participants from the non-belligerent countries suspicious, the names of the most prominent speakers perhaps should not appear on the program. The Foreign Ministry indicated that the congress should not be too conspicuous as to tendency lest it lose in resonance abroad. An accumulation of important political personalities might possibly impair the indirect efficacy [of the congress].

This argument, however, was parried by a paramount reason: everyone conceded that "of course the maximum success is to be sought," but "it was said that the Führer's entrusting the commission to Reichsleiter Rosenberg implied the preponderance of politics at the congress."

A copy of the minutes of the preliminary meeting was sent to the Propaganda Ministry where it was received with mixed feelings. In essence, needless to say, there was complete agreement. But some uneasiness was felt over the fact that their ministry had heard about the matter so late, when Rosenberg had already submitted the matter to the Führer; Goebbels did not like this rough treatment, nor should he have expected it, because he had been handled with much more courtesy since the serious reverses on the battle fronts had started. So the Propaganda Ministry wanted at least at this stage to become an equal partner. For this reason they felt that the congress should be called by two institutions simultaneously, namely the Frankfort Institut representing Rosenberg and Goebbels' Zentralforschungs-

institut (Central Research Institute) in Berlin. This suggestion, however, was not even taken up.

To talk over matters with Hans Frank, Hagemeyer went to Cracow and found the Governor General very cooperative. Frank felt that

> Cracow is particularly fit as a place for the congress because the Government General previously was the domain of Eastern Jewry and the Jewish power-reservoir for poisoning all of Europe.

He, therefore, instructed his subordinates to assist in every way possible and to cover from Government General funds all expenses involved. The opening of the congress was set, tentatively, for June 30 or, if that date was too early, for July 10; at any rate, it was agreed upon that by July 15 it should be over.

Since Paris and Bratislava had been eliminated, Rosenberg decided that Cracow definitely was a better choice than Prague. He obtained the Führer's consent and gave the order to proceed with the preparations. A committee consisting of representatives of Rosenberg's Office, the Propaganda Ministry, the Foreign Ministry, and Himmler's Reich Main Security Office went to Cracow to work with the Governor General on the particulars. As Hagemeyer reported, the preparations had advanced in the meantime. The Foreign Ministry had asked all German embassies and legations to submit lists of prospective participants. Rosenberg's Office, it was stated, contemplated about 450 invitations, including the former Swiss president Müsi, the leader of the Dutch Nazis Anton Mussert, the leader of the Rexist movement in Belgium, Léon Degrelle, three prominent Swedes, Giovanni Preziosi from Italy, and others.

For security reasons, it was deemed appropriate not to give out any communications before the congress was over. The meetings would be held in the rooms of the State Casino, a representative building which provided both a large assembly hall and a restaurant. On the fourth day of the sessions, the representatives of all participating nations would solemnly sign a resolution at the Wawel.[404] "The resolution would contain an unequivocal vow of allegiance (Bekenntnis) to Germany's Jew-policies and demand a Europe free from Jews"; this moment would mark the beginning of the press, radio, and newsreel propaganda of which the Propaganda Ministry was to take care.

[404] The time-honored beautiful castle of the Polish kings; called by the Germans "Die Burg."

The newsreel question was the matter of several meetings and letters. It was stated that it would take eleven days before the pictures found their way into the theatres. The contents of the movie presented serious difficulties:

> Congresses are very thankless subjects for the newsreels because they are boring. An attempt will be made to bring into the movie trick shots on the expansion of the Jews in Europe (Baruch, Morgenthau, Barmat) and new pictures from Jewish ghettos.

For political supervision of the movie, the Propaganda Ministry was to assign either Horst Seemann or Friedrich Löffler, both connected with the Antijüdische Aktion and its periodicals.

Complete unanimity was registered as to the presentation of "Fidelio" and the premiere of some "good German film" during the congress. Besides, two anti-Jewish films were to run at the time of the congress in the movie theaters of Cracow: "The Eternal Jew" (cf. p. 133) and "Jud Süss." Frank then proposed the inclusion in the program of some other "complementary items" which, as Oberregierungsrat Karl August Stuckenberg of the Goebbels' Ministry stated in his report, would give him the opportunity "to dissipate the atrocity propaganda which is being spread in the world concerning Germany's policies toward the Poles." He first recommended a performance of the Polish ballet but yielded when Stuckenberg, "in order not to put the Poles too much in the foreground," suggested the appearance of several ballet groups, such as German, Ukrainian, Polish, French, and one or two others. More serious was Frank's insistence upon having the Polish Philharmonic Orchestra play under the direction of "General-Musikdirektor" Furtwängler.[405] "Unfortunately, it has been impossible until now to dissuade the Governor General from this idea," Stuckenberg added in his secret report.

Goebbels, on the basis of the report submitted to him by Stuckenberg through Ministerialdirektor Alfred Berndt, insisted that Cracow was not the right place for the congress and that an appearance of the Polish Philharmonic Orchestra in this setting was inadmissible. He succeeded, however, only as to this latter point; the objection against Cracow he had to give up with an angry pencil remark on the report "All the same to me!" ("Mir gleich!") when his ministry was informed by Hagemeyer "that the place had been fixed by the Führer himself."

---

[405] As well known, *persona gratissima* with the Nazis.

When the date finally had been set for July 11-15, 1944, and the preparations were in full swing, Reichsleiter Martin Bormann in the middle of June in the name of the Führer ordered, "on the basis of the military developments," postponement of the congress until the beginning of September. Apparently, Hitler's alter ego felt that by September the invasion armies would have been forced into the sea. Proceeding on that assumption, Rosenberg envisaged September 6 as the first day of the congress and the preparatory work went on. On June 28, the day the Allies entered Cherbourg, Rosenberg's Office forwarded to the Propaganda Ministry a tentative list of persons to be invited. This "List of Participants Proposed for the anti-Jewish Congress in Cracow," compiled by Rosenberg's Office itself, the Foreign Ministry, and the Reich Main Security Office, consisted of two groups: A. German guests; B. Guests from abroad.

Obviously, the departments mentioned were concerned chiefly with political figures; of Nazi luminaries the following, among others, appear in the list: Martin Bormann, Hans Frank, Joseph Goebbels, Heinrich Himmler, Ernst Kaltenbrunner, Hans-Heinz Lammers, Robert Ley, Joachim v. Ribbentrop, Alfred Rosenberg, Fritz Sauckel, Xaver Schwartz, Arthur Seyss-Inquart, Helmut Sündermann. The Propaganda Ministry was supposed to add more names, "especially from the cultural sector." Still the original list carried a good many names that have become familiar to us. Of *German* professors, the list envisaged as participants Alfred Baeumler, Walter Gross, Walter Platzhoff, and Nikuradse, and reserved places for fourteen other professors to be named. From *France,* among fifty-one names of journalists, Vichy officials, jurists, and physicians the following seem to be of particular interest: Abel Bonnard, "Minister of Education"; Alexis Carrel, "known medical man, author of *L'homme cet inconnu*"; André Chaumet; Georges Claude, "renowned physicist and speaker for collaboration"; Henri Coston; Jean Drault, "publicist in Drumont's spirit"; Louis-Ferdinand Céline, "physician and anti-Semite writer"; Henri Labroue, "professor, anti-Semitic chair, Paris"; Charles Laville, "writer"; René Martel, "journalist, professor, specialist on the East"; René Martial, "race student, professor"; Georges Montandon, "professor, known race student"; Baron de la Meuse, "industrialist, former cagoulard, anti-Semitic champion, manager of the Rothschild estates, influential socially." *Hungary* was to be represented by at least 33 delegates, among them Zoltán Bosnyák, "Director of the Hungarian Institute for Research into the Jewish Question"; Dr. Alajos Dolanyi-

Kovács, "state secretary, retired, former Director, Office of Statistics"; Dr. Kultsar, "government commissar for the de-Judaization of employees"—both of them, it will be recalled, attended the 1941 Frankfort Conference—and eight university professors. *Italy* was supposed to send to Cracow, among others, Dr. Ettore Martinoli, "Rector of the Italian Center for Research into the Jewish Question, Trieste," and the famous anti-Semite, State Minister Giovanni Preziosi. From the *Netherlands* and *Belgium* five and fourteen participants, respectively, were expected, including Anton Mussert and René Lambrichts, who both had been at the Frankfort Conference, and Léon Degrelle, the Rexist leader. *Finland* and *Denmark* were to send four delegates each; *Norway,* one (but it was Vidkun Quisling himself, also a member of the Frankfort Conference); *Sweden,* three; *Switzerland,* six; *Spain,* three; Portugal, one delegate not mentioned by name but described as follows: "A Portuguese journalist (under a pseudonym as the Paris correspondent of *Esfera*), already has shown significant successes in German information work"; *Greece,* one; *Slovakia,* two— Propaganda Minister Sano Mach, who had been in Frankfort in 1941, and Prime Minister Tuka; *Serbia,* three, among them Sima Kerecki, "instructor, University of Belgrade, leader of the youth organization of the Zbor movement, correspondent of the Institut zur Erforschung der Judenfrage in Frankfort on-the-Main"; *Bulgaria,* thirteen, among them four professors and parliament member Peter Schischkoff who in 1941 had represented his country at the Frankfort Conference; *Rumania,* twelve, among them the Cuzas, who had been in Frankfort, and Luca Sindile, contributor to the *Weltkampf; Lithuania,* four, among them two professors and Bruzas, Director of the "Lithuanian Study Bureau for Research into Bolshevism"; *Latvia,* eleven, among them two professors; *Estonia,* one; *Ostland* (actually White Russia), five. *England* was accorded a representative in the person of "Dr. William Stranders, Sturmbannführer [of the SS], university instructor in medieval history, to be reached c/o SS—Main Office." Finally, *Iraq* was to be represented by Gailani, "[exiled pro-Hitler] Prime Minister", and *Arabia,* most fittingly, by Amin al-Husseini, "Great Mufti of Jerusalem." [406]

[406] The two Arab leaders, after their escape to Germany, were eagerly wooed by the Nazis, cf. footnote 247. Taubert's *Die Aktion* 3 (1942, March), 245-257, published an interview by N. H. Sanki under the title: "An Hour with the 'Faithful.' His Eminence the Great Mufti of Palestine speaks about the Arab National Aims." The following year, a book on the Mufti was issued: Kurt Fischer-Weth, *Amin al-Husseini, Grossmufti von Palästina* (Berlin, Titz, 1943, 95 pp.), and the Mufti was invited to write a preface to a Nazi source book on Britain's Palestinian policy: Mamun al-Hamui, *Die britische Palästina-Politik. Dokumente zur Zeitgeschichte,* her. von Prof. Dr. F. A. Six, Deutsches Auslandswissenschaftliches

In all, the Rosenberg Commissionership looked forward to 402 participants, of whom 189 were to be invited from abroad.

To comply with the request of Rosenberg's Office, the Propaganda Ministry set out to compile an additional list. The Propaganda Department under Stuckenberg was the first to work on that matter; it entrusted the job to Friedrich Löffler who supplied three foreign and twenty GeGrman names; then the Foreign and Literature departments were asked for additions, if any, but their reaction is unknown to us. The Propaganda Ministry also was furnished with a tentative list by the Frankfort *Welt-Dienst,* which had ample international connections through its anti-Semitic news service in twenty languages (Arabic, Bulgarian, Croatian, Danish, Dutch, English, French, German, Greek, Hungarian, Italian, Lettish, Norwegian, Polish, Rumanian, Russian, Serbian, Spanish, Swedish, Ukrainian); this list, however, has not come to our knowledge. The following names were submitted by Löffler; those not approved by Stuckenberg for one reason or another are marked with an asterisk: [467]

> Aldag, Peter (=Dr. Krüger), author of the books on the Jews in England;
>
> Bartels, Adolf, Professor of the history of literature, Weimar;
>
> Bertram, Dr. Georg, Professor, at present Director of the Institut zur Erforschung des jüdischen Einflusses auf das deutsche kirchliche Leben, Giessen;
>
> Euler, Dr. K[arl] F[riedrich], author of several publications against Jewry;
>
> Euler, Wilfried, Reichsinstitut für Geschichte des neuen Deutschlands; [468]
>
> Fischer, Dr. Eugen, Professor, race student, Freiburg-Breisgau;
>
> * Freisler, Roland, President of the People's Court, state secretary, etc.;
>
> Gruehn, Dr. Werner, Professor, psychologist of religion, author of the book *Der Zar, der Zauberer und die Juden* ["The Czar, the Sorcerer, and the Jews"], Berlin;
>
> Kindermann, Dr. [Heinz], Professor, historian of literature, Münster;
>
> Kittel, Dr. Gerhard, Professor, theologian, Tübingen and Vienna;
>
> Koch, Dr. [Franz], Professor, historian of literature, Berlin;

Institut, Band I (Berlin, Junker und Dünnhaupt, 1943, 365 pp.).—"Great Mufti of Jerusalem, Health Resort of Oybin (Grossmufti von Jerusalem, Kurort Oybin)" is mentioned in a Propaganda Ministry document of March, 1944 (now in the Yivo archives), in a mailing list of pro-German volunteer formations receiving literature from the ministry.

[467] The list has been rearranged in alphabetical order.

[468] A slip of paper in the file, apparently in Stuckenberg's handwriting, entitled "Vorschläge f[ür] Einladungen," contains the name Euler (without the first name), with a pencil remark opposite it: "Jewish family relationship? (Jüdisch versippt?)." But it seems that the grave suspicion proved baseless, because the two Eulers did figure in the final list.

Herrn ORR. Stückenberg.

Betr.: Gästevorschläge für M. 44.

Gegen die vom Walt=dienst gemachten Vorschläge sind – soweit ich darüber urteilen kann
– keine Einwendungen zu machen.

Weitere Vorschläge:

Ausländische Gäste

Frankreich: Boissel, Jean, Leiter des „Réveil
du Peuple", bekannter Juden-
gegner.

Norwegen: Aall, K.H., namhafter Jurist und bekannter Freund Deutschlands.

Ägypten: Fakoussa, Hassan, journalistisch und als
jüdischer Schriftsteller.

228

Deutsche Gäste

Freisler, Roland, Präs. d. Volksgerichtshofs, Staatssekretär a.D.

Rüttke, Falk, Prof., Verfasser der Nürnberger Gesetze.

Fischer, Eugen, Prof. a.D., Rassenforscher, Freiburg i.Br.

Kittel Gerhard, " " Theologe, Tübingen u. Wien.

Güldehn Werner, " " Religionspsychologe, Berlin; Verf. d. Buches "Das Tao, der Zauberer und die Juden".

Euler, Wilhelm Reichsinst. z. Gesch. d. neuen Deutschl.

Euler. Dr. K. F., Verfasser mehrerer Schriften gegen das Judentum.

Bertram, Hg., Prof. a.D., z.Zt. Leiter der Abteilung zur Erforschung des jüd. Einflusses auf das deutsche kirchliche Leben; Eisenach.

Meyer-Christian, W. , Verf. d. Buches "die englisch-jüdische Allianz".

Aldag, Peter (= Dr. Krüger), Verf. d. Bücher über die Juden in England.

Koch, Prof. a.D., Literaturhistoriker, Berlin.

Kindermann, Prof. a.D., " Münster.

Lenard, Prof. a.D., Physiker, bek. Judengegner.

229

X Roth, Alfred, Schriftsteller, ... u. Leiter des ...
deutschen völkischen Schutz- u. Trutzbundes.

X Bartels, Adolf, P.P., Literaturhistoriker, Weimar.

Sauerbruch, Prof. Dr. P.P. ..., Berlin.

Mollison, P.P. ..., Rassenforscher, München.

Reche, Otto, " " , " , Leipzig.

X Willrich, Maler, Verf. d. Buches, Säuberung
des Kunsttempels."

Strauß, Werner, Schauspieler.

Ich hoffe, in Kürze noch weitere Vorschläge
machen zu können.

Löffler 3.7.
44.

Krauss, Werner, actor;

Lenard, Dr. [Philipp], Professor, physicist, known adversary of the Jews;

Meyer-Christian, W[olf], author of the book *Die englisch-jüdische Allianz* ["The English-Jewish Alliance"];

* Mollison, Dr. [Theodor], Professor, race student, Munich;

* Reche, Dr. Otto, Professor, race student, Leipzig;

Roth, Alfred, editor, founder and director of the former Deutsch-völkischer Schutz- und Trutzbund (German Folk Defensive and Offensive Association); [469]

Ruttke, Falk, Professor, author of the Nuremberg Laws;

* Sauerbruch, Dr. [Ferdinand], Geheimer Regierungsrat, Professor, Berlin;

Willrich, painter, author of the book *Reinigung des Kunsttempels* ["Cleansing of the Art Temple"].

To the list of guests from abroad, Löffler had three names to add, and all of them were approved:

France: Boissel, Jean, Editor-in-chief, *Réveil du Peuple,* known adversary of the Jews;

Norway: Aale, H. H., well-known jurist and known friend of Germany;

Egypt: Fakoussa, Hassan, journalist and anti-Jewish writer.

The program of the congress as early as in June was prepared in all details and submitted for approval to all agencies concerned. The particulars presented here are taken from the secret report submitted to Reich Minister Goebbels by Oberregierungsrat Stuckenberg. For four days, a morning and an afternoon session were to be held each day, with the fifth day devoted to informal entertainment. The following were expected to be chairmen: Reichsstatthalter Sprenger of Frankfort on-the-Main; State Minister Professor Preziosi, Italy; Envoy Schleier of the Foreign Ministry; University Professor Dr. Martial, France; Ministerialdirektor Berndt of the Propaganda Ministry; President Drault, France; Dienstleiter Hagemeyer of Rosenberg's Commissionership, and Stabsleiter Dr. Stellrecht.

Each day was to be marked by the address of a high-ranking speaker in the following order: Hans Frank, "Greetings"; Alfred Rosenberg, "Biological Humaneness"; Joseph Goebbels, "The Agitation Methods of World Jewry"; Joachim von Ribbentrop, "Jewish World Diplomacy and the Present World War." Rosenberg also

---

[469] An anti-Semitic and anti-labor organization founded in 1919, at one time a promising competitor of the Deutsche Arbeiterpartei (German Labor Party) which later grew into the NSDAP. Cf. Hugo Bieber, "Anti-Semitism in the First Year of the German Republic," to be published in *Yivo Bleter,* Journal of the Yiddish Scientific Institute, XXVIII (1946).

was to close the congress after the adoption of the anti-Jewish resolution (cf. p. 223).

Papers were to be presented by the following eleven persons who
are here enumerated in alphabetical order:

Amery, John: "Jewish Influence in the English Ruling Stratum
(Herrschaftsschicht)."

Amin al-Husseini, Great Mufti, Jerusalem: "Palestine, a World-
Political Pivot of Jewish Drive for Power."

Anastasius, Metropolitan, Belgrade: "The Rôle of the Jews in
South-Eastern Europe."

Gross, Dr. Walter, University Professor: "The Parasitic Quali-
ties of the Jews."

Günther, Dr. Hans, University Professor: "The Invasion of the
Jews into the Cultural Life of the Nations."

Härtle [Heinrich], Oberreichsleiter: "Ideology and Practice of
Jewish bolshevism."

Hunke, Dr. [Heinrich], University Professor: "The Jew in the
Economic Life of the Nations."

Martial, Dr. [René], University Professor: "The Jew in the
Public and Social Life of France."

Müller, Dr. Karl Alexander von, University Professor: "The
Part of Jewry in the History of Germany and the Struggle against
It."

Pohl, Dr. [Johann]: "Religion and Moral Law of Judaism."

Preziosi, [Giovanni], State Minister: "The Rôle of Jewry in
Freemasonry in Italy's Past."

Tannenberg, Ministerialrat: "The UNNRA as a World-Political
Power System of Jewry (Including the Morgenthau World Exchange Plan)."

Several persons were conspicuous by their absence from the list,
such as the two antagonists Walter Frank and Wilhelm Grau; our
material does not offer any hint as to the reasons for ignoring them.

During the congress, an exhibition, "The Jew in Contemporaneous
World Politics," was to be shown. A meeting held in Berlin on
May 16, 1944, entrusted the preparations to Rosenberg's Office;
material also was to be furnished by the "Jew Achives (Juden-
Archiv)" of Taubert's Anti-Comintern and the *Welt-Dienst*. A committee consisting of Hagemeyer, Oberstudiendirektor Köster, Dr.
von Werder, Dr. Pohl, and H. Lichtnau, an expert in illustrating,
agreed upon the following subdivisions: (1) Where does the Jew
come from; (2) The emancipation of the Jews; (3) Jewry in the
modern world. A mural "The face of the eternal Jew" was to round
up the exhibition. After a month in Cracow, the exhibits were to
be shown in other cities.

The "by-program" also was to include other educational items.

The foreign guests are to be shown on one hand the German Cracow with its famous buildings, all of them traceable to German origin but, on the other hand, also institutions proving that Germany carries on quite a fair policy toward the Poles....

Nevertheless,

it is to be avoided by all means that the participants of the congress get into closer contact with the Polish population. The Reich Main Security Office prepares adequate measures for the security [sic] of the participants.

Then the secret report submitted to Reich Minister Goebbels by Oberregierungsrat Stuckenberg took up the very important matter of supplying the foreign guests with a suitable... brothel. The agency directly in charge was the SD (Sicherheits-Dienst) which we previously have seen assigned to other duties:

In addition, it is planned, in view of the sad experience of other congresses, to install in Cracow for the time of the event a brothel with non-Polish women. Party member Ohlenbusch [the representative of the Propaganda Ministry in the Government General], on instructions of the Governor General, continues to confer about this matter with the SD and then will submit a report.

This question of the brothel later was taken up in a confidential telegram addressed by Ohlenbusch on June 14 to the Propaganda Ministry, Department of Propaganda, attention Oberregierungsrat Stuckenberg, which read in part:

In accord with the SD there are no doubts as to the establishment of a bawdyhouse for the purposes mentioned. Polish or Ukrainian material [sic] must not be used. Practical steps must be taken at your end.

A pencil remark on the telegram, in Stuckenberg's hand, reads: "Rosenberg," and accordingly Ohlenbusch was instructed on the matter by wire on June 20 over Stuckenberg's signature preceded by "Heil Hitler":

The supply of the material will be effected by the Rosenberg staff. On principle, there is agreement here as to the establishment of a house.

As indicated, the congress, after the initial postponement in June, was tentatively planned for September 6. The preparations for the function (which in the correspondence often was referred to as K[rakau] 44), such as the work on a newsreel with new ghetto pictures, went on for some time. But as the last entry on the matter in the Propaganda Ministry file was made on July 27, it may be assumed that with the deterioration of the military and political

Es muß auf jeden Fall vermieden werden, daß die Kongreßteilnehmer mit der polnischen Bevölkerung in näheren Kontakt kommen. Das Reichssicherheitshauptamt bereitet entsprechende Maßnahmen zur Sicherung der Kongreßteilnehmer vor. Außerdem wird auf Grund der trüben Erfahrungen, die man mit anderen Kongressen gemacht hat, erwogen, für die Dauer der Veranstaltung in Krakau ein Bordell mit Nichtpolinnen einzurichten. Pg. Ohlenbusch verhandelt auf Weisung des Generalgouverneurs in dieser Angelegenheit noch mit dem SD und gibt dann nach hier Bericht durch.

---

akau   14.6.44.   18.00 uhr
uptabtlg. propaganda
  pm,
teilung pro
  hd. herrn oberregierungsrat stuckenberg.
ldung nr 20.011
==

     v e r t r a u l i c h.
   +++++++++++++++++++++++++++++++

tr.: sonderaktion rr.

.) im einvernehmen mit dem sd. bestehen gegen einrichtung ines oeffentlichen hauses fuer den besprochenenezwecke keine denken.polnisches oder ukrainisches material darf nicht erwendet werden.praktische voraussetzungen muessen von ihrer eite getroffen werden .

ch bitte um moeglichst bescheunigte stellungnahme zu den inzelnen punkten .

                    o h l e n b u s c h .

234

situation the whole idea of the congress had to be dropped. So much mastery in planning, so much understanding for lovely details had been spent in vain.

XXXX

ANTI-SEMITISM AN AVOWED "SECRET WEAPON"

We might have closed our survey with this report that so convincingly reveals the nature of Hitler Germany except for a document of a more theoretical character that, also, was discovered in the charred remnants of the Ministry of Propaganda in Berlin. It is entitled: "The Treatment of the Jewish Question in the German Press," but its scope is much broader than the title suggests. Written in March, 1944, i.e., before D-E Day, it still boldly envisaged the future and outlined long-range plans. But although antiquated in this respect, the document continues to be most instructive in that it sets forth the tenets of anti-Semitism, and not of the Nazi brand only, in almost classical form.

The eleven-page memorandum[470] was submitted to Goebbels' ministry by Oberstleutnant Wolf Meyer-Christian, an incisive writer already known to us as the author of a book on the "Anglo-Jewish alliance."[471] In a sense, the memorandum reverted to the same subject in that it intended to show that Zionism was the most menacing of all Jewish movements and the Jewish Agency for Palestine in effect was a world Jewish government striving for world domination. But whereas the ideology of the document may appear boring, the strategy advocated in it commands attention.

Meyer-Christian began with the statement that the German press only reluctantly dealt with things Jewish; "ordered actions . . . are being conducted without spirit." One reason, he believed, was that

[470] *Die Behandlung der Judenfrage in der deutschen Presse.* The covering letter was written on June 13, 1944, by Oberregierungsrat Walter Koerber to Stabsleiter Helmut Sünder-mann. On the authority of Oberregierungsrat Karl August Stuckenberg and Dr. L. Franz Gengler, it confirmed the reliability of the material supplied by Meyer-Christian and concluded: "Although at present other matters are in the foreground of press policies, I believe that along these proposals a long-range action should be prepared." Meyer-Christian's suggestions about the intensification of the anti-Jewish propaganda were well received, as shown, e.g., by the quotations from Goebbels' *Deutscher Wochendienst* on pages 204-206. During the second half of 1944, this news service also carried at least four unsigned articles under the general title: "Hinweise für die antijüdische Pressearbeit" ("Hints for anti-Jewish Journalist Work") which so carefully followed Meyer-Christian's memorandum that they might have been written by himself. The chronological table on the history of Zionism attached to the memorandum was published, slightly enlarged, under the compiler's name, in *Weltkampf* IV (1944), 149-152, under the title: "Hauptdaten der zionistischen Politik."

[471] See p. 86. Dr. Gengler's review of the book in *Die Judenfrage*, November 1, 1940, pp. 176-177, introduced the author as a "trusty contributor of *Die Judenfrage* for many years" and praised his "detailed knowledge of world-Jewish aspirations" as well as his "scholarly thoroughness."

after 1933 too many parallel institutes to study the Jewish question were established: the Party institute (Institut zur Erforschung der Judenfrage in Frankfort), the Propaganda Ministry institute (Institut zum Studium der Judenfrage), and the Reichsinstitut für Geschichte des neuen Deutschlands.[472] This was the reason that

> the research into the Jewish question . . . did not attain the same momentum and publicity as the part of the research work concerning foreign policy which, incidentally, possesses a considerably older tradition; the results of research are scattered and not accessible without effort for the lack of central coordinating agencies,[473] the old anti-Semitic material of the period of the struggle [for power] is purely polemical and unreliable.

But there is another reason for the lack of interest, Meyer-Christian continued: The legislative and administrative measures of the Reich which led to the elimination of the Jews have made people believe that there was no more immediate danger in Jewry: "the public at large (die breite Masse) considers the Jewish question settled."

> This would be of no consequence at all, had the Jewish problem really become past history through Germany's measures. Actually, however, only the domestic German side of the Jewish problem has been settled by the Reich's policy toward the Jews. In its entirety the problem not only continues to exist, but since 1933 it has acquired a most tremendous acuteness and poignancy, and must therefore be brought to view more than ever and with greater force than ever.

"Leaving out the six million European Jews"—the theorist of the murderers did not say why they might be left out—

> there are now 10-12 million Jews politically committed (im Einsatz) against the Reich. Their disproportionately strong intelligentsia with its exponents stands directly behind the political management of the enemy and, despite all its internal differentiations, constitutes the connecting link with and among England, the USA, and the Soviet Union. These hints suffice at least to outline the fighting front of world Jewry against Germany, which today is actually no longer a phrase. The front remains, but its center of gravity has shifted. A question of [German] domestic politics has become one of foreign politics.

[472] One more institute is mentioned as founded by the SD (Sicherheits-Dienst). Perhaps, its traces will be uncovered in the Nazi archives; or did Meyer-Christian have in mind the Institut für deutsche Ostarbeit in Cracow, which might have passed under the auspices of the SD?

[473] Oberregierungsrat Koerber in this statement scented an opportunity for his agency and remarked in his covering letter: "The most important premise . . . no doubt would be the achievement of close collaboration and a uniform line [of action] for all pertinent institutions of the Party and the State. This, at least as far as fixing the propaganda aims is concerned, is possible only through the Propaganda Ministry."

This change in situation should have necessitated a change in tactics, but no change occurred. And here was the negative result, as the author saw it:

> Young officers of twenty declare upon inquiries that they have never yet consciously seen a Jew. Consequently they find no interest, or only slight interest, in the Jewish problem, as it has been presented to them up to now. The designation, "typically Jewish," sufficient to us older people, carries no more meaning for them than the words "typically Chinese." Therefore the danger arises that the speeches of the Führer, who always begins his political messages with a detailed summary (Abriss) of the Jewish problem, lose so much in penetrative power for the younger generation, and in their view assume the character of a historical lecture.

It could happen, therefore, that the Jewish question would be buried with the older generation. Fortunately, the opponent had not yet noticed this growing indifference.

In Jewish circles, Meyer-Christian went on, the "correct idea" is frequently being expressed "that anti-Semitism is not only one of the foundations of national socialism but at the same time its most important propaganda weapon."

> Frequently, one finds, anti-Semitism is prettily and appropriately called the Führer's secret weapon. Consequently, the attitude of personalities and organizations, even of governments, toward the Jewish problem is considered, primarily in America, a measure of political reliability. This attitude also holds good among those neutrals whom we are interested in influencing.

At this, Meyer-Christian maintained, the question arises:

> How do we make use of our secret weapon? What does a Swede of good will find in the German press of fundamentals and material on the Jewish question as he sees it, material that concerns him and interests him, and that he can utilize? What does our radio, or our foreign-news system, both of which reach listeners in the very camp of the enemy, offer the dissatisfied and opposition circles in England, say, in the way of powerful material, appropriate to and important for England, which could exert its splitting effect there and continue its effect as oral propaganda? How, and by what means do we, the heartland (Kernland) of anti-Semitism, steer and strengthen the available defense forces against Jewry in England and North America?

> There is, unfortunately, no answer to these questions. We hold a weapon in our hands without steadily controlling or maintaining its sharpness and without a smashing plan for applying it.

The time has come to pass again from defense to attack, the memorandum insisted. It is by no means too late. "Moreover, success can be predicted for certain" if a considered plan underlies the action.

> Like every attack, this one requires
> 1. Steadfast leadership
> 2. A clear-cut task
> 3. A center of gravity
> 4. Examination of all arms available
> 5. Cooperation of all weapons
> 6. Minute preparation.

Point 5—cooperation of all weapons—was elaborated this way:

> The newly organized fight against world Jewry as Germany's and Europe's enemy must ostensibly—but without its *organization* being ostensible—be carried by the whole German people and its European friends. It will not do in any case if well-informed, but unknown, specialists dominate the field as editorial writers. The services of journalists who are known as experts on foreign politics, who are not of outspokenly National Socialist derivation or brand, should be enlisted in this effort, and not at random but according to capacity and circumstance.

> Apart from this group, however, all circles of the population, representatives of intellectual life, well-known poets and scholars, actors and film stars, painters and musicians, generals, bearers of the Knights' Cross, engineers, officials, retailers, housewives, and former functionaries of the SPD [Social Democratic Party of Germany] and other anti-national-socialist parties, should be drawn into this struggle.

The Jewish question must again be placed in the center of public interest, the author concluded, and real knowledge must be put to work. "If anywhere, knowledge in our struggle means power, and accurate information in this case is as important as munitions." To the German public, world Jewry must be made visible, because only the concrete enemy evokes interest. But even more important is public opinion abroad:

> On the outer front: the effect [of anti-Jewish propaganda] as explosive ammunition for the fifth column of the 20th century. Because opposition against the Jews, it so happens, is the secret cue by which all those who have understood the signs of time recognize each other. Should we, especially we, refuse to lead it?

Thus spoke an exacting German scholar at a time when the death furnaces were operating on a non-stop basis.

XXXXI

summary and conclusions

The foregoing analysis and discussion may be summarized as follows:

1. German scholars, who as a rule already in the Second Reich had done their best to foster German imperialism, from the end of World War I supplied nazism with the ideological weapons which any movement, but particularly a German movement, needs for its success.

2. The Jewish issue from the very outset was recognized as a decisive weapon in Germany's strife for conquest.

3. Pre-Nazi anti-Semitic literature was found by the Nazis to be unreliable and unsatisfactory in form and contents. But they soon succeeded in streamlining theory and adjusting it to the new circumstances of a totalitarian state headed for world domination.

4. Six periods can be discerned in the development of Germany's crimes against the Jewish people after Hitler's seizure of power:

a. From the establishment of the regime (January, 1933) until the promulgation of the Nuremberg Laws in the autumn of 1935.

b. From the Nuremberg Laws to the November, 1938, pogrom wave, which period is marked by an intensification of anti-Jewish legislation and practice within Germany and growing penetration of racial anti-Semitism into other countries as part of the fifth-column program.

c. From the end of 1938 until the attack on Poland. This period, which culminated in Hitler's prophecy of January 30, 1939, in connection with the preparations for war, was devoted to preliminary planning for *Ausmerze*.

d. From September, 1939, to the first half of 1941, when the German rulers seem to have anticipated the *Ausmerze* of the Jewish population by enslavement and starvation supported by occasional violence.

e. From the attack on the Soviet Union until the middle of 1942, when the Jewish population of Eastern Europe was decimated through outright murder of hundreds of thousands.

f. From July, 1942, until the end of the war, when the *Ausmerze* of millions was perpetrated.

At each of these successive stages the German rulers had theorists at hand who praised their achievements in reducing the Jews and supplied the academic formulae and the scholarly backing for each further step in German policies, until the "extinguishment" of the "eternally hostile forces" was accomplished to the best of the murderers' abilities. Nor did this last step lack theoretical backing.

5. Not mere second-rate writers or sham scholars participated in waging war on the Jews. The Nazis set out with a comparatively small number of outsiders but soon they were joined by mounting numbers of people of regular academic standing, some of them scholars of note. As time progressed, the bulk of university scholars, of scholarly periodicals, of publishing houses was entirely Nazified.

6. Apart from the scholars who served the regime as individuals, several special research institutions and publications were created as instrumentalities in Germany's war against the Jews.

7. No discipline of science that could be of use to the regime failed. The hundreds of names we have dealt with range from physical and cultural anthropologists to philosophers, historians, jurists, economists, geographers, and demographers, to theologians, linguists, and medical men. Only the names of the engineers who so ingeniously constructed the gas chambers and death furnaces for the time being remain in obscurity; but their deeds speak for their efficiency.

8. German scholars, in conspiracy with German politicians and military, did their utmost to spread Nazi anti-Jewish theory and practice to the occupied and satellite nations, and also to any other country within their reach.

9. Just as Nazi anti-Jewishness was part of a global program, anti-Jewish science of the Nazi era was no insular, self-contained branch of knowledge and instruction; it was embedded in the whole of German scholarship which had placed itself at the service of the Third Reich.

10. Nothing is gained by calling the perpetrators and accomplices madmen and their deeds "collective madness." There was too much method in this madness, too much premeditation and planning.

When Justice Robert H. Jackson in his opening statement at Nuremberg said: "History does not record a crime ever perpetrated against so many victims or one ever carried out with such calculated cruelty," he made no overstatement. There were in the memory of mankind Jenghiz Khans and Eugen Fischers but never before had a Jenghiz Khan joined hands with an Eugen Fischer. For this reason, the blow was deadly efficient. In 1939, there were 16,723,800 Jews in the world; 9,479,200 of them lived in Europe; of the latter, 7,950,000 belonged to Eastern Jewry.[474] Six million Jews in Europe are no more. Thus, thirty-six per cent of world Jewry, sixty-four per cent of European Jewry, seventy-five per cent of the Eastern-European Jewish group in Europe have been murdered by Germans, or by mercenaries on German order. Had the war lasted one year more, probably not a single Jew in Europe would have remained alive. If the murdered be placed one behind the other in marching order, the column of skeletons would extend all the way from New York to San Francisco, and then all the way back from San Francisco to New York, and then again from New York to Chicago. And if these victims of the "New Order" could have a casual glance at post-war Europe, what could prevent them from remarking with grim satisfaction: it seems as if there is still some trouble though we, the alleged troublemakers, are no more....

What is to be gained by this recital of agony and crime? No one of our murdered six million will be reawakened to life. But perhaps man is capable of learning from experience. Because of that chance, one is duty bound to rummage the piles of that unsavory literature of the Nazi era. Because of that chance, one must go through the pain of translating "extinguished" parents, brothers and sisters, and life-long friends, one's *people,* into impressive comparisons and percentages.

Here are some of the questions that confront us regarding the future:

Is the germ of Nazidom destroyed in Germany with the crushing of the Nazi state? Can German scholarship, even if technically de-Nazified, be made an instrument of re-educating the German people? [475]

Is nazism a German problem only? Is its menace over for the world at large, both as an instrumentality of Germany's national

---

[474] Figures compiled by Jacob Lestchinsky, Section of Economics and Statistics, Yiddish Scientific Institute, as also the estimates given on p. 87.

[475] The following item from the *New York Times* of August 14, 1945, is instructive: "Paris, August 13.—The *Figaro* will report tomorrow that one of Gen. Jean de Lattre de Tassigny's last acts as commander of the French First Army before he became inspector general of the French army was to release the late Field Marshal Gen. Erwin Rommel's son from a prison camp near Lindau on condition that he study at the University of Tübingen.

'I do not ask you to renounce all that a good German can legitimately love in his country," the General said. "I ask you merely to reflect in this place, where so many great philosophers have lived, and to evaluate the inhuman ideas that have led your country to its present condition.' "

politics and as a supra-national appeal to the meanest in human nature?

Is the menace of nazism over for the Jews in all the lands?

Are the Jews the only minority that is threatened by nazism and all it stands for? Is it too academic to ask: what minority is next to be singled out—or is it a group that is still to be molded into and elevated to the rank of a minority?

Our survey does not intend to provide a satisfying answer to these searching questions. It confines itself to submitting part of the factual evidence and urging the necessity of further study although the material here presented seems to point in a definite direction.

And now the final question that has been the subject of this survey: are Germany's intellectual leaders guilty of complicity in the crimes against humanity for which Germany's top politicians and generals have been brought to trial? It seems that only one answer is possible. With the political and military leaders, the intellectual leaders first declared Germany the final judge of her own acts and then renounced accepted morality. With the political and military leaders, they arrogated to themselves the right to dispose of millions of people for their own and their fatherland's greater glory. With the political and military leaders, they prepared, instituted, and blessed the program of vilification, disfranchisement, dispossession, expatriation, imprisonment, deportation, enslavement, torture, and murder. Some of them even took part in executing the program.

The question of legal responsibility is for a United Nations Tribunal to decide. Before the world's conscience, German scholarship stands convicted.

FACSIMILES OF EXCERPTS

CF. P. 5

'der internationale Jude! Ich wäre kein Nationalsozialist mehr gewesen, wenn ich mich von dieser Erkenntnis je entfernt hätte. Wir haben seine Spuren verfolgt durch so viele Jahre, wir haben wohl in diesem Reich zum erstenmal planmäßig wissenschaftlich dieses Problem und Phänomen der Menschheit geklärt

CF. P. 8

Die Arbeit des Instituts fühlt sich sowohl der methodisch kritischen Richtung, die in der deutschen Wissenschaft in den letzten hundert Jahren entwickelt worden ist und den Ruf Deutschlands in der Welt erhöht hat, wie der großen zusammenfassenden Darstellungskraft der besten und begnadetsten unter den deutschen Gelehrten verpflichtet, dem Geist der Gründlichkeit und Wahrhaftigkeit ebenso wie dem kühnen Fragen nach den letzten Urgründen des Lebens und der Geschichte.

CF. P. 12

Die jüdische Physik, die so in den letzten drei Jahrzehnten entstanden ist und sowohl von Juden wie von ihren nichtjüdischen Schülern und Nachahmern gemacht und propagiert wurde, hat folgerichtig auch in einem Juden ihren Hohenpriester gefunden, in Einstein. Aus ihm hat jüdische Reklame den größten Naturforscher aller Zeiten machen wollen. Einsteins Relativitätstheorien waren aber im Grunde nichts weiter als eine Häufung von gekünstelten Formeln auf Grund von willkürlichen Definitionen und Transformationen der Raum= und Zeitkoordinaten.

Der jüdische Formalismus in der Naturforschung ist unter allen Umständen zu verwerfen.

CF. P. 13

Auf dieser biologischen Erkenntnis ist nämlich ein wichtiger Teil des nationalsozialistischen Gedankengutes begründet. Und aus ihr entnimmt die nationalsozialistische Staatsführung die Richtlinien für ihre volkspolitischen Maßnahmen zur rassischen Aufartung des deutschen Volkes. Ihre Maßnahmen zur Ausschaltung des volksschädlichen jüdischen Einflusses auf das deutsche Volk sind biologisch=wissenschaftlich begründet

CF. P. 28

In der Nachkriegszeit versuchten jüdisch-demokratische und klerikale Kreise, vor allem in Berlin, die Rassenhygiene unter dem Namen Eugenik zu neutralisieren. / Mit dem Erstarken der nationalsozialistischen Bewegung entstanden dann auch gleich neue Schriften, die der Verbreitung des rassenhygienischen Gedankens dienen sollten

CF. P. 42

Ausrottung des Judentums? Eine gewaltsame Ausrottung des Judentums kommt für eine ernsthafte Betrachtung nicht in Frage: wenn sie den Systemen der spanischen Inquisition oder den russischen Progromen nicht gelungen ist, wird sie für das 20. Jahrhundert erst recht nicht möglich sein. Der Gedanke entbehrt auch des inneren Sinnes. Ein geschichtlicher Tatbestand, wie er mit diesem Volk gegeben ist, wird höchstens in demagogischen Schlagworten, niemals aber in der Geschichte selbst durch Ausrottung des Volkes gelöst. Der Sinn einer geschichtlichen Lage ist immer, daß sie uns eine Aufgabe stellt, die wir meistern sollen. Alle Juden totschlagen aber heißt nicht, die Aufgabe meistern.

CF. P. 45

Wir werden dafür sorgen, daß niemals mehr in Deutschland, dem Herzen Europas, von innen oder durch Emissäre von außen her die jüdisch-bolschewistische Revolution des Untermenschen entfacht werden kann. Unbarmherzig werden wir für alle diese Kräfte, deren Existenz und Treiben wir kennen, am Tage auch nur des geringsten Versuches, sei er heute, sei er in Jahrzehnten oder in Jahrhunderten, ein gnadeloses Richtschwert sein.

CF. P. 50

Die deutsche Judenfrage stellt sich heute im besonderen als wirtschafts- und außenpolitisches Problem dar. Ob sie in den kommenden Jahren auf diesen Gebieten mit Erfolg gesteuert wird, entscheidet darüber, ob Deutschland für immer seine Judenfrage gelöst hat und ob die Welt auf dem Weg zur Lösung ist.

CF. P. 51

Eine weitere methodische Neuerung bedeutete die aktive Teilnahme geschichtlich handelnder Männer an einer geschichtswissenschaftlichen Tagung. Im Zuge dieser Entwicklung wurden auch die Vorträge von Gauleiter Streicher: Mein politischer Kampf gegen das Judentum, und von Oberst a. D. Nicolai: Wie hat der Chef des Nachrichtendienstes der obersten Heeresleitung im Weltkrieg den Einfluß des Juden während des Weltkrieges gesehen? eingesetzt. Diese Vorträge zeigten, wie wichtig es ist, daß der heutige Historiker auch in Berührung mit geschichtsgestaltenden Persönlichkeiten die Überlieferung der gegenwärtigen Geschichte pflegt, die infolge des Fernsprechers und der „reisenden Diplomatie" vielfach ohne schriftlichen Überrest verlorenzugehen droht. Darüber hinaus dient diese Fühlungnahme zwischen Wissenschaft und Politik der Einheit des geistigen Lebens der Nation, indem der Historiker dem Politiker Waffen schmiedet und ihm die Übersicht über das geschichtliche Ringen der Gegenwart von der vergangenen Geschichte her vertieft und zugleich seinerseits vom Politiker neue Fragestellungen und Einsichten empfängt.   *ho.*

CF. P. 52

Erstmals wurde auf dieser Arbeitstagung der Forschungsabteilung eine methodische Neuerung eingeführt, der wir für die Geschichtsforschung der Zukunft grundsätzliche Bedeutung beimessen: Zum erstenmal sprachen im Rahmen einer wissenschaftlichen Körperschaft führende Männer des handelnden Lebens — der ehemalige Chef des Nachrichtendienstes der Obersten Heeresleitung, Oberst Walther Nicolai, und der Gauleiter Julius Streicher — über Gegenstände aus der Geschichte der letzten zwei Jahrzehnte, nicht auf Grund literarischen Quellenstudiums, sondern als Menschen, die das Geschehen an führender Stelle miterlebt und mitgestaltet haben.

CF. P. 54

Wohl aber habe ich in meiner Eröffnungsrede am 5. Juli erklärt, daß sich das Reichsinstitut für Geschichte des neuen Deutschlands als „den Mittelpunkt des Antisemitismus in der deutschen Wissenschaft" betrachte.

CF. P. 54

Gauleiter Julius Streicher rief in seinen mehrstündigen, lebendigen und packenden Ausführungen die deutschen Geschichtsschreiber auf zur unmittelbaren Fühlung mit der Natur und mit dem Volk
Adolf Hitler habe in den Anfängen der Bewegung gesagt: „Ein Kämpfer doziert nicht, er spricht aus dem Herzen." Der Gauleiter freute sich feststellen zu können, daß im Kreise des Reichsinstituts ein neuer Geist herrsche, hier seien Männer. die sich jung fühlten und auch den notwendigen Mut hätten, die Geschichte aus dem Herzen zu schreiben.

CF. P. 56

Deutsche Wissenschaft im Kampf gegen das Weltjudentum!

Wie auf die Freveltat des Weltjudentums der politische und wirtschaftliche Gegen-
schlag des Reiches gefolgt ist, wird auch in der Wissenschaft darauf geantwortet
werden, indem wir den antijüdischen Flügel unserer Forschungsarbeit immer
weiter verstärken. (Walter Frank a. d. Berlin. Tagung d. Reichsinstituts am 1. 12. 38)

CF. P. 57

Spinoza war, wie Grunsky
nachwies, ein Handelsjude wie seine Rassegenossen, der,
lediglich getarnt als germanisch-mystischer Denker, eine
neue Thora zu schaffen trachtete, die alle Völker unter
das Gesetz des Talmud bringen sollte.

CF. P. 63

Bei der Tätigkeit des Institutes handelt es sich um die Heraus-
arbeitung der wissenschaftlichen Folgerungen aus den rassisch-
völkischen Erkenntnissen der nationalsozialistischen Weltanschauung für den religiösen Sektor des deutschen Lebens. Die im
Institut zusammengeschlossenen Männer haben sich als Nationalso-
zialisten von vorn herein auf diesen Boden gestellt im Unterschied zu der bisherigen Theologie und Religionswissenschaft,
die sich diesen Erkenntnissen verschließt und darum für die religiöse Zukunft des deutschen Volkes unfruchtbar ist.

CF. P. 76

Es muß jedenfalls die Fest-
stellung hier getroffen werden, daß die Führer des Bolschewismus, soweit sie nicht-
jüdischer Abstammung sind, rassisch und geistig vorderasiatisch-orientalisch bestimmt
sind.

CP. P. 78

Eine Tatsache ist jedenfalls für alle antisemitischen Bewegungen
Osteuropas bezeichnend: es fehlt eine einheitlich ausgerichtete
Weltanschauung, die den Juden als rassisch bestimmte Gruppe
faßt und ihm gegenüber eine ganz besondere Haltung fordert. Der
Antisemitismus Osteuropas ist vorwiegend eine Folge des
wirtschaftlichen Gegensatzes, gemischt mit gefühlsmäßiger oder
auch religiös-sittlicher Ablehnung. Nationalistisch-minderheitenfeindliche
Zielsetzungen und Sentiments sind aber keine Weltanschauung
und können nie die Stoßkraft einer solchen besitzen.

CF. PP. 81-82

Und eines möchte ich an diesem vielleicht nicht nur für uns Deutsche denkwürdigen Tage nun aussprechen: Ich bin in meinem Leben sehr oft Prophet gewesen und wurde meistens ausgelacht. In der Zeit meines Kampfes um die Macht war es in erster Linie das jüdische Volk, das nur mit Gelächter meine Prophezeiungen hinnahm, ich würde einmal in Deutschland die Führung des Staates und damit des ganzen Volkes übernehmen und dann unter vielen anderen auch das jüdische Problem zur Lösung bringen. Ich glaube, daß dieses damalige schallende Gelächter dem Judentum in Deutschland unterdes wohl schon in der Kehle erstickt ist.

Ich will heute wieder ein Prophet sein: Wenn es dem internationalen Finanzjudentum in- und außerhalb Europas gelingen sollte, die Völker noch einmal in einen Weltkrieg zu stürzen, dann wird das Ergebnis nicht die Bolschewisierung der Erde und damit der Sieg des Judentums sein, sondern die Vernichtung der jüdischen Rasse in Europa!

Denn die Zeit der propagandistischen Wehrlosigkeit der nichtjüdischen Völker ist zu Ende. Das nationalsozialistische Deutschland und das faschistische Italien besitzen jene Einrichtungen, die es gestatten, wenn notwendig, die Welt über das Wesen einer Frage aufzuklären, die vielen Völkern instinktiv bewußt und nur wissenschaftlich unklar ist.

CF. P. 83

Das Reich der germanischen Rassenseele erhebt sich gegen das Gegenreich des semitisch-bolschewistischen Chaos. Der Kampf gegen Versailles und Moskau war der Kampf um das germanische Gottesreich, um die neue Weltordnung des Reiches. Die klare Erkenntnis des tiefsten Wurzelgrundes des gegenwärtigen Zeitalters ließ alle Feinde der nationalsozialistischen Idee als ein und denselben weltanschaulichen Willen begreifen, als den Willen des semitisch-jüdischen Weltgesetzes. Als der Führer das deutsche Volk zum organisierten Widerstand gegen das Judentum aufrief, war der Entscheidungskampf um das Dritte Reich, um das germanische Volksreich der Deutschen, angebrochen.

CF. P. 83

Es darf in der Zukunft keine deutsche Hochschule geben, auf der es nicht mindestens einen Lehrstuhl für die Judenfrage gibt, der jedem Hörer das Judenproblem zugänglich macht, der aber auch weltanschaulich gegen den protestantischen und katholischen Konfessionalismus ausgerichtet ist, um eindeutige Stellungnahmen zu den großen religiösen Fragen des deutschen Volkes im Sinne der nationalsozialistischen Revolution zu gewinnen.

Cf. p. 87

Das Schicksal hatte über diese Juden in dem Augenblick entschieden, in dem das Gebiet in den Verband des Großdeutschen Reiches eintrat. Nur noch die Durchführung der Entjudung war eine Frage der Zeit.

Cf. pp. 88-89

Herbert Poller

Die Zerschlagung der Ostghettos
Das größte Ghetto der Welt unter deutscher Kontrolle

Zwei Quellgebieten entstammt im wesentlichen das Judentum der Welt: Marokko-Spanien und Polen-Westrußland-Rumänien. Das erstere spielt für den Nachschub für das Weltjudentum heute nur noch eine unbedeutende Rolle. Mit ihm allein läßt sich heute nicht mehr Macht und Bestand des Judentums halten. Ganz anders ist es beim Ostjuden. So bangt heute das Judentum um seinen Nährquell. Die englische Forderung nach Wiederherstellung des alten polnischen Staates ist nichts anderes als der Wunsch des Weltjudentums, unerbittliche nationalsozialistische Grunderkenntnisse, die sich bereits heute zum Segen der gesamten arischen Menschheit auszuwirken beginnen, nicht erst zur Anwendung in Polen kommen zu lassen.

Deutschland, das durch seine Erkenntnisse über die Rassenfrage und den Wert eines jeden Volkstums ein Volk nach dem andern zum Erwachen bringt, das nach der Zerschlagung aller so schön ausgebauter jüdischer Festungen in Mitteleuropa heute die Entscheidung über Sein oder Nichtsein der jüdischen Weltherrschaft in der Hand hat, muß vernichtet werden, auf alle Ewigkeit, damit der ewige Jude zur Ruhe kommt. Wir kennen das Ziel des Juden und werden danach handeln. Wie sagte doch der Führer einmal: Ein neuer Weltkrieg wird das Ende des Judentums bedeuten!

Cf. p. 89

Worum anders haben wir gekämpft, Not und Entbehrung auf uns genommen, worum anders sind die tapferen Männer der SA. und ⚡⚡, die Jungen der HJ. gefallen, als darum, daß das deutsche Volk eines Tages antreten könne zu seinem Befreiungskampf gegen seinen jüdischen Unterdrücker. In dem Kampf sind wir begriffen.

Nicht Jude noch Freimaurer werden den Krieg beenden mit Verträgen, die neues Unheil in sich bergen. Den Sieg wird erringen Adolf Hitler, und er wird Europa einen Frieden bescheren, der dem jüdischen Untermenschen für immer versagt, Menschen und Völker zu zersetzen und gegeneinander auszuspielen.

CF. P. 89

Der Nationalsozialist hat erkannt: Der Jude ist kein Mensch. Er ist eine Fäulniserscheinung.

CF. P. 89

Wie bereits erwähnt, ist der Kreis Lowicz seit April 1941 judenfrei. Der ehemalige Kreis Lowicz war der erste Kreis im Generalgouvernement, der Wohngebiete für Juden einrichtete. Schon im Mai 1940 waren die ungefähr 13 000 Juden des alten Kreisteiles an fünf verschiedenen Orten des Kreises in geschlossenen Wohngebieten untergebracht.

CF. P. 91

Für die deutschen Behörden in dem besetzten Gebiet existiert der einzelne Jude nicht, es wird grundsätzlich nicht mit dem einzelnen Juden verhandelt oder mit einer Mischpoche, sondern ausschließlich mit den jüdischen Aeltestenräten, die neben der polnischen Selbstverwaltung einen ähnlichen Selbstverwaltungskörper für die Angelegenheiten der Juden unter der deutschen Leitung darstellen. Die Juden können mit Hilfe ihres Aeltestenrates ihre internen Angelegenheiten, auch die Angelegenheiten ihrer Religionsgemeinden, völlig für sich und unter sich ordnen, sie haben auf der anderen Seite in voller Verantwortlichkeit die Aufgaben und Anforderungen der deutschen Verwaltung durchzuführen. Die Mitglieder des Aeltestenrates, meist sind es die Reichsten und Angesehensten der Gemeinde, haften persönlich für die Durchführung. Zweifellos erinnert dieser jüdische Aeltestenrat entfernt an die Kahale, der sich die russische Judenpolitik bediente, doch mit dem einen großen Unterschied: die Kahale erhielten und verteidigten jüdische Rechte, die Aeltestenräte im Generalgouvernement erhalten und verteilen jüdische Pflichten.

CF. P. 91

Aber wir brauchen uns mit dieser Frage heute noch nicht weiter zu beschäftigen. Vorläufig gibt uns der Krieg seine Aufgaben, und der Sieg wird das deutsche Volk vor neue, noch größere Aufgaben stellen, von denen die meisten wichtiger sein werden als das Problem des Judenreservates. Noch ist das letzte Wort nicht gesprochen, aber es wird gesprochen werden zur rechten Stunde aus maßgeblichem Mund'

Cf. p. 94

Man pflegt darauf hinzuweisen, daß diese Lösung die historisch gegebene sei, da bereits im Mittelalter der jüdische Wohnbereich, das Ghetto, bestanden habe. Diese historische Beweisführung erscheint unzutreffend. Das Ghetto des Mittelalters war in weit höherem Maße ein Recht der Juden als eine Zwangsmaßnahme. Das Ghetto des Mittelalters war seinem inneren Gehalt nach eine wesentlich freiwillige Wohngemeinschaft, die zudem keineswegs eine geschäftliche Berührung von Juden und Nichtjuden ausschloß. Das heutige Ghetto wäre somit, wenn es einen Sinn haben sollte, anders als das mittelalterliche Ghetto, ein Zwangsghetto, ohne Berührung oder Berührungsmöglichkeit mit den Nichtjuden.

Cf. p. 94

Die Juden führen jetzt als äußeres Kennzeichen ihrer Stammeszugehörigkeit — je nach Anordnung des Landrates — einen gelben Davidstern oder ein gelbes Dreieck oder eine gelbe Scheibe o. ä. auf Brust und Rücken. Der Gesamteindruck, den man von dieser Menschenmasse erhält, ist erschütternd. Und man kommt wohl sehr schnell zu der Überzeugung, daß man es hier mit einem vollkommen degenerierten, minderwertigen Teil der menschlichen Gesellschaft zu tun hat.

Cf. p. 106

ersteht hier, geschaffen von der stärksten politischen antijüdischen Kraft, die es in Europa gibt, nämlich von der NSDAP., eine geistige Kraftzentrale, deren Aufgabe es ist, die großen Sicherungslinien für die Zukunft zu legen und die gewonnenen Positionen geistig zu halten.

CF. PP. 107-108

Praktisch bedeutet das nicht nur die Errichtung einer Ghettomauer, sondern die ständige polizeiliche Bewachung der gesamten Ghettogrenze, das Verbot für Nichtjuden, das Ghetto zu betreten oder sich ihm zu nähern. Das Ghetto nähert sich hier dem Typus einer jüdischen Isolierungszone, wie beispielsweise (aber ausgesprochen als Übergangslösung) der Versuch einer Ghettobildung für die Juden in Litzmannstadt. Soweit ein solches streng geschlossenes Ghetto nicht geschaffen, sondern nur eine Mauer errichtet wird (wie anfangs in Warschau), eine Reihe wichtiger Behörden aber ihre Amtssitze nach wie vor in dem zum Ghetto erklärten Stadtteil haben, Hauptausfallstraßen durchs Ghetto gehen, sein Betreten also nicht verhindert werden kann, ist das Ghetto praktisch in starkem Maße unwirksam.

CF. P. 108

Eine städtische Ghettobildung ist praktisch ungemein schwierig. Die Städte sind organische Einheiten: Verkehrslinien, Autobusse, Straßenbahnen sind zur Bedienung des gesamten Stadtgebiets angelegt. Fernstraßen kreuzen oder schneiden das Ghetto. Wasser-, Gas-, Elektrizitätsversorgung sind einheitlich; der Verbrauch muß abgelesen, Reparaturen müssen hergestellt werden. Es ist unmöglich, ein räumlich so bedeutendes Stück einer Kommune (bis zu ein Drittel der Wohnfläche) einfach aus dem Kommunalkörper herauszuschneiden. Tut man das, so bleibt auch der übrige Teil ein Torso! Das Ghetto als Stadtteil innerhalb einer Stadtgemeinde bedeutet aber auch in mancher anderen Beziehung eine Gefahr. Seuchenübertragung ist auch trotz einer Mauer möglich! Schließlich beansprucht die ständige polizeiliche Überwachung des Ghettos unverhältnismäßig starke Kräfte. Diese zu vermindern, hieße aber wieder die Gefahr einer praktischen Übertretung der Ghettogrenze anwachsen lassen.

CF. PP. 108-109

Ein weiterer Einwand gegen das geschlossene Stadt-
ghetto folgt aus wirtschaftlichen Überlegungen: das Stadt-
ghetto kann sich selbst aus sich weder mit Industriewaren
noch mit Rohstoffen und Heizmaterialien noch auch mit
Lebensmitteln versorgen.

Es müßte also die Gesamtheit des Bedarfs eingeführt
werden. Diese Einfuhren könnten je Kopf des Ghetto-
bewohners gering sein und das Existenzminimum nicht
überschreiten — in ihrer Gesamtheit stellen sie aber eine
ständige merkliche Zufuhrbelastung dar und bedeuten
praktisch eine Ernährung und Erhaltung der Juden durch
die Nichtjuden. Eine Ernährung des Ghettos ist aber
selbstverständlich ohne eine wirtschaftliche Gegenleistung
des Ghettos undenkbar. Möglichkeit der Gegenleistung besteht nur in der Nutzbarmachung jüdischer Arbeitskraft.
Es widerspricht dem Prinzip des geschlossenen Ghettos
und der Ausgliederung der Juden, diese Arbeitskraft
außerhalb des Ghettos zu verwenden. Ihre Verwendung
im Ghetto ist aber nur möglich, wenn Maschinen und
Rohstoffe ins Ghetto geliefert werden, eine Arbeitsdienst-
pflicht eingeführt und ihre Durchführung überwacht wird,
kurz, wenn man zur äußeren Bewachung des Ghettos
eine ausreichende Innenüberwachung, Organisation und
Kontrolle durch eine sicher nicht kleine Zahl nichtjüdischen
Aufsichtspersonals hinzufügt. Das wirtschaftliche Ergebnis
bleibt immer zweifelhaft, da die ausgenutzte Arbeitskraft
ausschließlich durch äußeren Zwang angetrieben wird.
Das Resultat von Zwangsarbeit bleibt aber ökonomisch
immer unbefriedigend.

CF. P. 110

In Osteuropa ist der Jude
durch Rechtssatzung und Verwaltungsmaß-
nahmen in dem Tempo in den Städten durch
Nichtjuden zu ersetzen, als qualifizierte
Nichtjuden für diesen Ersatz zur Verfügung
stehen. Oberster
Leitsatz bleibt: Der Jude muß weichen, wenn ein gleich-
qualifizierter Nichtjude zur Verfügung steht!

CF. P. 110

diesem Problem nun ein für allemal in diesem Jahrhundert auf dem europäischen Boden eine endgültige Lösung zu geben. Es darf nicht zweifelhaft sein: Das 20. Jahrhundert, das an seinem Beginn den Juden auf dem Höhepunkt seiner Macht gesehen hat, wird am Ende Israel nicht mehr sehen, weil es aus Europa verschwunden sein wird.

CF. P. 112

Wir sehen das Judentum als eine durchaus reale Erscheinung an, die sich auf das irdische Leben außerordentlich gut verstanden hat, aber ebenso auch dem geschichtlich-irdischen Tod unterworfen ist. Und soweit es sich um die historische Erscheinung des Juden in Europa handelt, glauben wir, daß diese Todesstunde unwiderruflich gekommen ist.

CF. P. 132

Doch die Juden dürften dann nicht vergessen: wer an die harten Dinge, die sie so selbst für sich geschaffen hätten, aus sittlichen und sauberen Notwendigkeiten der Selbsterhaltung und der Verantwortung gegenüber Deutschland und dem Schicksal Europas herangeht und einzig aus diesem Gesichtspunkt tut, was getan werden muß, und nicht ein Haarbreit darüber oder darunter, der kann bestehen vor dem eigenen Gewissen und vor der Geschichte. Nur darf kein Stäubchen niederer Instinkte das harte Werk verschmutzten. Hart, sauber, blitzeblank und scharf sei es dann, wie das Schwert und wie die Pflicht, die dieses Werk verrichten müssen. So wird das Konto ausgeglichen hier auf Erden und der gerechten Sache entsteht keine Schuld!

CF. P. 141

Das Ende der Judenherrschaft

Gefreiter Heinrich Sachs in einer Nachr.-Komp. im Osten an den Obergemeinschaftsleiter Friedrich, Gr. Strehlitz:

Lieber Pg. Friedrich!

Durch den Rundfunk, die Wochenschau und die Zeitungen werden Sie in Wort, Bild und lebendiger Schilderung ein kleines Bild von den Vorgängen im Osten haben. Jedoch: Vor der brutalen Wirklichkeit verblassen ja alle diese wohlgemeinten Kommentare zu einem Geschehen von einmaliger Wucht. Ein Kapitel für sich ist die Tatsache, wie die Judenfrage augenblicklich mit einer imponierenden Gründlichkeit unter dem begeisterten Beifall der einheimischen Bevölkerung gelöst wird. Wie sagte doch der Führer in einer seiner Reden kurz vor Ausbruch des Krieges: „Wenn es dem Judentum noch einmal gelingen sollte, die Völker Europas in einen sinnlosen Krieg zu hetzen, so wird dies das Ende dieser Rasse in Europa bedeuten!". Der Jude mußte wissen, daß der Führer mit seinen Worten Ernst zu machen pflegt und hat nun die entsprechenden Konsequenzen zu tragen. Sie sind unerbittlich hart, aber notwendig, wenn endlich Ruhe und Frieden unter den Völkern einkehren sollen.

CF. P. 144

Fern von allen politischen Erwägungen der Zukunft hat der Soldat zweierlei zu erfüllen:

1.) die völlige Vernichtung der bolschewistischen Irrlehre, des Sowjetstaates und seiner Wehrmacht,

2.) die erbarmungslose Ausrottung artfremder Heimtucke und Grausamkeit und damit die Sicherung des Lebens der deutschen Wehrmacht in Rußland.

Nur so werden wir unserer geschichtliche Aufgabe gerecht, das deutsche Volk von der asiatisch-jüdischen Gefahr ein für allemal zu befreien.

Der Oberbefehlshaber:

gez. v. Reichenau

Generalfeldmarschall.

CF. P. 147

Referent	Arbeitsgebiet	Bearbeiter	Stellen-zahl	Ber Ver.
F. (röens¦. Maskow	Judentum a) Begriff u. Erfassung b) Mischlinge c) Zwischenbehandlung d) Mitwirkung bei Zwangsarbeit e) Endloesung			

CF. P. 162

Vergeßt nicht, daß es ja der Jude ist, der gegen uns den Kampf führt. Man muß nur ein einziges Mal den Juden in seinem alttestamentarischen Haß kennengelernt haben, dann weiß man, was uns blühen würde, wenn der Jude an uns Rache nehmen könnte. Was glaubt ihr, was mit eueren Frauen, eueren Bräuten, eueren Töchtern geschehen würde!

CF. PP. 163-164

Es fehlt in der Kampfesweise unserer Feinde unter der jüdischen Führung jenes Maß an Ritterlichkeit, das auch in härtesten Kriegen der Vergangenheit oft auch den bittersten Kämpfen einen gewissen geschichtlichen Glanz verlieh. Das scheint heute verloren und vergessen zu sein. Die Schmutzflut der jüdischen Presse, die langjährige Beschimpfung unserer Staatsoberhäupter und Führer, das alles findet heute seinen Höhepunkt in der infernalischen Kriegführung, die bewußt von britischen Fliegern auf Befehl des jüdisch-amerikanischen Kapitalismus begonnen wurde und heute sich bemüht, höchste Denkmäler menschlichen Schöpfertums in Schutt und Asche zu legen.
                                    ist der heutige Krieg unserer Feinde ein Kampf gegen die Grundlagen aller Nationen Europas. Ein von politischen Gangstern abgesandter Flieger, der seine Bomben auf schönste Kulturstätten Europas niederläßt, weiß ja nicht, was er tut, ist gänzlich ahnungslos dem gegenüber, was überhaupt Kultur bedeutet. Und wenn in letzter Zeit die USA. ihre Bomber bereits mit Negern besetzen, dann zeigt das, wie tief dieses einst von Europäern gegründete Land gesunken ist.
    Die Brücken sind hinter den Völkern Europas abgebrochen. Es gibt in dem Kampf, in dem wir alle stehen, nicht zwei oder gar drei Wege, sondern nur den einen Weg des Kampfes und des Krieges.

CF. P. 181

b) Eine zweite Lösung würde darin bestehen, diese 15 Millionen
durch eine Radikalkur auszumerzen. Auch diese Lösung ist abzu-
lehnen.

Gewiß kann es vor der Geschichte gerechtfertigt werden, einmal
aus biologischen Gründen zu derartigen Radikalmaßnahmen zu
schreiten, wie es beispielsweise gegenüber dem Judentum notwendig gewesen ist. Aber ein fremdes Volkstum von 15 Millionen
einfach auf diese Weise zu beseitigen, ist einer Kulturnation
unwürdig. Der Plan eines Amerikaners, die männliche Bevölkerung des deutschen Reiches zu sterilisieren, ist mit Recht von
der gesamten deutschen Presse als Kulturschande gebrandmarkt
worden.

Wir Deutsche sollten uns auch zu stark fühlen, mit derartigen
Maßnahmen das Polenproblem lösen zu wollen.

CF. PP. 182-183

                              Die ganze Stadt ist empört über die
Aktion. Viele Polen äusserten sich: "Haben wir nicht recht gehabt,
dass die Aussiedlung über den Bug kommen wird. Sie ist eher gekommen,
als angenommen wurde. Pünktlich am 1. Oktober früh hat sie begonnen."
Als Beweis für die Aussiedlung nach dem Bug wird die Tatsache
angesehen, dass die Leute nach dem Alter und Geschlecht regi-
striert wurden. Weiter wird behauptet, dass die Evakuierten nur
25 kg Gepäck mitnehmen durften. Das sei ein Beweis dafür, dass
eine Aktion wie mit den Juden beabsichtigt ist. Die Polen kommen
jetzt genau wie die Juden zur Seifenproduktion dran.

CF. P. 205

Themen der Zeit

Wer regiert in den USA?

Warum wichtig:

Inland und Ausland müssen erkennen, daß die halb- und dreiviertelbolschewistische korrupte Rooseveltgruppe auf Grund ihrer moralischen Minderwertigkeit unfähig ist, die Welt zu ordnen. — Die Machtfestsetzung der Amerikaner in Europa muß den europäischen Völkern als tiefste Schande, die Beherrschung durch die Rooseveltgruppe als brennende Schmach dargestellt werden.

Ausrichtung:

BETONEN: Die Rooseveltgruppe ist die alte Wilsongruppe, verstärkt durch neue Juden und Schieber, zum großen Teil bereits mit stark bolschewistischem Vorzeichen. — Die Demokratie der USA. wird ihrem Wesen nach stets Korruptionisten, Spekulanten, War-Hawks (Kriegshetzer) und Agitationsgewinnler nach oben bringen. — Die jüdische Beherrschung und Durchsetzung der USA. müssen kraß herausgestellt werden.

VERMEIDEN: Allgemeine Schlagworte zu gebrauchen. — Falsche Objektivität zu treiben und die demokratischen Spekulanten an der Spitze der USA. als Staatsmänner zu behandeln. — Den Haß gegen das Volk der USA. offen auszusprechen (so widerlich uns die Yankees auch sind, muß es uns darauf ankommen, zwischen sie und die Rooseveltgruppe Keile zu treiben, um dort drüben Führung und Volk voneinander zu trennen). — Eine Beschimpfung der Bevölkerung der USA. insgesamt.

CF. P. 211

Wir müssen den Kampf nun besonders in diesem Kriege bestehen, der uns von den jüdischen und plutokratischen Mächten aufgezwungen worden ist. Sie neideten uns alles, was wir uns durch unsere Weltanschauung in beständigem Kampf und rastloser Arbeit des einzelnen wie des Volksganzen mühsam erworben hatten: unsere nationalsozialistische Volksgemeinschaft, unseren Sozialismus, unsere Arbeitsleistungen, die Erfindungen unserer erstarkten Wirtschaft, unser hohes Volkseinkommen, unsere Volksgesundheit, unsere Jugend, unsere Wehrkraft. kurz alles, was wir uns unter ungünstigsten Voraussetzungen durch eigene Kraft geschaffen hatten.

CF. P. 212

Es gibt heute noch in unserm Volk Menschen, die innerlich nicht ganz sicher sind, wenn wir von der Ausrottung der Juden in unserem Lebensraum reden. Bei uns bedurfte es der Charakterstärke und Tatkraft des größten Mannes unseres Volkes seit 1000 Jahren, um das jüdische Blendwerk von unseren Augen zu reißen.

Jüdische Plutokratie und jüdischer Kommunismus sind auf der Jagd nach dem seiner Sklaverei entsprungenen deutschen Volk.

Der Jude will uns zu einem Sklavenleben zwingen, damit e r bei uns als Parasit leben und uns aussaugen kann. Die g e s u n d e L e b e n s f o r m unseres Volkes steht gegen die p a r a s i t ä r e L e b e n s f o r m des Juden.

Wer kann in diesem Kampf noch von Mitleid, Nächstenliebe usw. reden? Wer glaubt daran, einen Parasiten (z. B. Laus) bessern oder bekehren zu können? Wer glaubt, daß es zu einem Ausgleich mit dem Parasiten kommen kann? Wir haben nur die Wahl, uns vom Parasiten a u f f r e s s e n zu·lassen oder ihn zu v e r n i c h t e n.

Der Jude muß vernichtet werden, wo wir ihn treffen!

Wir begehen damit kein Verbrechen gegen das Leben, sondern dienen seinem Gesetz des Kampfes, das immer gegen alles aufsteht, das dem gesunden Leben feind ist. So dient unser Kampf der Erhaltung des Lebens.

Der deutsche Sieg — Der Sieg der Schöpfungsordnung.

CF. P. 213

a) Beratung der Lagerkommandanten in der richtigen psychologischen Behandlung der Gefangenen zur Erhöhung ihrer Arbeitslust, zur Gewinnung von Gefangenen für die Aktivpropaganda in antibolschewistischem und antijüdischem Sinne und ganz allgemein zur Beeinflussung der Gefangenen als deutsche Propagandaträger nach Rückkehr in die Heimat.

CF. P. 213

Anfang 1944 sind 20.000 Exemplare der Broschüre "How odd of God", das vom Führer als das bestgeschriebenste, wirksamste antijüdische Material bezeichnet wurde, an englische Kriegsgefangene verteilt worden.

4.) Bücher.

Es sind viele tausend Bücher antijüdischen und für Deutschland werbenden Inhalts durch Vermittlung der Kriegsgefangenenorganisation an die Gefangenen verkauft worden. (Verschiedene in den Kriegsgefangenenlagern gemachte Erfahrungen zeigten, daß der Engländer für gratis verteiltes Schrifttum wenig Interesse zeigte, sondern es als Propaganda ablehnte. Daher werden seit längerer Zeit schon Bücher und Broschüren gegen geringe Bezahlung verkauft, oder es wird den Gefangenen Gelegenheit gegeben, sich dieses Schrifttum illegal zu beschaffen.)

CF. P. 217-218

Die Auffassung, daß Juden vor der blanken Waffe oder dem Kampf stets Angst hätten, stammt aus einer Darstellung, die den Juden verniedlicht. Brutale Gewalttätigkeit ist sogar bei Juden gar nicht selten. Was den Juden abgeht, ist der soldatische Sinn für Ritterlichkeit. Die abscheulichen Grausamkeiten, die das Alte Testament von der israelitischen Eroberung Palästinas berichtet, waren auch dem gewiß harten alten Orient fremd. So entsetzliche Dinge, wie sie Dio Cassius von dem Judenaufstand in Kyrene schildert, wo die Juden viele Römer und Griechen lebendig zersägten, ausdärmten und sich mit ihren Eingeweiden umwickelten, sind einfach verbrecherisch. Darum galten die Juden, auch wo sie zäh kämpften, niemals als eigentlich ehrliche Gegner. Kaiser Titus lehnte darum auch nach der Eroberung von Jerusalem den Titel „Judaicus" ab. Gefangene Juden wurden nicht mit dem Schwert hingerichtet (sie hatten im römischen Sinne kein caput, also keine Ehre, man konnte ihnen nicht nehmen, was sie nicht hatten), sondern erlitten den Sklaventod der Kreuzigung.

CF. P. 219

Der gegenwärtige sich immer stärker ausweitende Kampf der Völker muß dahingehend gedeutet werden, daß er eine weltschöpferische Auseinandersetzung ist, zu der neben dem Schwert auch geistige Waffen gehören. Es geht nicht nur um neue Grenzziehungen und vernünftige Wirtschaftsformen, nicht nur um das Auslöschen ewig feindlicher Elemente, sondern vor allen Dingen um ein neues geistiges Europa, ein neues Weltbild, ein Sichverstehen der Völker und eine wahre Freundschaft. Der Führer selbst hat den geistigen Einschlag unseres Kampfes neben dem eigentlich Kämpferischen immer wieder in seinen Reden betont.

CF. P. 237

Sehr hübsch und treffend findet man häufig den Antisemitismus als die Geheimwaffe des Führers bezeichnet.
Folgerichtig wird, vor allem in Amerika, die Einstellung von Persönlichkeiten und Organisationen, sogar
von Regierungen, zur Judenfrage als Maßstab für ihre
politische Zuverlässigkeit gewertet.
Das gilt auch für die Neutralen, auf deren Beeinflussung wir Wert legen.

CF. P. 238

Zu 5) Zusammenwirken aller Waffen heisst hier:
Der neuorganisierte Kampf gegen das Weltjudentum als
Feind Deutschlands und Europas muss sichtbar – aber
nicht organisatorisch-sichtbar – vom ganzen deutschen
Volk und seiner Freunde in Europa getragen werden. Auf
keinen Fall genügt es, wenn kundige, aber unbekannte
Spezialisten als Leitartikler das Feld beherrschen.
Gerade die als Aussenpolitiker bekannten Journalisten
nicht ausgeprägt nationalsozialistischer Herkunft und
Abstempelung sind für diesen Einsatz mit heranzuzie-
hen, und zwar nicht schlagartig, sondern nach Eignung
und Anlaß.
Darüber hinaus aber sollten alle Kreise der Bevölkerung, Vertreter des Geisteslebens, bekannte Dichter
und Gelehrte, Schauspieler und Filmstars, Maler und
Musiker, Generäle, Ritterkreuzträger, Ingenieure, Be-
amte, Einzelhändler, Hausfrauen und ehemalige Funktio-
näre der SPD und anderer antinationalsozialistischer
Parteien für diesen Kampf herangezogen werden

CF. P. 238

Nach aussen:
Wirkung als Sprengmunition für die fünfte Kolonne des
20.Jahrhunderts. Denn die Judengegnerschaft ist heute
nun einmal das geheime Stichwort, an dem sich alle
erkennen, die die Zeichen der Zeit verstanden haben.
Sollen wir, ausgerechnet wir, darauf verzichten,
sie zu führen?

INDEX
OF PERSONS AND INSTITUTIONS

This index of persons and institutions contains some material that does not appear in the text, particularly data on the age, the affiliation, and some writings of the persons concerned. Still, no exhaustiveness was attempted; as a rule, only the last university at which the person taught is mentioned and the bibliographical items are restricted to those bearing upon the subjects of this study.

In addition to the sources mentioned in the text and in the index itself, the following handbooks have been used:

Das Deutsche Führerlexikon 1934/35 (Berlin, Stollberg [1934], 552+148 +8 pp.).

Kürschners Deutscher Gelehrtenkalender 1935, her. von Dr. Gerhard Lüdtke, 5. Ausgabe (Berlin, de Gruyter und Co. [1935], 1923 pp.).

Deutsches Biologen-Handbuch, her. von Prof. Dr. Ernst Lehmann und Dr. Otto Martin. 2. Auflage (München, Lehmann, 1938, 261 pp.).

SS. Dienstalterliste der Schutzstaffel der NSDAP. Stand vom 1. Dezember 1938. Bearbeitet von der SS-Personalkanzlei (Berlin, 1938, 530 pp. 4°).

Kürschners Deutscher Gelehrtenkalender 1940/41, her. von Dr. Gerhard Lüdtke, 6. Ausgabe, 2 Bände. (Berlin, de Gruyter und Co., 1941; 1. Band, A-K, 1066 pp.; 2. Band, L-Z, Nachträge, 1476 pp.).

SS. Dienstalterliste der Schutzstaffel der NSDAP (SS-Oberst-Gruppenführer— SS-Standartenführer). Stand vom 20. April 1942. Her. vom SS-Personalhauptamt (Berlin, 1942, 48 pp., 4°).

Der Grossdeutsche Reichstag. IV. Wahlperiode. Beginn am 10. April 1938. Verlängert bis zum 30. Januar 1947.... November 1943.... (Berlin, Decker's Verlag, 1943, 575 pp.).

Many catalogues (*Vorlesungsverzeichnis...*) of German universities covering the war years.

Abbreviations used:

> FzJ — *Forschungen zur Judenfrage*
> NSMon — *Nationalsozialistische Monatshefte*
> Jfr — *Die Judenfrage*
> Wk — *Weltkampf*
> * — born.

INDEX

OF PERIODICALS, SERIALS, AND PUBLISHING HOUSES